SPECIAL ISSUES

SPECIAL ISSUES VOLUME 1 *is a topical compilation of current scholarship published in journals of the National Council of Teachers of English.*

TITLES IN THE SERIES

RACIAL LITERACY

Vol. 1: Implications for Curriculum, Pedagogy, and Policy

CRITICAL MEDIA LITERACY

Vol. 1: Bringing Lives to Texts

TRAUMA-INFORMED TEACHING

Vol. 1: Cultivating Healing-Centered ELA Classrooms

VOLUME 1 RACIAL LITERACY

IMPLICATIONS FOR CURRICULUM, PEDAGOGY, AND POLICY

EDITED BY DETRA PRICE-DENNIS

Editor: Detra Price-Dennis
Series editor: James Sitar
Cover and interior design: Ash Goodwin
Cover images: Marvin Young
Typesetter: Jim Gallagher

ISBN: 978-0-8141-4492-3
eISBN: 978-0-8141-4493-0

It is the policy of NCTE in its journals and other publications to provide a forum for the open discussion of ideas concerning the content and the teaching of English and the language arts. Publicity accorded to any particular point of view does not imply endorsement by the Executive Committee, the Board of Directors, or the membership at large, except in announcements of policy, where such endorsement is clearly specified.

NCTE provides equal employment opportunity to all staff members and applicants for employment without regard to race, color, religion, sex, national origin, age, physical, mental or perceived handicap/disability, sexual orientation including gender identity or expression, ancestry, genetic information, marital status, military status, unfavorable discharge from military service, pregnancy, citizenship status, personal appearance, matriculation or political affiliation, or any other protected status under applicable federal, state, and local laws.

Every effort has been made to provide current URLs and email addresses, but, because of the rapidly changing nature of the web, some sites and addresses may no longer be accessible.

Library of Congress Cataloging-in-Publication Data applied for.

NCTE
340 N. Neil Street, Suite 104 | Champaign, IL 61820
www.ncte.org

VOLUME 1 RACIAL LITERACY

IMPLICATIONS FOR CURRICULUM, PEDAGOGY, AND POLICY

EDITOR'S INTRODUCTION

DETRA PRICE-DENNIS

My Racial Literacy Journey

As a young Black girl growing up in West Virginia, I remember spending a lot of time thinking about race. My earliest memory involves showing off my knowledge of the color wheel to my family, as we gathered in the living room after dinner. I handed my father a brown piece of construction paper, my mother a yellow piece of construction paper, my grandmother a black piece of construction paper, and my grandfather a white piece of construction paper. In my mind, the colored papers represented how I saw their racialized identity. While I don't remember what anyone said, I recall many stories I have been told about this moment and how their smiles, silence, and looks to each other spoke volumes.

Prior to this moment, I was intrigued by the varying skin tones in my family and spent a lot of time trying to make sense of those variations. Though I do not remember using the word race, it was something that I was not afraid to question, discuss with others, and draw attention to in my community. I noticed all of the spaces and places where I was the only Black child—and where my family were the only Black people—as well as the spaces and places where everyone was Black. My observations did not make me feel sad, angry, or afraid, and they never got in my way of making friends and having enjoyable experiences. However, I do remember wondering why people were grouped together in those ways. My observations and questions evolved as I got older, and I would ask my dad excessively why we never saw Black people on hikes, at the beach, or at this magical toy store that was nestled on top of a mountain. I also wondered why there were no white people at our church, whether you had to be white to work at the bank or jewelry store, and why white people did not live in my grandparents' neighborhood. Out of all of those questions, I remember one response: my father told me that when he was little, the city opened up a tract of land for Black people to purchase and build homes. Before this time, Black families could not own property. I also learned that the Black families who lived on his parents' street were business owners, coaches, teachers, and nurses: they were the first Black people to live in a planned community within the city. The original families stayed in the neighborhood in the homes they built, which is why my grandparents did not have white neighbors. Although I do not recall how I reacted to this information, I do remember thinking that race and power were connected.

As I reflect on those memories now, I recognize the tentative—and then more confident—steps I was taking on my path to racial literacy development. My early experiences talking about race opened up conversations with my family about historical literacies, power, financial disparities, labor, colorism, diversity, stereotypes, racism, and social class, to name a few topics. During this formative time, no one told me to avoid these discussions because I was too young or that talking about race made people uncomfortable. Consequently, these conversations informed the narrative I was developing about living in a racialized society and what that meant for me and my family. The preceding vignette illustrates my personal history related to activating my racial consciousness. According to Sealey-Ruiz, this is a first and necessary step in the archaeology-of-self process that educators committed to racial equity move through to better understand how our racial literacy pedagogy is connected to our life experiences (Price-Dennis & Sealey-Ruiz, 2021; Sealey-Ruiz, 2020).

What Is Racial Literacy?

Racial literacy is a construct that foregrounds the relationship between race and power. Price-Dennis and Sealey-Ruiz define racial literacy as "a skill practiced when individuals are able to probe the existence of racism and examine the effects of race as it intersects with institutionalized systems" (2021, p. 14). Racial literacy can be used to analyze how being raced (e.g., through racial profiling, discrimination, or violence) in our society has material consequences for people of color that impact employment, housing, health care, finances, and education. The origin of the concept of racial literacy can be traced back to the work of sociologist France Winddance Twine (2004; 2010) and her research on racial socialization. Scholars in the field of literacy education have drawn on racial literacy to better understand the ways educators and students navigate and make sense of race and racism and the ways they affect student participation, pedagogical choices, curriculum development, policies, and experiences that shape identity construction.

Sealey-Ruiz (2020) and Guinier (2004) engage racial literacy as a heuristic that exposes structural racism to better understand how racial identity shapes experiences in our society, specifically in schools. Accordingly, Sealey-Ruiz & Greene argue that racial literacy is a "skill and practice in which individuals are able to discuss the social construction of race, probe the existence of racism and examine the harmful effects of racial stereotypes" (2015, p. 60). K–12 literacy educators have been effective advocates for curriculum, school policy, and pedagogy that support this approach to racial literacy in their classrooms. This collection shows how teaching from a racial literacy perspective is in conversation with antiracist, culturally responsive, equity-oriented frameworks that uplift curriculum design and instructional strategies to help educators (re)imagine the classroom as a space that supports the development of racial literacy skills and practices with their students.

Why Focus on Racial Literacy in K–12 Literacy Education?

There's a great deal of uncertainty, discord, and increased volatility across a number of critical institutions in our society. Each day on social media and tv news outlets we read, listen to, and/or watch events unfold that are linked to political, economic, health, legal, and educational inequities that can be traced to racist ideologies and practices political, economic, health, legal, and educational inequities that can be traced to racist ideologies and practices. Public schools across the country are being subjected to pending state legislation and new laws that seek to limit how race—among other markers of identity—can be taught in K–12 classrooms. Policy groups and grassroots organizers have circulated talking points and manifestos about critical race theory; culturally responsive education; equity education; social-emotional learning; diversity, equity, and inclusion programs; and LGBTQ+ rights. The common denominator across these topics, which have garnered a lot of public interest, is the need for educators to design curriculum and engage in instructional strategies that not only meet the educational needs of their students but also generate the capacity for them to build critical thinking about power, equity, and justice as civic-minded citizens in our country. This book takes up this charge as it relates to adopting an antiracist stance, reflecting on experiences with race and racism, becoming reflexive about how those experiences shape teaching and learning, and drawing on this information to disrupt and dismantle systems of racial inequality in education.

In the field of literacy education, Price-Dennis and Sealey-Ruiz envision racial literacy as "the ability of students to identify, in professionally published and student-generated texts, concepts related to race and racism, and exercise their skills in discussing the complexity of these topics" (2021, p. 14). If educators consider intentional approaches to this idea, fostering racial literacy among K–12 students will offer significant opportunities for teachers and learners to explore new strategies as a means to identify, disrupt, and work toward dismantling racist ideologies that circulate in their communities and cause harm in our society. In this capacity, racial literacy functions as a blueprint to support teachers and learners as they acquire the skills and practices to question assumptions about race and racism, engage in conversations with their peers to trace how power and social inequities tied to race impact liberation and justice, and become more reflexive as a means to sustain an antiracist ideology that informs how they interact in the world.

Curating the Edited Volume

The authors featured in this collection illustrate approaches that foster racial literacy through research, pedagogy, and curriculum development. These previously published articles were selected from NCTE publications using a three-phase process. In phase one, NCTE journal articles written about one or more of the following areas were identified as possible chapters for this book:

- Racial literacy
- Critical race theory
- Antiracist pedagogies
- Social or racial justice and equality

Roughly 250 articles were identified through this process. In phase two, I read the articles and created a matrix that aligned with the following six components of racial literacy development outlined in Sealey-Ruiz's 2021 policy brief on racial literacy: critical love, critical humility, critical reflection, historical literacy, archaeology of self, and interruption.

This process identified 35 articles as possible chapters for the book. In phase three, I revisited and sorted each article based on grade level, the component/s of racial literacy development, and the type of journal in which the article was published. The goal in this final phase of the process was to identify 18 articles that would appear as chapters in this book. In addition to the components of racial literacy development, I kept track of the range of grade levels, the number of practitioner-based articles, research articles, and columns across the publications to ensure representation among those factors.

The authors of these recent articles provide a comprehensive examination of race in K–12 literacy education. The collection opens with a focus on policy, shifts to examine classroom practices, and then explores community-based learning spaces that support the components of racial literacy development. The remaining chapters highlight (1) specific ways teacher education can focus on race and racism in service of advancing racial equity, (2) how educators can engage in self-reflexive action, and (3) the roles that solidarity and dialogue have in pushing forward an agenda for education that is grounded in humanizing pedagogies centered on racial equity, healing, and antiracism.

Overview of this Volume's Contents

Sealey-Ruiz's policy brief introduces us to racial literacy as a catalytic theory that can create opportunities for more equitable and inclusive literacy pedagogies. She outlines the components of racial literacy development and makes recommendations for educators and administrators to move theory into practice. In the next article, Johnson demonstrates how race functions as a mediator in literacy pedagogy. He puts forth a theory of Critical Race English Education (CREE) to make visible how educators can leverage humanizing pedagogies to work against white supremacy and anti-Blackness in the classroom. Then Germán makes the case for discussing racism in classrooms. She encourages readers to build on the questions and concerns students bring into the classroom about race and racism in order to develop intentional lesson plans that create an informed and agentive approach to dismantling racial oppression connected to white supremacy. Webb examines colorism in English language arts instruction. Polleck and Spence-Davis share insights into how incorporating themes connected to racial justice, equity, and social change support students' perception of advocacy in their daily lives. Grinage unpacks key moments in a lesson about racial progress in America that exposes the trauma Black students may experience when asked to defend or justify their position on topics connected to their humanity. Beschorner, Burnett, and Ferrero share details and lessons learned from a program they created to foster students' racial consciousness in support of antiracist actions. Kelly provides conceptual tools to support white teachers and students in discussing race and racism as part of their work to dismantle racism in our society. Dunn and Love make the case for Black joy as an anchor for antiracist English language arts pedagogy. Johnson and Sullivan make the case for drawing on Black intellectual thought with high school students to honor the rich cultural literacy practices those students bring to the classroom. Pennell offers insights into how a group of middle school educators created a course for their students that examines issues of race and social justice. Ohito and the Fugitive Literacies Collective introduce us to the concept of fugitive literacy practices as emancipatory tools from whiteness and anti-Blackness. Greene amplifies the lives and literacies of Black girls through their work on podcasting. Player introduces a feminist of color writing pedagogy she employed with girls of color in an after-school writing club. Turner and Griffin, as well as Player, offer additional insights and questions that urge us to draw connections among race, gender, and power as a means to unveil how "institutional and environmental forces" (Guinier, 2004, p. 115) impact the experiences Black girls and girls of color navigate in our society. Wetzel addresses the ways research and policy can inform the intentional approaches that teacher preparation programs use to address race, racism, and racial literacy. Neville's essay centers racial literacy as a heuristic to guide how teacher educators mediate discussions connected to power, race, oppression, and resistance. And the volume concludes with Martinez, Baker-Bell, Eagle Shield, and Lee's dialogue about working across diverse communities committed to racial equity, liberation, and justice. Each chapter in the volume adds to the complexity of racial literacy by layering various identity markers such as class, gender, language, and culture.

Racial literacy provides an entry point for analyzing the impact that race has on our daily lives in a manner that foregrounds the realities of living in a racialized society. K–12 schooling is uniquely positioned as a dynamic site for examining the construction of race, which manifests in our literacy curriculum, pedagogy, and policies that impact classroom instruction. With these realities in mind, this collection addresses elements of racial literacy including fluid definitions, skills, practices, instructional strategies, lesson plan design, and insights gained from merging theory with practice. The chapters in this book reflect the urgent need for educators, literacy researchers, students, and school communities to move "toward constructive conversations about race and antiracist action" (Sealey-Ruiz, 2021) as part of a broader effort to create and sustain humanizing spaces for teaching and learning.

REFERENCES

Guinier, L. (2004). From racial liberalism to racial literacy: Brown v. Board of Education and the interest-divergence dilemma. *Journal of American History*, 91(1), 92–118. https:/doi.org/10.2307/3659616

Price-Dennis, D., & Sealey-Ruiz, Y. (2021). *Advancing racial literacies in teacher education: Activism for equity in digital spaces.* Teachers College Press.

Sealey-Ruiz, Y. (2020). The racial literacy development model. Arch of Self. https://www.yolandasealeyruiz.com/archaeology-of-self

Sealey-Ruiz, Y., & Greene, P. (2015). Popular visual images and the (mis)reading of Black male youth: A case for racial literacy in urban preservice teacher education. *Teaching Education*, 26(1), 55–76.

Twine, F. W. (2004). A white side of black Britain: The concept of racial literacy. *Ethnic and Racial Studies*, 27(6), 878-907.

Twine, F. W. (2010). *A white side of black Britain: Interracial intimacy and racial literacy.* Duke University Press.

This article originally appeared
in *Policy Statement on Racial Literacy (2021)*

RACIAL LITERACY: A Policy Research Brief produced by the James R. Squire Office of the National Council of Teachers of English

What Is Racial Literacy?
Racial Literacy in Teacher Education
Enacting Racial Literacy
Racial Literacy Development Model for Teaching and Learning

YOLANDA SEALEY-RUIZ

This publication of the James R. Squire Office on Policy Research offers perspectives with implications for policy decisions that affect literacy education, teaching, and learning. Ernest Morrell, professor and director of the Notre Dame University Center on Literacy Education, directs the Squire Office on behalf of NCTE and creates research and reports with the involvement of literacy education leaders in the field. All policy briefs from the Squire Office are available at NCTE.org.

For information on this publication, contact NCTE at executivedirector@ncte.org.

What Is Racial Literacy?

In schools, healthy conversations involving race across class, culture, and other characteristics of diversity are possible. The use of multiple texts and modalities to engage students in these conversations is readily facilitated by digital technologies. To develop racial literacy among students, educators can draw from historical, fictional, and poetic texts most effectively. Teachers who are able to engage their students in the topic of race are most successful when they employ self-exploration and honest assessments about the role they may play in perpetuating racist ideas. Once specific behaviors are recognized, it becomes easier for racially literate individuals to interrupt those behaviors in the future. Racially literate teachers develop curricula that are centered on fostering open-mindedness, commitment to inquiry and reflection, and exploration of ideas connected to the concepts of democracy and equity in schooling. Racially literate teachers make evident their deep commitment to social justice in the ways they interact with students, families, and their BIPOC colleagues.

Racial literacy is a skill and practice by which individuals can probe the existence of racism and examine the effects of race and institutionalized systems on their experiences and representation in US society (Rogers & Mosley, 2006; Sealey-Ruiz,

2011; Sealey-Ruiz, forthcoming; Skerrett, 2011). Students who have this skill can discuss the implications of race and American racism in constructive ways. A desired outcome of racial literacy in an outwardly racist society like America is for members of the dominant racial category to adopt an antiracist stance and for persons of color to resist a victim stance. Thus, racial literacy in English classrooms is the ability to read, discuss, and write about situations that involve race or racism. Scholarship that informs the concept of racial literacy identifies race as a signifier that is discursively constructed through language (Hall, 1997); fluid, unstable, and socially constructed (Omi & Winant, 1986) rather than static; and not rooted in biology, but having "real" effects in individual lives (Frankenberg, 1996). The architect of the concept of racial literacy, Harvard Professor Lani Guinier (2004), implored a shift from racial liberalism to racial literacy. She critiqued racial liberalism as an inactive, deficit approach to racial equality that subjugates Black people to the position of victim and does not activate the required antiracist stance that white people must take against their own racist ideals and actions.

THUS, RACIAL LITERACY IN ENGLISH CLASSROOMS IS THE ABILITY TO READ, DISCUSS, AND WRITE ABOUT SITUATIONS THAT INVOLVE RACE OR RACISM.

Racial Literacy in Teacher Education

Several scholars have written about the discomfort many white preservice teachers experience when teaching students of color (Cochran-Smith, 2004; McIntyre, 1997; Tatum, 1997), particularly male students of color in urban schools. Often this discomfort is expressed in the form of "color blindness" as preservice teachers deny the salience of race by adopting a color-blind approach and view the experiences of students of color as if the were white ethnic immigrants who would eventually assimilate into mainstream society (Johnson, 2002). The end result of this "Pedagogy of Discomfort" (Boler & Zembylas, 2002) is a diminishing of the social makeup of present and future students of color with whom these future teachers will interact. Scholars of racial literacy (Sealey-Ruiz, 2012, 2013; Sealey-Ruiz & Greene, 2011; Skerrett, 2011; Rogers & Mosley, 2006) offer approaches to developing racial literacy in ways that move an individual or group of individuals toward constructive conversations about race and antiracist action in schools. Embedded in the concept of racial literacy is the significance of opening and sustaining dialogue about race and the racist acts we witness in schools, home communities, and society writ large. Racial literacy urges educators to take a close look at an institutionalized system like school and examine it for the ways in which its structure affects students of color. Educators who develop racial literacy are able to discuss with their students and with each other the implications of race and the negative effects of racism in ways that can potentially transform their teaching. Racially literate teachers can distinguish between real and perceived barriers in their classrooms that may be linked to institutionalized systems that govern schools and society. These teachers also develop an ability to resist labeling students as "at-risk" based on race and social status; rather, they are more likely to view racialized students as "at-promise" individuals who need and deserve increased educational opportunities (Milner, 2020). Two specific outcomes of racial literacy in a historically racist society like America are for members of the dominant racial category to adopt an antiracist stance and for persons of color to resist a victim stance (Gilroy, 1990). In practice, racial literacy allows preservice teachers to examine, discuss, challenge, and take antiracist action in situations that involve acts of racism.

RACIALLY LITERATE TEACHERS CAN DISTINGUISH BETWEEN REAL AND PERCEIVED BARRIERS IN THEIR CLASSROOMS THAT MAY BE LINKED TO INSTITUTIONALIZED SYSTEMS THAT GOVERN SCHOOLS AND SOCIETY.

Developing the racial literacy of all teachers, but specifically preservice teachers who will teach Black and Brown youth, is significant. Preservice teacher education programs are critical sites for foregrounding the discussion of race and problematizing the ways in which the social and academic behaviors of Black and Brown students are misread. At its best, the preservice experience allows preservice educators

PRESERVICE TEACHER EDUCATION PROGRAMS ARE CRITICAL SITES FOR FOREGROUNDING THE DISCUSSION OF RACE AND PROBLEMATIZING THE WAYS IN WHICH THE SOCIAL AND ACADEMIC BEHAVIORS OF BLACK AND BROWN STUDENTS ARE MISREAD.

to practice an integrative and holistic pedagogy, incorporating the most effective methodological and instructional practices into their teaching. Effective teacher education programs allow for rich clinical experiences where preservice students are able to hone their craft to address complex issues under the tutelage of seasoned professionals. However, once in service, the occasional professional development experiences are often "one-shot" skills-based exercises that are disconnected from the integrative complexities of culture and society. Teacher education candidates who instead receive an education that adequately prepares them for the classroom challenges they will encounter and builds their self-confidence and self-efficacy will stay in the profession longer (Darling-Hammond, Chung, & Frelow, 2002). Preservice programs, as Latham and Vogt (2007) have argued, better equip students to persist in teaching. Teacher education programs that diminish the gap between theory and practice provide extensive experience in schools that immerse preservice teachers in the school climate and thus prepare new teachers for the challenges they face. With these unique features and possibilities for learning, preservice teacher education programs have the potential to develop the racial literacy skills of their candidates and prevent teachers from relying on biased, stereotypical visual images of Black and Brown youth. Instead, these programs make it common practice to critique and interrupt the images of their students of color that they see in the media.

Enacting Racial Literacy

A teacher education program that fosters racial literacy must provide spaces for teachers to talk about their fears and uncertainties in embracing this type of pedagogy. Schools of education can embrace the following tenets as they move their students toward deep self-reflection, an equity mindset, and development of racial literacy. Specifically, teacher education programs must encourage both preservice and inservice educators to do the following:

- Engage the reading of critical texts (e.g., writings about race, racism, diversity) across the curriculum as a method of acquiring language to discuss, problematize, and refute racial stereotypes and racist hierarchical systems in society and in their schools (i.e., the school-to-prison pipeline).
- Understand that before becoming culturally competent and culturally responsive teachers, they must engage in self-examination around notions of race, Black children, and other children of color.
- Recognize the need for and accept the task of holding students accountable for practicing racial literacy in their teacher education classrooms and in classrooms where they will observe and teach.
- Discuss and critique personal experiences with race and racism. This is an essential component of developing racial literacy.
- Take action against racist or discriminatory practices that cause negative outcomes for their Black students and other students of color in the schools where they will ultimately teach.

Racial literacy in teacher education promotes deep self-examination and requires actions that can lead to sustainable social justice and educational equity for all students, and Black students in particular. Without racial literacy, teacher educators and their students will continue to find themselves powerless in systems based on race.

Racial Literacy Development Model for Teaching and Learning

Research has revealed that conversations about race, when conducted effectively, provide education professionals with the confidence they need to alter their pedagogy in more culturally responsive and culturally sustaining ways. They become skillful at engaging their students in essential conversations that relate to their learning and social development. The six components of racial literacy development prepare and support educators in their journey to becoming racially literate and eventually taking action to interrupt racism when they see it happen in their schools and classrooms.

RACIAL LITERACY IN TEACHER EDUCATION PROMOTES DEEP SELF-EXAMINATION AND REQUIRES ACTIONS THAT CAN LEAD TO SUSTAINABLE SOCIAL JUSTICE AND EDUCATIONAL EQUITY FOR ALL STUDENTS, AND BLACK STUDENTS IN PARTICULAR.

Sealey-Ruiz (2020) has conceptualized Six Components to Racial Literacy Development: critical

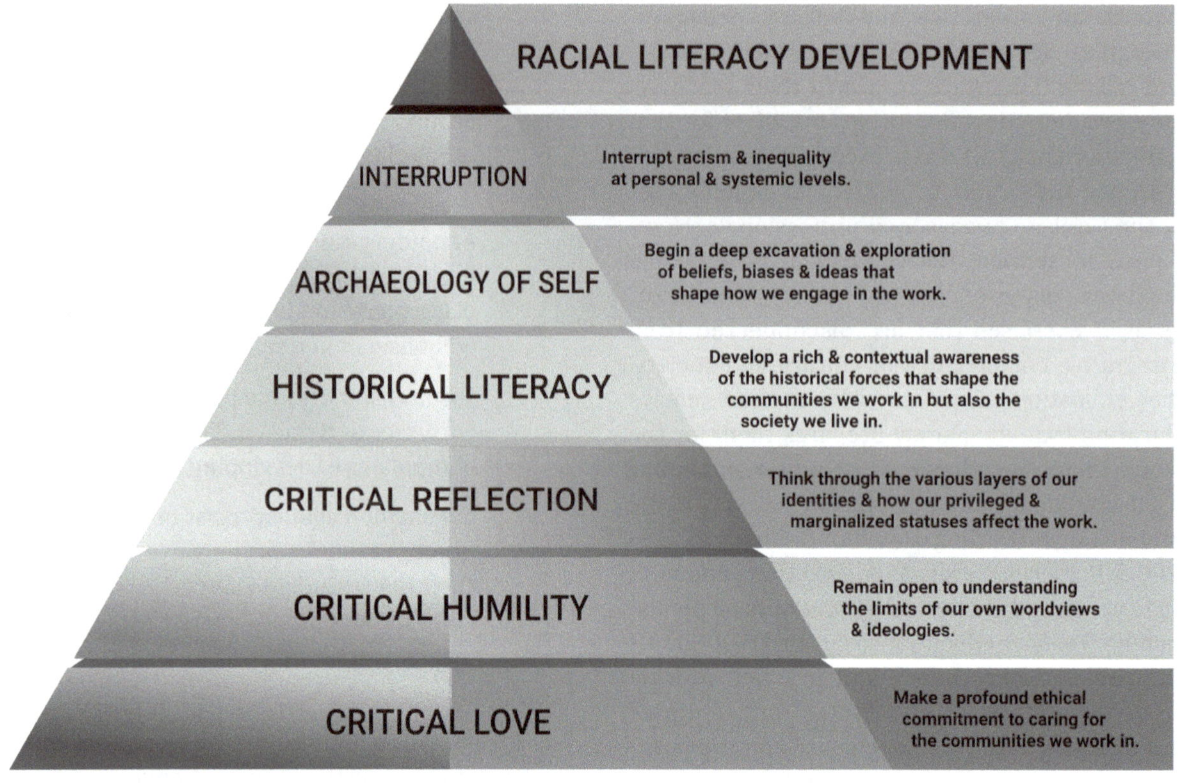

© Yolanda Sealey-Ruiz, 2020 | Angel Acosta

love, critical humility, critical reflection, historical literacy, archaeology of self, and interruption.

REFERENCES

Boler, M., & Zembylas, M. (2002, August 12). On the spirit of patriotism: Challenges of a "pedagogy of discomfort." *Teachers College Record*. Retrieved October 21, 2008, from http://www.tcrecord.org, ID Number: 11007.

Cochran-Smith, M. (2004). *Walking the road: Race, diversity, and social justice in teacher education*. Teachers College Press.

Darling-Hammond, L., Chung, R., & Frelow, F. (2002). Variation in teacher preparation: How well do different pathways prepare teachers to teach? *Journal of Teacher Education*, 53, 286–302. doi:10.1177/0022487102053004002

Frankenberg, R. (1996). *White women, race matters: The social construction of Whiteness*. University of Minnesota Press.

Gilroy, P. (1990). The end of anti-racism. *Journal of Ethnic and Migration Studies*, 17, 71–83. https://doi.org/10.1080/1369183X.1990.9976222

Guinier, L. (2004). From racial liberalism to racial literacy: Brown v. Board of Education and the interest-divergence dilemma. *Journal of American History*, 91(1), 92–118. https:/doi.org/10.2307/3659616

Hall, S. (1997). *Race, the floating signifier*. Media Education Foundation. http://www. mediaed.org/cgi-bin/commerce.cgi?preadd=action&key

Johnson, L. (2002). "My Eyes have been Opened": White teachers and racial awareness. *Journal of Teacher Education*, 53(2), 153–167. https://doi.org/10.1177/0022487102053002007

Latham, N. I., & Vogt, P. W. (2007). Do professional development schools reduce teacher attrition? Evidence from a longitudinal study of 1,000 graduates. *Journal of Teacher Education*, 58(2), 153–167. https://doi.org/10.1177/0022487106297840

McIntyre, A. (1997). *Making meaning of whiteness: Exploring racial identity with white teachers*. State University of New York Press.

Milner, H. R. (2020). *Start where you are, but don't stay there: Understanding diversity, opportunity gaps, and teaching in today's classrooms* (2nd ed.). Harvard University Press.

Omi, M., & Winant, H. (1986). *Racial formation in the United States: From the 1960s to the 1980s*. Routledge.

Rogers, R., & Mosley, M. (2006). Racial literacy in a second-grade classroom: Critical race theory, whiteness studies, and literacy research. *Reading Research Quarterly*, 41(4), 462–495. https://doi.org/10.1598/RRQ.41.4.3

Sealey-Ruiz, Y. (2020). *The racial literacy development model*. Arch of Self. https://www. yolandasealeyruiz.com/archaeology-of-self

Sealey-Ruiz, Y. (forthcoming). The critical literacy of race: Toward racial literacy in urban teacher education. In K. Lomotey & R. H. Milner (Eds.), *The handbook of urban education* (2nd ed.). Routledge.

Sealey-Ruiz, Y. (2011). Learning to talk and write about race: Developing racial literacy in a college English classroom.

English Quarterly: The Canadian Council of Teachers of English Language Arts, 42(1), 24–42.

Sealey-Ruiz, Y. (2012). Dismantling the school-to-prison pipeline through racial literacy development in teacher education. *Journal of Curriculum Pedagogy*, 8(2), 116–120. https://doi.org/10.1080/15505170.2011.624892

Sealey-Ruiz, Y. (2013). Building racial literacy in first-year composition. *Teaching English in the Two-Year College*, 40(4), 384–398.

Sealey-Ruiz, Y., & Greene, P. E. (2011). Embracing urban youth culture in the context of education. *The Urban Review*, 43(3), 339–357. doi:10/1007/s11256-010-0145-8

Skerrett, A. (2011). English teachers' racial literacy knowledge and practice. *Race, Ethnicity and Education*, 14(3), 313–330. doi:10.1080/13613324.2010.543391

Tatum, B. (1997). *Why are all the black kids sitting together in the cafeteria?* Basic Books.

YOLANDA SEALEY-RUIZ is an associate professor of English education at Teachers College, Columbia University. She is the founder and faculty sponsor of Columbia's Racial Literacy Roundtables Series and also cofounder of the Teachers College Civic Participation Project. With Detra Price-Dennis, she is the coauthor of *Advancing Racial Literacies in Teacher Education: Activism for Equity in Digital Spaces* (2021).

This article originally appeared
in *Research in the Teaching of English 53.2*

WHERE DO WE GO FROM HERE? Toward a Critical Race English Education

LAMAR L. JOHNSON

In this article, I propose Critical Race English Education (CREE) as a theoretical and pedagogical construct that tackles white supremacy and anti-black racism within English education and ELA classrooms. I employ autoethnography and counterstorytelling as methods that center my multiple identities and lived realities as I document my racialized and gendered experiences in relation to my journey to Ferguson, MO and my experiences as a secondary ELA teacher. I aim to expand English education to be more synergistically attuned to racial justice issues dealing with police brutality, the mass incarceration of Black people, and legacies of grassroots activism. This analysis suggests implications that aim to move the pedagogical practices around the intersections of anti-blackness and literacy from the margins to the center of discussion and praxis in ELA contexts.

Prelude: The Other Trayvon

On February 26, 2012, many people were numbed or in pain following the murder of Trayvon Martin. It's still hard to believe that Trayvon's life was taken away from him in just a matter of seconds by the hands of a man who viewed him as not fully human and by a society that saw his black hoodie and his Black skin as threats. Trayvon's murder happened two days after my 23rd birthday. My soul remembers (Greene, Boutte, & Hightower, 2018).

Trayvon Martin—a name that reminds me of the state-sanctioned racial violence that physically and symbolically abuses and kills the bodies and spirits of Black children and youth.

Trayvon Martin—a name that reminds me that Black Lives do Matter, in this particular case, even in English language arts classrooms and language and literacy education.

Trayvon Martin's unjust and horrendous death—as well as the taking of other Black, Brown, and transgender lives—influences my journey and shapes who I am as a critical race English educator. That Monday morning in 2012, during my first year of teaching, a timid 15-year-old Black male student, whose name coincidentally was also Trayvon, raised a question to me. He asked, "Mr. J., have you heard about the shooting of Trayvon Martin?" With a look of confusion, I replied, "No, I haven't." Trayvon proceeded to explain the story of Trayvon Martin's murder and how the neighborhood watchman racially profiled and physically abused him.

As Trayvon continued to share the story about Trayvon Martin, a few students gave head nods of affirmation while echoes of "yeah, I heard about that" permeated the room. Aaron, a Black male teenager, yelled, "Why did that watchman do him like that?" While I facilitated the critical conversation, I simultaneously searched the web for a news media clip that would help explain the racial incident. In a space of contestation, I witnessed my 14- and 15-year-old Black students wrestling with the misperceptions, stereotypes, and racial violence that are inflicted upon Black lives. The students and I watched a CNN news report that attempted to explain the events that took place between Martin and the neighborhood watchman. After the clip ended, I asked my students the following questions: *What can we do to speak back and to speak up about the police brutality that transpires in communities? Should a person be able to defend themselves if they are in danger of being hurt or even killed? Do you feel that people of different races are treated equally in today's society? Give an example of a time when you have experienced or seen unequal treatment. What is your definition of justice?*

My soul remembers.

Introduction

The above story sheds light on how Black youth are thinking about racial violence, on the relationship between how Black bodies are positioned in and out of school, and on the implications for English education. I didn't hear about the killing of Trayvon Martin from watching the news or through social media—my students informed me. If I hadn't genuinely listened to their words, I could have perpetuated further violence upon them by not incorporating critical questions and activities centered on their experience with racial injustice. This particular critical incident helped me to realize how imperative it is for educators to pay attention to the events unfolding in the world and how they affect the lives and learning of Black youth.

This story sheds light on the racial violence against Black youth that continues to sweep across the country. The physical violence that unfolds in out-of-school spaces (e.g., churches, neighborhoods, parks, playgrounds, gas stations, etc.) is connected to the symbolic violence (defined later) that is constitutive of PreK–20 classrooms and institutions (e.g., high suspension and expulsion rates for Black youth, overrepresentation in special education courses, underrepresentation in gifted education courses, and the hidden curriculum). Simply put, ELA classrooms, language and literacy studies, and English education are not exempted from the racial violence that Black youth encounter.

In this article, I extend the #BlackLivesMatter movement to language and literacy studies, ELA classrooms, and English education because we, as educators, cannot allow these pressing issues to go unaddressed. English education and ELA classrooms are dominated by eurocentric ideologies which are acts of violence that constantly remind Black children and youth that their language, literacies, culture, race, ethnicity, and humanity don't matter. Therefore, I take a close look at the ways in which educators can counteract the racial violence that erupts in ELA classrooms and in language and literacy studies through humanizing curricula and pedagogical practices that reject anti-black racism. The research questions guiding this study are the following:

1. As a Black male English educator and language and literacy scholar, how am I implicated in the struggle for racial justice and what does it mean for me to teach literacy in our present-day justice movement?
2. How are Black lives mattering in ELA classrooms?
3. How are we using Black youth life histories and experiences to inform our mindset, curriculum, and pedagogical practices in the classroom?

From these research inquiries, I trace how the unjust killing of Michael Brown, my journey to Ferguson, and my experiences as a Black male, as a former secondary ELA teacher, and now as a teacher educator shape my understanding of how we, as a field, are interconnected with the #BlackLivesMatter movement, anti-blackness, and the violence that unfolds in communities. I aim to show how critical race English education (CREE) can be operationalized to better understand the #BlackLivesMatter movement in its historical and contemporary dimensions and expand English education and ELA classrooms to be more attuned to racial justice issues dealing with police brutality, the mass incarceration of Black people, and legacies of grassroots activism. I propose CREE as a conceptual framework that informs research and pedagogy, including the methods by which I interpret data and the methods of designing and facilitating an ELA class. CREE is not only connected to the #BlackLivesMatter movement, but in this particular study, the #BlackLivesMatter movement was a data reference point for analysis. I utilized CREE as an analytical and pedagogical tool to help me understand and explicate the #BlackLivesMatter movement in relation to education, literacy, curriculum, and pedagogy.

It would be disingenuous of me to discuss #BlackLivesMatter without paying homage to the contributions, labor, and love of three Black queer women who created the movement—Alicia Garza, Opal Tometi, and Patrisse Khan-Cullors. They created #BlackLivesMatter after George Zimmerman was acquitted for murdering 17-year-old, unarmed Black male teenager Trayvon Martin (http://blacklivesmatter.com/about/). #BlackLivesMatter is an action-oriented movement that unveils the operation of white supremacy and works to dismantle a system that has a deep history of state-sanctioned violence (Dumas & ross, 2016; Rogers, 2018). The recent killings of Trayvon Martin, Jordan Davis, Michael Brown, Renisha McBride, Rekia Boyd, Stephon Clark, and Aiyana Stanley-Jones have sparked a much-needed conversation between national educational organizations such as the National Council of Teachers of English and the Literacy Research Association, and the broader field of English education. Scholar-activists within these organizations are leading the way and, through their position statements, have challenged the field of English education and language and literacy studies to (re)consider how they are implicated in the tragic killings of Black people. In making this statement, NCTE Black Caucus urges the field of English education to (re)imagine ELA curriculum as a revolutionized space that actively works against hegemonic language and literacy practices that further oppress and wreak violence against the bodies of Black students in classrooms. Building upon this argument, the Literacy Research Association states, "Children and youth in our schools today are living in a time of heightened racial violence, and these are the contexts in which literacy research examines issues that affect literacy learning and achievement" (Literacy Research Association, 2016).

In the following sections, I employ autoethnography to analyze my journey to Ferguson, Missouri, after the unjust killing of Michael Brown in light of the wider movement and social media response. Drawing from my personal experiences, observations, interviews, autobiographical narratives, social media artifacts, and images, I examine how literacy researchers, English educators, and ELA teachers can learn from the #BlackLivesMatter activism in ways that can inform research and practice. In doing this, I aim to move critical conversations and the pedagogical practices around the intersections of anti-blackness, violence, language, literacy, and education from the margins to the center of discussion and praxis in ELA contexts.

Theoretical Frameworks: Conceptualizing Critical Race English Education

I now turn to the theoretical underpinnings of CREE: critical race theory (CRT), Black critical theory (BlackCrit), and critical literacy frameworks. It is worth mentioning that I'm not proposing CREE as a replacement for CRT or BlackCrit; instead, as I explore in the coming section, CREE should be viewed as a member of the critical race family. I then turn to the literacy lineages of CREE, discussing the historical contributions of Black women language and literacy scholars and critical orientations to literacy as a social practice and in English education specifically.

CRT AND BLACKCRIT

Critical race theory informs my research and teaching because, contrary to postracial discourses, race *still* matters and racism is *still* alive and well. Decades ago, Ladson-Billings and Tate (1995) introduced CRT to the field of education. The authors argued that race was undertheorized in education; therefore, CRT would be an analytic tool to explicate race, racism, and white supremacy, and how these constructs contribute to the oppression of minoritized groups. In doing so, they also utilized CRT to examine curriculum, instruction, assessment, policy, and school funding (Ladson-Billings & Tate, 1995). Due to minoritized groups' personal encounters with racial oppression, Solórzano and Yosso (2002) emphasize that a key component of CRT is the centralization of the voices and lived experiences of people of Color. This crucial dimension gives rise to the voices that are often unheard throughout US schools by allowing marginalized people to speak their pain and to tell their racialized and gendered stories.

Extending the conversation, Dumas and ross (2016) argue that CRT fails to explicitly address "the Black experience" and the racial oppression of Black people. That is, CRT does not adequately address anti-black racism. BlackCrit is a response to CRT and other "crits"—specifically, LatCrit, AsianCrit, and TribalCrit, which have all developed as attempts to better identify and respond specifically to the racial oppression of Latinx, Asians and Pacific Islanders, and Indigenous groups (Brayboy, 2005; Chang, 1993; Hernandez-Truyol, 1997). Building on the tenets of CRT, Dumas and ross (2016) propose BlackCrit as a theory to better understand "the Black experience" and how anti-black racism is located in laws, policies, and the everyday lives of Black people.

BlackCrit in education can assist educators in understanding how social structures, policies, and practices are influenced by anti-blackness. Jeffries (2014) states that anti-blackness "is not merely about hating or penalizing Black people. It is about the debasement of Black humanity, utter indifference to Black suffering, and the denial of Black people's right to exist" (p. 1). Moreover, this anti-black violence derives from anti-black policies and practices, which continue the pain and suffering of Black children and youth in schools. Although CRT and BlackCrit are used in higher educational spaces and research (see Baszile, 2006; Bell, 1992; Stovall, 2015), CRT and BlackCrit as theoretical and action-oriented frameworks to understand race and anti-black racism are underutilized in PreK–12 contexts.

CONTRIBUTIONS OF BLACK WOMEN, CRITICAL ENGLISH EDUCATION, AND LITERACY STUDIES

There is a historical lineage of scholars who have called for racial justice work within ELA contexts. The work of CREE builds on the foundational contributions and stands on the shoulders of Black women language and literacy scholars such as Geneva Smitherman, Arnetha Ball, and June Jordan, to name a few. Black women have always been at the forefront of many justice-oriented movements (e.g., slave uprisings, women's suffrage, the Black Arts Movement, the Black Freedom Movement, women's rights, the Civil Rights Movement, and LGBTQ movements). Historically and contemporarily, Black women continue to carry the torch of justice-oriented work. In a similar vein, I believe the social projects and epistemologies of Black women intellectuals provide robust frameworks for helping literacy studies understand the interconnection between language, race, identity, power, and pedagogy.

For example, Smitherman's (1979, 1995) body of work has historicized Black language and literacies in relation to the Black Arts Movement and the Black Freedom Movement. Black movements have shaped Black peoples' beliefs and imagination, and have "fundamentally reimagined and re-landscaped Black writing and reading" (Kynard, 2013, p. 127). Smitherman's work challenges past and existing theories that demonize Black youths' language and literacy practices while privileging white mainstream ways of speaking, reading, and writing. During the late 1960s and 1970s, Smitherman (1979) understood that the ELA classroom had been engaging in fraudulent schemes against Black youths' linguistic repertories. Smitherman (1995) asserts that "the game plan has always been linguistic and cultural absorption of the Other into the dominant culture, and indoctrination of the outsiders into the existing value system (e.g., Sledd 1972), to remake those on the margins in the image of the patriarch" (p. 25). Her research demonstrated that through the ELA curriculum, schools reinforced racial and linguistic subjugation by protecting white norms and values.

Since then, language and literacy educators, composition studies scholars, and ELA teachers have been building on and adding to the conversation (see Baker-Bell, 2017; Kinloch, 2005; Kynard, 2013). This intergenerational dialogue is urgent, especially in a world that strives to erase the identities of Black girls and women (Butler, 2017). For example, Arnetha Ball and Ted Lardner (1997) theorize the interconnection between literacies, identity, and power through research on the preparation of teachers to work with youth who come from racially and linguistically diverse backgrounds. Ball and Lardner (1997) argue that teachers' uncritical and unconscious knowledge and attitudes about Black language affect Black youths' learning experiences in writing classrooms. Given the racial and linguistic differences in language-use patterns and styles, many classroom teachers' negative attitudes toward Black language develop from their lack of linguistic knowledge and utilization of narrow pedagogical techniques for teaching language skills (Ball & Lardner, 1997). Ball calls for writing teachers, literacy researchers, and ELA teachers to reenvision literacy and writing classrooms as transformative spaces that move toward more inclusive pedagogies that better support and sustain the oral and written literacies of Black youth.

The research of Geneva Smitherman and Arnetha Ball resonates with Caribbean poet, educator, and scholar June Jordan's 1982 keynote address to the National Council of Teachers of English, in which she queried, "What to do? What to do? . . . English education acts as a gatekeeper . . . closes down opportunities . . . narrows rather than opens possibilities of social meaning and social action" (Stuckey, 1990, p. 97). In a time of racial chaos, when Black people are losing their lives at higher rates than any other racial and ethnic group as a result of state-sanctioned violence, white supremacy, and anti-black racism, what is English education to do? Where do we go from here? Decades later, these questions continue to linger.

As a counterhegemonic tool, Morrell (2005) proposes that the field increase its emphasis on critical English education in order to be "explicit about the role of language and literacy in conveying meaning and in promoting or disrupting existing power relations" (p. 313). Critical English education is intentional about the role social context plays in students' meaning-making practices. It also provides youth with the knowledge base to deconstruct canonical literature and popular culture texts such as media, art, and film, "while also instructing them in skills that allow them to create their own texts that can be used in the struggle for social justice" (Morrell, 2005, p. 313). Critical English education welcomes multiple languages, literacies, and modalities that are reflective of societal changes.

In conjunction with critical English education, I draw upon literacies studies scholars who are attentive to issues of race and identity (e.g., Kynard, 2013; Haddix, 2015). These frameworks view literacy as a political act that reflects one's racial, social, cultural, and geographical context. Furthermore, in contrast to prevalent skills-based approaches, these frameworks treat literacy as "something that people do, rather than something that they have or do not have" (Kynard, 2013, p. 32). Literacy studies has helped me to gain a better sense of how Black students have fought to be seen, heard, and humanized. I specifically draw upon critical orientations to literacy that refer to "the process of reading texts in an active, reflective manner in order to better understand power, inequality, and injustice in human relationships and contexts" (Boutte, 2015, p. 79). An essential element of critical literacy is Freire's (1970) notion that literacy is not only about reading the word but also about reading the world—societal events are texts that must be read, interrogated, and interrupted. Scholars such as Haddix (2015), Kirkland (2013), Paris (2010), and Sealey-Ruiz (2016) are all working at the intersections of English education and literacy studies, and have called for research and pedagogy to honor the literacies of Black youth and work to dismantle oppression.

CREE

These historical legacies and the continued state of racial violence have led me to propose CREE as a means of (re)imagining English education. CREE is a theory and pedagogy that:

- Explicitly addresses issues of violence, race, whiteness, white supremacy, and anti-black racism within school and out-of-school spaces.
- Explores the intimate history and the current relationship between literacy, language, race, and education by expanding the concept of literacies to include activist contexts and social movements.
- Seeks to dismantle dominant texts (i.e., canonical texts, art, and media texts) while also highlighting how language and literacy can be used as tools to uplift the lives of people who are often on the margins in society and PreK–20 spaces.
- Builds on the Black literacies that Black youth bring to classrooms. Black literacies affirm the lives, spirit, language, and knowledge of Black people and Black culture. In addition, Black literacies are grounded in Black liberatory thought, which supports and empowers the emotional, psychological, and spiritual conditions of Black people throughout the African Diaspora (Grant, Brown, & Brown, 2016). Further, Black literacies move beyond the traditional understanding of texts (Kirkland, 2013) and may include tattoos, poems, novellas, graphic novels, technology/social media sites, oral histories/storytelling, body movements/dance, music, and prose. This particular component of CREE counters anti-blackness by showcasing an *unapologetic*, *unashamed*, and *unconditional* love for Blackness and for Black lives.

CREE's contribution is its unwavering focus on the ways in which anti-blackness and violence, historically and currently, permeate ELA classrooms, and are deeply embedded within curriculum, standards, and routine pedagogies. Love (2017) explains that when Black youth are taught from a curriculum that stifles their voice and experiences, symbolically, it kills their humanity. Love explains how this form of symbolic violence leads to spirit-murder. Spirit-murder is the psychological and emotional death Black youth experience due to living in a world that embraces anti-black racism. ELA teachers and literacy educators must understand that choosing eurocentric texts that omit the lived realities of Black people or misrepresent the multiple ways of being Black leads to anti-blackness and the devaluation of Black life. Similarly, racial violence also occurs in *who* and *what* educators include (or do not include) in classrooms. Educators have to consider the countless Black students who experience racial fatigue and spirit-murdering from sitting in classrooms where Black students are typically invisible (e.g., in curriculum and pedagogy) yet hypervisible (e.g., in suspension, expulsion, and overrepresentation in special education classes), as well as begin to consider instructional practices that actively stand against the physical and symbolic violence perpetrated against Black bodies.

CREE is not only connected to the #BlackLivesMatter movement, and other movements can inform and be viewed through CREE, such as slave uprisings, the Black Arts Movement, the Black Freedom Movement, the Civil Rights Movement, and the Black Panther movement. Historically, literacy and Black protest movements have gone hand-in-hand. The social movements of Black youths' protests and resistance are also examples of literacies, from chants and phrases that were created to speak back to and against the debasement of Black humanity, to digital technologies that foster affinity spaces and collective actions for change.

#BLACKLIVESMATTER IN ENGLISH EDUCATION AND ELA CLASSROOMS

Racism is etched within ELA classrooms and explicitly and implicitly influences the academic and social experiences of Black children and youth. As such, in order to disrupt racism, the structures, policies, and procedures that uphold racism must be named and unveiled. Teaching about white supremacy, whiteness, and anti-blackness is not for the faint of heart. It takes a deep level of critical consciousness and awareness of social and racial injustices against oppressed communities. Educators' hearts and minds have to change as well. This requires teachers who aren't afraid to resist the school-sanctioned language, literacy, and writing curriculum. ELA teachers committed to this vision should engage youth in humanizing racial dialogue (Matias, 2016).

Shipp (2017), for example, argues that if ELA classrooms revolutionize the traditional literary canon, then, essentially, we are revolutionizing the English classroom. Therefore, "Let us shift from focusing exclusively on required texts to equally acknowledging the urgent need for consciousness and activism from our students" (Shipp, 2017, p. 39). Shipp engages in an autobiographical narrative of her experiences teaching high school English in the wake of racial violence and injustices. The author demonstrates how she infuses Black music and Black artists (e.g., Kendrick Lamar and Beyoncé) into her curriculum, not only as a means for teaching ELA skills such as literary devices, figurative language, and literary analysis, but also to engage youth in critical discussions pertaining to the United States's past and current-day issues with racial inequities. In addition, Shipp also incorporates present-day cultural movements like #BlackLivesMatter, Black Is Beautiful, #BlackGirlMagic, and #BlackExcellence into her English classroom, as well as Black contemporary authors, artists, poets, orators, and activists invoking powerful symbols and messages pertaining to Blackness, language, culture, and humanity.

Muhammad, Chisholm, and Starks (2017) examined the textual, communal, and sociopolitical partnerships of kinship writing as Black youth composed protest poetry. As they note, "kinship writing carries significance in the Black literary community as the history of Black education has been interlaced with ideals of social learning, community, family, and kinship" (Muhammad, Chisholm, & Starks, 2017, p. 347). Through a four-week summer writing program, the authors engaged 15 Black youth in sociopolitical writing workshops that centered on anti-blackness, Blackness, Black love, and solidarity. Their research demonstrates what it looks like to create critical writing pedagogies for youth by incorporating texts from the Black protest movements and from the past to our current historical insurgence known as the #BlackLivesMatter movement. By critically reading and engaging with Black youths' kinship poems, Muhammad, Chisholm, and Starks found that the Black youth wrote across various topics that affect Black people and communities (e.g., gun violence and police brutality, the distorted depictions of Black lives, the conceptions of Black beauty, and the importance of revolutionary love and freedom). The authors call for English education classrooms to move from a narrow, linear approach to one that educates Black youth on how to use their words and "pens" as epistemic weapons to speak back/against racial oppression and marginalization.

In addition, my colleagues and I have conducted several conceptual studies pertaining to the theoretical and pedagogical conceptualizations of CREE (Baker-Bell, Butler, & Johnson, 2017; Johnson, Jackson, Stovall, & Baszile, 2017). The current study is an empirical example of how the literacy practices, events, and artifacts of the #BlackLivesMatter movement help ground and specify the construct of CREE and how CREE contributes to existing research directed toward equity in language and literacy studies and English education.

Research Methodology: Autoethnography and Counterstorytelling

This article is a counterstory that seeks to disrupt positivistic orientations to language and literacy research that privilege scientifically based reading methods and methodologies and align with race-neutral theories, frameworks, and methodologies (see Paris & Winn, 2014). Taking a positivistic paradigmatic approach to research often objectifies communities of Color; perpetuates class stratification; continues the discriminatory treatment of people who speak other languages than white mainstream English; and silences the experiences of LGBTQ communities. There is a long history of scholarship from a range of paradigms that has pushed against positivistic approaches to qualitative research. For example, Black feminist epistemologies (see Baker-Bell, 2017; Butler, 2017), CRT (see Bell, 1992; Ladson-Billings & Tate, 1995), LatCrit (Hernandez-Truyol, 1997), and critical Indigenous methodologies (Tuck & Yang, 2014)—just to name a few—take a stance against discriminatory and dehumanizing research methods and methodologies. This study builds on traditions that challenge notions of research neutrality and "objectivity." My theoretical grounding in CREE necessitated that I reconceptualize how I make sense of the research process, methodology, methods, and data analysis to be more humanizing. Paris (2010) defines humanizing research as "a methodological stance, which requires that our inquiries involve dialogic consciousness-raising and the building of relationships of care and dignity for both researchers and participants" (p. 141). In this light, CREE challenged the ways I participated and engaged in my research design, leading me to ask questions such as "What counts as theory? What counts as research? What counts as data? And what counts as analytical methods?" (Johnson, Gibbs Grey, & Baker-Bell, 2017, p. 5).

To consider the roles that anti-blackness, violence, and literacy play in ELA spaces and within communities in out-of-school contexts, I used CREE as a theoretical lens that helped me to share and analyze my racialized stories, and that worked hand-in-hand with methods such as autoethnography and counterstorytelling. For this qualitative study, I leaned on my personal racialized and gendered memories, autobiographical narratives, journal writings, social media interactions, pictures, and conversations with colleagues, family, and friends to help me to *tell*, *analyze*, and *theorize* my stories (Baker-Bell, 2017). Haddix (2015) argues that Black children's, youths', and women's stories matter and that Black peoples' stories illustrate how we are producers and holders of knowledge. I have selected stories from my journey to Ferguson, Missouri, and a specific teaching moment from my experience teaching secondary ELA to share in this article in order to analyze activist out-of-school literacies and moments where CREE might be operationalized in the classroom. The selected stories illuminate how racial violence is connected to language and literacy studies and English education while simultaneously showcasing humanizing and critical approaches to teaching ELA and conducting literacy research.

Utilizing CREE as a theoretical overlay to analyze my stories required me to ask various overarching questions that specifically pertained to the data: *In my stories as a language and literacy scholar or as an ELA teacher, whose identities are included and reflected in ELA curricula and pedagogies, and how are our curricula and pedagogies inclusive of Black youth? How is literacy being used in our current justice-oriented movements? Through a CREE-informed lens, what types of literacy modalities are being used to reposition what counts as literacy and to speak back to anti-blackness and dehumanization? What language and literacy practices have evolved in our current justice-oriented moments (i.e., #Black-LivesMatter and #SayHerName) and how do these current literacy practices connect to language and literacy practices from the justice-oriented movements of the past?* These types of questions were used to interrogate and interpret my racialized stories, and served as entry points to begin to consider the connections between self, literacy, race, and racism. Layering these questions over my stories allowed me to reflect on my teaching experiences, reformulate how I view the research process, and reimagine how I center the humanity of Black youth and Black people in the classroom.

It is noteworthy to mention that many of my stories stem from my experiences visiting Ferguson, Missouri, during the 2014 Ferguson Uprising. While visiting Ferguson, I was well aware that I had entered a community that was not immediately my own. Before I delve into the (re)telling of my stories, I have to recognize the tension of entering that space as a Black male but also as a Black male researcher who comes with certain privileges. Oftentimes, researchers enter marginalized communities without examining their positionalities, multiple identities, biases, and ideologies. In my case, I aim to make sure that I'm not exploiting or misrepresenting the stories that shaped me while in Ferguson.

In this journey, my positionality was also in many ways hypervisible. As a Black male, how my body is perceived by white communities mattered in that exact moment. Visiting the community of Ferguson underscored to me how the personal becomes political and the political becomes personal. While narrating this memory, I articulate how this particular experience not only affected me as a Black male and as a Black son but also as a Black English educator. I employ autoethnography and counterstorytelling as methods that center my multiple identities and lived realities as I document my racialized and gendered experiences in relation to my journey.

AUTOETHNOGRAPHY

Brooms and Brice (2017) state that autoethnography foregrounds "writing from the 'I' perspective . . . to write about our own choices, decisions, and experiences in ways that traditional methodological approaches do not allow" (p.148). Drawing upon a reflexive autoethnographic account enables me to view my personal experience as a larger cultural experience—"a convergence of autobiography, narrative, and ethnography" (Martin, 2014, p. 240). As I have argued (Johnson, 2017), however, "autoethnographic work does not necessarily center racism, whiteness, and white supremacist patriarchy" (p. 483). I have sought to bridge this gap by juxtaposing autoethnography with CREE. Qualitative researchers delineate different types of autoethnographies, including "confessional (Ellis, 2004), evocative (Ellis, 1997), and analytical (Atkinson, 2006)" (Martin, 2014, p. 240). For this study, I utilize an analytical autoethnographic method.

Analytical autoethnographies interweave personal narratives into a theoretical depiction of a particular phenomenon (Baszile, 2006). Engaging in a humanizing ethnographic study of my(selves) in relation to my shared experiences with other Black people provided me with the language to name and analyze broader phenomena in ELA education. I believe it is worth situating the analytical autoethnographic approach within a Black literary legacy where autobiography has been used to expose white supremacist patriarchy while asserting one's full humanity. In particular, I am reminded of the Black literary legacy of Frederick Douglass, Harriet Jacobs, Anna Julia Cooper, Malcolm X, Audre Lorde—Black literary scholars, educators, orators, and writers who shared and wrote their stories into existence by discussing ways for Black people and society at large to understand the nuances of oppression, white supremacy, marginalization, literacy, education, and power (see Grant et al., 2016; Perry, Steele, & Hilliard, 2003). Building upon the autobiographies of Black literary scholars provided me with the knowledge to utilize writing as a tool to heal myself and to write myself free (Baker-Bell, 2017). In short, writing about my experiences through autoethnographic and autobiographical accounts has helped me to reflect on several questions: *Who am I? As a Black male English educator and language and literacy scholar, how am I implicated in the struggle for racial justice and what does it mean for me to teach literacy in our present-day justice movement?* To answer these questions, I wedded autoethnography and counterstorytelling as methods to help me collect, share, and write my stories.

COUNTERSTORYTELLING

Dominant narratives—or stories—often sustain whiteness, white supremacy, and anti-blackness by privileging the stories and voices of white people (Bernal & Villalpando, 2002). In contrast, counterstorytelling as a methodological tool can counter these ideologies and the narrow claims that educational institutions, educators, and society make about people who are often on the margins (Delgado, 1989). Counterstorytelling tackles white supremacy, rejects notions of neutrality, and centers the voices and knowledge of people of Color. Oftentimes in ELA classrooms, Black youth encounter curricula and texts that sustain the dominant narratives; these dominant stories send Black youth negative messages and inaccurate depictions about their identity, race, culture, and language. What I find striking is that novels such as *The Scarlet Letter, Animal Farm, Huckleberry Finn, The Odyssey, Lord of the Flies*, and *The Great Gatsby* dominate the past and current landscape of many middle school and high school ELA classrooms. Therefore, ELA classrooms must become spaces that counter dominant narratives by centering the voices of youth of Color and creating assignments that allow youth of Color to speak back to the dominant narratives by writing or telling their stories.

In the sections that follow, I unpack three research stories to analyze the dehumanization of Black bodies such as Michael Brown, my own racialized experiences during my visit to Ferguson, Missouri, during the 2014 Ferguson Uprising, and my attempts to infuse these realities into a secondary ELA classroom.

Research Findings

RESEARCH STORY 1: MICHAEL BROWN

I did not initially enter the community of Ferguson with the intention of engaging in research. I entered as a Black man who wanted to be in solidarity with a community. My research grew from a hurt heart and with pain; it did not start with a set of research questions. My embodied experiences led to the formation of my research inquiries. I understand there is no distance between Michael Brown, other Black Brothas, and myself. I call them Brothas from the soulful and rich language of Black people—a language that intricately connects family, community, and personal identity. I call them Brothas because I, too, am a Black male whose flesh has been scarred by the pain and the wounds of racism throughout educational spaces and society at large. I understand my Black male body is not exempted from the physical and the symbolic racial violence that runs rampant throughout society. Even when Black males sit in privileged positions (e.g., tenure-track appointments, department chair, dean, president), our bodies are still subjected to racial violence (Johnson & Bryan, 2016).

On August 9, 2014, Michael Brown, an unarmed 18-year-old Black youth, was brutally murdered by a white police officer, Darren Wilson, in Ferguson, Missouri. According to Michael Brown's friend and key witness, Dorian Johnson, Brown and Johnson were walking on the street just a few feet from their destination when Darren Wilson exclaimed, "Get the fuck on the sidewalk or get the fuck out the street" (Jefferson-Griffen, 2015, p. 45). According to Johnson, he and Brown responded that they were only a minute away from their final destination (McLaughlin, 2014). Many believed that Wilson was not pleased with the youth simply because they did not respond to him, a white law enforcer, in what society deems a respectful manner (Fasching-Varner & Hartlep, 2015; McLaughlin, 2014). Consequently, Wilson's dehumanizing request and language only exacerbated the situation.

Immediately, Wilson became physically aggressive with the young men, which led to the murder of Michael Brown (Fasching-Varner & Hartlep, 2015). I am in agreement with Stovall (2015) when he states, "the officer's response is not to discharge the weapon to stop or frighten Michael Brown. The intent is to put the 'target' down. Brown is no longer human. He is the target. He is state property. If he cannot be contained, he is to be killed" (p. 68). Although the reports leading up to the death of Michael Brown are unclear, no one should lose their life for walking in the street. Brown's body lay in the stifling summer heat for over four hours. This horrendous act led the citizens of Ferguson to stand firm in the quest for racial justice. During this historical moment, the world witnessed the city of Ferguson pushing back against a system that not only physically and spiritually killed a Black life (Michael Brown) but also abuses and kills Black lives in general.

During this troubling time, we saw a kinship, revolutionary struggle, and acts of solidarity between Ferguson protesters and Palestinian activists and citizens (Davis, 2015). The pain and suffering experienced (as a result of racism, mass incarceration, the prison industrial complex, displacement of land, etc.) was illustrated through Palestinians' words of encouragement, empathy, and solidarity, such as the references made to tear gas produced in the United States (see Figure 1). Social media and Twitter provided an interactive view of the streets of Ferguson. As Twitter notifications of #Ferguson flooded people's timelines, another stream of tweets began to

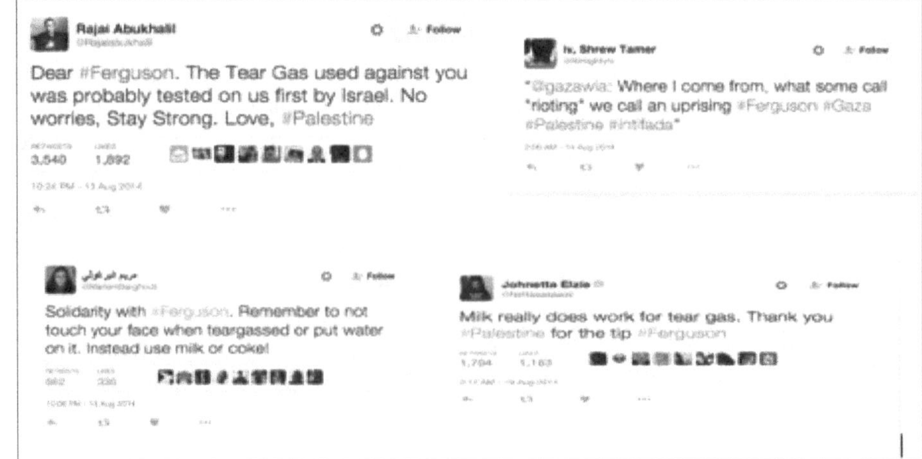

FIGURE 1

circulate comparing the streets of Ferguson to the Palestinian uprising that was simultaneously unfolding. It is beyond the scope of this paper to unpack the ongoing history of Palestinian oppression and the conflict between Palestine and Israel (see Davis, 2015); however, it is important to note that prior to the 2014 Ferguson uprising, Palestinians resisted control, repression, and violence through peaceful protests and marches. Many times, the Palestinian protesters were disrupted by military troops and police officers who entered their communities with battle tanks, tear gas, and weapons of mass destruction (Davis, 2015). Palestinians utilized social media and Twitter to create and express international solidarity *for* and *with* Black folks who were uprising in Ferguson.

Reflecting upon Michael Brown's story, I acknowledge the pivotal role literacy plays in the response to racial violence. The transnational solidarity between Black and Palestinian communities illuminates how Black and Brown communities have used Black Twitter as a form of literacy to fight against police brutality, anti-blackness, and racial violence. Black Twitter is a digitized space that promotes political organizing, solidarity, protest, critical literacy, and both physical and symbolic resistance to anti-black violence and police brutality within the United States (Hill, 2018). Hill (2018) explains that Black Twitter is a digital counterpublic—"any virtual, online, or otherwise digitally networked community in which members actively resist hegemonic power, contest majoritarian narratives, engage in critical dialogues, or negotiate oppositional identities" (p. 287).

After the unjust killing of Michael Brown, Black people expressed their frustration and anger through participation in real-time discussions pertaining to the dehumanization of Black lives in the United States, anti-black racism, the school-to-prison pipeline, Black culture, and Black politics. At the same time it was used to engage in critical and humanizing dialogue, Black Twitter was utilized as a space that focused on the body in practices of resistance. The tweets show how activists and community members protected themselves against the physical violence of tear gas. A CREE lens draws attention to how activist movements both in the United States and abroad center race and racial violence in their societal analysis and how literacies might also be mobilized for resistance. I decided I needed to learn firsthand from the on-the-ground movement in Ferguson.

RESEARCH STORY 2: MY JOURNEY TO FERGUSON

On September 27, 2014, I took a journey to Ferguson. After the unjust killing of Michael Brown, the city of Ferguson became a space where Black lives continued to be rejected through the enforcement of national guardsmen and militarized police officers who shot rubber bullets and tear gas at protesters. Although the residents of Ferguson and the nonresidents who were there in solidarity encountered militarized forces, they continued to write, speak, draw, sing, and chant their struggle and presence into existence. As I walked through the community, I took pictures of memorial plots, protest signs, and the Michael Brown paraphernalia that hung from the windows inside of homes. One such sign encapsulated much of the sentiment in the city, stating, "R.I.P. Mike Brown"; "They can burn, shoot rubber bullets, throw tear gas, but you can't stop us!!"; "No Justice, No Peace"; and "Arrest Darren Wilson" (see Figure 2).

One particular spot ignited a blaze of emotions within me (see Figure 3). There were red, white, and

FIGURE 2

FIGURE 3

blue balloons that, to me, symbolized the United States; teddy bears and stuffed animals that symbolized childhood and innocence; a graduation picture of Brown that represented young, Black males and the pursuit of education. These symbolic images were resting on the words "R.I.P. MIKE BROWN" written on the concrete in black and red spray paint over the preserved remnants of his blood.

As a Black male, I knew Brown was not murdered by a single police officer as much as he was killed by the system in the United States (Hill, 2018; Taylor, 2016). I am reminded of the children, youth, and adults who have actively engaged in the pulling apart of Brown's humanity through the adoption of racist stereotypes and oppressive ideologies as they view(ed) his murder as just another Black male teenager being responsible for his own death. Michael Brown's body signifies the struggle of living and of moving freely in a society where Black bodies are deemed less than worthy of human life. In many ways, his body illustrates the past and present dehumanization of Black lives.

The Black body has been and continues to be painted as violent and dangerous. Black peoples' bodies have encountered physical abuse and disdain since chattel slavery (e.g., Fanon, 2004; Matias, 2016; Woodson, 1933/2000). The negative discourse and (mis)readings of Black bodies continue to be perpetuated by whiteness and sustained by the white gaze. Yuan (2017) reminds us of the importance of understanding the Black body from a sociopolitical perspective and seeing the Black body as a form of resistance and an embodied action. Thus, the coupling of the body and literacy makes for a generative line of inquiry. The pictures and artifacts from my journey to Ferguson represent the multimodal nature of the literacy practices around the #BlackLivesMatter movement. The graffiti visuals, protest signs, and memorial plots are all complex counterhegemonic texts that disrupt the dominant white discourse around Black bodies while simultaneously illuminating the realities of racial violence pertaining to Black lives.

Looking at the multimodal nature of the literacy practices around the #BlackLivesMatter Ferguson experience led me to focus on the various ways knowledge is represented and how meaning is made through semiotic resources (e.g., language, images, gesture, etc.) (Fei, O'Halloran, Tan, & Marissa, 2015). In this particular case, the spray painting of activist slogans on the pavement still marked with blood is a vivid image and multimodal text that speaks to the horrific violence that is perpetrated on Black bodies. Semiotic modes such as art, language, gesture, and the body are mobilized in revolutionary ways that protest against and draw attention to dehumanization, violence, anti-blackness, and political and economic inequities. In this case, the memorial plots, protest signs, and graffiti tags that were highlighted in Ferguson challenged the dominant discourse of how the world saw Michael Brown, and represented various modes and media used to express concerns such as Black suffering, stop-and-frisk policies, militarized police, and the oversurveillance of Black bodies. The visit to Ferguson prompted me to reconsider the fundamentals of the ELA classroom, including what counts as literacy, what counts as text, whose knowledge and experiences matter, and what values drive the curriculum.

RESEARCH STORY 3: CREE IN THE CLASSROOM

As a former secondary ELA teacher and a survivor of the traditional model of school, I knew I had to incorporate a critical race curriculum that dismantled the conventional curriculum and standards, objectives, and instructional practices that permeate ELA classrooms. We know all too well that the traditional ELA curriculum mirrors westernized perspectives. It does not provide us with the resources to discuss race and racial disparities in manners that are beneficial and liberating to those who are oppressed by racism.

To address this, I strategically infused a critical race analysis of anti-blackness, whiteness, power, and white supremacy throughout my daily lessons and instructional practices. Prior to my journey to Ferguson, I had begun to teach from a critical race standpoint. The following vignette occurred in the freshman ELA classroom featured in my prelude to this article, before my trip to Ferguson: As for most secondary-aged students, *To Kill a Mockingbird* (Lee, 1960) was a required text (this is still true in the current ELA curriculum). Although this book engaged the topic of race, it focused on race from a eurocentric stance. The character of Atticus Finch could be viewed as a white savior—the *heroic* upper-middle-class white male who *saves* the innocent Black male who is on trial for allegedly raping a white woman. The savior mentality blocks white people from being conscious of their own privilege and of systemic oppression (Matias, 2016). Knowing the discussion of the white savior complex is often absent from secondary ELA classrooms, I believed it was essential for me to problematize Atticus Finch's character and how the savior complex perpetuates racial subjugation and the omission of voices of Color.

In preparation for a lesson on character analysis in *To Kill a Mockingbird*, the students and I read an excerpt from Matias (2016) about the white savior complex. I showed them clips from the movies *The Blind Side* (2009) and *Freedom Writers* (2007). In these Hollywood films, white women are portrayed as saviors or missionaries who have come to "rescue" youth from low, impoverished Black communities. After critically reading multiple texts, the students and I discussed whether or not Atticus Finch was truly a protagonist and the hero. In South Carolina, where I taught high school English, Standard 8.1 indicates that students must analyze how characters or a series of ideas or events are introduced, connected, and developed within a particular context (South Carolina Department of Education, 2015). I created critical race objectives because they were not included in the original standard objectives. Matias (2013) states that critical race objectives "strategically and directly link the content objective to an overarching CRT analysis of how oppressions of race, class, and gender are operating within that content itself" (p. 191). For example, if the content objective is that students will be able to analyze characters, settings, and ideas as they unfold and intersect across a particular context, then from a critical race English educator's stance, students will be able to critically discuss the role the white savior complex plays in the character development of Atticus Finch and how the geographical context of the South during the 1930s influences his development as a character. Critical race objectives create a contested space within ELA classrooms that works to counter the normativity of whiteness and racism in the curriculum and standards while promoting racial dialogue, justice, and healing.

As I reflect on these three stories, my criticality about what English language arts is and what English language arts classrooms should look like has deepened. Schools are riddled with the misperception that ELA is about skill and drill and teaching students how to read. Now that I have fleshed out the CREE perspective, I understand that humanization should be at the nexus of ELA classrooms. Similarly, the above vignettes and CREE have demonstrated to me that justice movements are connected to ELA classrooms. Concordantly, the social movements of Black youths' protests and resistance are also examples of New Literacies movements that include the chants and phrases that are created to speak back to and against the debasement of Black humanity, an artistic component that illustrates not only the ongoing struggle of being Black but also the beauty of Blackness. The redesign of curricula and policies has the potential to redefine literacy (i.e., critical media awareness) by connecting students to on-the-ground social movements, incorporating activist literacies and texts, building curricula off students' own testimonials, creating a classroom culture of collective care and action, etc. (see Kynard, 2013; Richardson, 2003).

CREE: Insights for Literacy Classrooms

This section is not intended to be a "how-to guide" or a "cookie-cutter" demonstration of how to *do* CREE. Oftentimes, when it comes to equity-based pedagogies such as culturally relevant pedagogy (Ladson-Billings, 1995), culturally responsive teaching (Gay, 2000), and culturally sustaining pedagogy (Paris, 2012), many educators want step-by-step instructions. In order for one to understand how CREE looks in practice, I surmise that one's state of *being*, *heart*, and *mind* has to change. I am in agreement with Palmer (1998) that "teaching, like any truly human activity, emerges from one's inwardness for better or worse" (p. 2). As we teach, we invariably cast our beliefs and values onto our students, our content, our instructional practices, and our ways of being together. Thus, educators are doing a disservice to all children, in particular Black children, when our knowledge base of other people's children (Delpit, 1995) remains static.

CREE BEYOND BLACK LIVES

Although CREE highlights anti-black racism and speaks to the experiences of Black lives, I want to make clear that this is not to negate anti-brown racism, the experiences of other minoritized groups, or other lines of inquiry around Latinx, Asian, Pacific Islander, and Indigenous youth. CREE is a movement of solidarity. I am also talking to my Brown and Indigenous brothers and sisters. Understanding CREE as an act of solidarity can assist teachers' pedagogical practices by helping them explore and illuminate the historical, political, cultural, racial, ethnic, and linguistic solidarity that exists between Black, Latinx, and Indigenous groups. Furthermore, educators must provide Black and Brown students with in-school and out-of-school spaces that allow them to make sense of their shared and collective experiences. Martinez (2017) argues, "Unquestionably, Black and Latinx youth experience violence on a daily basis, in and out of schools, as their bodies are racialized, their utterances marked, and their dispositions questioned for not aligning with the expectations of dominant culture" (p. 182). The unjust killings of Jessica "Jessie" Hernandez (Colorado), Jonathen Santellana (Texas), and Pedro Villanueva and Anthony Nuñez (California) illustrate how racial violence can be extrapolated across other minoritized groups.

I contend that CREE can sharpen our understandings about Black struggle and freedom, shed light on the humanity of Black lives through already developed constructs that work to better educate Black people and extend the conversation about English education's role in the struggle for racial justice in a time when Black lives are continuously debased. In an effort to move from racial violence to racial justice, I charge educators across all disciplines to cultivate CREE as part of their conceptual frameworks for teaching and learning.

(RE)IMAGINING ELA CLASSROOMS

Literacy scholars, English educators, and ELA teachers cannot fully utilize CREE if they do not embrace and live within the radical imagination. To (re) imagine ELA classrooms, educators have to work to create the world that we hope to see. Embracing the radical imagination requires English educators, literacy scholars, and ELA teachers to humanize English courses and language and literacy education (Johnson, 2017) and to foster a love of Blackness as a counternarrative to prevailing discourses of deficit. This love for Blackness must be poured into curricular decisions. Furthermore, this deep-seated love can move us toward humanization and away from oppression and marginalization. hooks (2003) illuminates love as a pedagogical tool and action that should be expressed in classrooms. Ultimately, CREE supports educators in (re)imagining how Blackness is highlighted and employed in classroom spaces.

I envision classrooms where the stories of Black people are told through liberatory literacy practices such as movement, media, art, song, dance, and poetry. I envision classrooms where educators *love* the multiple ways people from different racial and ethnic backgrounds express their pain and work toward liberation. I imagine classrooms where Black children are taught to love every ounce of their Blackness and that, as Africa's children, they are born from generations of kings and queens, scientists, writers, and mathematicians, from resilience and determination. I imagine classrooms where educators believe in the possibility of Black children and youth—classrooms where Black students know their Black skin, education, health, spirit, voice, life, and humanity *do* matter. Lastly, I imagine classrooms where the teachers and students all have riots in their souls (Baszile, 2006) and are not afraid to join the revolution in a time of racial chaos by making a commitment to racial justice—a commitment to *their* cause, *our* cause, and the cause of human freedom.

TEACHING TIPS

Johnson engages in autoethnographic methods to outline his vision for critical race English education (CREE). In addition to the multimodal ideas for supporting students in this work that are shared in this article, you can ask students to curate a Spotify playlist that speaks to their:

1. ***love of Blackness,***
2. ***complexity of loving Blackness in a society informed by white supremacy, and***
3. ***journey in learning to love Blackness.***

This type of strategy supports Johnson's call for liberatory literacy practices in the classroom.

NOTE

I have purposefully chosen to capitalize *Black* and other racialized language to show a radical love (see hooks, 2003) for Black and Brown people who are constantly wounded by white supremacy. In conjunction, I have chosen to disassemble white supremacy in my language by lowercasing the "w" in *white* and *white supremacy* as well as the "e" in *eurocentric*. Furthermore, see Cheryl E. Matias's (2016) "White Skin, Black Friend: A Fanonian Application to Theorize Racial Fetish in Teacher Education."

REFERENCES

Baker-Bell, A. (2017). For Loretta: A Black woman literacy scholar's journey to prioritizing self-preservation and Black feminist-womanist storytelling. *Journal of Literacy Research*, 49, 526–543.

Baker-Bell, A., Butler, T., & Johnson, L. L. (2017). The pain and the wounds: A call for critical race English education in the wake of racial violence. *English Education*, 49, 116–129.

Ball, A. F., & Lardner, T. (1997, March). *Dispositions toward literacy: Constructs of teacher knowledge and the Ann Arbor Black English case.* Paper presented at the Conference on College Composition and Communication Annual Convention, Phoenix, AZ.

Ball, A. F., & Lardner, T. (2005). *African American literacies unleashed: Vernacular English and the composition classroom.* Carbondale, IL: Southern Illinois University Press.

Baszile, D. T. (2006). Rage in the interest of Black self: Curriculum theorizing as dangerous knowledge. *Journal of Curriculum Theorizing,* 22(1), 89–98.

Bell, D. (1992). Faces at the bottom of the well. New York: Basic Books.

Bernal, D. D., & Villalpando, O. (2002). An apartheid of knowledge in academia: The struggle over the "legitimate" knowledge of faculty of color. *Equity & Excellence in Education,* 35, 169–180.

Boutte, G. S. (2015). *Educating African American students: And how are the children?* New York: Routledge.

Brayboy, B. M. J. (2005). Toward a tribal critical race theory in higher education. Paper presented at the meeting of the Association for the Study of Higher Education, Richmond, VA.

Brooms, D. R., & Brice, D. A. (2017). Bring the noise: Black men teaching (race and) white privilege. *Race and Justice,* 7(2), 144–159.

Butler, T. T. (2017). #Say[ing]HerName as critical demand: English education in the age of erasure. *English Education,* 49, 153–178.

Chang, R. S. (1993). Toward an Asian American legal scholarship: Critical race theory, post-structuralism, and narrative space. *California Law Review,* 81, 1241–1323.

Davis, A. (2015). *Freedom is a constant struggle: Ferguson, Palestine, and the foundations of a Movement.* Haymarket Books, 2015.

Delgado, R. (1989). Storytelling for oppositionists and others: A plea for narrative. *Michigan Law Review,* 87, 2411–2441.

Delpit, L. (1995). *Other people's children: Cultural conflict in the classroom.* New York: Norton.

Dumas, M. J., & ross, k. m. (2016). "Be real Black for me": Imagining BlackCrit in education. *Urban Education,* 51, 415–442.

Fanon, F. (2004). *The wretched of the earth.* New York: Grove Press.

Fasching-Varner, K., & Hartlep, N. D. (Eds.). (2015). *The assault on communities of color.* Lanham, MD: Rowman & Littlefield.

Fei, V. L., O'Halloran, K. L., Tan, S., & Marissa, K. L. E. (2015). Teaching visual texts with multimodal analysis software. *Educational Technology Research and Development,* 63, 915–935.

Freire, P. (1970). *Pedagogy of the oppressed.* New York: Continuum International Publishing.

Gay, G. (2000). *Culturally responsive teaching theory, research, and practice.* New York: Teachers College Press.

Grant, C. A., Brown, K. D., & Brown, A. L. (2016). *Black intellectual thought in education: The missing traditions of Anna Julia Cooper, Carter G. Woodson, and Alain LeRoy Locke.* New York: Routledge.

Greene, G., Boutte, G. S., & Hightower, D. (2018). "How can I be like you?": A tri-vocal account of intergenerational mentoring and queen mothering. In R. Jeffries (Ed.), *Queen mothers: Articulating the spirit of Black women teacher-leaders.* Charlotte, NC: Information Age.

Haddix, M. (2015). *Cultivating racial and linguistic diversity in literacy teacher education: Teachers like me.* New York and Urbana, IL: Routledge and National Council of Teachers of English.

Hernandez-Truyol, B. E. (1997). Indivisible identities: Culture clashes, confused constructs, and reality checks. *Harvard Latino Law Review,* 2, 199–230.

Hill, M. L. (2018). "Thank you, Black Twitter": State violence, digital counterpublics, and pedagogies of resistance. *Urban Education,* 53, 286–302.

Jeffries, M. (2014, November 28). Ferguson must force us to face anti-blackness. Retrieved from https://www.bostonglobe.com/opinion/2014/11/28/ferguson-must-force-face-anti-blackness/pKVMpGxwUYpMDyHRWPln2M/story.html

Jefferson-Griffen, L. (2015). Skittles, Arizona iced tea, and cigarettes: The price of Black lives in a "post-racial" America. In K. Fasching-Varner & N. D. Hartlep (Eds.), *The assault on communities of color* (pp. 43–49). Lanham, MD: Rowman & Littlefield.

Johnson, L. L. (2017). The racial hauntings of one Black male professor and the disturbance of the self(ves): Self-actualization and racial storytelling as pedagogical practices. *Journal of Literacy Research,* 49, 476–502.

Johnson, L. L., & Bryan, N. (2016). Using our voices, losing our bodies: Michael Brown, Trayvon Martin, and the spirit murders of Black male professors in the academy. *Race Ethnicity and Education,* 20, 163–177.

Johnson, L. L., Gibbs Grey, T. M., & Baker-Bell, A. (2017). Changing the dominant narrative: A call for using storytelling as language and literacy theory, research methodology, and practice. *Journal of Literacy Research,* 49, 467–475.

Johnson, L. L., Jackson, J., Stovall, D. O., & Baszile, D. T. (2017). "Loving blackness to death": (Re)Imagining ELA classrooms in a time of racial chaos. *English Journal,* 106(4), 60–66.

Kinloch, V. F. (2005). Revisiting the promise of students' right to their own language: Pedagogical strategies. *College Composition and Communication,* 57, 83–113.

Kirkland, D. (2013). *A search past silence: Literacy, Black males, and the American dream deferred.* New York: Teachers College Press.

Kynard, C. (2013). *Vernacular insurrections.* Albany: State University of New York Press.

Ladson-Billings, G. (1995). Toward a theory of culturally relevant pedagogy. *American Educational Research Journal,* 32(3), 465–491.

Ladson-Billings, G., & Tate, W. F. (1995). Toward a critical race theory of education. *Teachers College Record,* 97(1), 47–68.

Lee, H. (1960). *To kill a mockingbird.* Philadelphia: Lippincott.

Literacy Research Association. (2016). The role of literacy research in racism and racial violence statement endorsed by the Literacy Research Association. Retrieved from https://www.literacyresearchassociation.org/assets/docs/the%20role%20of%20literacy%20research%20in%20racism%20and%20racial%20violencejanuary2017final.pdf

Love, B. L. (2017). Difficult knowledge: When a Black feminist educator was too afraid to #SayHerName. *English Education,* 49, 192–208.

Martin, M. (2014). A witness of whiteness: An autoethnographic examination of a white teacher's own inherent prejudice. *Education as Change*, 18, 237–254.

Martinez, D. C. (2017). Imagining a language of solidarity for Black and Latinx youth in English language arts classrooms. *English Education*, 49, 179–193.

Matias, C. E. (2013). Tears worth telling: Urban teaching and the possibilities of racial justice. *Multicultural Perspectives*, 15(4), 187–193.

Matias, C. E. (2016). White skin, black friend: A Fanonian application to theorize racial fetish in teacher education. *Educational Philosophy and Theory*, 48, 221–236.

McLaughlin, E. C. (2014). What we know about Michael Brown's shooting. Retrieved from http://www.cnn.com/2014/08/11/us/missouri-ferguson-michael-brown-what-we-know/

Morrell, E. (2005). Critical English education. *English Education*, 37, 312–321.

Muhammad, G. E., Chisholm, M. G., & Starks, F. D. (2017). Exploring #BlackLivesMatter and sociopolitical relationships through kinship writing. *English Teaching: Practice & Critique*, 16(3), 347–362.

Palmer, P. J. (1998). *The courage to teach: Exploring the inner landscape of a teacher's life.* San Francisco: Jossey-Bass.

Paris, D. (2010). "A friend who understand fully": Notes on humanizing research in a multiethnic youth community. *International Journal of Qualitative Studies in Education*, 24, 137–149.

Paris, D. (2012). Culturally sustaining pedagogy: A needed change in stance, terminology, and practice. *Educational Researcher*, 41(3), 93–97.

Paris, D., & Winn, M. T. (Eds.). (2014). *Humanizing research: Decolonizing qualitative inquiry with youth and communities.* Thousand Oaks, CA: Sage.

Perry, T., Steele, C., & Hilliard, A. (2003). *Young, gifted, and black: Promoting high achievement among African-American students.* Boston: Beacon Press.

Richardson, E. (2003). *African American literacies.* New York: Routledge.

Rogers, R. (2018). *Reclaiming powerful literacies: New horizons for critical discourse analysis.* New York: Routledge.

Sealey-Ruiz, Y. (2016). Why Black girls' literacies matter: New literacies for a new era. *English Education*, 48(4), 290–298.

Shipp, L. (2017). Revolutionizing the English classroom through consciousness, justice, and self-awareness. *English Journal*, 106(4), 35–40.

Smitherman, G. (1979). Toward educational linguistics for the first world. *College English*, 41, 202–211.

Smitherman, G. (1995). Students' right to their own language: A retrospective. *English Journal*, 84(1), 21–27.

Solórzano, D. G., & Yosso, T. J. (2002). Critical race methodology: Counter-storytelling as an analytical framework for education research. *Qualitative Inquiry*, 8, 23–44.

South Carolina Department of Education. (2015). South Carolina college- and career-ready standards for English language arts. Retrieved from https://ed.sc.gov/scdoe/assets/file/programs-services/59/documents/ELA2015SCCCRStandards.pdf

Stovall, D. O. (2015). Normalizing Black death: Michael Brown, Marissa Alexander, Dred Scott, and the apartheid state. In K. Fasching-Varner & N. D. Hartlep (Eds.), *The assault on communities of color* (pp. 67–71). Lanham, MD: Rowman & Littlefield.

Stuckey, J. E. (1990). *The violence of literacy.* Portsmouth, NH: Boynton/Cook.

Taylor, K. Y. (2016). *From #BlackLivesMatter to Black liberation.* Chicago: Haymarket Books.

Tuck, E., & Yang, K. W. (2014). R-words: Refusing research. In D. Paris & M. T. Winn (Eds.), *Humanizing research: Decolonizing qualitative inquiry for youth and communities* (pp. 223–248). Thousand Oaks, CA: Sage.

Vera Institute of Justice. (2015). Translating justice. Retrieved from http://www.vera.org/project/translating-justice

Winn, M. T. (2013). Toward a restorative English education. *Research in the Teaching of English*, 48, 126–136.

Woodson, C. G. (2000). *The miseducation of the Negro.* Chicago: African American Images. (Original work published 1933)

Yuan, T. (2017). The teaching of "dangerous" school bodies: Toward critical embodied pedagogies in English education. *English Journal*, 106(4), 67–72.

LAMAR L. JOHNSON is an associate professor of Language and Literacy for Linguistic and Racial Justice in the Department of English at Michigan State University. His work explores the intricate intersections of language, literacy, anti-Black racism, Blackness, and education. He was the recipient of the 2017 Promising Researcher Award, the recipient of the 2018 Edwin M. Hopkins Award, and 2019 honorable mention for the Alan C. Purves Award. He was a coeditor of *African Diaspora Literacy: The Heart of Transformation in K-12 Schools and Teacher Education.*

This article originally appeared
in *English Journal 108.4*

TO DISMANTLE RACISM, WE MUST DISCUSS IT

LORENA GERMÁN

I TEACH NINTH-GRADE ENGLISH at an urban independent school with predominantly White students, and sometimes the characters in the books we read are the only other people of color with me in the classroom. I invite them into the classroom intentionally. Their voices fill our space and bring depth to our conversation. In ninth grade, the students are especially concerned with their social lives and the conundrum of who they are becoming. I use this common age-based stress to design the motif of our English class: Identity. The characters in books lead us into engaging and far-reaching explorations. The texts I present are purposefully selected to open dialogue across difference and offer us salient vantage points. In this feature, I introduce readers to some of the characters my students have "met" in our classroom.

Gabi, from *Gabi, a Girl in Pieces* by Isabel Quintero, talks to us about her body. She critiques it, she loves it, she struggles with it, she wrestles it, she tries to fix it. We walk and laugh with her. We also cry with her. We question our own bodies with her. Her concerns are especially obvious when she crosses the US-Mexico border. She demands that we think critically with her about the fact that she "doesn't look Mexican enough" because her skin is light. She is White-presenting and this proves to be an important element of her identity. She knows what others think of her: the looks, the doubts, the hesitations she gets because of the color of her skin. While the majority of my students don't share that experience with Gabi, we do have a population of students (because we're in Texas) that can identify with her. I, too, have relatives who could easily pass as White people. Gabi's experience, then, becomes real and relatable for us as a class. Immediately, this fictional character presents us with a conversation that involves invested classmates and friends. We discuss how issues of skin tone can surface tensions of beauty and acceptance within a family. We think about the ways that friends we have had for years may have been struggling with this concern about skin color silently and how we can go about broaching the conversation to offer them support. My White students often want to know how they can affirm the identity of a person of color who is White-presenting. It's complicated and lifelong work, but we must get started sometime and somehow. Gabi's voice is honest, and her truth-telling is an open door.

We also meet Jin Wang from Gene Luen Yang's *American Born Chinese*. Jin takes Gabi's struggle a step further: he makes the *choice* to pass as White. Jin is a great example of what racism and the supremacy of Whiteness can accomplish when internalized. Jin's desire to fit in socially and to be accepted are so strong that he represses his own identity. He resists his culture, his language, his family, himself. The conversation about racism is often limited to the Black/White binary, yet racism is more than that. The experience of Asians and Asian Americans is important to understanding color hierarchies. Identifying the "model minority" myth, which we also discuss in this unit, allows students to see the sinister way racism can be masked and presented as something good, flattering even. The term *model minority* refers to a minority group perceived to be academically and socioeconomically successful, especially in contrast to other minoritized groups. At our school, we have a recognizable number of Asian exchange students from Korea, China, and other countries. They experience some of the microaggressions Jin experiences, and our White students commit the mistakes and express the biases that the characters exhibit in the text. This book allows us to engage in demystifying those interactions, face the tension, and unpack this cultural phenomenon.

Starr, the main character in *The Hate U Give* by Angie Thomas, is another young woman who comes to our classroom and helps us discuss race, White supremacy, and the color hierarchy so prevalent in our society. Starr's friend Khalil is killed by a police officer. What's unique about Starr's story is that her friend dies because of circumstances related to the color of his skin. We talk and think about the ways that people's skin tone unconsciously informs our perceptions and beliefs about them. I talk about the ways that as a teacher, I've often been confused to be a student or confused to be a Spanish teacher because of my youthful appearance and my name. I know that my White colleagues aren't delegitimized in the same way. The idea of a Brown English teacher is so foreign that well-educated adults misidentify a thirty-five-year-old Dominican woman as a student. I know this is also not a unique experience; I've talked with other educators, including college professors, who share this experience. Too often, our role as academics seems far-fetched; it doesn't exist as a possibility in the imagination of others. Starr helps us see how racism affects our imagination and therefore influences our biases.

Shakespeare's *Othello* also presents us with a reason to pause and empathize. We meet Othello, a Black man living alone in Europe who falls prey to an evil White man who eventually tears him down. Othello reveals to us how isolating color hierarchy can be. My students and I discuss the ways that it can be difficult to be the only person of color or the only "fill-in-the-blank" in a social space. Othello's pain and loneliness allow my students to peer into that experience and imagine what some of their peers, as well as my colleagues of color and I, may feel. We talk about the situations we find ourselves in and we discuss the ways that it can affect our sense of self. When you are the "only one," trauma from experiencing racism throughout your life bubbles up, often at the slightest trigger. You may doubt your intelligence, your strength, your power, even your rights. You may ask yourself: Should I be here? Should I just leave? Can I do this?

Not discussing the subtleties of issues of race and racism in the classroom is irresponsible. If we are preparing our students to engage with other humans in empathic and respectful ways, then we must do our part to address racism. If we are preparing young people to build a future that doesn't yet exist, then we must explain the need to dismantle racism. If we are supporting our young people as they seek to change the world—because they can, because it's doable—then we must play our role well and imagine that future with them. I encourage you to invite these characters and others into your classroom. Let's work toward imagining new possibilities with and for our students. How will we ever help them rid the culture of racism without discussing it first?

TEACHING TIPS

Germán presents a message about dismantling racism that speaks to the urgency of doing this work with youth. Drawing on the examples from her article, you can begin engaging students in conversations about lessons they learned connected to race and racism from characters in the books you have read in class as a way to support their racial literacy development. As you read books with your students, curate an audit trail (Harste & Vasquez, 1998) that focuses on how critical encounters with race and racism that provide insight into how the characters made sense of race and racism in the book. This approach can model for students how to name racial inequities in texts and consider specific ways they can disrupt these practices in real life.

WORKS CITED

Quintero, Isabel. *Gabi, a Girl in Pieces*. Cinco Puntos, 2014.

Shakespeare, William. *Othello*. Simon and Schuster, 2004.

Thomas, Angie. *The Hate U Give*. Balzer + Bray, 2017.

Yang, Gene Luen. *American Born Chinese*. Square Fish, 2008.

LORENA GERMÁN is a two-time nationally awarded Dominican American educator focused on antiracist and antibias education. She's been featured in the *New York Times*, NPR, PBS, *Rethinking Schools*, *EdWeek*, *Learning for Justice Magazine*, and more. She published *The Anti Racist Teacher: Reading Instruction Workbook, and Textured Teaching: A Framework for Culturally Sustaining Practices* about curriculum and lesson development focused on social justice. She's a cofounder of #DisruptTexts, Multicultural Classroom, and chair of NCTE's Committee Against Racism and Bias in the Teaching of English.

This article originally appeared
in *English Journal 108.4*

EVERYDAY COLORISM: Reading in the Language Arts Classroom

The author provides an overview of colorism, addresses colorism in the English language arts classroom, and shares ideas for responding to colorism beyond the classroom.

SARAH L. WEBB

"DEE IS LIGHTER THAN MAGGIE, with nicer hair and a fuller figure," says the narrator in Alice Walker's short story "Everyday Use" (49). A significant aspect of this classic text is the conflict between the two sisters, Dee and Maggie. Some readers might infer that a large source of this conflict stems from the difference in Dee's and Maggie's appearance, as did one of my African American male students, who concluded that "Dee is lighter than Maggie, so that means Dee can smash her." While it may seem like a huge leap to go from Walker's sparse description of Maggie's appearance to such an overt judgment about the meaning of her complexion, we must remember that students do not read skin color neutrally or objectively. Particularly for students of color, the nuances in skin tone among members of their race are loaded with cultural baggage due to the ubiquitous phenomenon of colorism. The same may be true for us as teachers. As a dark-skinned African American woman with a lighter-skinned sister, I readily perceived the archetypal relationship between Walker's characters. However, even readers who do not have such mirroring experiences are likely to recognize what is popularly labeled the "light skin versus dark skin" dynamic.

While teaching high school in Louisiana between 2010 and 2012, I occasionally witnessed instances of explicit colorism among my students in their conversations about themselves and others. Beyond the above student response to Walker's short story, I heard several of my other ninth and tenth graders make unsolicited value judgments about skin color in casual conversations outside of instructional time:

> "I wish I was light-skinned like my momma."
>
> "I'm less proud of myself because I got darker over the summer."
>
> "I don't like this picture; I look too black on here."
>
> "I don't like dark-skinned people when I first meet them, maybe once I get to know them."

Some of these statements were even told directly to me, and every time I heard something like this, my heart broke. Students took for granted and assumed a consensus that light skin shades are preferable, if not outright superior, to darker skin shades. Much like an everyday household item, colorism was something that my students took for granted as just a typical element of daily life, something they could simply accept at face value, something innocuously mundane. This article provides teachers with a basic understanding of colorism and how it commonly affects students, how to incorporate lessons or discussions about colorism into a typical high school English curriculum, and strategies for continuing conversations about colorism beyond the singular classroom.

Understanding Colorism

The origins of colorism are linked to European colonialism, American slavery, class hierarchies in Asia, and White supremacy in general (Hunter 238). Alice Walker, in fact, writes extensively about this hurtful dynamic in her 1982 essay "If the Present Looks like the Past, What Does the Future Look Like?" Walker coins and defines the term *colorism* as "prejudicial or preferential treatment of same-race people based solely on their color" (290). Researchers have since described this phenomenon using other terms such as *skin color bias* or *color complex* (Russell-Cole et al.). In the decades following Walker's testimony on colorism, scholars have conducted research on colorism in fields such as education, economics, law, and social work and in cultures spanning the globe in places such as Canada, Brazil, and India (Hunter 238). Colorism is indeed a global issue.

Colorism is also associated with prejudice based on other physical traits, such as hair texture, eye color, and shape or size of the nose and lips (Blair et al.). All of these features have historically been racialized in the United States, meaning we typically associate these features with certain racial categories, and also certain ethnic groups. Colorism is based on the degree to which one's outward appearance matches or does not match the expected or archetypal (and stereotypical) appearance of one's designated race. The general pattern is that society extends greater privileges to people of color who appear less like their racial archetype and more like a European racial archetype. In my discussions about colorism with White people from around the world, many of them also report social pressure among Whites to meet certain standards of racial appearance, such as blonde hair and blue eyes. Though in recent decades a Western standard of beauty among Whites has been tanned skin, for centuries the ideal beauty feature for White women was pale skin (Blay 21).

Throughout her epistolary essay, Walker elaborates on the historical conflict of colorism among Black women in the United States and asserts that colorism is as harmful as the more well-known issues of racism and sexism. Walker's beliefs about colorism as expressed in that essay are connected to her short story in how, for example, the sisters' complexions correspond with their relative confidence, social status, and financial success. The overwhelming majority of research has confirmed and elaborated on the issues Walker raises in her short story and essay, including income and wealth inequality—as much as a 14 percent gap between earners with lighter skin compared to those of the same race with darker skin; implicit (unconscious) employer discrimination—such that job applicants with light skin fared better even when they had less education; disparities in marriage rates; and differential health outcomes (Goldsmith et al.; Hamilton et al.; Harrison and Thomas; Kreisman and Rangel; Udry et al.). Here are some findings we should be particularly aware of in an educational setting:

- Light-skinned individuals often report painful awareness of privilege that results in "survivor's guilt," or alienation/antagonism from their own community (Cunningham). Teachers should understand this dynamic because it can often be one cause of interpersonal conflict among students.
- People perceive Blacks and Latinos with more Caucasian features as more intelligent (Lynn). This means that teachers of any race or ethnicity are likely to have some bias in their perceptions of student intelligence based on skin tone. As teachers we should honestly assess our own biases about darker skin tones and lighter skin tones, for example, or curlier hair versus straighter hair. Harvard's suite of implicit bias tests includes a test on color bias (implicit.harvard.edu/implicit/takeatest.html). This is a useful tool for helping teachers become more self-aware regarding colorism.
- Dark and very dark-skinned Black students continue to experience educational disadvantages well after the Civil Rights era (Loury).
- Very light skin corresponds with a greater likelihood of going to college and finding a full-time job (Ryabov).
- Girls with very dark skin tones are three times more likely to be suspended from school than girls with very light skin tones who engage in the same behaviors (Hannon et al.). This is another example of implicit bias. Whereas above, people tend to view dark-skinned people as less intelligent, this finding about school suspensions is based on the stereotype that dark-skinned girls are more delinquent.

This research—which reveals the existence of color-based stereotypes, implicit biases, economic disparities, educational inequalities, and other forms of social discrimination—illustrates why it is necessary to discuss colorism with all students, not just students we believe are most directly affected. I recommend teaching all students about colorism just as we would teach all students about racism. Regardless of a student's race, ethnicity, nationality, or other cultural background, having critical education about colorism helps them become more empowered, responsible global citizens who can help redress color-based social inequalities. In the remainder of this article, I return to the text "Everyday Use" to illustrate one possible approach to addressing colorism in our classrooms.

Addressing Colorism in the ELA Classroom

A culturally responsive way to introduce the topic in class is through the literary texts we choose to teach. Walker's short story "Everyday Use" is one good choice for exploring the topic of colorism within the framework of literary analysis. Focusing on the dynamic between the two sisters allows teachers to connect colorism to other themes in the text: sibling rivalries, self-esteem, bullying, social status, and class discrimination, to name a few. However, I caution against diluting conversation about colorism by lumping all forms of discrimination or bullying into one discussion. Rather, I urge teachers to hold space for students to learn about and discuss colorism as a specific issue. I urge this primarily because colorism, compared to more widely recognized -isms, often gets glossed over or dismissed outright in public discourse.

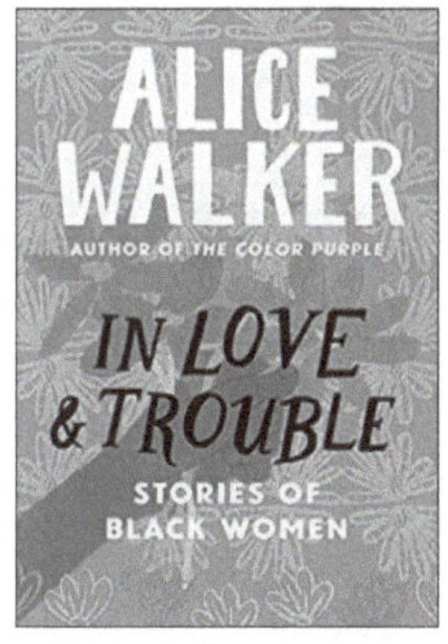

FIGURE 1
The short story "Everyday Use" appears in Walker's 1973 short fiction volume *In Love and Trouble: Stories of Black Women.*

Though recent attention to colorism by celebrities such as Gabrielle Union and Amara La Negra is helping to change this, I still believe that our students will rarely, if ever, have other opportunities outside of our classrooms to have informative or productive conversations about colorism.

Beginning with the brief and deceptively simple statement, "Dee is lighter than Maggie, with nicer hair and a fuller figure," teachers might ask: *What does the narrator mean by "lighter" and "nicer"?* A common obstacle to understanding colorism is the use of the word *color* as a euphemism for the word *race*. As stated earlier, certain physical traits are stereotypically associated with certain races, complexion and hair texture being first and foremost of those traits. So, starting here in a discussion of colorism can help students see that as biological siblings Dee and Maggie are the same race, yet they have different physical features. Their skin colors and hair types are unique, though both are African American. This is key to distinguishing between racism and colorism: people of the same racial category can have different skin tones and hair textures, and people of different racial categories can have similar skin tones and hair textures.

REGARDLESS OF A STUDENT'S RACE, ETHNICITY, NATIONALITY, OR OTHER CULTURAL BACKGROUND, HAVING CRITICAL EDUCATION ABOUT COLORISM HELPS THEM BECOME MORE EMPOWERED, RESPONSIBLE GLOBAL CITIZENS WHO CAN HELP REDRESS COLOR-BASED SOCIAL INEQUALITIES.

The next step, after recognizing the difference in the sisters' skin tone and hair texture, is asking students: *How might the sisters' different appearances have affected their lives?* Students can begin to explore this question by making inferences from details in the story as they read closely. Key passages and descriptions to highlight in response to this question include the following:

- **An introduction:** "Maggie will be nervous until after her sister goes: She will stand hopelessly in corners, homely and ashamed of the burn scars down her arms and legs, eyeing her sister with a mixture of envy and awe. She thinks her sister has held life always in the palm of one hand, that 'no' is a word the world never learned to say to her" (Walker 47).
- **Body language:** "Dee, though. She would always look anyone in the eye. Hesitation was not part of her nature" (49) and "'Wa-su-zo-Tean-o!' [Dee] says, coming on in that gliding way the dress makes her move" (52) versus "Have you ever seen a lame animal, perhaps a dog run over by some careless person rich enough to own a car, sidle up to someone who is ignorant enough to be kind to him? That is the way my Maggie walks.

She has been like this, chin on chest, eyes on ground, feet in shuffle, ever since the fire that burned the other house to the ground" (49) and "She stoops down quickly and lines up picture after picture of me sitting there in front of the house with Maggie cowering behind me" (53).

- **Education:** "I used to think she hated Maggie, too. But that was before we raised the money, the church and me, to send her to Augusta to school. She used to read to us without pity, forcing words, lies, other folks' habits, whole lives upon us two, sitting trapped and ignorant underneath her voice . . . to shove us away at just the moment, like dimwits, we seemed about to understand" (50) versus "Sometimes Maggie reads to me. She stumbles along good-naturedly but can't see well. She knows she is not bright. Like good looks and money, quickness passed her by" (50).

- **The climax:** "'She can have them, Mama,' [Maggie] said, like somebody used to never winning anything or having anything reserved for her. 'I can 'member Grandma Dee without the quilts.' I looked at her hard. She had filled her bottom lip with checkerberry snuff, and it gave her face a kind of dopey, hangdog look. It was Grandma Dee and Big Dee who taught her how to quilt herself. She stood there with her scarred hands hidden in the folds of her skirt. She looked at her sister with something like fear, but she wasn't mad at her. This was Maggie's portion. This was the way she knew God to work.

  "When I looked at her like that, something hit me in the top of my head and ran down to the soles of my feet. Just like when I'm in church and the spirit of God touches me and I get happy and shout. I did something I never had done before: hugged Maggie to me, then dragged her on into the room, snatched the quilts out of Miss Wangero's hands, and dumped them into Maggie's lap. Maggie just sat there on my bed with her mouth open" (58).

After completing close readings of these passages and thinking about colorism as a factor in the sisters' relative confidence, education, and overall life outcomes, I recommend teachers continue with a third phase, which is to introduce critical context. The primary resource I recommend for providing critical context to high school students is Walker's essay "If the Present Looks Like the Past, What Does the Future Look Like?," which students can read as a companion text.

FIGURE 2
The essay "If the Present Looks Like the Past, What Does the Future Look Like?" appears in Walker's 1983 volume *In Search of Our Mothers' Gardens: Womanist Prose.*

For middle school students, I recommend teachers provide them with a summary or excerpts from the essay. Combining Walker's fiction with her nonfiction is a good way of exploring themes across genres. Questions that help facilitate the cross-genre analysis between Walker's two texts might include the following:

- **How is Walker's focus on sisterhood in the essay reflected in her short story, "Everyday Use"?** Walker claims in her essay that colorism is particularly harmful to the relationships among women, causing division and antagonism. This is reflected in the story by her choice to focus on the sibling rivalry between two actual sisters.

- **How do the essay and short story each illustrate the relationship between colorism and class among African Americans?** In the story, the lighter-skinned sister Dee has moved into a middle-class lifestyle and exhibits prejudice against the poor and working-class lifestyle of her mother and sister, who happen to be darker skinned. In the essay, Walker calls out the Black middle class as being especially problematic in overtly discriminating against dark-skinned women.

- **How does "Everyday Use" differ from Walker's criticism of early nineteenth-century novels by African American authors?** Walker's essay includes her analysis of earlier novels by African American authors that only feature "white-looking" female characters, and only including darker-skinned female characters on rare occasions and only in disparaging ways. Her own short story breaks from that old tradition by telling the stories of Black women with darker skin tones who have more traditionally Black hair textures.

- **Based on the many examples in Walker's essay, write an additional scene depicting an instance of colorism that Maggie might have faced growing up.** Walker's essay includes real-life examples of dark-skinned people being excluded from middle-class social activities at school, from dating circles, and from certain career paths, especially during the historical time period of the story.

The fourth phase and essential component of classwork related to the theme of colorism is personal self-reflection. It is the element of self-reflection that matters most for students in their personal development as citizens. Again, self-reflection is productive for all students, even those who have no overt personal experiences with colorism. In most cases, students of any background have likely observed colorism in popular media such as music, movies, television, magazines, and other literature. It is also likely that students might have a conditioned, implicit bias against dark skin as a result of their exposure to such media, whether or not they typically encounter dark-skinned people in their day-to-day lives. Self-reflection can be incorporated throughout a lesson and/or incorporated as a formal activity or assignment. The following questions will help spark student reflection and can be posed as general class discussion questions, as prompts for journal entries, or as topics for more formal and extended essays or research papers.

SELF-REFLECTION IS PRODUCTIVE FOR ALL STUDENTS, EVEN THOSE WHO HAVE NO OVERT PERSONAL EXPERIENCES WITH COLORISM. IN MOST CASES, STUDENTS OF ANY BACKGROUND HAVE LIKELY OBSERVED COLORISM IN POPULAR MEDIA SUCH AS MUSIC, MOVIES, TELEVISION, MAGAZINES, AND OTHER LITERATURE.

- How does "Everyday Use" and/or "If the Present Looks Like the Past" remind you of things you have seen, heard, or experienced in your own life or in other forms of media?
- In "Everyday Use," the mother, who is the narrator, finally decides to take a stand for her daughter Maggie by giving her the quilts instead of letting Dee take them. How might you and your peers act against colorism as upstanders?
- If racial categories did not exist, would problems like colorism still exist? Explain your reasoning.
- What advice would you give to someone who had a prejudice or bias against others because of their skin tone or hair texture? If your advice includes "appreciate all skin colors" or "don't judge people for how they look," explain ways that people can practice doing that. Use examples from the story or essay to explain your advice.
- What advice would you give to someone who is treated unfairly due to colorism? If your advice includes "love yourself" or "love the skin you're in," explain strategies for how people can learn to do so. Use examples from the story or essay to explain your advice.
- What attitudes or beliefs have you had about different skin tones, your own or others? Why or how did you get those ideas? Have they changed, and if so, why and how?

Thinking beyond the Explicit Curriculum

As ELA teachers, one of the most proactive ways we can address colorism is to directly address it within our curriculum. However, there may be times when we observe colorism outside of the curricular or academic context. I briefly offer tips for responding in these situations.

RESPOND

A teacher's failure to respond after an instance of colorism could be interpreted by students as approving or condoning colorism. While it might be tempting to say nothing out of fear of saying the wrong thing, our silence actually speaks volumes. Even the simple encouragement to "love the skin you're in" is better than a nonresponse.

OFFER RESOURCES TO THE STUDENTS INVOLVED

This applies to the person who is a target of colorism as well as the person who is perpetuating colorism. A list of recommended resources is provided.

KNOW WHAT COLORISM LOOKS AND SOUNDS LIKE

Teachers can familiarize themselves with the kind of nomenclature minority students might use to tease or alienate their classmates. Even without knowing the specific words, educators can pick up on context clues that alert them to insults, teasing, bullying, or harassment. Regardless of students' race or ethnicity, pay attention to when and how they discuss skin tone or hair texture. If you feel comfortable, ask students or other colleagues if they understand the meaning behind certain comments.

BRING THE TOPIC OF COLORISM INTO THE LARGER SCHOOL COMMUNITY

Partnering with other stakeholders to address colorism is a crucial next step because regardless of what we do within our individual classes, students will inevitably leave our classrooms and reenter a schoolwide atmosphere and community environment that condones and promotes colorism. Community engagement can include reciting poems at school assemblies, professional development for faculty and staff, or guest speakers. Teachers, administrators, support staff, professional development trainers, parents, students, researchers, and others can continue to educate ourselves and help spread awareness that colorism exists and how it manifests in our schools, classrooms, and communities. Just as colorism itself is an everyday part of society, so too must be our efforts to eradicate it.

TABLE 1

These texts and resources are recommended for the study of everyday colorism.

Title	Source/Author
Fall Secrets	Candy Dawson Boyd
Alice Walker in the Classroom: "Living by the Word"	Carl Jago
"Team Lightskinned"	CNN YouTube Channel
Colorism Poems	Colorism Healing
"A Girl Like Me"	Kiri Davi on Vimeo
The Skin I'm In	Sharon G. Flake
Implicit Association Test	Stanford University
"Shadeism: Part 1"	Nayani Thiyagarajah on Vimeo
"Shadeism: Digging Deeper"	Nayani Thiyagarajah on Vimeo
"In This Shade (Colorism)"	Youth Speaks YouTube Channel

Considering Teachers as Change Agents

The reason I've been focusing on colorism in the classroom through professional development, classroom visits, and instructional materials is because I believe teachers are one of the most powerful groups of change agents in the world. As educators, we hold a unique position to impact successive generations that will shape the future of our society and culture. I believe this is especially true of English teachers. I'm also aware of the overwhelming burden placed on teachers as we're implicitly asked to play so many roles—content experts, surrogate parents, nurses, therapists, activists, technical innovators, and so much more. If the concept of colorism is new, it could feel like just one more responsibility added to the load. However, I hope this article helps demonstrate how we can address colorism with the everyday strategies we're already adept at using.

WORKS CITED

Blair, Irene V., et al. "The Role of Afrocentric Features in Person Perception: Judging by Features and Categories." *Journal of Personality and Social Psychology*, vol. 83, no. 1, 2002, pp. 5–25.

Blay, Yabba A. "Skin Bleaching and Global White Supremacy: By Way of Introduction." *Journal of Pan African Studies*, vol. 4, no. 4, 2011, pp. 4–46.

Bodenhorn, Howard. "Colorism, Complexion Homogamy, and Household Wealth: Some Historical Evidence." *The American Economic Review*, vol. 2, no. 2, 2006, pp. 256–60.

Cunningham, Julie L. "Colored Existence: Racial Identity Formation in Light-Skin Blacks." *Smith College Studies in Social Work*, vol. 67, no. 3, 1997, pp. 375–400.

Goldsmith, Arthur H., et al. "From Dark to Light: Skin Color and Wages among African-Americans." *The Journal of Human Resources*, vol. 42, no. 4, 2007, pp. 701–38.

Hamilton, Darrick, et al. "Shedding 'Light' on Marriage: The Influence of Skin Shade on Marriage for Black Females." *Journal of Economic Behavior and Organization*, vol. 72, no. 1, 2009, pp. 30–50.

Hannon, Lance, et al. "The Relationship between Skin Tone and School Suspension for African Americans." *Race and Social Problems*, vol. 5, no. 4, 2013, pp. 281–95.

Harrison, Matthew S., and Kecia M. Thomas. "The Hidden Prejudice in Selection: A Research Investigation on Skin Color Bias." *Journal of Applied Social Psychology*, vol. 39, no. 1, 2009, pp. 134–68.

Hunter, Margaret. "The Persistent Problem of Colorism: Skin Tone, Status, and Inequality." *Sociology Compass*, vol. 1, no. 1, 2007, pp. 237–54.

Kreisman, Daniel, and Marcos A. Rangel. "On the Blurring of the Color Line: Wages and Employment for Black Males of Different Skin Tones." *Review of Economics and Statistics*, vol. 97, no. 1, 2015, pp. 1–13.

Loury, Linda D. "Am I Still Too Black for You?: Schooling and Secular Change in Skin Tone Effects." *Economics of Education Review*, vol. 28, no. 4, 2009, pp. 428–33.

Lynn, Richard. "Skin Color and Intelligence in African Americans." *Population and Environment*, vol. 23, no. 4, 2002, pp. 365–75.

Norwood, Kimberly Jade. *Color Matters: Skin Tone Bias and the Myth of a Post-Racial America*. Routledge, 2014.

Russell-Cole, Kathy, et al. *The Color Complex: The Politics of Skin Color among African Americans*. Anchor Books/Doubleday, 1993.

Ryabov, Igor. "Colorism and School-to-Work and School-to-College Transitions of African American Adolescents." *Race and Social Problems*, vol. 5, no. 1, 2012, pp. 15–27.

Udry, J. Richard, et al. "Skin Color, Status, and Mate Selection." *American Journal of Sociology*, vol. 4, 1971, pp. 722–33.

Veenstra, Gerry. "Mismatched Racial Identities, Colourism, and Health in Toronto and Vancouver." *Social Science and Medicine*, vol. 73, no. 8, 2011, pp. 1152–62.

Walker, Alice. "Everyday Use." In *Love and Trouble: Stories of Black Women*, Harcourt, 1990, pp. 47–59.

——. "If the Present Looks Like the Past, What Does the Future Look Like?" *In Search of Our Mothers' Gardens: Womanist Prose*. Harcourt, 1983, pp. 290–312.

SARAH L. WEBB launched the global initiative Colorism Healing in 2013 to raise awareness and foster individual and collective healing through creative and critical work. Dr. Webb's myriad efforts to address colorism include hosting an international writing contest, publishing anthologies, speaking, coaching, consulting, and mentoring students across the world from Sacramento, California to Sydney, Australia. Dr. Webb has been featured on regional NPR stations, Fox Soul TV, the *Illinois Times*, and on the TEDx stage.

This article originally appeared
in *English Journal 109.4*

CENTERING #BLACKLIVESMATTER TO CONFRONT INJUSTICE, INSPIRE ADVOCACY, AND DEVELOP LITERACIES

The authors provide a model to integrate themes of social justice, advocacy, and #BlackLivesMatter to develop students' sense of agency.

JODY POLLECK & TASHEMA SPENCE-DAVIS

OUTSIDE, the noise of the New York City streets tries to interrupt our agentic flow, horns blaring, someone shouting angrily at a double-parked car. But inside, students are seated quietly in a circle, shoulder to shoulder, books inches from their noses, as they eagerly await the final scene of *All American Boys* by Jason Reynolds and Brendan Kiely. As the main characters of the novel march to fight racial injustice, we ask students to read with them, to chant with Rashad and Quinn, our heroes in this narrative: "Black lives matter! Black lives matter!"

Our students, primarily recent immigrants from countries as close as Haiti and as faraway as Pakistan, tell us they have never marched for justice, have never protested in the United States nor in their own countries. However, through the powerful imagery and dialogue of *All American Boys*, they rehearse and enact what advocacy can look like through an opportunity in their English language arts (ELA) classroom. In this article, we demonstrate how the reading of a novel along with culturally sustaining and responsive instruction can enhance students' sense of agency and advocacy along with their literacy development. The characters in the young adult (YA) novel *All American Boys* grapple with police brutality, as Reynolds and Kiely center the #BlackLivesMatter movement and the ways in which different racialized groups process and confront racial injustices. Here we present our planning and decision-making processes, along with our rationales for these approaches, to reveal the ways in which students responded to the topics, text, and each other.

Instructional Context and Our Stance

We taught this instructional unit collaboratively during summer school in an alternative school district in New York City. Because #BlackLivesMatter and racial injustice pervade settings throughout the United States and our world, we believed that *All American Boys* would be relevant to our adolescent students. Despite the ages of our students (seventeen to twenty), they all read below the sixth-grade level, according to The Adult Basic Education (TABE) test, which is mandated by our school district. Thus, *All American Boys* became accessible to our students based on both the reading level and the relevance and immediacy presented by the authors on the topic. Our primary goals for the instructional unit were as follows: (1) build students' literacies (including their reading, writing, and discussion skills) and (2) develop adolescents' sociopolitical awareness and engagement.

The class consisted of seventeen students who came on a regular basis each week, for a total of six weeks. Of these seventeen students, eight were female and nine male. They came to us with the asset of multilingualism, and we engaged daily with their home languages that included Arabic, English, French-Creole, Mandarin, Punjabi, Spanish, and Urdu. Ethnically, students identified themselves as Middle Eastern, Caribbean, Latinx, and Chinese. While our article is grounded within this particular school context, we believe the practices we address here are transferable across a variety of school populations and communities. As such, our discussion concludes with some suggestions for educators to adapt their work to meet the diverse needs of their students and the contexts surrounding their communities.

We have more than three decades of combined teaching experience in literacy instruction. Jody identifies as White and as an ally in antiracism. She has taught urban adolescents for more than twenty years and is a teacher trainer at a local university. Tashema identifies as Caribbean American and has taught for fourteen years. She is currently a districtwide instructional coach.

Theoretical Framework for Instruction

What unites us, as ELA educators, is our commitment to instruction that uses culturally sustaining and responsive approaches (Paris). Our first pedagogical tenet is the belief that students' cultural and linguistic identities are not static, but fluid. Their identities include a diversity of identity markers and intersectionalities that are based on students' ethnicity and race, socioeconomic status, gender, abilities, languages, sexuality, immigration status, and youth cultures (Ladson-Billings). We also strive to set high expectations for our students, regardless of their reading test results, while also offering appropriate scaffolding and differentiation so that students feel successful in all of our classroom tasks. Further, we spend much of our time before, during, and after class getting to know the complexities of students' identities and communities. We believe their cultural assets and experiences are "funds of knowledge" in which to build our curriculum and instruction (Gonzalez et al. 10).

To be culturally sustaining also means that our instruction embodies sociopolitical and sociocultural stances (Paris). In this way, we use the classroom as a space where students can build critical consciousness to process and confront injustices in their lives and communities (NYSED). Specifically, we engaged in Lamar Johnson's framework for critical race English education (CREE). CREE asks that teachers explicitly address "issues of violence, race, whiteness, white supremacy, and anti-black racism"; simultaneously, CREE uses curriculum that explores the relationships among "literacy, language, race, and education by expanding the concept of literacy to include activist contexts and social movements" (108). Thus, we decided to center #BlackLivesMatter and use *All American Boys* as a narrative catalyst to uplift our students, using language and literacy for social justice, particularly for our historically marginalized youth.

Finally, culturally sustaining instruction asks educators to not just be relevant (Ladson-Billings) and responsive (Gay) to students, but also work to *sustain* their identities and languages (Paris). This means being mindful of students' bi/multiculturalism and bi/multilingualism so as to "foster—to sustain—linguistic, literate, and cultural pluralism" (Paris 93). As examples, we invite students to speak and write in their first languages each class day. For those students who are building their writing abilities, we encourage them to draw or use visuals to share their experiences and textual interpretations. We also ask students to make personal connections. Thus, they write, draw, and speak to ways in which they see their lives reflected in the novel, especially as it connects to racial injustices and #BlackLivesMatter.

YA Literature to Center #BlackLivesMatter

YA literature can reach young people in powerful ways, especially in their understanding and involvement in social justice within the ELA classroom. *All American Boys* is a young adult novel featuring two male adolescents, Rashad who is Black and Quinn who is White. The chapters exchange perspectives of both young men as they work to understand and confront racism within their communities. Rashad is a survivor of police brutality, after being beaten by a police officer named Paul who erroneously thinks he stole from a local store. Quinn, a longtime friend of Paul, is witness to the beating and grapples with his community alliances; his understanding of Whiteness, White privilege, and racial injustice; and his responsibilities to confront police brutality.

The novel is unique in that the authors offer dual perspectives, one of Rashad who must deal with racism directly, along with the physical and emotional trauma it carries, and Quinn who must learn to deal with his White privilege and the ways in which his position of power gives him access to resources and protection from racialized violence. In sharing both voices, the authors provide a dialogue between two different races, a dialogue that has been rare within the United States as controversies surrounding

#BlackLivesMatter have been divisive among racial communities. Thus, we selected this text to center youth and racial injustices while also offering multiplicity in perspective.

Building Classroom Community

As teachers of culturally sustaining practices, our first and most important task was to get to know our students. During the first week of school, students wrote "Auto-Literacy-Biographies" in their writing notebooks so that we could learn about their cultural backgrounds and literacies. Students chose their literary genres and thus were allowed to draw and/or use poetry to reveal aspects of themselves and their communities, literacies, and languages.

This initial writing entry was critical for getting to know students and also assessing their literacy abilities, experiences, and dispositions. Specifically, we learned about students' sense of self, which influences their confidence for writing and advocacy work. Below is an excerpt from Ralph, a young man from Guyana, who immigrated to the United States three years ago (see Figure 1). (All names are pseudonyms.)

I love to read when am bord reading make my bay
I read this book in the Pass talking a bout the
treat other kindly and that chang my life.
reading was verry hard for me baek in Guyana
I came to the united state and develop in my reading
reading mean alot for me I can see my name
and sine for a chick.
I dont like to write becaus I fink it too
ugly for People to read and understant

FIGURE 1

This is an excerpt from Ralph's auto-literacy-biography.

In just these few sentences, we learned why Ralph reads and how texts serve as an inspiration in his life. At the same time, we learned about his writing disposition, which can now guide us as we support him and build his confidence as he develops as a writer.

Before reading *All American Boys*, we also used students' background knowledge to develop their understanding about historical racism, social activism, police brutality, #BlackLivesMatter, and local and global racial injustices. To build context, we first introduced key vocabulary and concepts that included advocacy, racism, and social justice.

To engage students further in the conversation, they participated in a gallery walk. First, they selected a partner. (We recommended they choose a peer who shared their home language, so they could have more in-depth discussions if needed.) Around the room were photographs of local and global examples of social justice movements, including images of the US civil rights movement, #BlackLivesMatter, anti-apartheid in Africa, and the Puerto Rican Young Lords. We wanted to be inclusive of diverse examples so that these photographs served as mirrors of their communities and windows into advocacy movements they did not know (Bishop). Each photograph had two questions: (1) Which social justice movement is represented? (2) How are the people advocating for social change? Students walked about the room, talked to each other, and wrote their responses on sticky notes, which they placed next to the images. This opportunity allowed students to unearth and discuss power struggles within the United States and within their own countries, sharing tensions and inequities between and within various racial and civic communities.

The following day each student received a personal copy of *All American Boys*. We then asked students why they thought it was important to read a text about racial injustice and advocacy. Students talked with their partners, and we later discussed as a class why we would center #BlackLivesMatter for our unit of instruction. We focused their purpose further by sharing our essential questions:

- In what ways can young people advocate for change?
- How do our identities influence our ideas about social justice?
- How do we confront racism within our communities?

In small groups, students discussed each question. We explained that we would read the book together every day to support their comprehension and use these questions to guide their reading. We also addressed with students the sensitivity of the novel's content, preparing them for the physical and emotional abuse that would be discussed. Reading about racialized acts of violence can trigger deep trauma for students, so we wanted them to be aware of the content of our reading and ensuing conversations (Dutro). We encouraged students to share with us if they felt uncomfortable or unsafe so that we could support them emotionally as well.

Funds of Knowledge and Choice

Each day began with a writing or drawing prompt that centered #BlackLivesMatter, racial injustices, or advocacy. We selected questions based on the previous day's reading (to serve as review), or we selected questions that would provide entry points into the upcoming reading. Most of these questions asked students to make connections, and there was always choice so as to differentiate our instruction. Sample prompts and scenarios included the following:

- Quinn is feeling conflicted about Paul. What would you do if you were in Quinn's shoes? How could he confront Paul or work toward social justice? What is his responsibility?
- In the United States or in your home country, where have you seen protesting? What were people fighting for?
- Yesterday we talked about racism that we've seen in New York City. What is another example that you have seen but were not able to share?
- Draw a picture of a sign you would use for a #BlackLivesMatter march.

We gave students three to five minutes to draw or respond in their choice language.

Because the purpose of these responses was for students to process the tensions in the novel, we did not grade these. Instead, students had the space and choice to grapple with difficult issues and concepts. Afterward, our discussions in pairs and as a whole group were grounded in the students' writings, so we could assess their understanding of the topics and the text. While a few students wrote in their home language, most of our emergent multilingual students opted to improve and practice their English. In this way, students experienced choice to honor their voices and the ways in which they learn best.

Literacy Scaffolding and Advocacy

Part of our intentional practices was integration of explicit reading instruction that was contextualized within the novel and our themes of advocacy and social justice. Strategies included visualizing, asking questions, making connections and predictions, summarizing, and annotating. For each mini-lesson, we explained what the strategy was to our students and why it was important to the reading process. We then modeled the strategy by reading a selection from the novel and demonstrated our use of the strategy. Two examples are below:

- Today as we read, focus on visualizing the text—making a movie in your mind. Mark at least one place with your sticky note where you see an act of racism happening.
- Today as we read, make a connection, either a text-to-self or a text-to-world connection. Think about where you have also seen oppression or discrimination or think about when you have been conflicted about a situation. Be sure to use your sticky note to mark that spot.

Once we gave students a purpose for their reading, we then read *All American Boys* together, opting for the audio version, so students could listen and follow along. For our emergent multilingual readers and writers, this kind of scaffolding provided support in fluency and comprehension. We read approximately one chapter per day, and the entire reading of the YA novel took four weeks.

Another strategy we modeled was annotation, demonstrating why and how to underline for significance and make notes in the margins. For these learning experiences, we made copies of the chapters, so students could actively engage with the text. Figure 2 offers examples of student annotations.

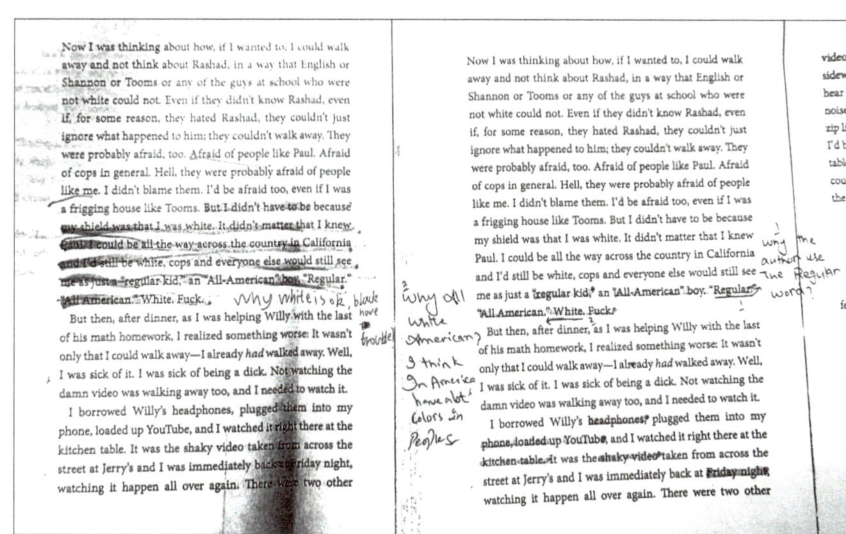
Now I was thinking about how, if I wanted to, I could walk away and not think about Rashad, in a way that English or Shannon or Tooms or any of the guys at school who were not white could not. Even if they didn't know Rashad, even if, for some reason, they hated Rashad, they couldn't just ignore what happened to him; they couldn't walk away. They were probably afraid, too. Afraid of people like Paul. Afraid of cops in general. Hell, they were probably afraid of people like me. I didn't blame them. I'd be afraid too, even if I was a frigging house like Tooms. But I didn't have to be because my shield was that I was white. It didn't matter that I knew Paul. I could be all the way across the country in California and I'd still be white, cops and everyone else would still see me as just a "regular kid," an "All-American" boy. "Regular." "All American." White. Fuck.

But then, after dinner, as I was helping Willy with the last of his math homework, I realized something worse: It wasn't only that I could walk away—I already *had* walked away. Well, I was sick of it. I was sick of being a dick. Not watching the damn video was walking away too, and I needed to watch it.

I borrowed Willy's headphones, plugged them into my phone, loaded up YouTube, and I watched it right there at the kitchen table. It was the shaky video taken from across the street at Jerry's and I was immediately back at Friday night, watching it happen all over again. There were two other

FIGURE 2
This figure is a sample of two student annotations of the same page of the text.

Annotating the text is an effective way to differentiate instruction, because students then have choice in the ways in which they want to respond. They can highlight passages that spoke to them and write questions they personally have as they read. Annotation is also another example of cultural responsiveness, as students' identities will certainly affect the ways in which they interpret and connect to the text.

Student-Led Discussions and Journaling

On completing the reading, students wrote daily in their journals. These written assessments were usually based on the reading strategy we taught and allowed students to process the content of the novel and our larger themes of advocacy and social justice. Figure 3 provides two examples: Kayla as she uses the reading strategy of visualization and Donald as he makes a personal connection to the text.

Once students recorded their responses, they shared their journal entries with a peer. Sometimes we discussed issues as a whole class; however, we believe it was important that each student had a voice and opportunity to be heard on their reading interpretations, connections, and questions. By using turn and talks on a daily basis, students participated in critical moments of engagement and connections with their peers.

Our formalized whole-class discussions occurred every Friday, when students participated in a Socratic seminar. In preparation for the seminars, students crafted questions and selected passages they wanted to discuss. As an example, Sabu asked the following to his peers: "Why are people who are different colors writing this book? What is the reason?" Students then discussed why having different perspectives was important in understanding the complexities of race and racism within the United States. For our emergent multilingual students, we offered question starters to guide them in their writing.

During discussions, we also paired students by home languages, so they could support one another. One challenge was with Zhang who was the only student who spoke Mandarin. He used his phone for Google-translating and often worked with Rachelle, a Haitian female, who helped him on a daily basis, especially during times when we were conferencing with other students. The interaction between these two students speaks to the high leveraging of community-building where students become resources for each other.

Authentic Writing Experiences

For the summative assessment, students wrote narratives about a time when they were an advocate or witnessed an act of advocacy. Students developed their writing throughout our six weeks together. Using *All American Boys* as our mentor text, we offered writing mini-lessons to guide students to construct their stories. Mini-lessons included how to brainstorm or plan for our narratives; how to develop opening hooks, conflict, and character; and how to conclude our stories. We demonstrated the writing techniques through the novel and our own teacher-created stories as well.

Students worked in pairs, in groups, or independently on their narratives. For independent writing, students wrote on their own, while we conferred with them one on one. Sometimes students worked in pairs to give each other feedback, while other times, we worked in small guided writing groups, based on student need. For example, one day, we had five students working on descriptive imagery; at the same time, five worked on editing, and the other five worked on developing their characters. Students could self-select their group based on what they needed the most as emerging writers. Regardless of the structure, we always concluded our writing workshop with a "share out," which could be with the whole class or with a peer. The purpose of this routine was to build students' confidence in writing through positive feedback and daily celebration. The space also allowed us to develop our ELA classroom as a community of

Visualization

Images	Meaning
Rashad in a hospital he is in an emergency room I hear machine beeping. I see him in the bed, I smell some medicine. The room is cold because he have a AC.	he was injuried thats sound bad.

• What connections did you make to Quinn today?
My connection that I make with Quinn today is that I'm nervous to tell people whats up and what happen if I have any thing on my mind.

• Can you relate to anything that happened to Quinn in this chapter?
Yes I can and it is to see someone get beat up from a family of mines and I was so afread, I don't tell anyone what happened.
afraid

FIGURE 3

On the left, Kayla visualizes the text; on the right, Donald makes a personal connection.

writers where students could build trust and provide powerful models of writing for each other.

On the last day of school, students shared polished versions of their stories. Their narratives explored a variety of issues including advocating for their families, bullying behaviors, violence in their homelands, immigration, and Islamophobia. In groups, students talked to each other about the writing process and what they learned. They also read each other's final narratives and gave each other feedback.

In Tyler's final reflection, he wrote, "I love my writing because I am the hero in my story because I advocated for my friend." Similarly, Donald reflected, "I love how I advocated in a way of love and happiness through my words." He also told his group that he wanted to write a new short story called "All American Girls," so that young Black women could provide their perspectives and experiences with racism. (Consequently, Donald finished this narrative over the summer and shared it with us on the first day of our fall semester together.)

Finally, we must return to where we started, with Ralph, who originally wrote: "I don't like to write because I think it too ugly for people to read and understand." On the last day of school, his sense of self as a writer changed. He explained, "I love how I write like it's happening right before me."

When Rachelle asked him how he grew as a writer, Ralph responded, "Very much. I didn't realize how much talent I had."

Using relevant texts and student-centered instruction, ELA teachers can help develop students' writing confidence, particularly for our emergent multilingual students, whose experiences are often marginalized in school communities. Culturally responsive and sustaining literacy instruction is the foundational work that can lead to developing both students' literacies and sense of agency.

Final Reflections

Culturally sustaining pedagogies can be achieved in conjunction with the development of students' literacies. We can use the roots of students' diverse cultures and experiences to build meaningful and powerful curriculum that our students care about. As educators, we need to situate students' learning within issues that are important to them, so that they are the knowers and the driving force behind our instructional decisions. In doing so, we connect students' home and community cultures and languages to their school lives and identities.

We understand, however, that there is greater diversity within our US schools, and not every classroom will be as culturally and linguistically diverse as ours. What might, for example, this unit of instruction look like in suburban communities with primarily White students? We encourage use of *All American Boys* for the same reasons we taught it: the duality of perspectives and experiences. Whereas our students connected more with Rashad, White students might connect with Quinn. Students can then learn from Rashad's perspectives and experiences and from Quinn's tensions around White privilege. Most importantly, White students can discuss how they can become critical and active citizens who work to deconstruct and confront racial injustices. For teachers and students who need additional information on #BlackLivesMatter, please refer to the resources in Figure 4.

CULTURALLY RESPONSIVE AND SUSTAINING LITERACY INSTRUCTION IS THE FOUNDATIONAL WORK THAT CAN LEAD TO DEVELOPING BOTH STUDENTS' LITERACIES AND SENSE OF AGENCY.

The teaching of #BlackLivesMatter and racial injustices is not just a curriculum for young people of color, but a curriculum for all young people around the world. For our marginalized students of color, it is a story of hope and advocacy, and for our White students, it is a story of unpacking privilege and

Black Lives Matter at School. Black Lives Matter at School, blacklivesmatteratschool.com.

"Black Lives Matter at School—Resources." National Education Association EdJustice, neaedjustice.org/black-lives-matter-school-resources.

Garza, Alicia. "A Herstory of the #BlackLivesMatter Movement." *The Feminist Wire*, 7 Oct. 2014, thefeministwire.com/2014/10/blacklivesmatter-2/.

Khan-Cullors, Patrisse, and Asha Bandele. *When They Call You a Terrorist: A Black Lives Matter Memoir*. St. Martins, 2018.

Taylor, Keeanga-Yamahtta. *From #BlackLivesMatter to Black Liberation*. Haymarket, 2016.

Watson, Dyan, Jesse Hagopian, and Wayne Au. *Teaching for Black Lives*. Rethinking Schools, 2018.

Yancy, George, and Judith Butler. "What's Wrong with All Lives Matter." *The New York Times*, 12 Jan. 2015, opinionator.blogs.nytimes.com/2015/01/12/whats-wrong-with-all-lives-matter/.

FIGURE 4

This figure provides resources to teach #BlackLivesMatter.

TEACHING TIPS

Polleck and Spence-Davis present insightful information about how they planned to read and respond to the book* All American Boys *by Jason Reynolds and Brendan Kiely with their high school students. Building on the ideas in the article, ask students to work in pairs to make a list of events from the news that are connected to social justice and activism. Next, have your students rank the list based on their level of interest. Using the ranked list, ask students to select one topic they want to investigate and generate a list of questions related to the topic. Then have students begin exploring the topic with the goal of generating a multimodal text set that responds to the questions. Students can post their text sets on a class website or on padlet.com. Polleck and Spence-Davis's work with their students is an example of teaching informed by a culturally responsive stance that is designed to promote racial literacy, equity, and social change.

power and finding methods for combatting racism. These political movements require participation by all races and ethnicities if we truly want to overcome systematic racism and xenophobia.

The YA novel *All American Boys* offers adolescents visions of courage and transformation. For adolescent readers, the characters can serve as powerful models to invoke students' sense of agency and advocacy, as we saw through their daily interactions, their engagement with the novel, and personal narratives. If we return to that final day when students chanted together in unison, we can also see how these novels can inspire both unity and community.

For ELA teachers, using texts such as these and developing culturally sustaining pedagogies also requires courage and transformation. If we truly want to inspire agency and advocacy within our classrooms, then we must do the work as well. Our movement toward more justice-oriented instructional practices is a critical journey that requires hope, love, and intentional pedagogical decisions, all key contributors to enhancing civic engagement and community building in our ELA classrooms.

WORKS CITED

Bishop, Rudine Sims. "Mirrors, Windows, and Sliding Glass Doors." *Perspectives*, vol. 1, no. 3, 1990, pp. ix–xi.

Dutro, Elizabeth. *The Vulnerable Heart of Literacy: Centering Trauma as Powerful Pedagogy*. Teachers College P, 2019.

Gay, Geneva. *Culturally Responsive Teaching: Theory, Research, and Practice*. 2nd ed., Teachers College P, 2010.

Gonzalez, Norma, et al., editors. *Funds of Knowledge: Theorizing Practices in Households, Communities, and Classrooms*. Erlbaum, 2005.

Johnson, Lamar. "Where Do We Go from Here? A Critical Race English Education." *Research in the Teaching of English*, vol. 53, no. 2, 2018, pp. 102–24.

Ladson-Billings, Gloria. "Culturally Relevant Pedagogy 2.0: A.K.A the Remix." *Harvard Educational Review*, vol. 84, no. 1, 2014, pp. 74–84.

New York State Education Department (NYSED). *The Culturally-Responsive Sustaining Educational Framework*. University of the State of New York, 2019.

Paris, Django. "Culturally Sustaining Pedagogy: A Needed Change in Stance, Terminology, and Practice." *Educational Researcher*, vol. 41, no. 3, 2012, pp. 93–97.

Reynolds, Jason, and Brendan Kiely. *All American Boys*. Atheneum, 2015.

JODY POLLECK is an associate professor in literacy at Hunter College in New York City. She began her work with adolescents in 1994 as an outreach counselor, and since 1999 has been teaching literacies within urban contexts. Polleck has published in over 25 books and journals and is currently working on her first book with Teachers College Press, *Book Clubs as Transformative and Inclusive Spaces*. She was also a 2019 Fulbright scholar. Her research focuses on culturally sustaining literacy instruction.

TASHEMA SPENCE-DAVIS is an instructional coach and educator in New York City, where she teaches and provides coaching, mentoring, curriculum, and offers professional development to teachers and staff. Dr. Spence-Davis research focuses on urban adolescents and culturally responsive and sustaining approaches to literacy instruction. She has been a member of NCTE since 2009 and can be reached at tspence3@schools.nyc.gov.

This article originally appeared
in *English Education 51.2*

REOPENING RACIAL WOUNDS: Whiteness, Melancholia, and Affect in the English Classroom

This article critiques a classroom encounter between a Black student, Richard, and a white student, Nick, that complicated the white English teacher, Mr. Turner's, attempt to facilitate a discussion about racial progress in America. Students positioned their bodies on a continuum between 1, no racial progress since the 1930s, and 10, full racial equity. When Richard positioned himself at the low end of the continuum and Nick located himself on the high end, a disruption occurred after Mr. Turner moved his body toward Nick while verbally validating Richard's perspective. I argue that the classroom's affective register was altered by racial melancholia, reopening racial wounds and reproducing whiteness, evoking emotions I call "melancholic affects."

JUSTIN GRINAGE

So we may walk into the room and "feel the atmosphere," but what we may feel depends on the angle of our arrival. Or we might say that the atmosphere is already angled; it is always felt from a specific point. The pedagogic encounter is full of angles.

—SARA AHMED (2010), "HAPPY OBJECTS"

RESPONDING TO BAKER-BELL, Butler, and Johnson's (2017) call for a critical race English education and following the theme of this special issue, critical whiteness in English education, this article explores how whiteness disrupted an English teacher's attempt to facilitate a dialogue about racial progress in America since the 1930s. Stemming from a larger yearlong critical ethnographic research project that I conducted in a high school English classroom, this study uses racial melancholia (Cheng, 2001; Eng & Han, 2000) and affect (Massumi, 2015) as theoretical tools to uncover the subtle and insidious ways that whiteness operated when students engaged in this dialogue concerning racial progress (or a lack thereof) and as a result exposed the persistent reality of racial violence in contemporary American society.

Often, when we evoke the connections between past state-sanctioned racial violence and how this violence continues to haunt Black, Brown, and indigenous people, it produces racial melancholia, the reopening of racial wounds that have festered for centuries, having never fully healed. Tensions arise when exposing this wound, highlighting the complex relationship between history and racism. An imperceptibility often surrounds this tension; feelings slowly emerge within us or sometimes suddenly appear, seemingly in ways that we cannot explain. These tensions manifest in the feeling that people of color unexpectedly acquire when realizing they are being followed by a police squad car or the dread they feel when being racially profiled in a department store. During these moments, there is a shift in atmosphere: A casual joy-ride turns into an anxiety-riddled car trip; the department store clerk transforms a fun shopping spree into a nightmarish reminder of one's skin color. Alternatively, sometimes the atmosphere is predetermined to contain a racial register, for example, when one finds oneself driving below the speed limit on the highway or making sure to keep hands out of pockets while strolling through the jewelry store—all in hopes of avoiding racially motivated encounters. As Ahmed (2010) notes in the epigraph, these situations are "angled."

Of the upmost importance for the purposes of this article is Ahmed's (2010) assertion that "the *pedagogic* encounter is full of angles" (p. 37, emphasis added). Ahmed's description of the critical formulation of pedagogic maneuvers as "angled" contains significant implications for teaching and learning about race in the English classroom. For instance, in what ways are affects racially angled, how do these angles influence the teacher, and what emotions are produced as a result of these angles that may either inhibit or promote classroom learning opportunities? I analyze this series of questions by examining a specific classroom pedagogical encounter where the white classroom teacher, Mr. Turner,[1] Nick, a white student, and Richard, a Black student, clashed during a discussion about racial progress that was contextualized by what I term *melancholic affects*, which produced intensified emotional responses during the conversation.

I first describe what is commonly known as the "affective turn" (Clough & Halley, 2007) recently taken up in the social sciences and humanities and place it within the context of educational scholarship on race and racism. I then more closely study how formations of racial melancholia are influential to understanding affect and the pedagogical encounter. Using Mr. Turner's conflict with Nick and Richard as the source of my analysis, I illustrate the aforementioned incident, which involved students positioning themselves on a continuum between 1 and 10—1 representing no racial progress since the 1930s and 10 representing full racial equity. When Richard positioned himself at the low end of the continuum and Nick located himself on the high end, a conflict ensued and Mr. Turner had to make a split-second decision as to how he was going to handle the encounter. The ensuing conflict occurred when Mr. Turner agreed verbally with Richard's perspective while simultaneously moving his body away from Richard to stand next to Nick. During this decision, I argue that racial melancholia mediated the affective environment and influenced the emotional responses of the teacher and students in the classroom. I demonstrate how racial melancholia is a useful tool for uncovering methods in which technologies of whiteness are mobilized to interrupt critical race dialogues in the English classroom. I end with a discussion of how "working" the pedagogical angles can be used to disrupt hegemonic constructions of whiteness through the production of alter-accomplishments (Massumi, 2015) that represent affective practices of antiracism.

Affect, Race, and (Classroom) Space

The study of affect has experienced a reemergence in the past decade within the social sciences and humanities where scholars have sought to better understand and theorize the context and transmission of bodily energies, intensities, feelings, and emotions (Brennan, 2004; Seigworth & Gregg, 2010). Theories of affect have also been used to understand race in ways that consider ontologies of racialization in conjunction with epistemological, material, and discursive forms of racism (Lim, 2010; Saldanha, 2006, 2010). Still other studies define affective formations within the realm of psychoanalytic accounts of race and subjectivity (Ahmed, 2004; Hook, 2005). These various studies are characteristic of the many theories of affect that encompass the field of critical affect studies (Rice, 2008) as there is not one single generalizable theory of affect, nor should there be, considering "the tensions, blends, and blurs" of affective environments (Seigworth & Gregg, 2010, p. 4). What may be the most enduring contribution to the affective turn is the recognition of the corporeal as dynamically interconnected to the sociopolitical (Zembylas, 2015).

Originating from Spinoza's (1677/2001) proclamation that affect is defined as the body's capacity to affect and be affected, I make central the modes in which bodies are mobilized within classroom spaces as inextricably linked to theorizing racial encounters through a psychosocial lens. Centralizing the movement of bodies within racial interactions foregrounds an analysis of affective formations in the classroom and enables an articulation of the ways in which affective forces are organized to achieve certain ends. This theorization of the corporeal dimensions of the classroom allows for representations of race that uncover ontological conceptualizations of racialized bodies rather than solely focusing on the discursive, emotional, and/or ideological modes of racism. In other words, we cannot fully comprehend epistemological theories of race without considering ontologies of racialization. The study of affect instead positions historical assemblages (Zembylas, 2015) as the critical backdrop for the methods in which epistemologies of race are deployed in classroom spaces, including the ways we think, talk, and feel about racism. Racial melancholia illuminates these affective formations and exposes the often-hidden linkages between racialized bodies and affective energies and intensities within classroom spaces.

Melancholic Affects

The concept of racial melancholia as a "constellation of affect" illuminates the "tension between the past and the present, between the dead and the living" (Eng & Kazanjian, 2003, p. 1). Race scholars have used the Freudian (1917) concept of melancholia, or the harmful act of mourning loss, as a framework for making connections between the traumatic effects of racial violence on racial identities (see Cheng, 2001; Eng & Han, 2000). Racial melancholia's relationship to trauma and history enables an ontologically based analytical device that can be used to unveil normatively structured affective formations in the classroom. The repeated aggravation of past and present racial wounds that come to frame racial encounters, bodily movements, and the feelings that these movements and encounters conjure underscore the psychosocial reproduction of trauma. Racial melancholia's connection to affect highlights the notion that "every *intra*subjective process is potentially an intersubjective exchange" (Cheng, 2006, p. 126, italics in original).

The intrasubjectivity of racial melancholia refers to how the dead remain inside us—how the history of our racial losses becomes the formation of the ego itself. The encryption of these losses within us is significant when theorizing intersubjective racial encounters and how these encounters are shaped by racial preconceptions. The "angling" of affects is psychosocially linked, considering the American history of racial transgressions and the ways in which these transgressions continue to haunt society. For example, as Cheng (2006) illustrates, "The 'personal' or the 'individual' is always potentially colored by historical relations and contingencies" (p. 126). Thus, bodies, behaviors, and feelings are not separate or outside of the nation's complex racial history; rather, they are shaped by these histories and form the manner in which we interact racially.

The racially melancholic subject is tormented by the festering of past racial wounds through the inability to work through and properly mourn the internalization of grief. As a result, this grief is often repressed and driven into the unconscious as a means of resisting conscious recognition of the terror of white supremacy. However, what happens when racial realities are brought to the forefront of one's consciousness, where racism cannot be ignored any longer? These instances of confronting racial traumas engage the interplay between the intrasubjectivity of psychic processes and the intersubjective context of racial encounters. Affect's role in these encounters establishes the *potential* (dis) connectivity of the subject(s) within a given relational field. Massumi (2015) explains, "So what you are, affectively, isn't a social classification—rich or poor, employed or unemployed—it's a set of potential connections and movements that you have, as a function of those classifications, but always in an open field of relations" (p. 40). The most prominent "social classification" when directly confronting racism is indeed our racial identifications, which function affectively by providing or restricting a certain degree of freedom or power within a given encounter depending on one's racial identity.[2] For instance, these gradations can be as faint as an airplane passenger's subconscious nervous reaction to sitting next to someone wearing a turban or as penetrating as the bullets of a police officer's weapon firing at a 12-year-old boy playing with a toy gun.[3] Either way, racial affects play a key part in the movements, behaviors, and feelings of social interactions.

Within the classroom racial affects operate in multifaceted, complex, and often subtle ways through bodily movements, sensations, and feelings mediated by our racial classifications. The dynamics of racial melancholia include the shifting of affective intensities and energies in relation to the (re)aggravation of our racial wounds. That is, the force of our feelings regarding race is affectively connected to the emergence of past racial injuries in the present. Underscoring Cheng's (2001) proclamation that we feel the most melancholic when we are confronted with the shamefaced reality of racism, I call these intensities *melancholic affects*. To further explain, when we are confronted with the ghosts of our racial past, when the racial trauma we have repressed bubbles to the surface, the affective register is altered and, in an instant, there is a micro-perception (Massumi, 2015) or a sensation that takes place bodily before it reaches conscious recognition. Then our perception of the affective event is expressed through feelings because emotion translates into our conscious perception of an affective experience. A melancholic affect can be described as the moment when the atmosphere in the room changes or what Brennan (2004) refers to as the *transmission of affect*. The intensity of the room is altered by confronting racism: There is an occurrence of collective discomfort, anxiety, or nervousness, similar to when one describes the energy of a situation as so intense that one could cut the (racial) tension with a butter knife.

Classroom melancholic affects embody Ahmed's (2010) assertion that pedagogy is full of angles through the evocation and transmission of racial trauma within teaching and learning. The pedagogic encounter in the context of teaching and learning about race in the English classroom has the potential to reproduce normative racial dynamics, but it also has the potential to elicit an alter-accomplishment (Massumi, 2015) that disrupts hegemonic formations of racialization, indicating that perhaps a fundamental element of antiracist pedagogy may be to better understand how affective classroom politics function in the context of racial melancholia. The persistent barrier to this type of pedagogy is that the normative response to having discussions about racial issues is typically resistance, discomfort, and disengagement. The consequence is that the deeper we dive into learning about race, the more we unlock previously repressed racial trauma and thus the more difficult learning sometimes becomes. For example, often during surface-level race conversations, whites feel as though they have made progress and that learning has occurred, while people of color often become frustrated with the lack of racial literacy that whites exhibit. The end result is only the illusion of equality—the affective environment simply becomes a reproduction of whiteness. Then, when race conversations begin to go more in-depth, white students often become resistant to learning by using a plethora of affective techniques to avoid their culpability in perpetuating racism—what I describe later as "white intellectual alibis" (Leonardo & Zembylas, 2013). The task of the antiracist pedagogue is to adjust the relational field to allow for the potential for alter-accomplishments to take place within the classroom for critical race dialogues to evolve and progress. As the rest of this article illustrates, this is by no means easy to achieve and involves much effort, but it is nonetheless vital to disrupting hegemonic racial constructs.

Method and Positionality

This article draws from a yearlong critical ethnographic study I conducted in a 12th-grade English classroom at Sumner, a large Midwestern suburban high school. Critical ethnography strives to challenge dominant ideologies, discourses, and narratives that disenfranchise and indoctrinate people in a world with unequal power dynamics (Carspecken, 1996; Madison, 2005; Thomas, 1993). This type of research espouses an overtly political message that seeks to be a catalyst for social change and contribute to emancipatory knowledge in the quest for social justice. As such, my usage of critical ethnography enabled me to illuminate and decipher the presence of whiteness and affect during the classroom discussion concerning racial progress.

The data I collected during the 2014–15 school year included (1) field notes, (2) semistructured interviews, and (3) the gathering of classroom artifacts including curriculum documents, student writing/homework assignments, and online discussion forums. In particular, I relied heavily on field notes and an audio-recorded transcript taken during the classroom encounter, as well as interviews with Mr. Turner and Richard that I conducted after the incident to further contextualize the conflict.

The classroom in which I conducted my research contained racial dynamics that uncovered how racial ideologies functioned to influence the ways whiteness shaped classroom practices. This specific classroom was ideal for this type of exploration because of the white classroom teacher, Mr. Turner, and his commitment to openly discussing race with his students. The students were also quite accustomed to talking about race as they had been in the same English class together since ninth grade, where learning about racism had been a focal point of the curriculum. The racial demographics of the class reflected the wider student population of Sumner, a large Midwestern suburban high school, whose student of color population increased steadily over the course of the previous decade from approximately 11 percent to 45 percent. Mr. Turner's class was composed of 33 students, 16 of whom were students of color and 17 who were white. Not only were students familiar with one another, but they also had a previous relationship with me, as I had served as their English teacher in both ninth and tenth grade. There was also a rapport between Mr. Turner and me, as we had been friends and colleagues for six years.

Inside the classroom, this level of familiarity among the students, the classroom teacher, and me allowed for a high level of comfort. The closeness of the group enabled a depth of social history through the interconnectedness of the relationships. Students in the class possessed a tacit link with one another; every student was able to recall past stories, jokes, and incidents that had occurred over the course of the past four years of being in the same English class together. The family-type atmosphere, established because of the intimacy of the class, also generated a high level of trust. The students felt comfortable enough to be uncomfortable with their classmates. The students trusted each other enough to be vulnerable, and because they were able to be vulnerable, they engaged in discussions about race despite instances of discomfort.

Although in general terms the classroom environment was a comfortable location for students, comfort and trust are not fixed variables. There were times when students felt varying levels of discomfort and times when students did not trust one another. My researcher positionality is important to mention here considering the fluid nature of the researcher and participant relationship. Because I had past relationships with the students as their former English teacher, it was possible for certain participants to be more candid about their racial experiences—something that may not have happened without an already established previous relationship. Still, my insider research status went deeper than past student relationships because of my extensive involvement in curriculum writing for Sumner's English department. As a result, I was able to contribute significantly to the established curriculum that the students were engaging with in Mr. Turner's class.

The English curriculum at Sumner reflected my philosophical standpoint of incorporating a social justice-focused framework for teaching about critical issues and fostering critical consciousness, with learning about race and racism at the forefront. The students not only understood that race scholarship was my main focus as a researcher, but they also knew that I identified as Black and often could guess where my allegiance lay on matters of racism occurring in society. Yet, students were often not afraid to challenge my perspective or disagree with my opinions on race-related issues. These facets of my researcher identity help to provide further context for the classroom dialogue, outlined in the next section.

Context and Background of the Encounter

The class had just completed a unit on the Richard Wright (1940) novel *Native Son*. In this unit, Mr. Turner taught lessons related to racial violence, race and capitalism, and the history of 1930s Chicago, including the growth of communism within Black spaces. I greatly admire and respect Mr. Turner's willingness to incorporate these topics into the curriculum. I believe he has demonstrated a genuine commitment to antiracist teaching and has made significant progress developing antiracist pedagogy. I am explicitly declaring his commitment to antiracism here to illustrate that despite my critiques of his pedagogy later in this article, my intention is not to portray him as an unsuccessful racial pedagogue. Instead, my point is that *any* teacher may make similar missteps in the process of practicing antiracism.

Mr. Turner proceeded to devise a lesson that would enable students to discuss how far the nation has progressed in achieving racial equity since the 1930s. He wanted to find a method for students to think and talk critically about the overt violence of the Jim Crow era and connect this violence to issues involving police brutality and other forms of public displays of racism occurring in present-day American society. To achieve this level of analysis, he instructed students to write their opinion about the topic by posing the following question:

> What would Richard Wright say about the progress (or lack thereof) we have made as a society since the publication of Native Son?

The next class period, he asked students to identify a number on a scale from 1 to 10 as to how far they believe the country has progressed racially since *Native Son*. He then asked the students to locate themselves on an imaginary continuum around the room, with one corner of the room representing 1 (no progress since the 1930s) and the opposite corner representing 10 (racial equity has been achieved). Mr. Turner chose this structure for the discussion because he thought it would provide a visual representation that would allow the students to see where everyone stands on the topic, but also, he encouraged students to change their position on the continuum if their classmates' responses were persuasive enough.

The students rose out of their desks to move to their prospective spots on the continuum. The majority of the class was clustered between about 4–6 on the scale, while just a few students located themselves on the opposite ends of the continuum in the 1–3 or 7–10 range. Mr. Turner facilitated the discussion by asking students to volunteer their opinions. After a student offers a thought, his customary pedagogical strategy during discussions is to summarize the response in his own words to ensure he understood what the student was saying and also to make sure the rest of the class understood the student's answer. The most common thoughts students gave referred to racial progress being made over time. For example, one student said:

> I think what we are learning now in school about race is what we are going to teach our children. Like the younger generations are less racist than our grandparents.

The discussion took place over about 15 minutes with no students changing their positions on the continuum. I could sense an overall feeling of nervousness during the discussion through the body language of several students and the careful, reluctant responses being given, as if students were afraid of saying something that would offend or challenge someone's viewpoint. Even I felt a certain level of tenseness as students shared their perspectives. The conversation culminated with an interaction between Mr. Turner and two students on opposing ends of the continuum, Nick and Richard. The interaction is important to consider here.

Mr. Turner's Racial Encounter

Mr. Turner's pedagogical approach during classroom discussions is to stay neutral, especially when the topic concerns race. He believes that it is critical for classroom teachers not to impose their viewpoints on students and, as a result, I observed him interjecting his opinions on the topic of race only on rare occasions. Following this neutral pedagogical strategy, Mr. Turner deliberately refused to position himself on the continuum for fear of influencing student opinions.[4] Noticeably present throughout the dialogue were the two students at the opposing ends of the spectrum, a white male student, Nick, and a Black male student, Richard. Neither student verbally offered his opinion, yet Mr. Turner, as well as the rest of the class, was anticipating their contributions. I observed many students glancing at both of them over the course of the discussion, expecting some sort of conflict to occur. Nick and Richard have a history of clashing over their opposing ideas on race, and both students are strong-willed and opinionated. It was not until the conversation began to stall that Mr. Turner decided to ask Richard if he would like to share his opinion.

Richard was sitting in a stray desk located around the 2 area on the continuum. With an inflection of passion in his voice, he explained that although forms of racial progress have been achieved since the publication of *Native Son*, recent police shootings similar to Michael Brown's are proof that not much has changed since this era. Mr. Turner, who was standing in the center of the horseshoe, paraphrased Richard's words and then paused to see if any student would volunteer to respond to Richard. When no student offered a response, Mr. Turner turned to face Nick, who was standing on the opposite end of the continuum around 8, and asked Nick for his opinion. Nick, with a shaky tinge in his voice, reluctantly stated that he believes much progress has been made and as a country we are close to achieving racial equality. Richard became visibly frustrated as Nick shared his opinion, and he began shaking his head back and forth in opposition. Nick ended his response by saying:

> The people on the other end [of the continuum] are smarter at talking about this [race] so I guess since I am on this end I'm just not very smart.

The class observed Richard still shaking his head, and Mr. Turner, noticing Richard's frustration, asked if he would like to respond. Richard expressed his frustration by stating:

> How could you say this when police are shooting Black people?! How could we have possibly made this much progress?

Mr. Turner, who at this point was still standing calmly in the middle of the horseshoe, offered a verbal acknowledgment of Richard's response:

> This is a very good point that Richard brings up and it seems to be in contrast to what you are saying, Nick, about racial progress. How do we as a country explain all of this violence, yet claim to have made so much progress?

As Mr. Turner spoke this statement, he walked from the middle of the horseshoe to stand about a foot away from Nick on the end of the continuum. Immediately, as Mr. Turner walked toward Nick, Richard put his head down on his desk and covered his face with his arms.

Mr. Turner, still standing next to Nick as he looked around at the class, noticed that Richard put his head down, and the rest of the class noticed too. The conversation halted after this occurred, and the intensity in the room became palpable. The students fell silent. Mr. Turner asked if there were any more comments, and no one responded. I noticed many students shaking their heads as if to indicate they did not want to talk anymore. So, Mr. Turner proceeded to end the conversation by thanking students for engaging in the difficult discussion and indicating that there would be conversations about the topic over the next couple of teaching units. With about 10 minutes remaining, the class moved on to an activity unrelated to race. Richard still had his head down on his desk, and when class ended, he did not leave as students filed out of the room. Mr. Turner and I both approached him to see how he was feeling. He lifted his head off the desk and with an agonized look lamented:

> I can't do this anymore. I don't know what to do. I don't know what to do. I was in the car for the Trayvon Martin verdict and I didn't know what to do. During Michael Brown and Eric Garner, those verdicts, I was in the car too. This keeps happening again and again, and again. I don't know what to do. I feel hopeless.[5]

Reopening Racial Wounds

If racial melancholia can tell us one thing, it is that the past does not always stay in the past. The context of the discussion, racial progress in the wake of present-day racial violence, constitutes an affective relational field where the national espousal of disarticulated racial grief rises to the surface. Melancholia's seething presence reveals our affective attachments to past histories of violence through the reopening of the nation's racial wounds. Ruti (2005) explains:

> In the same way that nations and other collective entities owe their current shape to complex and at times highly conflicted histories, the lived present of each of us is traversed by a countless number of invisible threads that connect us to our pasts. (p. 638)

These interwoven threads connecting our racial pasts are largely invisible to us because our psyches find ways to repudiate the past on a conscious level, resulting in these disavowals being more aggressively reasserted in the unconscious (Ruti, 2005). However, the discussion brought the class face-to-face with grief that had been previously distorted and repressed and asked students to make sense of what has been lost by exposing the invisible threads attached to old racial wounds. The discussion embodies what it means to face those immaterial objects that haunt us through the transmission of affect, igniting past traumas that engulf the present—a melancholic affect. The "angling" of pedagogical encounters underscores how race and trauma converge and emerge within the classroom as the discussion represents the class's exposure to the nation's infected racial wounds.

What is at stake here is much more than simply identifying oneself on a continuum since the discussion engages the core of the nation's racial traumas. As a student aptly described during the discussion:

> I just think that we can't put ourselves even at a 5 because it starts with institutionalized racism and then it bleeds out into society and if you don't get rid of the source you can't address other problems. It is like a wound. You can clean the wound out, but it is still there.

The imagery of bleeding out and wounding is a suitable metaphor for racial injury. The tension in Nick and Richard's encounter certainly illuminates the apprehensive nature of the exchange and also points to a central conflict for the antiracist pedagogue. The conundrum involves how one navigates a situation where there is a confrontation with the painful history of racial violence and how this confrontation often becomes a barrier to antiracism. Cheng (2001) states, "It can be damaging to say how damaging racism has been. Yet it is surely equally harmful *not* to talk about this history of sorrow" (p. 14, italics in original). Our racial wounds persist even if we choose to ignore them. The antiracist pedagogue must make the choice to address racial injury, but with this choice comes much pain and sorrow. The discussion that Mr. Turner wanted the class to engage in was an attempt to confront our racial traumas, but the clash between Nick and Richard disrupted further engagement as the affective dynamics of the encounter reinforced racial hegemonies. During the encounter, the pain of racial trauma was evident; however, the process of facing racial injury is a necessary component of antiracism. A closer examination of the encounter between Mr. Turner's pedagogy in relation to Nick and Richard's disagreement can provide valuable insights into how the opening of racial wounds produces melancholic affects that often disrupt antiracist agency.

Affective Economies and the Rippling Effect of Emotion

The most crucial aspect of the exchange among Nick, Richard, and Mr. Turner was not so much what they were saying, but where their bodies were positioned in the classroom. The tipping point of this encounter is Mr. Turner's movement away from Richard to be closer to Nick, which prompted Richard's disengagement. Bundled within Mr. Turner's movements and Nick and Richard's reactions to those movements are the histories of their bodies—"the lived past of the body" bound up within the affective event (Massumi, 2015, p. 49). These histories encompass assemblages of both their past interactions (including the ways their bodies have existed previously within the classroom) but also interactions that predate the existence of their bodies. This predated history refers to the racialization of the body or what Fanon (1967) identifies as a "historical-racial schema" that constitutes the racialized body as being woven "out of a thousand details, anecdotes, and stories" by whiteness (p. 95). Here the body has a predetermined objectification where one's skin has already been contextualized through the prism of race. There is a layering effect of histories for Nick, Richard, and Mr. Turner—the history of their marked racial bodies and their history of past interactions within classroom and school space that help formulate the affective register.

THE MOST CRUCIAL ASPECT OF THE EXCHANGE AMONG NICK, RICHARD, AND MR. TURNER WAS NOT SO MUCH WHAT THEY WERE SAYING, BUT WHERE THEIR BODIES WERE POSITIONED IN THE CLASSROOM.

To grasp the intensity of the moment, Nick and Richard's history within the classroom needs to be further explored. For as long as I have known Nick and Richard, ever since ninth grade, they often disagreed on topics related to race. Their polarizing perspectives made discussions edgier as they clashed over the reality of racism. Nick's viewpoints came to represent traditional white conservative values where racism is a relic of the past and everyone has an equal chance of succeeding in life as long as they work hard enough. Conversely, Richard's views reflected those of a staunch social activist; at his core lies a spirit for antiracism and he strives to fight against racial injustice. Over three years, their frequent conflicts had a lightning-rod effect in the classroom. Whenever race was a topic of study, Nick and Richard came to symbolize conductors of racial static that attracted the energy for the proverbial strike.

Ahmed's (2004) theorization of affective economies contextualizes how the history of Nick and Richard's interactions became the catalyst for the intensification of affective space. Affective economies, as Ahmed (2004) suggests, allow for emotions to accumulate much like capital accumulates in an economic sense. That is, emotions accumulate over time through "the movement between signs: the more signs circulate, the more affective they become" (p. 45). Much like how the circulation of commodities increases in magnitude over time, "the movement between signs or objects converts into affect" (p. 45). Nick and Richard's frequent disagreements signify an accruement of affective value where the sign becomes the positioning of Nick and Richard at opposite ends of the continuum. The lightning rods and the object become the charge of emotionality during the encounter, the lightning strike. The undercurrent of racial static pervades the affective environment, with Nick standing in support for racism (or at least a postracial society) at one end of the continuum and Richard in support of antiracism at the other, symbolizing opposing poles of the ideological struggle for control of racial knowledge.

For Ahmed (2004), the affective value of signs, subjects, and objects underscores what she calls the "rippling effect of emotions" that involve a process of movement mediated by history (pp. 44–45). The circulation of emotions moves both sideways between signs, subjects, and objects as well as backward and forward through the past and into the present. Within the context of Nick and Richard's conflict, feelings spread as part of both the affective accumulation of their previous confrontations as well as through the reopening of the nation's racial wounds. These "*feelings take us across different levels of signification, not all of which are admitted in the present*" (Ahmed, 2004, p. 44, italics in original). Thus, the interaction between the intrasubjective and the intersubjective is at work here: The circulation of feelings is psychosocial in nature. These emotions are not contained within sign, subject, or object but are instead only produced as a result of the relationality between Nick and Richard (that is, the linkages between signs, subjects, and objects) and the expression of repressed racial trauma created through the pedagogy of Mr. Turner. Khanna (2003) asserts that the distressing return of the inassimilable lost object into psychic life produces an affective state as the lost object is unable to be mourned. In this case, the lost object represents the nation's festering racial wounds that are typically suppressed, but in this instance become transparent because students were asked to consider the connections between past and present racism on the continuum. The intrasubjective then refers to the psychic recurrence of past and present racial losses, while the intersubjective illuminates the racial dynamics of social encounters; both the "intra" (the psyche) and the "inter" (the social) merged to manifest melancholic affects during Nick and Richard's confrontation.

Whiteness as Technology of Affect

Having established that affective formations can accumulate value through the circulation of emotion, what ultimately are the effects of this accumulated value? The emergence of affect and the production of feeling as a result of affective encounters are concomitantly imbued with structures of power that Hook (2005) identifies as "hegemonies of affect." Here my analysis turns toward a particular hegemonic construct: whiteness. Leonardo and Zembylas (2013) emphasize the reproduction of whiteness as intimately connected to emotional and bodily reactions. Their analysis maintains that the hegemony of whiteness is upheld in part through affective investments in white identities and through insidious patterns of operationalized emotions that aim to disrupt classroom race dialogues, which they label as "technologies of affect." Whiteness as technology of affect engages the Foucauldian (1977) term *technology*, which is defined as a set of techniques and practices used by individuals, either on themselves or on others, to accomplish certain objectives. Affective technologies pertain to the arrangement of affects and emotions within a given field of relations that are mobilized in ways that reify hegemonic constructs. Whiteness as technology of affect has implications for antiracist praxis through the theorization of the methods whites use to preserve racial power dynamics within classroom spaces.

An explanation of the subtle reification of whiteness during Mr. Turner's encounter with Nick and Richard requires us to consider the emotional and bodily dimensions of affective technologies. Recalling Nick's response to positioning himself at the higher end of the continuum (close to achieving racial equity), he justified his placement by replying that he was simply "not smart enough" to discuss the topic. His appeal to ignorance is a stark example of an affective technique called "white intellectual alibi" where whites "attempt to project a nonracist alibi for themselves to maintain equilibrium" (Leonardo & Zembylas, 2013, p. 152). For example, white intellectual alibis resemble the behavior patterns that researchers have identified as commonplace responses to critical race dialogues, where white people express an array of techniques to avoid the heightened anxiety associated with discussing race including awkwardness, silence, anger, and incoherence (Bonilla-Silva, 2003; Pollock, 2004). In this instance, Nick's white intellectual alibi was ironically to claim to be unintellectual, which I interpreted as a ploy to avoid looking racist to the rest of the class for placing himself at the highest point on the continuum. There was a discursive element to his strategy where Nick accounted for his perceived racism by appearing incoherent, but the other side of the affective coin reveals the emotional subtext of his statement as crucial to the movement of Mr. Turner's body toward him during the interaction. Stemming from an understanding of Mr. Turner's willingness to remain neutral during race dialogues, I read Nick's emotional disposition as a plea for white empathy. If we are to believe that Nick desired Mr. Turner's emotional support, not only did Nick want to be seen as not smart enough, he wanted to be consoled for feeling this way. I think he was appealing to Mr. Turner's empathetic nature and banking on the likelihood that Mr. Turner had perhaps felt the same way as a white person at some point in his own life.

Helping Nick's case for empathy was Richard's angry response. Certainly, Nick anticipated Richard acting as such; after all, they had had plenty of past experience disagreeing with one another. This prompted Mr. Turner's next movements, which unveil the power of both whiteness and affective technologies in the classroom. Mr. Turner, a veteran teacher who is by no means a novice antiracist pedagogue, had to make a split-second decision. He had two students, one white and the other Black, who are in conflict over the reality of racism. His choice reflects the nuanced angling of the pedagogic encounter and the blending of bodies, emotions, and discourse within affective formations. Choosing to move his body to stand by Nick while verbally supporting Richard is a white intellectual alibi in its own right. His movement toward Nick was a method for maintaining equilibrium during a heightened moment of anxiety. This is where Mr. Turner's pedagogical strategy of neutrality works against his antiracist efforts, since he literally and ideologically cannot be in two places at once. Leonardo and Zembylas (2013) affirm, "Affectively, within a white subject's self-understanding, he cannot be racist and antiracist at the same time" (p. 156).

The formation of Mr. Turner's white intellectual alibi takes place on two fronts. The first involves his psychic management through his attempt to support both viewpoints: his verbal support for antiracism and his bodily support for racism. Within this contradictory space the alibi serves an emotional purpose: "It allows white subjects to establish stability in the face of destabilizing situations, such as critical race dialogue" (Leonardo & Zembylas, 2013, p. 156). The second comprises the literal matter of being unable to stand in two places at once, stressing the power of the corporeal in light of Mr. Turner's verbal support for Richard. In this instance, Mr. Turner's movement toward Nick represents both a social shielding (Mr. Turner's and Nick's bodies are protecting each other from the discomforting trauma of racial dialogue by virtue of standing next to one other) as well as a psychic shielding (Mr. Turner's bodily association with Nick provides the white empathy that Nick desired, but also Mr. Turner enables a certain level of comfort for himself by creating a sense of equilibrium during a particularly turbulent moment). I read this movement as ultimately securing a preservation of white safety for both of them. Indeed, it is illustrative that Hook (2005) refers to the affective resonance of whiteness as a "force-field of attachments" (p. 82). Nick's original white intellectual alibi thus sets off a chain of affects that ultimately curtails the discussion and effectively (and affectively) reproduces whiteness.

THE HEGEMONIC HOOKS OF WHITENESS PULL THE PUPPET STRINGS THAT COERCE MR. TURNER TO STAND NEXT TO NICK, THEREBY SYMBOLIZING AN EXPLICIT FORM OF WHITE SOLIDARITY IN RICHARD'S EYES, INDICATING THAT MR. TURNER'S BODILY MOVEMENT CAME TO MEAN MORE THAN HIS WORDS, PROMPTING RICHARD TO DISENGAGE FROM THE DISCUSSION.

After the discussion, Mr. Turner expressed his frustration concerning his facilitation of the encounter. He deeply regretted not silencing Nick more explicitly and in retrospect had a self-awareness about his movement toward Nick as causing Richard to put his head on the desk. Within his split-second decision to move closer to Nick, what forces compelled Mr. Turner to act in such a way? Hindsight is 20/20 for Mr. Turner, as he would have never made this decision knowing the consequences of his actions, but it is important to consider the question posed by Spillers (1996): "It would be useful to know, though, in general, how bodies respond to bodies not like their own, and what it is that 'sees'—in other words, do we look with eyes, or with the psyche?" (p. 79). I believe that Mr. Turner's pedagogical choice was not *consciously* motivated by the affective pull of whiteness since Mr. Turner recognized that his movement caused Richard's disengagement after reflecting on the incident (not during the incident), so the answer to the aforementioned question may indeed be that in this instance Mr. Turner was "seeing" with his psyche. My interpretation was that the shuttling of Mr. Turner's body may have had more to do with the body's skin color that resembled his own rather than the body's skin color that did not. Herein lies the essence of race and affect: The body's (in)ability to enter into relations with other bodies. Even for this brief instance affect "provides the invitational opening for a rationality to get its hooks into the flesh" (Massumi, 2015, p. 85). The hegemonic hooks of whiteness pull the puppet strings that coerce Mr. Turner to stand next to Nick, thereby symbolizing an explicit form of white solidarity in Richard's eyes, indicating that Mr. Turner's bodily movement came to mean more than his words, prompting Richard to disengage from the discussion.

These racialized affects have severe consequences for Richard's well-being. Richard's reaction to the movement of Mr. Turner's body illustrates the sinister repercussions of white intellectual alibis. Leonardo and Zembylas (2013) describe this impact as such:

> Whereas whites have the ability to put themselves in harm's way within the anti-racist project, minorities rarely have the power to voluntarily choose to experience discursive violence. People of color have no recourse for an alibi. They are guilty bodies. (p. 157)

In the process of Mr. Turner's shielding of Nick, the discursive violence, and I would also add the psychic violence, was absorbed by Richard. Richard reiterated these sentiments when he later clarified why he was angry:

> He [Mr. Turner] was understanding what I was saying but he kind of still sided with Nick's point of view even though he personally didn't feel that way. He wanted Nick to feel comfortable in expressing his viewpoints even though they were sort of dumb. He [Nick] made stupid viewpoints, so that angered me.

Richard also added another reason for his anger:

> I was fed up with Nick and his bullshit.

Let us not forget the melancholic connection to this incident; the intensity of Richard's anger is due to the high-stakes nature of the dialogue. For Richard, this discussion served as a means for validating that the racial violence he sees around him is a threat to all of humanity. My interpretation of this was that Richard was less concerned with where Nick placed himself on the continuum since I'm sure he suspected beforehand that Nick would be high on the scale. Instead, what mattered most to Richard was that Mr. Turner would refuse to validate Nick's point of view by not moving to stand next to Nick on the continuum. Richard needed Mr. Turner to put himself "in harm's way." A necessary part of critical discussions concerning race is confronting the unsettling and painful realization of racism. Yet, these confrontations are also when we are the most melancholic and the most vulnerable relative to the traumas that haunt us. Not only was Mr. Turner "seeing" through his psyche, but so were Nick and Richard. This form of "seeing" was not optical, but rather was the process of deciphering their unconscious traumas and working to come to grips with their racial grief.

Thus, in the context of affective strategies, white intellectual alibis serve a psychosocial purpose within the melancholic landscape. When the affective environment became the most melancholic, Nick and Mr. Turner each used alibis to escape the uncomfortable conscious presence of melancholy, which enabled a certain ability for both of them to produce feelings of safety in the face of suffering. However, the social aspect of this psychosocial encounter is a result of Nick and Mr. Turner needing each other to ensure the validity of their white alibis. Therefore, the guilty body in this incident was Richard, who could not obtain an alibi in the first place.

Conclusion: Affect Is a Synonym for Hope

To what extent should Mr. Turner's attempt at discussing race in the classroom be considered unsuccessful? Mr. Turner's assessment of the lesson was that it failed to advance the conversation concerning more current racial issues, and he greatly attributed the encounter with Nick and Richard as the main reason for which the dialogue was ineffective. My analysis of their interaction seems to back up his claims since affective technologies of whiteness disrupted the dialogue. However, if we take a closer look at the affective politics of classroom interactions, the perceived failure of the lesson may not be so apparent. Theorizing the relationship between affect and ideology is useful in understanding how power operates within the realm of the classroom. The dimensions of affect constitute a pre-ideological event where affects take shape *before* we are inculcated by ideology. Massumi (2015) further explains:

> To be in affect, ideological predeterminations have to enter the event and *take* effect. They have to reassert themselves to make themselves effectively ingredient to the event. Their effectiveness is always an accomplishment, a renewed victory, and what needs to be accomplished can fail. (p. 58, italics in original)

What Massumi's assertion tells us is that in the context of affective politics, there is always the potential that ideology will fail to indoctrinate us and reassert its control.

In classroom spaces, these affective events are plentiful, but the manner in which ideology interpolates us often renders affective formations imperceptible. Similar to Bourdieu's (1977) conception of *habitus*, we are duped into unconsciously repeating the script that ideology has written for us, often in ways that ensure our dominance. The potential for affect as a tool for the antiracist pedagogue lies in its ability to find the cracks in ideology's armor. The critical English educator must determine, in any given affective event, where there are openings for the power of ideology to be usurped. Lim (2010) summarizes this potentiality with his description of the relational field:

WHAT MATTERED MOST TO RICHARD WAS THAT MR. TURNER WOULD REFUSE TO VALIDATE NICK'S POINT OF VIEW BY NOT MOVING TO STAND NEXT TO NICK ON THE CONTINUUM. RICHARD NEEDED MR. TURNER TO PUT HIMSELF "IN HARM'S WAY."

> The range of things that might potentially be done, felt, or perceived is continually modified by what actually happens between all the different bodies on the field . . . It is because of this multiplicity and this constant modification that the virtual or potential field of affect guarantees an openness to difference and thus the momentum for change. (p. 2398)

Since affect guarantees a degree of openness for every situation, Massumi (2015) refers to affect as synonymous with hope. An understanding of affective politics emphasizes that the body is not fully predetermined to follow an ideological script. As a result, there is always the potential for actions that break the chains of hegemony.

The antiracist pedagogical alteration that perhaps should have been made during the encounter among Nick, Richard, and Mr. Turner was for Mr. Turner to either stay in place or move closer to Richard. In this singular encounter, Mr. Turner was unable to disrupt the hegemonic construction of whiteness as a result of his movement toward Nick. However, before we call this interaction a failure, we must consider that affects do not take place as singularities. There is a continual emergence of affects at any given pedagogical point in time. In other words, this interaction will not be the last opportunity Mr. Turner will have to make pedagogical alterations. What was most instructive for Mr. Turner was what he learned as a result of this pedagogical misstep. Sometime after the class period, Mr. Turner and I talked extensively about his thought process during the incident. He walked around the empty classroom and replayed the event:

> I remember walking away from this corner [standing in Richard's corner] and going to stand in this kind of like neutral territory over here [walks to the middle of the horseshoe]. And then as I walked over to Nick, I turned and Richard's head went down. Like it was this physical moment.

Mr. Turner then discussed with me the realization that he made a mistake by walking to stand by Nick:

> I watched Richard put his head down and I was like, *oh my god, what did I do*? And at what cost was I willing to do that? And that was my big feeling of depression; I feel like to preserve Nick, I destroyed Richard.

When determining whether the incident should be considered ineffective, we need to also consider the rigorous self-reflection that Mr. Turner engaged in after the event in question. During an interview that took place three months after the encounter, his final comment to me about the incident was this:

> I know my words are important during these conversations [about race], but now I realize how important my body is too. This idea of the power of my body is now something I am always going to be aware of in the future when we have these types of conversations.

Although the incident became a reproduction of whiteness, I would not necessarily qualify the encounter as hopeless. In light of the insights that Mr. Turner gained from the interaction, it can be classified as an alter-accomplishment insofar as it primed the potential for future alter-accomplishments. For Mr. Turner, the interaction "[amplified] a previously unfelt potential to the point of perceptibility" (Massumi, 2015, p. 58). It became the momentum for future change in that Mr. Turner now has the potential to be aware of his body in relation to his words during critical race dialogues. The learning resulting from this interaction gives Mr. Turner the capacity to adapt and redeploy his pedagogy when faced with similar interactions. There is now a space available in his pedagogical repertoire to make a habitual leap toward comprehending the importance of the corporeal; the memory of this pedagogical encounter enables Mr. Turner the possibility to enhance his recognition of bodily positioning in the classroom. He is now conscious of the power of his affective presence in classroom space.

Despite what Mr. Turner learned after the incident, there is still the question of "at what cost" with regard to Richard's melancholic reaction to the encounter. In Mr. Turner's words, he "destroyed" Richard while "preserving" Nick. These dynamics are characteristic of race dialogues that reproduce whiteness as students of color bear the burden of the provocation of racial trauma. Richard's feelings of hopelessness became heightened as a result of a layering of losses caused by the melancholic psyche: "The racially melancholic minority is doubly versed in the art of losing. The racially denigrated person has to forfeit the full security of his/her imaginary integrity . . . but is then forced to take in . . . and reidentify with that loss: a double loss" (Cheng, 2001, p. 175). In this instance, Richard's double loss is layered with the insecurity of his own integrity caused by Mr. Turner's bodily movement toward Nick as well as Richard's reidentification with the conscious racial injury that comprises the melancholic nation as a result of this movement. In the moment, this may have left Richard psychically destroyed (conversely, Nick was psychically preserved), but hope is not lost because the next day Mr. Turner was able to apologize to Richard and express his regret for not more explicitly defending his viewpoint. Although this apology did not erase the pain Richard felt, he did appreciate the fact that Mr. Turner acknowledged his mistake and was pleased that Mr. Turner vowed to be more aware of how his words and actions affect students of color during race discussions.

The implications for classroom practice that can be gleaned from Nick, Richard, and Mr. Turner's interaction are that confronting violence is a

TEACHING TIPS

Grinage offers us a glimpse inside a high school classroom discussion focused on racial progress, with important background information about the students, teacher, and pedagogical strategy to help us understand the dynamics during the discussion. Although the classroom teacher created space for students to share their opinion, it would helpful to make visible the information sources and experiences that have shaped those opinions. To achieve this goal, you can modify James Banks's (1993) knowledge construction chart to analyze a current event related to racism. Begin by posting four large pieces of chart paper around the room and pass out Post-it notes to the class. Use or modify the following headings (one per chart): media (television/internet), community, school, pop culture. As students walk around the room placing notes on the chart that list what the "knowledge source" has conveyed about the topic, remind them to skim the other Post-its and take note of common themes. After everyone has contributed ideas to the chart, give students three to four minutes to summarize the interesting ideas and patterns they read. Then, explain how discussions about race, racism, and racial violence can trigger emotions in some people that cause more pain. Offer suggestions for students who may find themselves in this position and ask for additional suggestions. If the class is prepared to move forward, then you can engage in a discussion about their ideas, with the intention of making visible how the event you selected exposes connections among the racism, history, and power. Pay close attention to how students react to each other and offer options to process the ideas individually.

necessary aspect of discussing race in the classroom (Leonardo & Porter, 2010), but being willing to continuously learn from these confrontations is also necessary for pedagogues to improve their ability to teach about traumatic subjects. For Mr. Turner to learn from his mistake, he had to have the courage to design a curriculum[6] that uncovered the nation's racial injuries to even be in the position to make this mistake in the first place. Antiracist pedagogy must include these types of conflicts. However, the unconscious is sometimes an unpredictable entity, and the pull of whiteness is strong. To say that Mr. Turner learned from this interaction is tenuous considering that he may unconsciously make the same pedagogical error when faced with a similar decision in the future, since we see the most clearly through our psyches when we are the most melancholic. Instead, Mr. Turner must learn through repetition; after all, whiteness cannot be abolished overnight. This requires that pedagogues repeatedly put themselves in situations where they are meeting racial trauma as a means of understanding the nuances and intricacies of affective formations of whiteness and the emotions that are produced as a result.

Still, simply meeting trauma cannot be enough, as Mr. Turner was only able to understand through a process of self-reflection, via the conversations he had about the incident with both Richard and me. This form of learning resembles Boler's (1999) conception of a *pedagogy of discomfort*, defined as "both an invitation to inquiry as well as a call to action" (p. 176). A pedagogy of discomfort seeks to highlight what can be gained from the repetitious commitment to traumatic learning. Mr. Turner not only sought to engage in this racial dialogue as a form of collective action, but he participated in critical inquiry through his conversations with me and with Richard. This type of pedagogical process is necessary when considering that alter-accomplishments need to be *primed*. The priming involves the hard work of finding the crucial pedagogical angles that produce social change. Working to produce these pedagogical alter-accomplishments is vital to antiracist orientations of teacher education and the advancement of critical race English education.

NOTES

1. All names and places are pseudonyms.
2. This is not to say that other social classifications do not intersect, overlap, and interlock with race, which speaks to the elaborate blends and blurs of affective politics.
3. As in the case of Tamir Rice, a 12-year-old Black boy shot dead by a police officer in 2014.
4. I typically acted as a participant-observer in the classroom and sought to participate in most activities, but for the same reason I chose not to locate myself on the continuum.
5. The description of this entire section is taken from my field notes and an audio-recorded transcript of the class period.
6. Curriculum design is not something I explicitly analyze here, but it is nonetheless important to note. Mr. Turner's decision to have students place themselves on a continuum made it likely that Nick and Richard would disagree, creating the space for some kind of conflict to occur. Although not discussed in this article, curriculum theory in the context of racial melancholia, whiteness, and affect opens new pathways for critique specifically in relation to critical race English education, but also more broadly in the field of critical literacy.

Could Mr. Turner's lesson be designed in a way that would promote more productive conversations? Levine-Rasky (2000) identifies a commonly used but ultimately unproductive approach to teaching about racism that she calls "white privilege pedagogy." This type of pedagogy emphasizes an individualized confessional model of professing one's material advantages as a white person rather than focusing on highlighting the social relations and systemic structures that solidify whiteness. Levine-Rasky (2000) states, "The body of the white individual resides at the fulcrum of the confessional model at the core of white privilege pedagogy" (p. 276). Mr. Turner's curricular choice to focus on body position to discuss racism may have trapped students into participating in this type of pedagogy.

REFERENCES

Ahmed, S. (2004). *The cultural politics of emotion*. New York: Routledge.

Ahmed, S. (2010). Happy objects. In M. Gregg & G. J. Seigworth (Eds.), *The affect theory reader* (pp. 29–51). Durham, NC: Duke University Press.

Baker-Bell, A., Butler, T., & Johnson, L. (2017). The pain and the wounds: A call for critical race English education in the wake of racial violence. *English Education*, 49(2), 116–128.

Boler, M. (1999). *Feeling power: Emotions and education*. New York: Routledge.

Bonilla-Silva, E. (2003). *Racism without racists: Color-blind racism and the persistence of racial inequality in the United States*. Lanham, MD: Rowman & Littlefield.

Bourdieu, P. (1977). *Outline of a theory of practice*. Cambridge, UK: Cambridge University Press.

Brennan, T. (2004). *The transmission of affect*. Ithaca, NY: Cornell University Press.

Carspecken, P. F. (1996). *Critical ethnography in educational research: A theoretical and practical guide*. New York: Routledge.

Cheng, A. A. (2001). *The melancholy of race: Psychoanalysis, assimilation, and hidden grief*. Oxford, UK: Oxford University Press.

Cheng, A. A. (2006). Ralph Ellison and the politics of melancholia. In R. Posnock (Ed.), *The Cambridge companion to Ralph Ellison* (pp. 121–136). Cambridge, UK: Cambridge University Press.

Clough, P. T., & Halley, J. (2007). *The affective turn: Theorizing the social*. Durham, NC: Duke University Press.

Eng, D. L., & Han, S. (2000). A dialogue on racial melancholia. *Psychoanalytic Dialogues*, 10(4), 667–700.

Eng, D. L., & Kazanjian, D. (2003). *Loss: The politics of mourning*. Berkeley: University of California Press.

Fanon, F. (1967). *Black skin, white masks*. New York: Grove Press.

Foucault, M. (1977). *Discipline and punish: The birth of the prison*. New York: Random House.

Freud, S. (1917). Mourning and melancholia. In J. Strachey (Eds.), *The standard edition of the complete original works of Sigmund Freud, vol. 14*. London: Hogarth Press.

Hook, D. (2005). A critical psychology of the postcolonial. *Theory & Psychology*, 15(4), 475–503.

Khanna, R. (2003). *Dark continents: Psychoanalysis and colonialism*. Durham, NC: Duke University Press.

Leonardo, Z., & Porter, R. (2010). Pedagogy of fear: Toward a Fanonian theory of "safety" in race dialogue. *Race Ethnicity and Education*, 13(2), 139–157.

Leonardo, Z., & Zembylas, M. (2013). Whiteness as technology of affect: Implications for educational praxis. *Equity & Excellence in Education*, 46(1), 150–165.

Levine-Rasky, C. (2000). Framing whiteness: Working through the tensions in introducing whiteness to educators. *Race Ethnicity and Education*, 3(3), 271–292.

Lim, J. (2010). Immanent politics: Thinking race and ethnicity through affect and machinism. *Environment and Planning A*, 42(10), 2393–2409.

Madison, S. (2005). *Critical ethnography: Methods, ethics, and performance*. Thousand Oaks, CA: Sage.

Massumi, B. (2015). *The politics of affect*. Cambridge: Polity Press.

Pollock, M. (2004). *Colormute: Race talk dilemmas in an American school*. Princeton, NJ: Princeton University Press.

Rice, J. E. (2008). The new "new": Making a case for critical affect studies. *Quarterly Journal of Speech*, 94(2), 200–212.

Ruti, M. (2005). From melancholia to meaning: How to live the past in the present. *Psychoanalytic Dialogues*, 15(5), 637–660.

Saldanha, A. (2006). Reontologising race: The machinic geography of phenotype. *Environment and Planning D: Society and Space*, 24(1), 9–24.

Saldanha, A. (2010). Skin, affect, aggregation: Guattarian variations on Fanon. *Environment and Planning A*, 42(10), 2410–2427.

Seigworth, G. J., & Gregg, M. (2010). An inventory of shimmers. In M. Gregg & G. J. Seigworth (Eds.), *The affect theory reader* (pp. 1–25). Durham, NC: Duke University Press.

Spillers, H. J. (1996). All the things you could be by now, if Sigmund Freud's wife was your mother: Psychoanalysis and race. *Boundary 2*, 23(3), 75–141.

Spinoza, B. (2001). *Ethics* (W. H. White & A. H. Stirling, Trans.). Ware, UK: Wordsworth Editions. (Original work published 1677)

Thomas, J. (1993). *Doing critical ethnography*. Newbury Park, CA: Sage.

Wright, R. (1940). *Native son*. New York: Harper & Brother.

Zembylas, M. (2015). Rethinking race and racism as technologies of affect: Theorizing the implications for anti-racist politics and practice in education. *Race Ethnicity and Education*, 18(2), 145–162.

JUSTIN GRINAGE is an assistant professor of literacy education in the department of curriculum and instruction at the University of Minnesota. With a particular focus on Black education, critical whiteness studies, and critical literacy, his research examines processes of racialization in school and classroom spaces alongside explorations of how curriculum and pedagogy can engender antiracism. His recent publications have appeared in *Harvard Educational Review*, *English Education*, *Journal of Curriculum Theorizing*, and *Curriculum Inquiry*. You can reach him at grin0060@umn.edu.

This article originally appeared
in *Voices from the Middle 28.4*

CREATING SPACE FOR MIDDLE SCHOOL STUDENTS TO DISCUSS RACE

BETH BESCHORNER, ROBBIE BURNETT
& KATHLEEN FERRERO

THE SYSTEM OF EDUCATION in the United States continues to operate largely from a colorblind ideology where race remains ignored and viewed as irrelevant. That is, educators, who are predominantly white and female (NCES, 2019), teach subject matter without consideration of their own racialized identities or their students' racialized identities. This type of "race neutral" or colorblind education can result in racially predictable outcomes (Choi, 2008). Thus, racism, both outrageous and ordinary (Harper, 2019), undergirds schooling and continues to perpetuate white supremacy and racist outcomes.

Therefore, it is necessary for teachers to take a color-brave (Hobson, 2014) approach to education. There are many ways to do so, including being racially conscious when selecting curriculum, making connections between content and racialized current events, and disrupting power relations between the teacher and students within the classroom. One specific action that educators can take involves bringing students together to discuss race/ism in ways that develop students' racial consciousness and encourage justice-oriented action.

This was the approach at one middle school in the Midwest, whose student population was approximately 30 percent students of color. This article describes the lessons learned when a white principal, Mary, initiated a group called Brave Space, which met once per month for an hour over the course of an academic year. The researchers were females, one Black and two white. The researchers conducted observations and interviews and analyzed the data, and one served as a mentor for the white girls. Mary selected approximately 30 students from the sixth, seventh, and eighth grades and six adult mentors to participate in monthly meetings that used the Courageous Conversations about Race (CCAR) protocol, which is explained extensively in *Courageous Conversations about Race* (Singleton, 2015). CCAR includes four agreements and six conditions for having intra- and inter-racial dialogue about race/ism. Mary identified students as Black, Hispanic, and white; whether they were and male or female; and she assigned them to an affinity group with a mentor who identified as a similar race and gender who, with the exception of the white female researcher, worked at the school. The staff at the school was participating in ongoing professional development that centered race/ism, so Mary was aware of how the adults identified.

ONE SPECIFIC ACTION THAT EDUCATORS CAN TAKE INVOLVES BRINGING STUDENTS TOGETHER TO DISCUSS RACE/ISM IN WAYS THAT DEVELOP STUDENTS' RACIAL CONSCIOUSNESS AND ENCOURAGE JUSTICE-ORIENTED ACTION.

The group regularly had small group and partner discussions about videos and other media that addressed race/ism. Through the initial year of Brave Space, we learned that the process of naming and discussing race/ism in middle school will be ongoing, imperfect, and will need to be adapted for specific contexts, school culture, and current events. As a result, we offer the following recommendations.

Plan for Collective Leadership

SETTING A PURPOSE

When Mary started Brave Space, she started small by intentionally inviting students and adults with whom she had already developed relationships, which allowed her to act with urgency. She brought the adult mentors together for one meeting before the school year started to discuss the format for Brave Space. Certainly, given the political context at that time, it was necessary to begin the work quickly, and educators, like Mary, felt as though they should not wait too long, thinking that they're not ready. However, Mary may have started too quickly, because adult mentors did not participate in any formal training. Anna, a Latina adult mentor explained, "I want to keep asking them questions, but I don't know if it's becoming too many questions" and Brittany, a biracial adult mentor who shared that her mother is white and her father is Black stated, "I was nervous about facilitating a group." The mentors may have benefited from learning more about the CCAR protocol or doing a common read of a book like *Not Light, but Fire* by Matthew Kay. Further, there was not time set aside for the adult mentors to come together to plan and reflect. Therefore, Mary did all of the planning from month to month with little formal feedback from the multiracial group of adult mentors, which allowed a white perspective and whiteness to dictate much of the content and approaches to facilitation. In retrospect, educators trying to establish a space for students to discuss race/ism would likely benefit from a slower start that includes collective multiracial efforts to set a purpose for the group and time set aside for regular planning and reflection.

IN RETROSPECT, EDUCATORS TRYING TO ESTABLISH A SPACE FOR STUDENTS TO DISCUSS RACE/ISM WOULD LIKELY BENEFIT FROM A SLOWER START THAT INCLUDES COLLECTIVE MULTIRACIAL EFFORTS TO SET A PURPOSE FOR THE GROUP AND TIME SET ASIDE FOR REGULAR PLANNING AND RELECTION.

MULTIPLE RACIAL PERSPECTIVES

It is essential to include multiple racial perspectives and a range of stakeholders in the planning and facilitation of the group. This is a critical because the curriculum must represent an array of experiences. For example, Anna explained that she sent a video to Mary that she wanted the kids in Brave Space to watch and discuss because the video was "like my whole life. . . . [a dad at a school board meeting] was saying his experience and then, yeah, a white guy said why don't you just go back to Mexico or something like that and so it's really upsetting, but it's what we hear, like, every day so it would be really interesting to see what people thought about that." Anna felt that the girls in her group would resonate with the video, perhaps more so than some of the other resources that focused on the lived experiences of Black and white people, which were often the focus of Brave Space. Her comments highlight the need to have multiple racial perspectives involved in developing the curriculum for the discussions. Mary shared that, because she often planned alone, the process was time intensive and excruciating, because she was not always confident in her choices. Involving others in the planning process may have led to a more robust and comprehensive planning process that reduced the burden from one person.

Another consideration when developing a group like Brave Space is determining who will facilitate the group. Mary facilitated Brave Space. She organized the activities and led the discussions. In retrospect, she should have taken a more collective approach to the facilitation of Brave Space that amplified Black and Latinx voices. Mary shared how important it was to have consistent, reliable, trusting adults as mentors. The adult mentors must also be "willing to be vulnerable and open themselves in conversation, [and be people] who the kids like to spend time with." Perhaps these adults should have been given more leadership in facilitation of Brave Space.

Rules of Engagement: Use a Protocol for Discussion

Mary introduced the Courageous Conversations protocol in each meeting (Singleton, 2015). Brave Space meetings began with a review of the protocol, definition of words like race, bias, power, etc., and provided an activity or piece of media to respond to (e.g., video, commercial, story, etc.). For example, during one of the early meetings the group watched a video where a Black male was clearly treated differently because of his race. Each student responded by describing their thoughts, feelings, or beliefs using "I" statements with a partner. Callie, a white female explained, "The people wanted to help the girl because like she seemed helpless . . . they were treating the Black guy like he was a murderer."

In thinking about how to develop a space for racial dialogue, educators should remember that middle school students require caring relationships with adults in order to thrive, so the space should feel protected and secure (Alder, 2002). Only then can educators encourage critical dialogue to address racism (Darder, 1991; Friere et al., 2018). Nearly everyone in Brave Space shared that initially conversations were awkward. Peter, a Black male adult mentor, indicated that the students were initially quiet, but "every time we were in there, it was a learning, fun experience for the kids, like kind of being out of their groups." It was important that kids participated in both inter- and intra-racial conversations. One of the students, Angelica, a Latinx female, explained that in talking with her intra-racial group, "We talk more about [racism] . . . maybe because like we've been through the same things and we know what each other . . . we know what we're going through."

Learning to Listen to Students: Let the Students Lead

All educators recognize the need for planning, and as indicated earlier, collective leadership helps to ensure that all voices are heard, but students' voices must not be forgotten. Students should be active participants in shaping the discussion while maintaining a focus on race. Andrew, the white male mentor, shared, "I think it was good, but also took us off topic a little bit . . . my group wanted to talk about gender inequality." In this instance, Andrew described how he brought the focus back to race since the move to talk about gender was likely meant to diminish the discomfort of talking about race. Adult mentors must let students lead, but also be able to gauge when to bring students back to race and let them sit in discomfort.

Students must also lead in creating groups. Mary created affinity groups based on race, which would allow students of color to be and exist in their own skin and allow the white students to examine their privilege (Tatum, 1997). Mary further divided the group by gender in order to provide the girls with opportunities to speak and use their voice, which is less likely to occur in mixed-gender groups (Sadker & Sadker, 1995). Unfortunately, Mary did not allow the students to self-identify either their race or gender. In order to provide an identity-sustaining environment, it would have been better to have students self-identify, because when adults label students' identities harmful misunderstandings can occur. For example, Mary labeled a group of mixed-race girls as Black. This caused the initial mentor for the group, a mother of one of the Black boys, to step away because she felt could not relate effectively with the young women. Mary recounted that a mother of one of the mixed-race girls tried to alert her to the potential issue by remarking, "You are including them in the Black female group, but I don't know if that's where they belong." Mary acknowledged that she

INVOLVING OTHERS IN THE PLANNING PROCESS MAY HAVE LED TO A MORE ROBUST AND COMPREHENSIVE PLANNING PROCESS THAT REDUCED THE BURDEN FROM ONE PERSON.

TEACHING TIPS

These authors share details and lessons learned after they created a space for students to discuss race and racism. The goal of this effort was to support students' racial literacy development as a means to foster action for racial equity. Attending to the lessons they learned from their work with students, you may decide to begin the process with your students by developing a multimodal survey to gauge interest in creating space to deepen their understanding of race and racism. Next, you can support students who want to proceed with this project by developing a plan to analyze and share the survey results with your school community. After everyone has a chance to look over the findings and add their comments and questions, you and your students can begin planning the first meet up. Refer back to the article for specific steps the authors took to create a shared purpose and to problem solve any issues that may arise as students learn to work through tension or difficult discussions related to race and racism in our society.

disregarded the mother's comment and that doing so was a mistake. In hindsight, it would have been prudent for Mary to, perhaps, have each student do some reflection that allowed them to describe their racial and gender identities in their own words. Then, the adult mentors could have used what they learned from the students to generate groups accordingly.

Discussion

When attempting to bring middle schoolers together to talk about race, several factors should be considered. First, it takes time to plan, implement, grow, and sustain initiatives that create space to discuss race. This work is not a quick fix, and will take collective organizing, strategic planning, and relationship development. Priorities for successful implementation include building collective leadership to establish purpose, incorporating multiple perspectives in shaping content, and identifying a framework to facilitate discussions.

Second, it is critical to center the voices of students of color and Indigenous American communities while forming inclusive relationships. Educators have to release some power and control as they shape and deliver program content. Students should have the opportunity to share their experiences and perspectives as a way to collaboratively plan curriculum. Participating as co-constructors has the ability to strengthen student empowerment, support relationship building, and create relevant responsive topics for discussion.

Lastly, educators must be aware of the racialized context within their school. This includes recognizing the racial makeup of the student population and how their multiple identities take shape. Understanding these components, and the related complexities, is required to successfully assign students into racial affinity groups. Following these recommendations and guidelines should be helpful when initiating a program that creates the space and conditions for racial dialogue that can lead to a more racially just middle school.

ENDNOTES

1. All names are pseudonyms.

REFERENCES

Alder, N. (2002). Interpretations of the meaning of care. *Urban Education*, 37(2), 241–66. doi:10.1177/0042085902372005

Choi, J. (2008). Unlearning colorblind ideologies in education class. *Educational Foundations*, 53–71.

Darder, A. (1991). *Culture and power in the classroom: A critical foundation for bicultural education*. Bergin & Garvey.

Freire, P., Ramos, M., Macedo, D., & Shor, I. (2018). *Pedagogy of the oppressed*. Bloomsbury.

Harper, S. (2019). The unacceptability of racism in schools. Urban Speaker Series. Michigan State University.

Hobson, M. (2014, Mar.) *Color blind or color brave?* [Video]. TEDTalk. www.ted.com/talks/mellody_hobson_ color_blind_or_ color_brave?language=en.

Kay, M. (2018). *Not light, but fire: How to lead meaningful race conversations in the classroom*. Stenhouse Publishers.

National Center for Education Statistics. (2019). *Characteristics of public school teachers by race/ethnicity*. nces.ed.gov/programs /raceindicators.

Sadker, M., & Sadker, D. (1995). *Failing at fairness: How our schools cheat girls*. Touchstone.

Singleton, G. E. (2015). *Courageous conversations about race: A field guide for achieving equity in schools*. Corwin, A SAGE Company.

Tatum, B. D. (1997). *"Why are all the Black kids sitting together in the cafeteria?" and other conversations about the development of racial identity*. Basic Books.

BETH BESCHORNER is an associate professor in the department of elementary and literacy education at Minnesota State University, Mankato.

ROBBIE BURNETT is Director of Innovation and Collaboration at Minnesota State system office.

KATHLEEN FERRERO is a doctoral candidate at Minnesota State University, Mankato.

This article originally appeared in *Voices from the Middle 27.4*

TOUGH TALKING: Teaching White Students about Race and Responsibility

CAROL KELLY

IT IS DIFFICULT to teach white students that a significant part of their personal identity—being white—is connected with the enslavement of African people, the damage done to Africa, and the history of slavery and discrimination of African Americans. These are heavy burdens to put on such young people. Yet it isn't accurate to teach about this history without covering how white people were the perpetrators of these acts. We know from the work of Robin DiAngelo that when a white person feels blamed or challenged their fragility will cause them to be defensive and even to turn to denial rather than to engage with these lessons. Teaching white students that the history of racism is a white issue is a tough lesson to deliver.

As a white teacher in a school where the majority of students are white, I was inspired when I came upon Jackson Katz's TED Talk, *Violence Against Women is a Men's Issue* (2012). Just as the issue of violence against women is a men's issue, the history of violence against people of color is a white issue. The white enslavement of Africans and African Americans often focuses on the victims and pays little attention to the subject of the action—white people. If we apply Katz's principle to the teaching of race, then we should teach that racism is a white issue, and our focus should be on how white people have acted, and continue to act.

Potential Problems

White fragility makes it clear that this teaching could raise problems, but as a white teacher I have the potential, and responsibility, to speak to white students. I teach in southeast Michigan where there is a broad political spectrum and a range of opinions about the relevance of teaching about race.

The main concern I have encountered from students is that the focus of this work is on reading and understanding. Some students have questioned this, and I refer them to the Common Core's anchor standards for reading. Being able to demonstrate clear learning objectives gives the work authenticity and encourages the idea that the process of learning is as meaningful as any written product.

TEACHING WHITE STUDENTS THAT THE HISTORY OF RACISM IS A WHITE ISSUE IS A TOUGH LESSON TO DELIVER.

I have not yet received any direct challenges from parents. I attribute this to two factors: Firstly, I am careful in the selection of my texts. Some of the excerpts I use do have to be prudently selected to ensure their suitability for a middle school audience, and I often consult colleagues about particular excerpts. Secondly, the teaching environment of our middle school is built on responsive classrooms, restorative practices, and inclusivity. This environment enables me to engage with a difficult dialog in my classroom and has, so far, avoided parental pushback.

Whole-School Approach

As an eighth grade teacher of English language arts (ELA) I am able to build on prior learning from colleagues in earlier grades and other subject areas. Before students begin their classes with me, I know that they have already studied American history, such as the civil rights movement, in social studies. As students study this in seventh grade, they simultaneously read the play script of Lorraine Hansberry's *A Raisin in the Sun* (1994) in language arts class. I am therefore confident that students are already aware of the history of race within the United States, and that it was studied through the lens of looking at the impact of racism from white Americans. Similarly, as I teach African literature in my class, students are learning how white Europeans colonized Africa. As all students take these same core classes there is a continuity of approach that is essential for effectively teaching a difficult topic.

In addition, electives are offered that study the history of race in America in greater depth. Although a relatively small number of students take these electives, it does create a group who has the knowledge and the language to discuss racism within the United States. If I were teaching in a school without this foundation, I would appoint considerably more time to establishing prior knowledge, and developing teaching techniques, before introducing the texts we study in eighth grade.

Topics Covered and Texts Studied

PRE-COLONIALISM: AN ACT OF INTERVENTION

To really understand the full impact of slavery, we should begin with what was lost when white Europeans chose to invade Africa and strip the continent of its resources. We start by looking at how complete Africa was before white people invaded. Before we read any books, we watch Chimamanda Ngozi Adichie's *The Danger of a Single Story* (2009) and use that to emphasize the importance of understanding a whole society, rather than a narrow, stereotyped version. After this introduction, we start to read some African literature.

We always begin with the opening chapter of Chinua Achebe's *Things Fall Apart* (2009). The chapter includes descriptions of many aspects of Igbo culture and clearly demonstrates that this was a rich and varied society. I then use a carefully selected excerpt from Yaa Gyasi's *Homegoing: A Novel* (2017). The second chapter of this book includes a description of the life of Esi before she is captured. It contains the same cultural depth as Achebe's work and clearly establishes how Esi was treated with privilege and respect: She was a princess among her people. Using these two texts effectively stages an intervention in the narrative of the history of Africa. By studying the cultural richness that existed before white people destroyed African societies we build a strong understanding of how life could have been. From this focus we can feel the loss of Africa's past more genuinely.

This is the easy part of the task: We are used to discussing race by focusing on people of color. As satisfying as it can be to see students engage emotionally with the loss of those communities, it does not address the responsibility of white people in the disruption of African history.

POST-COLONIAL AFRICA

When considering this work, I thought about how Germany teaches the history of the Second World War to its youth. In Germany it is a part of the curriculum to cover the Holocaust for all high school students, and anti-bias education is an intrinsic part of this teaching. This approach makes it possible for students to look at the past within the context of the times. It can help them to gain a sense of responsibility for the future without feeling shame for the past. A similar approach to colonialism means we can name white people as being the instigators and profiteers of slavery without laying blame onto the middle school students who we teach and care for.

To gain a sense of the impact of colonialism, we study a number of texts set in modern Africa. The full range of stories that I use gives many examples of life in Africa and steers away from a "single story" (Adichie, 2009) so that students can build a more complete idea of modern African lives. The stories and excerpts that we cover include topics such as economic inequality, racism, education, and personal relationships. A story that I frequently return to is Lauri Kubuitsile's *The Rich People's School* (2009) that manages to include all of these topics in one short, charming tale. I also include *Homeless* by Ovo Adagha (2009). This story highlights the practice of forced eviction and bulldozing of areas of temporary housing. Both stories are told from the perspective of children, and in each of them the characters face challenges that are, in part, caused by global

TEACHING TIPS

Kelly highlights the work she did with white students in her school to support their racial literacy development and emerging understandings of racism as a problem connected to whiteness. To support the ideas Kelly shares in this article, you can also curate multimodal text sets with your students that focus on institutions in your community. This practice can provide insight into historical and current manifestations of racism and possible antiracist practices connected to vital institutions your students and their families use each day. Ask students to engage these texts in ways that examine connections, questions, and tensions among developing racial literacy skills and practices to identify, discuss, and disrupt stereotypes and racist practices that are foundational to how institutions operate.

economic inequality. Trevor Noah's *Born a Crime: Stories from a South African Childhood (Adapted for Young Readers)* (2019) explicitly describes the effects of racism in modern South Africa. Investigating this range of stories engages students with the long-term effects of colonialism that still affect Africa.

By comparing the richness of the culture demonstrated in pre-colonial settings with these modern stories, students can grasp a better understanding of how Africa was and is affected by colonialism. This also leads us into how the story of Africa is linked to the wealth and privilege of America. The European invasion of Africa fed the slave trade and was integral to America's rise as a wealthy nation. However, students are still able to claim that it was "people in the past" who created colonialism and influenced American economic dominance. Discussing racism in modern America is an even harder conversation than discussing the past of racism, but it is still important to do this.

TEACHING ABOUT RACE IN MODERN AMERICA.

When bringing the discussion into the modern American context, I often find that students become reluctant to talk—this is, by far, the hardest part of the conversation to have. It is essential at this point to remind myself of bell hooks' belief that a good teacher "respects and cares for the souls of our students" (1994, p. 13). Before we can even start talking about problems with race in modern America, we need to address the identities of the students in the room. We talk about how race can be simultaneously a social construct and a lived reality, and how identity can at times be both fluid and complex. This introduction is necessary for students to be accepting of and confident within their own identity, which must happen before we can expect them to engage in difficult conversations.

The next lesson we cover is racial bias. We all absorb biases, and we need to learn to accept that we carry bias, including racial bias, with us. Although we can't be held responsible for the experiences that create these biases, we can still attempt to become aware of them and challenge them in our own lives.

Using these principles has enabled me to teach about race without bringing in conflict and blame to my classroom. This makes it possible to read books such as *All American Boys* (Reynolds & Kiely, 2017) and *Harbor Me* (Woodson, 2018) with my middle school students. I have also been able to address the Black Lives Matter movement and the issue of kneeling for the national anthem.

Student Work in Response to Texts

When teaching about these topics, I often place the main emphasis on reading and understanding the text rather than a formal written outcome. The Common Core emphasizes critical thinking and analytical skills, and these are the main focus of student work. As we read the opening of *Things Fall Apart*, I model a range of visible thinking routines. These include visual responses to the chapter, research into words or phrases that students didn't initially understand and having them explain how certain words or phrases made them respond. Finally, students reflect back on what they have learned about historical Igbo culture from this excerpt.

THE EUROPEAN INVASION OF AFRICA FED THE SLAVE TRADE AND WAS INTEGRAL TO AMERICA'S RISE AS A WEALTHY NATION.

After modeling this method of responding to writing, students are given another text to read, and then they choose from a variety of visible thinking routines to create a personal response. Each day they are required to write a brief journal entry to summarize their work. I frequently conference with students in small groups or individually in order to guide their responses and keep them engaged. At the end of this unit students submit all material that they have generated along with their journal. The grading rubric focuses on how well they have developed their ideas, responded to new thoughts, and made appropriate choices when selecting their visible thinking pieces.

Conclusion

Trying to teach white students that racism is a white issue is hard. We can't make middle school students feel burdened or shamed by the past, but we can give them a sense of responsibility and a belief in their own agency to be guardians against allowing the problems from the past to re-emerge, or even to work for greater equity and justice in the future. Middle school students are able to take on tough challenges, and teaching white students that race is a white problem should be a part of the middle school ELA curriculum.

[T]EACHING WHITE STUDENTS THAT RACE IS A WHITE PROBLEM SHOULD BE A PART OF THE MIDDLE SCHOOL ELA CURRICULUM.

REFERENCES

Achebe, C. (2009). *Things fall apart*. Anchor Books.

Adagha, Ova. (2009). "Homeless." In *One world: A global anthology of short stories* (pp. 169–174). New Internationalist.

Adichie, C. N. (2009, July). The danger of a single story. Retrieved May 24, 2019, from https://www.ted.com/talks/chimamanda_adichie_the_danger_of_a_single_story

DiAngelo, R. J. (2018). *White fragility: why it's so hard for white people to talk about racism*. Beacon Books.

Gyasi, Y. (2017). *Homegoing: A novel*. Vintage Books.

Hansberry, L. (1994). *A raisin in the sun*. Vintage Books.

hooks, bell. (1994). *Teaching to transgress*. Routledge.

Katz, J. (n.d.). Violence against women—It's a men's issue. Retrieved May 24, 2019, from https://www.ted.com/talks/jackson_katz_violence_against_women_it_s_a_men_s_issue?

Kubuitsile, L. (2009). "The rich people's school." In *One world: A global anthology of short stories* (pp. 47–52). New Internationalist.

Noah, T. (2019). *Born a crime: Stories from a South African childhood (Adapted for young readers)*. Pan Macmillan.

Reynolds, J., & Kiely, B. (2017). *All American boys*. Atheneum.

Woodson, J. (2018). *Harbor me*. Penguin Random House.

CAROL KELLY lives in southeast Michigan and has been teaching middle school students for 25 years.

This article originally appeared
in *Research in the Teaching of English 55.2*

ANTIRACIST LANGUAGE ARTS PEDAGOGY IS INCOMPLETE WITHOUT BLACK JOY

DAMARIS DUNN & BETTINA L. LOVE

IN THE DOCUMENTARY *What Happened, Miss Simone?* (Kelly & Garbus, 2015), there is a scene in which Nina Simone is sitting in a café wearing an oversized hat, her stunning flawless black skin is glowing, and her eyes speak to the soul of every Black child about the role of an artist and what art should reflect. She passionately and without hesitation tells the interviewer: "An artist's duty, as far as I'm concerned, is to reflect the times." Simone's words intend to push artists to create art that challenges the world to see humanity, to see justice and injustice, to convey the complexities of being human. Her words should also push educators and researchers who create antiracist language arts pedagogy not just to reflect Black folx pain and trauma, but also to center Black joy.

With good reason, antiracist language arts pedagogy is focused on dismantling the racism that is deeply ingrained in the field of language arts (Baker-Bell, 2013, 2020; Turner & Ives, 2013). However, we argue that antiracist language arts pedagogy is incomplete without Black joy. Centering Black joy within antiracist pedagogies allows Black people to be more than their struggles and setbacks, and to see Black folx creativity, imagination, healing, and ingenuity as a vital part of antiracism (Love, 2019). Black joy is the radical imagination of collective memories of resistance, trauma, survival, love, and cultural modes of expression, which push and expand antiracist pedagogies (Love, 2019). Language arts education must be a space where students write their future of resistance and joy.

The Schomburg Center for Research in Black Culture's Junior Scholars program in Harlem, New York, is the perfect example of a space that cultivates and nurtures Black joy. The Junior Scholars program is committed to teaching and learning Afrodiasporic historical literacies while engaging scholars in arts-based practices such as spoken word, dance, theater, and the visual arts. On Saturdays, scholars fill the halls of the Schomburg, with fervor and fearlessness, they reclaim their humanity, hone their artistic creativity, and envision freedom. In Nina Simone's (1967) song "I Wish I Knew How It Would Feel to Be Free" she contemplates freedom and a world unbound by segregation, she sings "I wish I could give, All I'm longin' to give, I wish I could live, Like I'm longin' to live." Like Ms. Simone, the scholars write and create the things they wished they could read and see in formal school settings where they take up language arts pedagogies. At the Schomburg freedom is not merely a word but a state of being. Freedom, to Nina, is no fear. Reckoning with their complex histories scholars and instructors heal and talk back to trauma and anti-Blackness. They are in constant conversation with the ancestors who walked the space before them: Maya Angelou, Amiri Baraka, Langston Hughes, Ella Baker, and Chadwick Boseman. Here their joy is affirmed and their freedom real, not simply a figment of their imaginations. It is in this space

TEACHING TIPS

Dunn and Love remind us that the foundation of antiracist pedagogy is Black joy. You can look more closely at a Nina Simone quotation in their article, as a way to provide a provocative stance for students to think with as they consider the need for representing Black joy: "An artist's duty, as far as I'm concerned, is to reflect the times." Share this Nina Simone quotation with students, then create small groups of three or four students. Each group will discuss this quotation and create a chart that shows how artists they follow have engaged in this practice to explore Black joy. Encourage students to add the art form and themes the artists address through their work, and have them share why they believe these artists' work is valuable to them and our society.

that they resist, dare to be free, and conjure up magic (Carruthers, 2018). This magic is riddled with love and a commitment to collective responsibility.

Thus, an antiracist language arts pedagogy creates space and a place, much like the Junior Scholars program has for the past twenty years. This space allows Black children to imagine, dream, create, resist, take up space, and be. They get to define themselves on their own terms, free from interruption and prescriptive identity markers placed on Black folx. If joy is our internal clarity and purpose (Cooper, 2018), then joy is also our healing, and most importantly our justice. What would it mean if every Black child could find their internal clarity and purpose? Like the artist, educators and researchers must reflect the times, we must craft and commit to antiracist language arts pedagogies, that seek truth, mutuality, love, and most importantly Black joy.

REFERENCES

Baker-Bell, A. (2013). "I never really knew the history behind African American language": Critical language pedagogy in an advanced placement English language arts class. *Equity & Excellence in Education*, 46, 355–370.

Baker-Bell, A. (2020). Dismantling anti-Black linguistic racism in English language arts classrooms: Toward an anti-racist Black language pedagogy. *Theory Into Practice*, 59, 8–21.

Carruthers, C. (2018). *Unapologetic: A Black, queer, and feminist mandate for radical movements*. Beacon Press.

Cooper, B. (2018). *Eloquent rage: A Black feminist discovers her superpower*. St. Martin's Press.

Kelley, L. & Garbus, L. (2015). *What Happened, Miss Simone?* [Motion picture]. Netflix.

Love, B. L. (2019). *We want to do more than survive: Abolitionist teaching and the pursuit of educational freedom*. Beacon Press.

Taylor, B., & Lamb, R. (1967). I Wish I Knew How It Would Feel to Be Free. [Recorded by Nina Simone]. On *Silk & Sou*. RCA Recordings.

Turner, K. N., & Ives, D. (2013). Social justice approaches to African American language and literacy practices: Guest editors' introduction. *Equity & Excellence in Education*, 46, 285–299.

DAMARIS DUNN is a Queens, New York native. She is a doctoral student in the Department of Educational Theory and Practice at the University of Georgia. She is a former social studies teacher and youth developer. She is committed to the joy of Black women teachers and girls in K–12 schools.

BETTINA L. LOVE is an award-winning author and the Athletic Association Professor in Education at the University of Georgia. She is one of the field's most esteemed educational researchers. Her writing, research, teaching, and activism meet at the intersection of race, education, abolition, and Black joy.

This article originally appeared
in *Research in the Teaching of English 54.4*

REVEALING THE HUMAN AND THE WRITER: The Promise of a Humanizing Writing Pedagogy for Black Students

LATRISE P. JOHNSON &
HANNAH SULLIVAN

Using a critical stance on place, literacy, and humanity in order to examine how the literacy learning and practices of ELA classrooms/schools might (de)humanize and (de)culturize Black students, this study examines the writing pedagogy of a professor who taught a semester-long creative writing class for students at West High School. Through a humanizing approach to teaching writing, the professor and students engaged in writing and being in ways that honored—as well as centered and supported—their individual, cultural, and writerly identities. This article offers ways that teachers of writing might tap into Black intellectual traditions and invite students to use writing as a way to connect to what they do and learn while at school.

The Promise of a Humanizing Writing Pedagogy for Black Students

Imagine that you have entered your third-period 11th-grade English class. Tables are arranged in neat rows, with two chairs per table—all facing the front of the room. Your teacher tells the class that you will continue listening to Jeannette Walls's *The Glass Castle*. The dry erase board is covered in the teacher's handwriting with notes from the previous day. The "warm-up" provides directions to copy each sentence and make corrections. After you and your classmates stumble through the sentences, the teacher provides the correct answers using call and response, and reiterates that you should have the correct version in your notes. "Y'all will see this on the ACT," she offers as another reminder. The teacher resumes the recording, stopping periodically to pose questions about plot. As the period nears its end, the teacher stops the recording and instructs the class to complete the exit slip. Today's question is, "Do you think Jeannette's parents are good or bad? Use at least one piece of textual evidence to support your answer." You pass your exit slip to your teacher on your way out.

It is important to note that the teacher and the students in the "regular" English class described above were Black. The teacher used both African American Language and American English to convey ideas, used call and response to check students' understanding, and tasked students with making a judgment about the characters using evidence from the text—practices that were linked to aspects of students' cultures and experiences. While such approaches provide opportunities for students to make connections between their lives and what they are learning in school, they fail to acknowledge students as contributors of knowledge or as creators of language and text worth engaging.

To some, the classroom experience described above may seem ideal. The teacher incorporated media and checked for understanding frequently as students followed along with the text. The class began and ended with a focused activity to ensure that students were engaged. However, when the teaching and learning are examined more closely, it becomes clear that these so-called best practices had little to do with students (or the teacher) engaging deeply with the content—a problem that inspired the line of inquiry guiding this work. Instead, the reading and writing could have served as methods for students to think deeply and authentically about how what they were learning connected to their pasts, presents, and futures. Opportunities to align and connect what they learn in schools with their lived experiences, as well as pedagogies that account for dehumanizing instructional and discipline practices of schooling, could have a lasting effect on the ways that Black students come to understand their intellectual and writerly selves.

For Black students in particular, cultural deficit perspectives and racist constructions of language, literacy, and literacy achievement (Anderson, 1988; Baker-Bell, 2019; Woodson, 1932) are used to explain why they do not do as well as their White counterparts (Rothstein, 2013). These damaging perspectives influence how Black students are educated in schools, as well as how teachers perceive and instruct them. Traditionally, literacy instruction for marginalized youth has been "data driven" (Neuman, 2016), grammar- and technical skills-focused (Tatum, 2006), and anti-Black (Baker-Bell, 2019), and has lacked the kind of engagement that leads to liberation (Ladson-Billings, 2005). Such approaches are offered as ways to improve the achievement of Black students and close the so-called gap between them and White students (Ladson-Billings, 2006).

The opening vignette also reflects several conflicts between the promise and the reality of literacy teaching for Black youth. First, the physical space of the classroom removed opportunities for students and teachers to engage as a community and did not reflect their literate identities or literacy development (e.g., book choice, no representation of Black authors on the walls). Second, the pedagogical approach of focusing on "correctness" limited opportunities for dialogue that could lead to analysis and synthesis of text and left little room to think deeply about language practice. And, finally, the little writing (and thinking) asked of the students missed the chance to connect their experiences to the content and context of what they learned. Such practices ignore the rich literate traditions of Black people (Fisher, 2009; Harris, 1992) and thereby (re)center whiteness in literacy teaching and learning (Gangi, 2008). Additionally, they exclude Black adolescent voices from the intellectual work of meaning-making that could happen in and through writing. In total, they do very little to fulfill the promise of quality public schooling for Black children (Morris, 2015).

Thus, the question guiding this research is: What happens when a teacher-scholar leverages historicized and humanizing views of Black orientations, identities, and literacy practices to teach writing? Moreover, this study examines the literacy practices of a creative writing class of Black students and Latrise, a Black teacher-scholar, (*the professor*[1], hereafter) in order to illuminate the writing pedagogical approaches used and the textual outcomes that centered and celebrated Black students' histories, identities, and experiences—practices that reveal the human and the writer. In addition, the professor considered the ways that Black people have been able to (re)write themselves into the world historically through language arts, included many of those traditions in the course as a way to decenter whiteness, and invited the students to read and write themselves into the context and content of their literacy learning (Winn, 2010).

Place, Literacy, and the (De)humanization and (De)culturization of Black Students: Theoretical Considerations

For this study, the authors consider critical stances on place, literacy, and humanity in order to examine how the literacy learning and practices of ELA classrooms/schools might (de)humanize and (de)culturize Black students. This triadic framework contends with the tensions that affect the educational experiences of students of color in public schools and is used to argue for more humanizing writing pedagogies that invite students to write themselves in and through their experiences as Black youth. For the sake of this article, Black orientations and cultural identities are understood as "inherited West African values, ideas, and beliefs" where individuals are (re)shaped and influenced by the experiences of the collective (Croft, Juergensen, Pogue, & Willis, 2018, p. 33). In other words, there is a Black cultural ethos where Black individuals shape and are shaped by a collective and communal understanding of elements like time, space, and expression. These collective and communal understandings of school(ing) situate the place of school and its practices as hostile (Meiners, 2007), anti-Black (Baker-Bell, 2019), culturally misaligned (Ladson-Billings, 2014), and dehumanizing (Goff et al., 2014).

School as place is "the embodiment of a purposefully created space that is a creation and enactment of the cultural and social conditions of the [people who occupy that place]" (Callejo-Pérez, Slater, & Fain, 2004, p. 1). School as place reflects a long and complicated history for Black people. And while the establishment of segregated public schools offered a glimmer of hope for Blacks during Reconstruction, several turning points (including but not limited to World War II, Brown v. Board of Education I and II, massive resistance to the integration of public schools, federal involvement, busing, the civil rights movement, resegregation) have positioned school as a hostile place for Black people (Anderson, 1988; Morris & Morris, 2002). In addition, the signs, symbols, and curricula that represent American school and schooling do not reflect the study of practical and scholarly contributions that Black people have made. In other words, school continues to be an antagonistic place for students of color as curriculum, discipline practices, achievement data reporting, and pedagogies tend to center whiteness and support White, middle-class constructions of what it means to be a "good" student. Understanding school as place in both historical and contemporary contexts requires researchers to attend to the signs, symbols, bodies, and practices (i.e., place matter) of schools and classrooms, as well as to examine the local contexts and meaning-making of place matter for the (under)education of students of color.

As this work privileges a historicization of literacy that acknowledges the rich and textured lives of youth broadly and Black youth specifically (Scribner & Cole, 1981; Winn, 2015), it also recognizes the relationship of school as place (with history) with the schooling of African Americans that "deemed [the] most appropriate education [to be one that] emphasized rudimentary literacy skills and the inculcation of an ideology that guaranteed caste-like status" (Harris, 1992, p. 276). While contemporary views suggest that literacy is not defined solely by the ability to read and write, but encompasses knowledges, actions, emotions, exchange of ideas, and communal experiences, comparison of the multiple literacies that youth practice against the practices of school literacies reveals much tension. Ideologies that inform the literacies most practiced in schools tend to be instrumental, as literacy is used to dispense the "best knowledge," the content consists of "good books," and the writing demonstrated is "formal" (Stuckey, 1991). According to Stuckey, comprehension of particular information and ideology is how schools "turn out proper conformity and regulate failure" (p. 54). The logic of literacy presented in this way denies Black youths' own proclivities, interests, experiences, and engagements with/in literacy practice. It also racializes literacy achievement, seeking to remedy failure by entry into mainstream literacy practice and participation—namely, White, middle-class, heteronormative, and cisgender forms of literate being and belonging (Austin, 2018).

Historical perspectives of Black conceptions of literacy position Black people as demanders, creators, funders, and maintainers of educational institutions that have (a) provided literacy for all; (b) apprised individuals of and prepared them for the dominating culture's institutions; (c) counteracted the pernicious and venal images of African Americans prevalent in popular culture; and (d) engendered group solidarity and commitment to uplift (Harris, 1992). These perspectives are reflected in texts that historicize and imagine the lives of Black people, as well as in the contemporary composition of authentic portraits of Black people that challenge monolithic, dominant, and damaging narratives. The production and centering of such texts represent what is possible for teaching writing to Black youth, in that these texts serve as a "re-appraisal of . . . aesthetic values . . . [that are] less influenced by the dominant standards" and allow Black youth to "be taught with real conviction the beauties of [their] own [lives]" (Johnson, 1936). These texts also provide models for how writing has been used to add the voices and perspectives of Black people to bodies of knowledge that have historically ignored their contributions.

Therefore, a humanizing writing pedagogical stance begins with the notion that students' knowledges (which encompass their collective and individual histories) are at the center of what they are expected to know and do while at school (Bartolomé, 1994; Donnell, 2007). Thus, a humanizing writing pedagogy provides a lens to view Black students' individual lives and creates opportunities for them to make personal, critical connections to a world where they share collective struggle related to the "circumstances of race status" (Johnson, 1936). With regard to writing instruction and the production of text, humanizing pedagogical processes require that pedagogues enact critical practices that interrupt normalized literacies and dominant ways of knowing and being. For instance, the full development of a writer depends on understanding oneself in relation to one's world (Johnson, 2017). That said, humanizing approaches to writing instruction and practice mean centering the writer in the processes and production of critically conscious writing—and, in this case, in ways that involve Black youth in the meaning-making that is part of a rich literary tradition. Indeed, Black people have historically "needed literacy in order to acquire freedom and power" (Harris, 1992, p. 278). And it is that history and re-centering of Black culture that is integral to humanizing writing pedagogies for Black youth as they (1) recall forms of literacy that privilege and are contingent upon students' sociohistorical lives, both proximally and distally; (2) are grounded in literate histories and traditions of Black people; and (3) invite Black students to compose and add their voices to various bodies of knowledges.

Writing in Place: Limitations of School-Sanctioned Writing for Black Adolescents

According to Yagelski (2009), "school-sponsored writing is about separating self from experience by changing an experience into a stylized textual artifact" (p. 19). In addition, the type of writing practiced in high school classrooms often requires that students remove, deny, and ignore important aspects of their writing identities. Specifically, English classrooms—and, consequently, writing instruction—reinforce hegemonic, heteronormative, patriarchal, and "standard" discourses as teachers center literature, practices, and skills aligned with normalized White, middle-class views of what it means to be intellectual (Johnson, 2017). According to Bartolomé (1994), "unless educational methods are situated in the students' cultural experiences, students will continue to show difficulty in mastering content area that is not only alien to their reality, but often antagonistic" to who they are or want to be (p. 191). This is true when students are learning to write. For Black students specifically, the reality is that the instruction they receive in schools is typically the result of the misinterpretation, denigration, and dismissal of their "languages, nonverbal cues, physical movements, learning styles, cognitive approaches, and worldviews" (Cooper, 2002, p. 48). As a result, Black students frequently experience the type of writing instruction that is tied to systemic inequities of literacy teaching, content, and expectations.

Recent scholarship that considers the writing lives of adolescents focuses on bridging their in- and out-of-school literacy practices by using innovative, digital tools and multimedia in order to respond to questions of identity, schooling, and being for historically marginalized students. Several studies describe novel projects that invite students to engage in writing processes that help them discover their voices, making meaning of the world around them in the process. Zenkov and Harmon (2009) conducted a study where "high school students of diverse backgrounds and living in poverty" were invited to compose a multimodal text to reflect on the purpose of school, supports they needed, and barriers to their success, with hopes that the students would "appreciate [their] English curricula" (p. 575). The researchers found that the use of images supported youths' ability to "paint pictures with words," which informed how ELA teachers might use visually based methods to "understand the points of view of urban youth and as tools in our writing activities" (Zenkov & Harmon, 2009, p. 583). A similar study conducted by Haddix and Sealey-Ruiz (2012) acknowledges the potential of digital tools to transform literacy learning. They encouraged digital composing that empowered students to be "producers and creators of knowledge within the classroom" (Haddix & Sealey-Ruiz, 2012, p. 190). What is different about these studies' approaches to writing instruction is that while the former study centered English curricula, the latter focused on empowering students as producers and creators of knowledge, was grounded in freedom, and aimed to improve the critical thinking and critical literacy skills students already had.

These studies, framed by sociocultural and sociopolitical understandings of literacy, illuminate the importance of developing literate identities in and beyond school. Researchers also recognize the need for paradigmatic shifts in the ways teachers of writing might use relevant approaches in order to reimagine what writing might look like for students with marginalized identities. However, the reality is that the dominant discourse of writing research and pedagogy urges teachers toward cognitive process models of writing and skills-based teaching (Gardner, 2018). Moreover, Cremlin and Oliver (2016) concluded that because teachers tend to have restricted views of writing and exhibit low confidence and negative writing histories, the teaching of writing is problematic. Confounded by the lack of writing teacher efficacy, standards for teaching writing outline an ambitious roadmap for what students should be able to do as proficient writers, but provide little direction on how writing benchmarks are to be achieved, and are "notably silent about the role of context" (Graham, Harris, & Santangelo, 2015, p. 501). And while both social/contextual and cognitive/motivational structures of effective writing instruction have potential in developing adolescent writers, these approaches do not fully attend to how the relationship to school as place for students with historically marginalized identities might affect efforts to "develop a writing environment that is motivating, pleasant, and nonthreatening, where teachers support students and their writing efforts" (Graham et al., 2015, p. 507).

Humanity Revealed in and through Writing with Black Youth on the Edges of School

In the past 10 years, an increasing amount of research has been conducted on the writerly lives of Black youth and how Black youths' literacies might be leveraged in ways that center their humanity (Everett, 2018; Johnson, 2015; Kirkland & Jackson, 2009). These and other studies make visible the contemporary literacy practices that are connected to the literacy legacies of Black people. By centering intellectual and ideological traditions of Black people, these scholars offer ways that Black youth, like their ancestors, have used writing in order to write themselves into the world in authentic ways, as well as to counter problematic narratives that plague society's collective consciousness about being Black.

In her work with Black boys, Haddix (2009) interrupts dominant framings of Black males as nonwriters and posits that "the dominant discourse of failure initiates and sustains the dehumanization and objectification of Black male subjects, positioning them as scapegoats for failed academic efforts" (p. 343). For example, Haddix centers one student's views on writing as a counterstory to the dominant framing of Black male failure by illuminating his prowess for intellectual performance. Like Haddix, Kirkland and Jackson (2009) focus on how Black males use writing, "cool talk," drawing, and dressing in order to construct ways of being Black that position them as creators of their own symbols and signals of literate identity. Another study showing Black males' construction of scholarly identities in and through writing is Everett's (2016) work with high school students, where one Black male used metaphor to interrogate his schooling experiences.

In studies that focus on Black girls, similar approaches have been used to understand how writing identities are developed by centering students' lived experiences as well as Black ways of doing literacy and being literate. Hall (2011) notes the ways Black girls used scene writing in order to "testify" about friendship and sisterhood in ways that included oral-aural traditions of Black culture. In a study focused on the digital literacies of Black girls, Price-Dennis (2016) posits that digital spaces have the potential to be transformative and helpful in constructing a model for being fully human in the world. Using "Black women leading thinkers such as Sojourner Truth, Ida B. Wells, Phillis Wheatley, and Anna Julia Cooper," Price-Dennis conceptualizes the social, political, economic, and historical contexts that are tied to Black girls' understanding of what it means to be literate. Such constructions of literacy for Black girls are important, as deficit perspectives of Black girlhood, like Black boyhood, dominate educational discourse. Price-Dennis (2016) found that the literate identities of the Black girl participants were "*tied to their identities as Black girls*" (pp. 357–358, italics in original). In other words, there is a Black collective identity to which the participants felt connected. Most importantly, this work offers an exploration of how digital spaces were used to help "Black girls create, control, and disseminate ideas that validate their understanding of what it means to be proficient, literate, excellent, thriving, and brilliant" (Price-Dennis, 2016, p. 360).

These studies are important in understanding how the relationship between literacy and blackness is connected to how Black youth experience school. Unfortunately, many of these studies center practices that are happening on the edges of school and reflect literacy work that is being done with youth, possibly in schools, but not as a part of their ELA (or other) curriculum or in collaboration with their ELA teachers. In this way, these studies highlight the fact that Black students' ability to write themselves into bodies of knowledge is more likely to occur outside of the classroom than inside it.

Methodology

This study is part of a larger ethnographic research project, in which Latrise has reimagined her role as researcher and located her teaching and research with/in one local school community. For this project, she has utilized practitioner inquiry to observe patterns and create conditions for imaging and enacting new possibilities (Cochran-Smith & Lytle, 2009). Hannah's expertise in literacy classrooms was important to the professor's delimitation as an ethnographer whose roles and work with/in a local high school had shifted and created more fortuitous research and teaching experiences (Green, 2014). The second author was integral in analyzing and interpreting the pedagogical approaches set by the professor, as they understand collaboration to be an element of humanizing approaches to teaching and conducting research.

SCHOOL CONTEXT AND PARTICIPANTS

The study took place at West High School.[2] At the time of the study, it served 752 students, approximately 95% of whom identified as African American, 4% as White, and less than 1% as Hispanic, Latinx, or multiracial; 63% of the student body qualified for free or reduced lunch. West was the only high school that offered the International Baccalaureate program in the school system. The school had 41 full-time faculty and housed numerous programs that focused on student achievement and social development. West also partnered with nearby colleges to offer dual-enrollment and early college. At the school, the professor also served as professor in residence, in which she was involved in research, teaching, and service with/in the school's community. Her role as professor in residence led to the opportunity to teach a one-semester English elective at the high school.

Out of 31 students, 30 identified as African American/Black and 1 identified as "mixed" or biracial. The class comprised 1 ninth grader, 7 tenth graders, and 23 eleventh graders; 2 students volunteered to take the course, while the others were enrolled by the school's registrar. The class represented a diverse group of students with different interests, abilities, and experiences. For example, Nagasi, a male in the 10th grade, described his writing as "ok," and his skill level was developing. He did not particularly enjoy writing. However, he loved to talk about his experiences growing up with cerebral palsy and bragged about his ability to walk even though doctors told his mom he would not. Fari, a biracial female in 9th grade, loved writing and described her own writing as "unique." Fari would write several pages per day. She wrote independently and would often share her fantasy narratives written outside of class with the professor.

To help the professor get to know the students, their first writing assignment was titled, "25 Things You Don't See When You Look at Me." They wrote about how old they were, favorite musicians, and least favorite subjects. Students also used the assignment to share insights into their worlds, as well as statements about what they hoped and dreamed for their lives. While the statements gave the professor insight into students' lived experiences, they also revealed a wide range of interests, traits, and ideas with which she connected. Incorporating this assignment early on in the course was instrumental in the students' first steps toward understanding and validating their realities as resources to draw on in their writing.

RESEARCHERS' POSITIONALITIES

The professor, Latrise, is a Black, queer educator with 17 years of teaching experience. She is an associate professor of literacy and professor in residence at West High School, where she explores local and broader questions related to (1) the in-, out-, and edge-of school literacy practices of nondominant and/or historically marginalized youth; (2) how educators leverage students' existing literacy practices in order to teach in ways that are liberating and empowering for all students; and (3) her role as teacher/researcher in posing questions and solving problems with/in nondominant and historically marginalized communities.

Hannah is a White PhD student, research assistant, and classroom teacher. She entered the project at the analysis phase to gain insight into various ways of conducting humanizing research—in this case, through interpretation of data. Her collaboration on this project was integral to co-constructing the ways humanizing pedagogies were understood in the context of the professor's work at West High School. While her contribution to this work was an opportunity to practice data analysis and writing for publication, her perspective was important to the meaning-making needed to understand the complexities of the pedagogical choices made by the professor, of the experiences of the students, and of the writing they did together.

DATA COLLECTION AND ANALYSIS

The professor began collecting data on day 1 of the semester-long course beginning August 4, 2017, and ending December 18, 2017. The class met Monday through Friday from 2:05 to 3:30 p.m. for 18 weeks. Artifacts from the entire course are a part of the data set. The professor wrote field notes after each class, including descriptions of what was observed throughout the class period. At times, the professor would jot notes during class if particular phenomena struck her as important. She also kept a notebook where she collected artifacts that were not student work. Some examples include pictures, personal notes, hall passes, and extra copies of handouts and readings. The professor's field notebook, artifacts, and daily writing journals were collected throughout the course and organized by type of artifact/writing example. The professor collected 19 of the 31 journals. All students' and professor's writing and work collected were considered data.

In analyzing the data for this study, the authors started with a list of codes that were grounded in the ways they were defining humanizing writing instruction and practice. Initial codes were revealed where the professor and students engaged in teaching and writing that allowed them to explore and compose identities, share important aspects of their being, grapple with experiences, and write toward deeper understandings of self in relation to schooling. Sample codes include *personal identity, social/collective (Black) identity, experiences* (named and categorized), *criticality, transformation*, and *healing*. Table 1 illustrates examples of how pedagogical decisions and texts were coded according to purpose, function, and context. For example, in the course's syllabus, the professor included, "Changing the World with Our Word" as one unit's title. "Our" was initially coded as *collective identity*, given that humanizing pedagogy for Black students was being developed and defined to include Black cultural ethological understandings. From these codes/coding, the authors created interpretive statements in order to identify themes in the data. These themes included *honoring Black ways of knowing and being* and *centering and supporting (Black) identity/writerly development*. Because of the nature of classroom teaching and learning, as well as the authors' thinking with (developing) theory, post-coding analysis was necessary for noting what was instrumental and salient to understanding the nature of participants' writing in relation to a humanizing pedagogy.

For the professor, being at West High School presented many opportunities to understand the data within and apart from larger contexts. In other words, making meaning of students' writing also took place while the professor was coming to understand West High School and the communities where she and these students were members. Being at the school for the semester in a teaching capacity made everything that occurred (before and beyond the class) viable data, and also made member checks possible throughout the data collection and interpretation processes. We conducted post-coding analysis in order to include what we now know and offer as humanizing writing pedagogy.

TABLE 1
Data Analysis Matrix

Research Question	What happens when a teacher-scholar leverages historical and humanizing views of Black orientations, identities, and literacies to teach writing?	
Unit of Data (e.g., one pedagogical choice/approach, one text)	The professor included language in the syllabus that referred to a collective identity.	The List—an assignment that invited students to compose a list and descriptions that were related to their lived experiences.
Themes	Honoring Black ways of knowing and being	Centering and supporting student (Black) identity/writerly development
Patterns	Purpose: To signal to students that Black students/writers have something to say that is significant	Purpose: To center students' individual experiences
	Function: A signal to students that their voices are included and important to issues *in* and beyond the classroom	Function: A way for students to critique and connect their experiences to larger ideas around being African American
	Context: Students rarely experienced opportunities to think of themselves as writers in the context of school(ing).	Context: Students were exposed to other ways of thinking and writing beyond those stressed in their ELA classrooms.
Post-coding Analysis	Students were reminded through the handouts, texts by Black authors, lessons, classroom discourse, and writing, that their voice was a legitimate part of bodies of knowledge.	Students were exposed to ways of writing themselves in the world that invited their lived experiences and centered what they knew and were finding out about being and being Black. The List offered a way into writing that allowed even the most reluctant writers to locate context in their lives to compose text.

Findings: Leveraging Historicized and Humanizing Views of Black Youth to Teach Writing

In the following sections, we describe the pedagogical choices made by the professor, exploring how specific pedagogical choices functioned in the classroom space and how they fit with/in broader school contexts. In addition, we shed light on the texts that resulted when students were invited to write their lives as well as to critique relevant broader issues. We then discuss why humanizing writing pedagogies for Black youth are important in remembering and reimagining school as a place where their literate legacies and writerly lives are honored.

REIMAGINING SCHOOL AS OUR PLACE: CENTERING BLACK LITERARY TRADITIONS

The professor was intentional about communicating to students that school was a place where she and her Black students belonged. She wanted to be sure that the space reflected and supported what Winn (formerly Fisher, 2003) calls *African diasporic participatory literacy traditions* (ADPLTs). The space needed to support fluid and critical literacy participation that was based on flexibility, responsibility, and intergenerational connections (Fisher, 2003; Pogue, 2015), and the students needed to "read" that the space was a reflection of their Black intellectual lineage. ADPLTs were reflected in the overall discourse of the class, as well as in the place matter—that is, the signs, symbols, bodies, and practices of the course.

Creating Communal Space and Sharing. The classroom contained six tables, each with six chairs; each table was furnished with a small metal bucket that contained markers, highlighters, colored pencils, pens, role tags for group activities, and a picture of one of six writers of color (Solange, Paulo Coelho, Tupac, Alice Walker, Toni Morrison, and James Baldwin). For the professor, providing students with equal access to tools for learning (e.g., pens, markers, composition books, etc.) daily was an intentional and important choice. While many of the students lived in impoverished neighborhoods on the city's west and south sides, the professor was most interested in providing access to the material wealth that she now had access to through employment as well as material resources from the university.

Many students brought earphones to listen to their own music. However, the professor often played music ranging from John Coltrane to Tupac from a Bluetooth speaker for the entire class. Many times, students would request music they wanted to hear and included the names of artists on the whiteboard under "Request for Class Playlist." Music, table chatter, and student movement created a relaxed and uninhibited classroom atmosphere that supported a sense of freedom, interaction, and sharing.

Belonging with/in Intellectual Spaces and Building Community. The arrangement of the desks was used to support collaboration and discussion, optimize students' ability to talk through their ideas, and support the transition of oral ideation to the written word (Pogue, 2015). At these tables, the professor encouraged students to talk through their ideas and share their writing with each other, and wrote with students to model how dialogue could be used as an authoring move. Intergenerational connection was also supported through this arrangement, as students were reminded to consult the writing (text creation) of seasoned writers they knew and were learning about in class.

The "25 Things You Don't See When You Look at Me" assignment invited students to compose 25 sentences/statements that reflected parts of their social and personal identities. For example, several students included family members who had passed away and how tragedies had affected their families. Four students wrote about their sexuality; two identified as gay, one said they were straight, and Delu, a 16-year-old female, proclaimed, "My sexuality is fluid." Other students used metaphor to provide insight into their personalities. Nilah, a 15-year-old female, declared, "I am an unfinished puzzle, put together and broken." From their statements, the professor learned that several of the girls in the class loved wearing "lashes." Five wrote statements about their hair, two of them wrote about their love of football, and Aire connected several statements to her love for basketball. The professor completed the same assignment in order to reveal parts of her own identity that students could connect with.

Centering Our Voices. The texts used in the course centered Black voices, and the approaches to teaching illustrated how text by and centering African Americans could be used to learn concepts and skills from students' "regular" English classes. According to Tatum (2006), "neither effective reading strategies nor comprehensive literacy reform efforts will [decrease the education debt] in a race- and class-based society unless meaningful texts are at the core of the curriculum" (pp. 47–48). The meaningful texts used in this course—that is, texts authored by writers who readers identified with on sociocultural and experiential levels—offered a way for students to see their current lives reflected in what they learned about and through writing.

Other opportunities to center Black composers as legitimate context for study included the use of an edited version of Tupac's "Me and My Girlfriend" in order to teach extended metaphor (Shakur, 1996, track 10). The professor referenced Black movies and art in class lectures and discussions. For example, the professor referred to movies, like *Friday* (Charbonnet & Gray, 1995), when explaining elements of story and used Black music to explain how writers experiment with language to make old concepts new. One discussion invited students to think of instances where their favorite songs, traditionally nonacademic texts, might serve as context for scholarly and intellectual inquiry.

The professor, who identified as a writer, wanted her students to witness the vulnerability involved in storying one's experience. For example, while drafting "Things My Dad Told Me," she shared that her list was a way to remember her father and highlighted that the meaning was located in her own feelings about those moments. Sharing personal stories and mutually constructing their work opened avenues of trust and vulnerability between students and the professor. It also invited them to think about the many ways they could write themselves into classrooms, schools, and the world. When Black students are invited to use the stuff of their everyday lives in their writing, they have the opportunity to add their experiences to classroom discourses, and—more importantly—to see their experiences as valuable content for teaching and learning. One example of this is Sapphire's journal entry, "The Flea Market," where she described "the crowded aisles of knockoffs and club clothes" and "getting grilled corn on the cob with my cousin." In her responses to students' writing, the professor often commented that particular lines were inspiring, funny, or "messed up"; in this case, she wrote to Sapphire that the above lines "belonged in literature."

The pedagogical approaches used to center students' lives and the contributions of Black people created a classroom environment that reflected a sense of freedom and intellectual engagement that was evident in students' writing. When the class discussed writing, little attention was given to using "standard" English or writing in strict formats. Instead, students were encouraged to experiment with language and learn to communicate in ways that spoke to their intended audiences. In addition, the professor wanted her students to recognize that much of what they encountered in the form of everyday music and youth culture could serve as content for intellectual engagement and good writing. Traditions like call and response, playing the dozens, writing from experience, sharing stories orally, and song were integral to carving a school space for Black students that fostered their intellectual development and considered their individual and collective identities. The signs, symbols, bodies, and practices of the course reflected a celebration of Black identity and were used to illustrate to students that the content of Black culture was worthy of study *in schools* and for gaining understanding of many matters of the world.

"ON A WHOLE OTHER LEVEL NOW": FOSTERING PERSONAL, SOCIAL, AND WRITERLY IDENTITIES FOR BLACK ADOLESCENTS

In and through writing, the professor and students centered and celebrated small things in their lives. For example, King wrote about things that were a part of him, including his scars, art, clothes, arm bands, and shoes that were "armor to protect my feet from the dangerous ground as I walk up the stairs of life"—a metaphor that he used throughout his writing. In his list, King celebrated himself, his choice of style, and his talent. Students wrote in ways that celebrated aspects of their lived experiences, while experimenting with form. What resulted was writing that was fresh, funny, and reflective as it showcased students' being and becoming. For example, in an assignment entitled "Remember Me," inspired by an assignment from Linda Christensen's (2017) *Reading, Writing, and Rising Up*, Aire wrote:

> I'm a bold young woman
> Dancing in my dreams.
>
> Writing and admiring.
> My critique:
> My writing sounds awesome to me.
>
> When performing
> Shy:
> I'll never be.
> I'm a star when my audience reads me.
>
> Brave and proud is what I aim to be.
> I am Aire
> What you thought?
> I know you remember me. (October 13, 2017)

Aire's poem reflected a confidence in herself, her writing, and who/how she aimed to be. There was also a sense of fearlessness in Aire's poem that showed up in other students' writing as well.

Students were not afraid to share aspects of their lives that could be misinterpreted, used against them, or dismissed by some of their teachers. For example, Jazz shared her poem, "Hiding the Truth":

> Sitting in the classroom
> laughing
> talking
> eating.
> WAIT!
> "[to teacher], may I go to the restroom?"
> I usually go to change my clothes for work.
> But this time,
> I went for another reason.
> What did I leave for this time?
> The world may never know. (September 29, 2017)

Similarly, Safi wrote freely about choices made throughout her life. Her list, "Things I Regret," read:

> Lying to my mom: I had homework and wanted to play—I got a bad grade and as a result I got in even more trouble.
> Calling my sister ugly: She made me mad and I said what I was thinking—It lowered her self-esteem.
> Watching Jeepers Creepers at Night: We were just having fun—I was four and couldn't go to sleep.
> Moving to Montgomery: It was after the house fire—worst school year of my life!
> Not Watching my dog: She attacked a smaller dog to protect her puppies—They put her down. Not keeping the Puppies: We didn't want to separate them from their mother—They put them down too.
> Skipping class: In Montgomery, I didn't like my teacher—I got caught.
> Not taking risks: I stay at home during fun events—I miss out.
> Eating undercooked yams: My great aunt cooked them—I got food poisoning.
> Contemplating suicide: After the fire we lost everything and I thought without me expenses would decrease—I almost gave up my future. (November 13, 2017)

At the intersection of celebrating other ways of knowing and being (in most cases, Black culture), writing from experiences, and freedom was the type of writing where the students took risks and shared aspects of their lives that made for engaging context.

Many times, students aligned larger issues of racism, classism, and inequity with local and personal issues that affected their own lives. For example, Nagasi used "The List" assignment to compare his identity to Black men who had been killed by police. His list, entitled "A List of How I Am Like Men Killed by Police," explained:

> Eric Garner and I are alike because he was a peacemaker.
> John Crawford and I are alike because he loved to help people out and he had a kind
> heart. Just like me.
> Ezell Ford and I are the same because we both have asthma.
> Rumain Brisbon and I are the same because he was a hard-working man who loved and
> took care of his family. (September 13, 2017)

Nilah celebrated the different figures of women. Her list, "Things Women Are Shaped Like," read:

> Milkshake: full figured, big bust, wide hips, large thighs—beautiful.
> Coca-Cola: hourglass, small waist, proportioned evenly—lovely.
> Hi-C: small frame, short, petite—gorgeous.
> Peppermint: classic, underestimated, saggy boobs, stretch marks—fabulous. (September 12, 2017)

Through the creation of her list, Nilah produced images of women that celebrated their different figures and shapes. Her writing honored women's physical appearance. Reading, writing, and discussion focused around issues relevant to Black lives inspired students' writing. Access to texts that celebrated Black culture, that critiqued systems of oppression and discrimination, and that provided models of different ways to add one's voice to larger discourses were integral to students' meaning-making and to their writing.

Messenger, an 11th-grade student, used the dedication page of her portfolio to comment on her growth as a writer:

> I would like to dedicate my writing to Ms. Johnson. Her encouragement and guidance have helped me out a lot. When my writing was bad she took notice and gave me advice on how to improve by leaving sticky notes in my journal. Believe it or not I really did read each and every one of them and took into account

> what she was saying. Because of that I am on a whole other level now. She teaches because she loves to share her knowledge with the students and enhance our minds. Before taking creative writing, I would just throw words on to the paper. Now I delve into the deepest parts of my mind when I write. (December 13, 2017)

Messenger's dedication illustrated how she had grown to be more thoughtful and introspective in her writing, and how she had improved as a writer who was "on a whole other level now."

School as the *Write* Place: A Discussion on Developing Black Student Writers in ELA Classrooms

There is a growing body of research that has explored the literacy participation of Black people in light of broader discourses, institutions, and relations of power, particularly in out-of-school contexts (Fisher, 2009; Kinloch, 2010; Muhammad & Behizadeh, 2015). Scholars have noted the need for what Hill (2011) refers to as *literacy counterpublics*, "spaces in which written texts are central to the engagement of social practices that enable participants to challenge the authority of the state, develop oppositional politics, reinterpret dominant social narratives and counternarrate their own lived experiences" (p. 41). Understanding school as a space where curriculum, policies, and practices work to deculturize and dehumanize Black students is necessary for undoing the damage that has been done by privileging mainstream intellectual, cultural, and political ways of being and knowing found in schools (Hill, 2011). In order to counter some of the practices the professor observed in other ELA classrooms, her efforts to center Black ways of being and knowing were intentional and informed primarily by the collective identities of the students. The professor acknowledged and used the cultural backgrounds of students in literacy and language instruction (Delpit, 2006; Ladson-Billings, 2014; Paris, 2012); she also named and located opportunities to incorporate African American language features and linguistic registers into literacy teaching and learning processes—practices used to include Black students as legitimate and valued participants in the teaching and learning that happens in schools.

Each writing opportunity encouraged students to explore who they were and prompted them to use their experiences to communicate who they were becoming. In writing, the students exposed who they were as humans and who they were as writers—both worthy of attention and development. Furthermore, their stories and texts became a part of the curriculum as their epistemic privilege was centered in their writing development. For example, students wrote about personal content that, at times, offered "forbidden knowledge or critique" and made possible the inclusion of "fugitive knowledge and counterhegemonic perspectives" that were imperative to their critical consciousness (Nelson, 2011, p. 475).

For Black students, being invited to write oneself into classrooms is a necessary prerequisite for writing oneself into the world. Providing students with guidance and mentorship in writing well, and centering Black literary traditions within teacher practice, invite students to locate places in their own ways of knowing that serve as content and context for their writing development and literate being (Fisher, 2009; Hill, 2011; Johnson, 2017).

Decentering Whiteness in ELA Teaching and Learning: Implications for Theory, Research, and Practice

The history of schooling in the United States is driven by racialization, and Black students have been subjected to institutionalized conditions that contradict their humanity (Kohli, Pizarro, & Nevárez, 2017). Given this, it is important that we locate ways to attend to the intellectual needs of Black students in our schools. The English language arts classroom provides a significant place to begin as ELA scholars and teacher educators are illuminating the ways white supremacy of language (Baker-Bell, 2019; de los Ríos et al., 2019), of literature (Thomas, 2019; Webb, 2019), and of discipline (Milner, Cunningham, Delale-O'Connor, & Kestenberg, 2019; Winn, 2018) policies and practice devalue Black ways of knowing, being, and doing in schools. Such scholarship can inform more equitable and transformative ways forward for the teaching of English language arts.

Teachers must first reject deficit perspectives used to pathologize the literacy abilities, practices, and participation of Black students (Bartolomé, 1994). Doing so will require that teachers research and read texts by Black authors beyond the select few that have made it into the cannon. Teachers will also have to engage with these texts in ways that prepare them to make pedagogical and contextual connections in order to teach relevant content. To help students become better writers, teachers might consider assignments that invite students to share aspects of their lived experiences. For instance, instead of assigning writing for the purposes of understanding students' command of language and idea development regarding arbitrary topics, instructors could begin with writing assignments that invite students to reveal themselves as humans and as writers. In engaging writing that centers students' epistemic privilege, teachers of writing must look inward at their own assumptions about what counts as good writing and interrogate their own instructional practices that might be grounded in racist, heteronormative, and classist language systems designated as normal or standard. Instead, teachers can help students understand how their language use compares with other forms, and encourage them to push the boundaries of language by considering how to engage particular audiences.

Most of the structures of school and schooling, as well its professional workforce, center whiteness. When teachers of writing require "standard English" or focus on normalized content, many students are unable to locate themselves with/in the teaching and learning of literacy classrooms. In other words, in classrooms that center colonized literacy practice—that is, practices that determine who is (and who is not) literacy-proficient, ignore students' funds of knowledge, mandate banking and normalized pedagogies, and deny cultural relevancy—students sacrifice essential parts of their humanity (Del Carmen Salazar, 2013; Shelton & Altwerger, 2015). For Black students, this reality is starker.

On the other hand, instructors who teach students to write well by centering and privileging their realities and languages facilitate the types of learning/doing/being that shape intellectual identities and encourage personal and societal transformation. As a result of a humanizing approach to teaching writing, students in the course featured in this study affirmed their joy, pain, ideas, and experiences. Through meaningful mentor texts, they learned to write well from writers who had similar experiences and ways of being in the world. It is important that teachers acknowledge and invite students to write themselves into teaching/learning landscapes that reflect their identities, histories, cultures, and values. When teachers of writing use students' everyday experiences to teach writing and see them as part of a rich literate tradition, they tap into students' intellectual heritage and invite students to connect to what they do and learn while at school.

TEACHING TIPS

Johnson and Sullivan's approach to humanizing pedagogy for Black students centered individual and collective community knowledge rooted in Black culture. To expand on the pedagogical strategies they share in the article, you can invite students to brainstorm a list of "25 Things You Don't See When You Look at Me." Next, ask them to create a multimodal representation of their list (or a part of their list) to share with class. Invite students to share in pairs or small groups and discuss the implications of what they learned for creating a space that fosters racial literacy.

Humanizing writing pedagogies support the development of a critical consciousness and center the everyday lived experiences of youth of color. So much of what students read, do, and study in school is devoid of images, languages, and texts that remind them of their intellectual lineage. For students of color in particular, humanizing environments and practices have the potential to transform their relationship with learning and writing as they come to understand that their experiences provide context and content toward critical examination of their worlds. With such an understanding, writing becomes a way for them to confront racism, injustice, and structural disadvantages in their lives, within communities, and around the world. And, in doing so, writing becomes a way for students to reclaim and assert their own beautifully complex humanity.

NOTE

1. We use *the professor* to embody what Walker (2009) delineates as a uniquely positioned conduit of ideas, knowledges, and tools to support schools and deploy resources with the primary goal of uplifting Black communities.

2. The names of the school and participants are pseudonyms.

REFERENCES

Anderson, J. (1988). *The education of Blacks in the South: 1860–1935.* Chapel Hill: University of North Carolina Press.

Austin, J. (2018). Literacy practices of youth experiencing incarceration: Reading and writing as points of regulation and escape. *Libri*, 69, 77–87.

Baker-Bell, A. (2019). Dismantling anti-Black linguistic racism in English language arts classrooms: Toward an anti-racist Black language pedagogy. *Theory Into Practice*, 59, 8–21.

Bartolomé, L. A. (1994). Beyond the methods fetish: Towards a humanizing pedagogy. *Harvard Educational Review*, 64, 173–194.

Callejo-Pérez, D. M., Slater, J. J., & Fain, S. M. (2004). *Pedagogy of place: Seeing space as cultural education*. New York: Lang.

Charbonnet, P. (Producer), & Gray, F. G. (Director). (1995). *Friday* [Motion picture]. United States: New Line.

Christensen, L. (2017). *Reading, writing, and rising up: Teaching about social justice and the power of the written word* (2nd ed.). Milwaukee, WI: Rethinking Schools.

Cochran-Smith, M., & Lytle, S. L. (2009). *Inquiry as stance: Practitioner research for the next generation*. New York: Teachers College Press.

Cooper, P. (2002). Does race matter? A comparison of effective Black and White teachers of African American students. In J. Irvine (Ed.), *In search of wholeness: Black teachers and their culturally specific classroom practices* (pp. 47–63). New York: Palgrave.

Cremlin, T., & Oliver, L. (2016). Teachers as writers: A systematic review. *Research Papers in Education*, 32, 269–295.

Croft, S., Juergensen, M., Pogue, T. D., & Willis, V. (2018). A pedagogy of intentionality: Developing Black scholars dedicated to social justice. *The SoJo Journal: Educational Foundations and Social Justice Education*, 4(1), 31–43.

Del Carmen Salazar, M. (2013). A humanizing pedagogy: Reinventing the principles and practice of education as a journey toward liberation. *Review of Research in Education*, 37, 121–148.

de los Ríos, C. V., Martinez, D. C., Musser, A., Canady, A., Camangian, P., &. Quijada, P. D. (2019). Upending colonial practices: Toward repairing harm in English education. *Theory Into Practice*, 58, 359–367.

Delpit, L. (2006). *Other people's children: Cultural conflict in the classroom*. New York: New Press.

Donnell, K. (2007). Getting to we: Developing a transformative urban teaching practice. *Urban Education*, 42, 223–249.

Everett, S. (2016). "I just started writing": Toward addressing invisibility, silence, and mortality among academically high achieving Black male secondary students. *Literacy Research: Theory, Method, and Practice*, 65, 316–331.

Everett, S. (2018). "Untold stories": Cultivating consequential writing with a Black male student through a critical approach to metaphor. *Research in the Teaching of English*, 53, 34–57.

Fisher, M. T. (2003). Open mics and open minds: Spoken word poetry in African diaspora participatory literacy communities. *Harvard Educational Review*, 73, 362–389.

Fisher, M. T. (2009). *Black literate lives: Historical and contemporary perspectives*. New York: Routledge.

Gangi, J. M. (2008). The unbearable whiteness of literacy instruction: Realizing the implications of the proficient reader research. *Multicultural Review*, 17(1), 30–35.

Gardner, P. (2018). Writing and writer identity: The poor relation and the search for voice in personal literacy. *Literacy*, 52, 11–19.

Goff, P. A., Jackson, M. C., Leone, D., Lewis, B. A., Culotta, C. M., & DiTomasso, N. A. (2014). The essence of innocence: Consequences of dehumanizing Black children. *Journal of Personality and Social Psychology*, 106, 526–545.

Graham, S., Harris, K. R., & Santangelo, T. (2015). Research-based writing practices and the Common Core: Meta-analysis and meta-synthesis. *The Elementary School Journal*, 115, 498–522.

Green, K. (2014). Doing double Dutch methodology: Playing with the practice of participant observer. In D. Paris & M. Winn (Eds.), *Humanizing research: Decolonizing qualitative inquiry with youth and communities* (pp. 147–160). London: SAGE.

Haddix, M. (2009). Black boys can write: Challenging dominant framings of Black adolescent males in literacy research. *Journal of Adolescent & Adult Literacy*, 53, 341–343.

Haddix, M., & Sealey-Ruiz, Y. (2012). Cultivating digital and popular literacies as empowering and emancipatory acts among urban youth. *Journal of Adolescent & Adult Literacy*, 56, 189–192.

Hall, T. (2011). Designing from their own social worlds: The digital story of three African American young women. *English Teaching: Practice & Critique*, 10, 7–20.

Harris, V. (1992). African-American conceptions of literacy: A historical perspective. *Theory Into Practice*, 31, 276–286.

Hill, M. L. (2011). A different world: Black bookstores as literacy counterpublics. In V. Kinloch (Ed.), *Urban literacies: Critical perspectives on language, learning, and community* (pp. 38–52). New York: Teachers College Press.

Johnson, C. S. (1936). The education of the negro child. *American Sociological Review*, 1(2), 264–272.

Johnson, L. P. (2015). The writing on the wall: Enacting place pedagogies in order to reimagine schooling for Black male youth. *Discourse: Studies in the Cultural Politics of Education*, 36, 908–919.

Johnson, L. P. (2017). Writing the self: Black queer youth challenge heteronormative ways of being in an after-school writing club. *Research in the Teaching of English*, 52, 13–33.

Kinloch, V. (2010). *Harlem on our minds: Place, race, and the literacies of urban youth*. New York: Teachers College Press.

Kirkland, D. E., & Jackson, A. (2009). "We real cool": Toward a theory of Black masculine literacies. *Reading Research Quarterly*, 44, 278–297.

Kohli, R., Pizarro, M., & Nevárez, A. (2017). The "new racism" of K–12 schools: Centering critical research on racism. *Review of Research in Education*, 41, 182–202.

Ladson-Billings, G. (2005). Is the team all right? *Journal of Teacher Education*, 56, 229–234.

Ladson-Billings, G. (2006). From the achievement gap to the education debt: Understanding achievement in U.S. schools. *Educational Researcher*, 35(7), 3–12.

Ladson-Billings, G. (2014). Culturally relevant pedagogy 2.0: a.k.a. the remix. *Harvard Educational Review*, 84, 74–84.

Meiners, E. (2007). *Right to be hostile: Schools, prisons, and the making of public enemies*. New York: Routledge.

Milner, H. R., IV, Cunningham, H. B., Delale-O'Connor, L., & Kestenberg, E. G. (2019). *"These kids are out*

Morris, J. E. (2015). *Troubling the waters: Fulfilling the promise of quality public schooling for Black children*. New York: Teachers College Press.

Morris, V. G., & Morris, C. L. (2002). *The price they paid: Desegregation in an African American community*. New York: Teachers College Press.

Muhammad, G. E., & Behizadeh, N. (2015). Authentic for whom? An interview study of desired writing practices for African American adolescent learners. *Middle Grades Review*, 1(2), 1–18.

Nelson, C. D. (2011). Narratives of classroom life: Changing conceptions of knowledge. *TESOL Quarterly*, 45, 463–485.

Neuman, S. B. (2016). Code red: The danger of data-driven instruction. *Educational Leadership*, 74(3), 24–29.

Paris, D. (2012). Culturally sustaining pedagogy: A needed change in stance, terminology, and practice. *Educational Researcher*, 41(3), 93–97.

Pogue, T. D. (2015). Finding the written in unexpected places: Literacy in the maintenance and practice of Lukumí rituals and traditions. *Written Communication*, 32, 174–194.

Price-Dennis, D. (2016). Developing curriculum to support Black girls' literacies in digital spaces. *English Education*, 48, 337–361.

Rothstein, R. (2013). Why children from lower socioeconomic classes, on average, have lower academic achievement than middle-class children. In P. L. Carter & K. G. Welner (Eds.), *Closing the opportunity gap: What America must do to give every child an even chance* (pp. 61–74). New York: Oxford University Press.

Scribner, S., & Cole, M. (1981). Unpacking literacy. In M. F. Whiteman (Ed.), *Writing: The nature, development, and teaching of written communication* (pp. 77–88). Mahwah, NJ: Erlbaum.

Shakur, T. (1996). Me and my girlfriend. On *The don killuminati: The 7 day theory* [CD]. Los Angeles: Can-Am Studios.

Shelton, N. R., & Altwerger, B. (Eds.). (2015). *Literacy policies and practices in conflict: Reclaiming classrooms in networked times*. New York: Routledge.

Stuckey, J. E. (1991). *The violence of literacy*. Portsmouth, NH: Heinemann.

Tatum, A. W. (2006). Engaging African American males in reading. *Educational Leadership*, 63(5), 44–49.

Thomas, E. (2019). *The dark fantastic: Race and the imagination from Harry Potter to The Hunger Games*. New York: New York University Press.

Walker, V. S. (2009). *Hello professor: A Black principal and professional leadership in the segregated South*. Chapel Hill: Univ of North Carolina Press.

Webb, S. L. (2019). Everyday colorism: Reading in the language arts classroom. *English Journal*, 108(4), 21–28.

Winn, M. T. (2010). 'Our side of the story': Moving incarcerated youth voices from margins to center. *Race Ethnicity and Education*, 13, 313–325.

Winn, M. T. (2015). Exploring the literate trajectories of youth across time and space. *Mind, Culture, and Activity*, 22, 58–67.

Winn, M. T. (2018). *Justice on both sides: Transforming education through restorative justice*. Cambridge, MA: Harvard Education Press.

Woodson, C. G. (1932). *The mis-education of the Negro*. Washington, DC: Associated Publishers.

Yagelski, R. P. (2009). A thousand writers writing: Seeking change through the radical practice of writing as a way of being. *English Education*, 42, 6–28.

Zenkov, K., & Harmon, J. (2009). Picturing a writing process: Photovoice and teaching writing to urban youth. *Journal of Adolescent & Adult Literacy*, 52, 575–584.

LATRISE P. JOHNSON is an associate professor of secondary ELA and literacy at The University of Alabama.

HANNAH SULLIVAN is an assistant professor of Spanish at Charleston Southern University, though her experience includes teaching at both the middle and high school levels as well. She completed the Secondary Education (Curriculum and Instruction) PhD program at the University of Alabama and enjoys investigating the ways in which teacher education, student motivation, and language learning overlap.

This article originally appeared
in *English Journal 108.4*

READING REPRESENTATIONS OF RACE: Critical Literacy and Ferguson

Working as a team, three teachers created an interdisciplinary course for middle schoolers to examine issues of social justice.

SUMMER MELODY PENNELL

ON AUGUST 9, 2014, Darren Wilson, a White police officer, shot and killed Michael Brown, an unarmed Black teenager, in Ferguson, Missouri. Brown's death sent shockwaves across the nation, as people debated the issue of blame. Three activists—Patrice Khan-Cullors, Alicia Garza, and Opal Tometi—who founded the Black Lives Matter movement in response to the death of Trayvon Martin, another unarmed Black teen who was shot in Sanford, Florida, in 2012—quickly worked to organize protests and other plans of action ("Our Co-Founders"). Media coverage of the protests in Ferguson included a wide range of perspectives, from those who condemned the protests and referred to them as riots to those supportive of the Black Lives Matter movement who called for an end to racist policing practices. The protests intensified when, at trial, Wilson was found "not guilty" of any of the civil rights violations for which he had been charged, including first-degree murder. Brown's death and the trial's outcome continue to be discussed as a reminder of the country's ongoing unequal treatment of Black people.

As a response to the incident, educators representing a range of levels gathered resources to promote discussion of the tragedy of Brown's death in their classrooms. A crowd-sourced syllabus was born on social media, when Marcia Chatelain began using the hashtag #FergusonSyllabus and curated sources from scholars in education, sociology, and related fields. Literacy-related suggestions included Chimamanda Adichie's TED Talk, "The Danger of a Single Story," texts about the history of lynching, and contemporary articles on policing and police violence (Chatelain). Educator Christopher Emdin offered several ideas for teachers to discuss the Ferguson incident with students. Those most applicable to English classes include having students complete a KWL chart before and after reading about the case (where students write what they *know*, what they *want* to know, and then what they *learned* after the lesson), and having students write letters to those involved (such as politicians, police, and family members).

Soon after Brown's death, I began co-teaching and conducting research in an interdisciplinary literacy and mathematics course with the theme of social justice at The Anchor School (a pseudonym). In this article, I discuss how a fellow researcher, a classroom teacher, and I discussed Brown's case and racial injustice with a group of young adolescents using critical literacy, social justice pedagogy, and queer pedagogy to frame the instruction. I share elements of our Michael Brown unit, highlighting the literacy strategies we used to assist the students as they explored the idea of racial injustice through reading, reflection, and discussion.

Providing Context

The Anchor School is a private PK–12 Quaker institution in a southern state, located near two cities and with access to several large universities. As an element of the school's curriculum, students are taught to think of others as equal and to treat people with kindness.

With my collaborators (described below), I developed a course titled Math for a Cause framed by issues of social justice for the middle school, which housed students in the fifth through eighth grades. The interdisciplinary course purposefully paired math and language arts to allow students to explore social justice topics from more than one disciplinary perspective.

The student population of the school is predominately White: fewer than five Black students attended the middle school at the time of the study, which is unusual for the region, where the public schools include significant populations of Black and Latinx students. All of the faculty and staff at the middle school were also White. The twelve students in the class were ten to thirteen. Ten students in the class chose to participate in the study. In line with the demographics of the school at large, eight of the students were White, and two students identified as White and Asian.

Morgan, the classroom teacher (a pseudonym), Bryan Fede, a critical mathematics expert, and I collaborated to plan the course and the Michael Brown unit. We are all White and are dedicated to social justice education and racial justice. My research focuses on English education; Bryan's focuses on education and critical mathematics; and Morgan is a middle school math teacher. Morgan expressed interest in working with Bryan and me when we contacted the leaders at The Anchor School looking for collaborators for our research. She regularly incorporates social justice concepts into her teaching practices and was excited about the opportunity to teach a course that reflected that commitment. Morgan was the teacher of record, but we adopted a co-teaching model, each of us playing specific roles during instructional activities. I was the lead researcher and planned the majority of the course curriculum, with the exception of the explicit math instruction, which Bryan and Morgan developed. I led the literacy-related discussions following students' reading of news articles, and we typically co-facilitated other class conversations.

We chose to begin our course with a Michael Brown unit. We hoped that studying his death would help students understand systemic racism more broadly and address our goal of offering a social justice curriculum that highlighted instances of injustice as part of a system, rather than as individual moments of discrimination. For our predominately White students, whose school environment focused on embracing differences, the thought of being discriminated against or harmed physically because of a person's race was a difficult idea to grasp.

Identifying Theoretical Frameworks

Queer pedagogy calls not only for discussion of queer subjects in the classroom but also for a *queering*—that is, questioning and rethinking norms, boundaries, and structures—of pedagogy (Britzman). In our case, that meant trying to deemphasize classroom boundaries, particularly the idea of teachers serving as knowledge gatekeepers (which also aligned with our other critical pedagogical frameworks). Social justice pedagogy largely stems from Paulo Freire's influential educational model, Pedagogy of the Oppressed, which encourages the development of critical consciousness. Freire's ideas have influenced educators who want to support a critical mindset. He promotes thinking through teaching rather than a toolkit of specific techniques, and the model is inclusive of race, ethnicity, gender, sexual orientation, disability, and other areas of identity.

Critical literacy is an intentionally political framework that asks students to consider social and cultural contexts as they analyze texts (Janks; Luke). Hilary Janks discusses four interrelated domains of critical literacy:

- Domination (discerning how texts uphold and create control),
- Access (providing access to a variety of text types, even those that are dominating),
- Diversity (including diverse subjects and texts in different modalities), and
- Design (creating personal meaning from texts) (176–77).

Students reading with a critical literacy lens seek not only to comprehend the text but also to discern the inherent power relations. Important questions include "Who does the author show as having power?"; "How do authors portray antagonists or people who are different from them?"; and "Whose voices are heard?" These questions are vital for students working within a social justice framework, of which critical literacy is an important element.

Reading with a Critical Lens

The Michael Brown unit began on the second day of the class and took place over four days (our class met only twice a week, and we conducted three units over a ten-week trimester). Two of those days covered literacy elements. While discussing Michael Brown's death, we worked to reserve our opinions about social justice issues to allow the students to form their own opinions from their reading and research. To describe the unit in this article, I analyzed my fieldnotes and observations, notes from reflections with my collaborators, and student work from the sixth and seventh graders. The student talk included in this article is summarized from my notes.

To begin, we asked students to share what they knew about Michael Brown in a large-group conversation. Their list, which we recorded on the board, included the following: he was Black; maybe he was a victim of racial discrimination; he was shot multiple times; he was not resisting or armed; and his body was left in the street. A few students had heard about the Trayvon Martin shooting and related it to Michael Brown. In the previous class session, we had discussed the term *social justice* and noted that it referred to issues of equality and inequality among groups of people. Students decided that the Ferguson incident was a social justice issue because Michael Brown was Black and his death related to the deaths of other Black teenagers at the hands of White men.

After the whole-class discussion, we were confident the students were ready to read articles on the subject by themselves. Morgan divided students into small groups by grade level (sixth and seventh). Before the group work began, I led a discussion on what to look for as the students read their articles, focusing the students' attention on these questions: "Who has the power or is portrayed as having the power?" and "What beliefs are shown in the article?" A sixth grader, Sum Dood (students chose their pseudonyms), was quick to respond that "reporters show their beliefs in their articles" while others pointed out that the opinions of the writers were sometimes subtle. I suggested that reporters may not write, "This is a horrible person," but may, instead, choose words that could imply this idea. Ashley (a sixth-grade girl) said she had heard reporters "aren't supposed to do that, they're supposed to stick to the facts," which demonstrated that students had different expectations for informational texts. I encouraged the students to investigate this idea as they read. In addition to these guiding questions presented orally, students were given handouts I created that included the following instructions and questions (for full instructions, see Figure 1).

1. Write a two- to three-sentence summary of the article.
2. What do you think is the author's purpose for writing this article?
3. Who do you think is the audience for this article and why?

Directions: Read the roles below, and with your group decide who will do what. Read your group's article carefully, and answer the five questions.

Roles:

Recorder: While you should talk about your answers to the questions as a group, the recorder writes down your responses. If there are questions you don't agree on, you can write down all answers and specify who thinks what.

Navigator: You keep the discussion on track—these topics are complex and your discussion may take many directions, which is OK. But the navigator must get everyone back on point if it strays too far.

Highlighter: When your group is answering the questions, look through the article to find specific words, sentences, or impressions you get from the article that justify your groups' answers. Let the recorder know so they can include examples in your answers. (If the example is long, just explain where to find it, like "third paragraph.")

Write article title here:

____

1. In your own words, sum up this article in two to three sentences.

2. What do you think is the author's purpose for writing this, and why do you think so?

3. Who do you think is the audience for this article and why?

4. What math do you see in the article? Or, what kind of math would help you understand the article better, or show a different point of view? You do not need to do calculations yet, just describe the type of problems you see the potential for, being as detailed as possible.

5. What questions do you have for the class that would help you understand this article and/or issue better?

FIGURE 1

Student groups used a set of specific instructions as they discussed the readings in the Michael Brown unit.

Protests at Ferguson on August 14, 2014. Photo by LoavesofBread; used under Creative Commons license CC BY-SA 4.0.

We assigned each group an article that described Brown's death from a different perspective. The groups began reading after the class discussion and finished their reading during the following class meeting. The articles were diverse in scope: Anonymous' press release denouncing Brown's murder and threatening to attack the police department's online servers if they harmed protesters, a discussion of hip-hop artists speaking out and raising money for Brown's family (Associated Press), and an article blaming then-Attorney General Eric Holder for stirring up the protesters (Chavez). Some groups chose to read independently and then discuss the questions; others took turns reading aloud. The teaching team checked on groups periodically while they read the articles in their groups and answered questions they had, but we gave them space to come to their own conclusions.

Facilitating Critical Literacy Practices

When students answered the question "What do you think is the author's purpose for writing this?" and the question "Who do you think is the audience for this article and why?," some groups also addressed author beliefs and power relations. This was easier for the groups whose texts were opinion pieces or from activist groups than for the students who read news reports.

Morgan overheard Group One (three sixth-grade girls), who read Anonymous' "Operation Ferguson Press Release," exclaim, "This is so mean!" They were shocked that Anonymous threatened to release personal information about the police officers. They wrote that the purpose was "they're so annoyed and mad . . . they want to get more awareness." Because the tone of the press release is clear with phrases such as "The entire global collective of Anonymous is outraged at this cold-blooded murder of a young teen," it was easy for them to detect the purpose and author beliefs. Ashley, the student who said journalists were not supposed to state opinions but only facts, was shocked at this document written by activists who were not trying to remain neutral. The group also easily identified the audience as "the police who killed Mike Brown because they warned them about putting personal information on the internet." The press release made their audience explicit with this statement: "To the Ferguson Police Department . . . we are watching you very closely." However, the students did not mention that the writers also addressed "the good people of Ferguson" and offered to "support [them] in every way." This omission is likely because the Ferguson population is addressed only in one paragraph while the rest of the text is written to law enforcement.

Group Three (two seventh-grade girls), whose article was also inflammatory but favored Wilson and other police officers, said that "the author wrote the article as though Brown were at fault, that he turned on the police" and that the audience was "racist people." They discussed with me while reading that they thought the author was racist because she kept emphasizing Brown's size and age, calling the eighteen-year-old "an adult by all legal standards . . . [who] weighed nearly 300 pounds . . . with Brown looking to have a height advantage over Wilson and outweighing the officer by about 100 pounds" (Chavez). The students noted in their conversation that the author kept mentioning his size as if it was a justification for Wilson shooting him.

The other group's article, about hip-hop artists who created a song in tribute to Brown, was less inflammatory. This reading focused more on the artists' efforts than on Brown, which caused the group of sixth- and seventh-grade boys to note that it would have been "better if Michael Brown was the main focus." They wrote that the purpose of the author was "he likes Michael Brown, Pro-Michael Brown" and that the audience was "everyone on Fox news." Perhaps because the article was not focused on Brown's death, it may have not held the students' interest, as they did not consider a more specific answer like the ones their classmates generated for their articles. In this case, writing "hip-hop fans" or "Michael Brown supporters" would have indicated a deeper consideration of intended audience.

Several interesting student-generated questions emerged during their small-group discussions: "How might things have been different if Michael Brown were a woman?"; "Why did the cop shoot to kill, why not just try to slow him down, if he had to shoot at all?"; and, "What was Brown wearing, and did that impact the impression the cop had of him?" The seventh-grade girls who asked the latter question noted that if Brown were wearing a hooded sweatshirt, he may have been stereotyped as a gang member. These inquiries demonstrate the power of the student-to-student dialogue and the way it facilitated their reflection on this complex topic. By identifying questions rather than conclusions, the students were demonstrating their critical thinking skills and their curiosity. They were practicing an inquiry stance to learning, focusing on developing future directions for information-gathering and continuous investigation. Questioning is a key aspect of queer pedagogy and important for social justice pedagogy, as social issues are rarely easily solved and require continuous review.

Students Reflecting Together

To allow students to share their findings with each other on the day after they finished reading their article and answering the questions on their handout, we asked each group to write on the board their answers to these questions: "Who has the power?," "What are the author's beliefs?," and "How was Michael Brown addressed in their articles?" The third question was Bryan's idea. In talking with the groups, he realized that some articles called Brown "Mr.," while others called him a teenager, and Bryan wondered how the students might interpret these differences. Full student responses are noted in Table 1.

QUESTIONING IS A KEY ASPECT OF QUEER PEDAGOGY AND IMPORTANT FOR SOCIAL JUSTICE PEDAGOGY, AS SOCIAL ISSUES ARE RARELY EASILY SOLVED AND REQUIRE CONTINUOUS REVIEW.

After writing their responses on the board, each group provided the class a brief summary of their article and shared their answers to the questions; this reporting was followed by a class discussion. The teaching team facilitated the conversation, but the conversation was student-driven. We asked the students to share their knowledge and, at times, we posed questions, but we did not state whether we felt

TABLE 1

We recorded the groups' responses to the articles about Michael Brown on the board as part of the whole-class discussion.

		Student Responses: Reported in Whole-Class Discussion		
	Article title and author	**Who has the power?**	**What are the author's beliefs?**	**How was Michael Brown addressed?**
Group One: (sixth graders)	"Operation Ferguson Press Release" by Anonymous	The police had the power, and they chose to use it by shooting the boy.	They believe the police did something very wrong and threatened to invade the police's personal information online.	Unarmed teen, seventeen, future college student.
Group Two: (sixth and seventh graders)	"Ferguson Shooting: Hip-Hop Moves as a Strong Force for Michael Brown" by Associated Press	People have some power because they can protest and wrote songs about it.	The rappers are good and helping society.	Michael Brown
Group Three: (seventh graders)	"Eric the Arsonist: Holder Fans the Ferguson Flames" by Linda Chavez	The police	The author thought Michael was guilty. Maybe she's racist?	Author did not like how people called him an "unarmed black teen," pointed out he was eighteen and an adult, 6'4" and nearly 300 pounds.

an article was accurate in how it portrayed Brown and the incident that led to his death. We refrained from sharing personal beliefs.

As each group explained the power structures and beliefs found in their assigned article, the students gained a broader picture of how different individuals and groups reacted to Michael Brown's death. Many students said that they thought the cop was racist. Some were less sure than others, but no one thought Michael Brown should have been shot and killed, even if he did rob a convenience store beforehand, as the police claimed. They felt that any crime he committed should have resulted in arrest and a trial, as they assumed would be the case for someone who was not Black.

Students also concluded that the shooting was racially motivated and tied that to a history of racist violence in our country, based on a conversation on the first day of the unit about the history of police shooting Black men and teens. The seventh graders had also learned about the Civil Rights Movement the previous year and brought this knowledge to the conversation. Rather than buy into the racist narrative posed by authors such as Linda Chavez that Black men are inherently dangerous, judging from the comments described above, the students saw a counter-narrative of systemic racism that resulted in an unnecessary death.

The students were learning to read texts about racism in a critical way. They discerned the differences between how authors described Brown ("adolescent" or "unarmed Black teenager" compared to "large adult Black man") and inferred author biases from these differences in connotation. They also began to question the origins of racist stereotypes and pondered why White people thought Black men were frightening. Other students wondered how police officers are trained and wanted to know if most police officers were racist. Their ability to generate these kinds of questions indicated the students' emerging understanding of the importance of addressing systemic issues of social justice from a critical inquiry perspective.

Moving Forward: Suggestions for ELA Teachers

START WITH OPINION PIECES

When introducing critical literacy practices, particularly regarding social justice issues, teachers may want to begin with articles that have an easily discernible opinion, like the articles the sixth- and seventh-grade girls in our unit read. Perhaps after this introduction to a topic, students will have an easier time discerning the subtler ways power relations and author beliefs are reflected in more neutrally toned news articles. The students in this class were also better able to describe the power relationships when I included a direct question such as "Who has the power?" on their handouts, rather than saving that question for our larger discussion. Discerning the power relations in a text for the first time may be easier for students when they read a piece that has a clear point of view, thus scaffolding their ability to respond critically.

PRIORITIZE REFLECTION

We also learned from this initial unit that we needed to give students more space for written reflection. Students who did not naturally reflect on their reading needed time to pause and consider how they were feeling and thinking about the material. In the subsequent units, we implemented this adaptation by including questions on the group reading handouts such as "Are the opinions in the article different from your own?" and "What is your reaction to the article?" or "How do you feel reading this article?" These questions allowed for more intentional reflection and encouraged the students to discuss the articles more deeply in their small groups. The personal reflections also better prepared the students for whole-class reflections. While we wanted students to have as much freedom as possible within the curriculum, guided questions were necessary for the students to work through material, especially for topics that were outside of their own experiences.

CONNECT TOPICS TO RELATED EVENTS

Teachers may also want to ask students to connect the events in their news articles or other informational texts to related recent events, as suggested by Emdin. Identifying the relationship between incidents will help students understand that social justice issues are systemic, rather than individual. In our class, some of the students knew about Trayvon Martin, and the discussion of the similar incidents taking place in two different states—Florida and Missouri—helped the class see a pattern of violence against Black people. (The website Mapping Police Violence provides data and graphics that can assist with this conversation: mappingpoliceviolence.org/.)

Creating Allies through Critical Literacy

While this unit was a learning experience for the students, as teachers, it was our first attempt to discuss social justice with middle schoolers. It taught us that we needed more intentional scaffolding for activities that involve reflection and critical analysis of informational texts and allowed us to better plan for the rest of the course. By providing students a critical literacy framework with guiding questions and allowing them to engage with the text in student-centered groups, we invited students to create their own knowledge about the Michael Brown incident. They examined how an author's word choices expose biases and illustrate a point of view, and then, in turn, how these word choices imply power relationships.

BY PROVIDING STUDENTS A CRITICAL LITERACY FRAMEWORK WITH GUIDING QUESTIONS AND ALLOWING THEM TO ENGAGE WITH THE TEXT IN STUDENT-CENTERED GROUPS, WE INVITED STUDENTS TO CREATE THEIR OWN KNOWLEDGE ABOUT THE MICHAEL BROWN INCIDENT.

Students became better allies for racial justice after this unit. As the course continued, students expressed further opinions about racial justice issues and continued to improve their critical reading skills as well as their ability to articulate their arguments. They also kept asking questions, aligning with both our social justice and queer pedagogy goals of continued inquiry. This unit demonstrated that it is possible, and fruitful, to talk about racism with students (and teachers) who have never experienced it personally. If White students do not learn about institutionalized racism, they cannot be allies. Using critical literacy can be a first step in showing students the importance of being allies. This unit helped meet our goals of increasing student awareness of social justice issues and encouraging further learning and action. For our young students, this action took the form of speaking to others in the school community and paying closer attention to news stories they watched with their families. Social justice is a constant commitment and practice, one that we worked to foster for young learners through teaching about the tragic death of Michael Brown.

WORKS CITED

Anonymous. *Anonymous Operation Ferguson-Press Release*, 10 Aug. 2014, pastebin.com/KpmJKU8D.

Associated Press. "Ferguson Shooting: Hip-Hop Moves as a Strong Force for Michael Brown." *Fox News*, 30 Aug. 2014, www.foxnews.com/entertainment/2014/08/30/ferguson-shooting-hip-hop-moves-as-strong-force-for-michael-brown.html.

Britzman, Deborah P. "Is There a Queer Pedagogy? Or, Stop Reading Straight." *Educational Theory*, vol. 45, no. 2, 1995, pp. 151–65.

Chatelain, Marcia. "How to Teach Kids about What's Happening in Ferguson: A Crowdsourced Syllabus about Race, African American History, Civil Rights, and Policing." *The Atlantic*, 25 Aug. 2014, www.theatlantic.com/education/archive/2014/08/how-to-teach-kids-about-whats-happening-in-ferguson/379049/.

Chavez, Linda. "Eric the Arsonist: Holder Fans the Ferguson Flames." *NY Post*, 23 Aug. 2014, nypost.com/2014/08/23/eric-the-arsonist-holder-fans-ferguson-flames/.

Emdin, Christopher. "5 Ways to Teach about Michael Brown and Ferguson in the New School Year." 20 Aug. 2014, *The Huffington Post*, www.huffingtonpost.com/christopher-emdin/5-ways-to-teach-about-michael-brown-and-ferguson-in-the-new-school-year_b_5690171.html?utm_hp_ref=tw.

Freire, Paulo. *Pedagogy of the Oppressed*. Translated by M. B. Ramos, Bloomsbury, 1970.

Janks, Hilary. "Domination, Access, Diversity and Design: A Synthesis for Critical Literacy Education. *Educational Review*, vol. 52, no. 2, 2000, pp. 175–86.

Luke, Allan. "Critical Literacy: Foundational Notes." *Theory Into Practice*, vol. 51, no. 1, 2012, pp. 4–11.

"Our Co-Founders." *Black Lives Matter*, blacklivesmatter.com/about/our-co-founders/.

SUMMER MELODY PENNELL is a lecturer in Education at the University of Vermont. Her research and teaching interests include equitable educational practices in teacher education, interdisciplinary partnerships, and queer Young Adult literature. She has been a member of NCTE since 2014 and is the past chair of the Genders and Sexualities Equality Alliance (GSEA). Contact her at summer.pennell@uvm.edu or on twitter @summerpennell.

This article originally appeared
in *English Education 52.3*

"THE CREATIVE ASPECT WOKE ME UP": Awakening to Multimodal Essay Composition as a Fugitive Literacy Practice

This article details a self-study dissecting an interracial group of students' theories of Blackness in a postsecondary classroom. I begin by conceptualizing fugitive literacy practices *as tools with which to awaken and animate education as the practice of liberation from whiteness and anti-Blackness. I then approach multimodal essay composition as one such practice and illuminate its application in a classroom. I show how this practice affirmed students as empowered producers of knowledge. I contend that pedagogues must pivot away from the* disruption *of whiteness and anti-Blackness as a defined target, and turn toward the* destruction *of both as a desirable goal. I conclude by considering further inquiries that this provocation invites vis-à-vis curriculum and pedagogy in English teacher education.*

ESTHER O. OHITO & THE FUGITIVE LITERACIES COLLECTIVE

> **We must become undisciplined. The work we do requires new modes and methods of research and teaching; new ways of entering and leaving the archives of slavery . . . that live in the present.**
>
> —CHRISTINA SHARPE (2016, P. 13)

> **I believe art is our ability to create—which is the very essence of humanity. I believe art—whether painted, danced, written, spoken, sung, rapped, and/or expressed by hands, bodies and minds in various ways—is what allows us to explore our humanity, heal from pain, show love and embrace joy. Art . . . has the ability to move people emotionally, and also move people to action. When we lose our ability to create, to share our story and truth through a medium that we love, we lose our humanity.**
>
> —TONI MORRISON (QUOTED IN STELLA ADLER STUDIO OF ACTING, 2016)

> **The role of the artist is exactly the same role, I think, as the role of the lover. . . . If I love you, I have to make you conscious of the things you don't see.**
>
> —JAMES BALDWIN (1973, P. 41)

I AM, QUITE UNABASHEDLY, a hopeless romantic. Critical literacies were my first true loves. In the aftermath of a fortuitous rendezvous with interdisciplinarity during graduate school, I have woven my scholarship into a colorful tapestry composed of threads from multiple disciplines such as Black[1] studies, women's and gender studies, and curriculum studies. Critical literacies, however, linger at the heart of my "undisciplined" scholarship (Sharpe, 2016, p. 13). In my oeuvre, I "attend to the spectacular but also to those quotidian experiences of unbreathability where really the ability to fully live in a Black body is continually curtailed, foreclosed" (Sharpe, quoted in Lambert, 2017, p. 52). The Black body's relationship to Blackness lies in the innards of this article, which can be summarized as a letter to other lovers of Black literacies and knowledges (e.g., Baker-Bell, Butler, & Johnson, 2017; Coles & Powell, 2019; Emdin, 2017; Love, 2019; Lyiscott, 2019; Muhammad & Haddix, 2016; Price-Dennis, Muhammad, Womack, McArthur, & Haddix, 2017; Richardson, 2002, 2003, 2007; Sealey-Ruiz, 2016). Inspired by Baldwin's (1973) insistence that the doing of love requires equal parts devotion to and dissection of the object(s) of one's affection, I pen this epistle as a critique of whiteness and anti-Blackness in English teacher education, which is concerned with the preparation of future teachers of English(es).

Whiteness, Anti-Blackness, Literacy, and Fugitivity: A Conceptual Mélange

Researchers surmise that teacher education in the United States is submerged in the "overwhelming presence of Whiteness" (Sleeter, 2001, p. 94). Whiteness is an octopod, which may explain why scholars are yet to settle on one definition for this multi-limbed monster. Some scholars conceptualize whiteness as "a systematic production of power—as a normative social process based upon a history of domination, recreating itself through naturalized everyday acts—much like heteronormativity or misogyny" (Warren & Fassett, 2004, p. 411). Based on this definition, whiteness is a verb—that is, an action upheld by ideological beliefs that underpin processes used to hierarchize humans and justify oppressive disciplining tactics deployed in the maintenance of social stratification. Oppressive violence manifests in many forms, including as anti-Blackness. *Anti-Blackness* is a term describing "epistemic, ideological, material, and spiritual violences against Black peoples . . . contoured by a hyper-climactic obsession with and disregard for Blackness as bonded to Black bodies, experiences, and knowledges" (Curriculum Inquiry, n.d.). Whiteness and (anti-)Blackness entwine in the self-study (see Hamilton & Pinnegar, 1998, 2010; Loughran, 2007) detailed in this article. In this anti-Black world, Black people exist in "the wake"—that is, in proximity to social and material demise wrought by "the still unfolding aftermaths of Atlantic chattel slavery" (Sharpe, 2016, p. 2). Therefore, as Sharpe (2016) states, "to be *in* the wake is to occupy and to be occupied by the continuous and changing present of slavery's as yet unresolved unfolding" (pp. 13–14). It is to have (one's) Black life shaded by death's shadow. Like Sharpe (2012), I, too, wonder: "Will the fact of black studies ameliorate the quotidian experiences of terror in black lives lived in an anti-black world? And, if not, what will be the relationship between the two?" (para. 3).

This article links the world (re)making elements of Sharpe's line of inquiry to the thoughts of Paulo Freire and Donaldo Macedo. In their theories on the relationship between the learning process and the learner's experience of their world(s), Freire and Macedo (2005) maintain that reading and writing can increase learners' knowledges of the word and the world. Meek's (2005) foreword in the duo's canonical text proposes that "learning involves both culturally transmitted understanding joined to the use of tools (including reading and writing) devised to enlarge one's grasp of the world for purposes which the user intends" (p. vii). Reading and writing are mentioned often in common definitions of literacy, a concept conceivable as "the process of using reading, writing, and oral language to extract, construct, integrate, and critique meaning through interaction and involvement with multimodal texts in the context of socially situated practices" (Frankel, Becker, Rowe, & Pearson, 2016, p. 7). This quilt-like conceptual framework of literacy augments Frankel et al.'s (2016) explanation with Freire and Macedo's (2005) theorizing. These scholars define literacy as

> a meaningful construct to the degree that it is viewed as a set of practices that functions to either empower or disempower people. In the larger sense, literacy is analyzed according to whether it serves to reproduce existing social formation or serves as a set of cultural practices that promotes democratic and emancipatory change. (p. 98)

The desire for "emancipatory change" (Freire & Macedo, 2005, p. 98) underpins much Black critical and cultural theorizing of fugitivity. In the annals of U.S. history, fugitivity connotes myriad modes of resistance to and refusal of bondage vis-à-vis slavery. Black cultural and critical theorists have applied this analytic to investigate the precarity of the interstitial space between life and death that Black people inhabit in an anti-Black world. Campt (2014) contends that "the concept of fugitivity highlights the tension between the acts or flights of escape and *creative practices of refusal* [emphasis added], nimble and strategic practices that undermine the category of the dominant."

I present in this article multimodal essay composition as an example of creative *literacy* practices that refuse whiteness and anti-Blackness. It is a timely introduction: "As the nation grapples with heightened racial tensions and blatant institutionalized white supremacy, the work of examining and disrupting whiteness and privilege is unambiguously urgent" (Berchini, quoted in Davis, 2017, para. 3). My configuring of multimodal essay composition as a device for the pedagogic refusal of whiteness and anti-Blackness merges the idea of fugitivity (see Campt, 2014; Moten, quoted in Wallace, 2018) with that of literacy practices as "the broader cultural conception of particular ways of thinking about and doing reading and writing in cultural contexts" (Street, 2003, p. 79). Hence, I submit that *fugitive literacy practices* involve creative uses of reading, writing, and oral language as strategic tools for the curricular and pedagogic refusal of the hegemony of whiteness and anti-Blackness (Gramsci, 1971/1989). I re-view my use of multimodal essay composition as a fugitive literacy practice in a semester-long course comprised of an interracial group of undergraduate learners in a university setting.

Multimodal Essay Composition as a Fugitive Literacy Practice

Multimodal essay composition intertwines textual, aural, linguistic, spatial, and/or visual modes of communication. In this article, I theorize and operationalize this tool as a fugitive literacy practice through which education undertaken in pursuit of freedom from whiteness and anti-Blackness can be awakened in the classroom. I also contemplate what my findings from a self-study on the use of this device suggest for engagement with whiteness and anti-Blackness in critical English teacher education. Furthermore, I illustrate the function of multimodal essay composition as a practice powerful enough to elicit Black knowledges about Blackness and demonstrate how these knowledges epistemically trouble whiteness and anti-Blackness. My investigation asks, first, what does multimodal essay composition illuminate about an interracial group of college students' knowledges of Blackness? Second, how does students' theorizing provoke current discourse about the disruption of whiteness—and as attendant, anti-Blackness—in English teacher education? Relatedly, what are the implications for curriculum and pedagogy in English teacher education?

[A portion of this essay has been excised due to space needs. To read the article in full in English Education, go here: https://library.ncte.org/journals/EE/issues/v52-3/30596.]

Students' Theorizing of Blackness

"What is Blackness?" I asked my students. "Tell me," I urged; "show me," I stoked, adding, "be precise." By inviting students to theorize, I was eliciting both analysis and speculation of the concept of Blackness (Culler, 2011). In her artist's talk, Phoebe described her affective reaction to the collage-making aspect of the assignment, stating:

> I've always had a pretty clear understanding of Blackness, because my parents were very open with history and where we are positioned in America. . . . But I wanted to show how this class has really deepened my further understanding. . . . [The collage] felt like an emotional effect, because after I stepped back and looked at it I was like, "Oh my gosh!" It's kind of dark but at the same time there's . . . a lot of the things that I felt like I did subconsciously. And then I stepped back I was like, "Oh my gosh, these connections and all these things." It just makes me think how much I do really know.

Phoebe's realization that the collage "just makes me think how much I do really know" illustrates that the assignment was metacognitively beneficial for someone who "always had a pretty clear understanding of Blackness." For Isabelle, a white female student whose collage centered a Black woman's curvaceous body (see Figure 1), the assignment was a provocation to inquire into the size of her knowledge of Blackness. She stated, "this assignment also allows us to really reflect on [Blackness] again, and what we do and what we don't know." As she completed the assignment, she was shocked by the knowledge that "there's just so much that we don't know, and we think we do. I mean personally, so much that I don't know."

Rick's artist's talk also referenced the stimulation that had registered in his mind and body. In a

FIGURE 1

Isabelle's collage, in which a Marlon Riggs (1994) quote is incorporated.

genius demonstration of word play, he used the Black vernacular term *woke* to indicate that both his curiosity and social consciousness were provoked by the collage-creation process:

> I was going to say that the creative aspect of the collage woke me up; kind of—like they say, "[stay] woke"—it like, woke me up. It seems weird because every day, I know I'm Black. I'm Black, but I don't take time and think about my Blackness by sectioning it off like this. So [now] I'm like, "This idea of my Blackness. What does that mean?"

The incisiveness of students' reflections astonished me. Feelings of awe swirled within and around me during a conversation that Rick and I had at the conclusion of the class discussion:

> **Rick:** I was going to say, what did you take away from all of our collages?
>
> **Esther:** Yeah, I took away a lot. I don't know if you all remember, but the very first day of class I walked in and wrote on the board [with deference to Marlon Riggs (1994)] "Black is . . . / Black ain't . . ." and asked you to respond to that. My read of the mood of the room was . . . this sense that it felt like people were taken aback and kind of like there was something happening in terms of the affect or the emotion in the room. It felt like people were—I don't know if I want to say held back but were maybe scared or nervous or something. There was an energy there. So to go from that to now, where you all have not only very artistically—all of you—done this assignment, but are able to stand in front of your peers and say confidently some things that you think or you know or you've learned that Blackness is, is really tremendous. I think sometimes with learning, we think that, oh, we're going to go into classes, and we're just going to absorb information and then regurgitate the information back out. I think there's a different kind of learning that's been happening here. There's something about this assignment—for people who've embraced it—that seems to have almost led to a bit of a surprise for you all as learners. Like surprise about what you know or what you don't know, or surprise around the connections that you're making. That for me is really great. It's great in terms of how I teach and what I think teaching is. For me, teaching is not so much about dumping information in people's heads; it's saying, "You come into my classroom with a lot of knowledge. So how do I help you deepen that? How do I help you think critically about that? How do I help you really intellectualize that? Then, how do I push you beyond what you might think you already know? How do I help you be curious about what you don't know and be curious about what you do know? How do I help you learn and unlearn at the same time?" I think this is great. I think you all did a really fabulous job, and I'm deeply, deeply impressed. . . . Your collages and then your ability to talk like intellectuals about your thinking—that's pretty impressive. So, I'm excited to see where we go from here.

My lengthy response to Rick's question included my interpretation of students' reactions to my initial effort inviting their theorizing of Blackness. This tri-part essay assignment extended from that early endeavor. In the approximately five-week interim, students read the texts of mostly Black scholars such as Marlon Riggs (1994), Zora Neale Hurston (1928/2015), and Resmaa Menakem (2017). As I confessed to Rick, I was pleasantly surprised that overall, students, who seemed hesitant weeks prior, embraced the tasks required for this assignment. My answer to Rick was authentic but partial; I did not reveal that I was shocked by the unexpected discovery of corporeal provocation percolating as a theme across racial lines. This illuminated the embodied dimensions of their knowledge production and proved that all students involved in the study were stirred by the process of multimodal essay composition; however, there was also evidence of deep racial divides in the content of students' collages about Blackness.

BLACK STUDENTS' THEORIZING OF BLACKNESS

Later, as I reflected on my affective reaction to students' work, I realized that what struck me most about Black students' multimodal essay compositions was the *absence* or minimization of whiteness in their midst. Thematically, Black students conveyed comprehensions of Blackness as constructed yet unconstrained by and unhinged from whiteness.

Blackness Is a Thing. Marquis explained that his understanding of Blackness as "a thing"—that is, as a construct—paralleled his matriculation as a student in a mono-racial high school.

> Before I went to my high school, which was all-Black, I went to public schools that were mostly white. Usually, you don't think about those things. . . . You don't think about your Blackness in terms of other people sometimes as a young person. But going to an all-Black school I got to notice that there are other people who see these things, and other people who realize that *Blackness is a thing*, and that, in public spaces it's relevant to other people.

Marquis's sentiments mirror Moten's (2013) theorizing of Blackness as pre-ontological. Marquis interrogates what Moten might call the "black thing" (p. 745), theorizing that Blackness *becomes* a thing of relevance in relation to its configuration through intercorporeal encounters with "other people who see these things."

For Marquis, Blackness is a relational thing. For Phoebe and Miracle, Blackness is a thing of nobility. "At one point, we too had kingdoms," Phoebe posited, referencing Black people. "There were earthly kingdoms all throughout Africa. We had our own world." Similarly, when describing her collage (see Figure 2), Miracle explained:

> I thought about kings and queens. I believe that all Black people are all kings and queens, no matter what you [non-Black people] say. So, I have the King and Queen here just sitting high on their throne. . . . Some people might believe that Black people are just in America. But you have Black people everywhere, literally everywhere.

FIGURE 2
Miracle's collage

Blackness Is Many Things. Miracle and her Black peers also seemed to understand Blackness as diasporic—that is, unrestrained by nation-state boundaries. They knew that there are "Black people everywhere, literally everywhere" who comprise heterogeneous cultural groups. Phoebe used her collage to visually convey this point (see Figure 3):

> My background is a tree. I picked it as a background because it's like Blackness—and specifically, Black women. Because I am a Black woman, I think of how they affect the world, like trees with a lot of history. But also [a tree is] a complex system with a lot of diversity. It affects the world. Nature is kind of seen as a woman, like Mother Nature. . . . There's

FIGURE 3
Phoebe's collage, which includes multiple quotes from Zora Neale Hurston (1928/2015)

FIGURE 4
Marquis' collage

> different sorts of beauty, different kinds of Black women but in a way Black women affect the world. If we look at this one girl here with her natural voluminous hair and then curves—people are paying a lot of money for this now!

Phoebe's sentiments were mirrored by Miracle, who stated that "every Black person is different. No more than one Black person is the same. So, in this picture, you see the different outfits and different hair and different styles because I want to indicate how different we are." Marquis remarked that his road to "seeing that diversity" in Blackness was potholed, and for this reason, he chose images for his collage that represented Black struggle (see Figure 4). He further explained that those visual depictions allowed him to identify the variance in Blackness, and to illustrate strife as a single component of Black life. For Marquis, "seeing that diversity [in Blackness] and also recognizing it with a group of people that look like me was my struggle through adversity in one aspect of my Blackness."

Blackness Is Strength. Overcoming struggle and strife was evident as a strong theme in Black students' collages. Many Black students highlighted their knowledge of Black struggle and strife in their artist's talks. Rick spoke of his choice to center images that show "Black men striving and pushing on" (see Figure 5).

Likewise, said Phoebe:

> I have on this section [of my collage] just struggles because that also is a part of it. . . . Then here is a picture of . . . Black female punishment. She's high up the tree and she's hanging there. Then she has a rope. She has some blood on her head. It's just bad. Then we know about her struggle. Then here is a Black woman [slave] and her master in an uncomfortable situation. Then I have the [Zora Neale Hurston] quote that's throughout it all: "I'm still not tragically colored. There's no great sorrow damned up in my soul," [meaning that] even though we have to go through these things, I'm proud. It's amazing that we can do that.

Phoebe's collage incorporated a reproduction of a controversial Kehinde Wiley painting portraying

FIGURE 5
Rick's collage, which includes a Zora Neale Hurston (1928/2015) quote

a Black woman brandishing a brown-haired white woman's severed head (see Levine, 2018). When asked to speak about this image, Phoebe fidgeted slightly, then said descriptively, "this is a picture of a [Black] woman with a White woman's head. It's not meant maliciously, but it's just to show that if anything is going to change it needs to be through violence."

Miracle also pondered pride and violence in relation to Blackness, expressing delight in the knowledge of Black survival against great odds. "Our ancestors came from something great. They overcame something. They were able to be leaders. They were able to survive through horrible times," she asserted.

Blackness Is Untethered to Whiteness. Miracle carefully arranged the images in her collage to reduce the space claimed by whiteness. In other words, Miracle marginalized whiteness, and then mentioned that in her collage, "although you see white people, it's symbolic. It means something. That's why they're in there." Perplexed by this statement, I asked Miracle to elaborate. The following dialogue ensued between us:

> **Esther:** I have a question for you. When you were framing this you said that, "Even though we might see white people there, they are there for a reason." So, it sounds like you were trying to be intentional about minimizing how much space you gave to white people in your collage.
>
> **Miracle:** Yes.
>
> **Esther:** Can you talk a little bit about that? Why, what was your thinking?
>
> **Miracle:** I just thought about how I wanted Black people to be the center of attention. . . . In the middle you see a white man. However, I wanted to show—celebrate—[pause] obviously he is the one that everybody wants to celebrate and congratulate. And I just wanted to make sure that I reiterated that this was what I mean by celebration of Black people.
>
> **Esther:** So, you wanted to center Black people?
>
> **Miracle:** Yes, I wanted to make sure Black people were the focus.
>
> **Esther:** Why?
>
> **Miracle:** I love Black people.

WHITE STUDENTS' THEORIZING OF BLACKNESS

The affection for Black people that many Black students like Miracle expressed stirred me as much as the flat conceptualizations of Blackness articulated by most white students. Also striking was the dominant *presence* of whiteness in white students' creations. This is in sharp contrast to Black students, who decentered whiteness in their multimodal compositions.

As a reminder, the assignment prompted students to reply to the query, "What is Blackness?" Thematically, white students theorized Blackness as nothing without whiteness, and as nothing more than struggle and strife.

Blackness Is Nothing without Whiteness. With the curious exception of Isabelle, white students made sense of Blackness solely through whiteness. For the majority, Blackness became a thing *through* whiteness. In fact, students' meanings of Blackness sprouted mainly from their interpersonal relationships and encounters; therefore, Blackness came into being through *their* whiteness. For Henry, this displacement of Blackness and *re*centering of whiteness was intentional. He explained his rationale for thinking about Blackness through whiteness as follows:

> I was thinking about what Blackness means to me, I was thinking growing up . . . I didn't necessarily experience Blackness a lot neither did we talk about it in my home, not necessarily because we ignored it, but because we didn't need to talk about it. When I was thinking about that I was like, "How privileged am I that I didn't have to talk about it growing up." Instead it became the focus of my paper, and my collage was the privilege that I have as a white male . . . . So yeah, my paper was focused on the privilege that I have (see Figure 6).

Henry's response minimizes Blackness and maximizes the space allotted to his relationship to whiteness vis-à-vis white privilege. Like Henry, Sarahi—who identified racially as white/Latina—begins her explanation of her collage on Blackness (see Figure 7) with the *inter*personal:

> My poster, right . . . it's a little bit more personal. It may not seem personal, but it is definitely personal to me. . . . Up here is Cornell West and then James Conyers. These two people added a very important impact on my life, because . . . I had dinner with the both of them. This one

FIGURE 6
Henry's collage

dinner that I had particularly with both of them was just really powerful for me, because they were talking about their struggles through adversity. . . . Then for [this picture of] Nelson Mandela as well, one of my family friends is from South Africa, just recently gave me a piece of his work. And I started to read through it, I really felt connected to his work. . . . Then this woman: no one would really know her because she's a family friend, but she had to go through a lot in regards to her line of work. Being an African American woman, especially whenever I talk to her, I always feel that she's always very uplifting for me whenever she talks about what she's going through. Even though I can't personally feel what she's going through, she's always just a sign of hope for me.

Connor's conceptualization of Blackness was sewn together by interpersonal threads of a romantic nature. Connor placed his Black girlfriend at the center of his collage, which included many more photographs of the couple (see Figure 8).

FIGURE 7
Sarahi's collage

FIGURE 8
Connor's collage

Connor framed his artist's talk with the following remarks:

> I wanted to see how my views [of Blackness] changed over time . . . and also [connect to] things in my personal life. So, I'm going to start in the center and work out. That's my girlfriend. I've been dating her since around last semester. We have a good time. She's introduced me to a lot of her friends. . . . So I've met a lot of people who are from Africa or have African roots or Caribbean roots, which she has.

Although sutured to an interpersonal romantic relationship, Connor's theorizing of Blackness contained more layers than the knowledges displayed by his white peers. This became apparent during his artist's talk, when he stated:

> I think that one of the things that [my relationship] really taught me about Blackness is just the diversity in it. It's not necessarily just an African-American experience. That there's also African experiences and Caribbean experiences. Not only that, but there are larger differences between these groups and other groups in terms of sexuality, gender, class, etc.

Blackness Is Struggle. White students' understandings of Blackness primarily rotated around the personal. For most, personal connections to Blackness informed their knowledge of Blackness as struggle. In contrast, Black students primarily held perceptions of Blackness as struggle *through* adversity to perseverance, resilience, and resistance. Blackness was known to white students as a static condition of struggle; however, to Black students, Blackness was known as a dynamic circumstance to struggle through. White students also knew Blackness to be perpetually under siege. For example, Connor inserted visual representations of the Black Lives Matter social movement into his collage, which also depicted

BLACKNESS WAS KNOWN TO WHITE STUDENTS AS A STATIC CONDITION OF STRUGGLE; HOWEVER, TO BLACK STUDENTS, BLACKNESS WAS KNOWN AS A DYNAMIC CIRCUMSTANCE TO STRUGGLE THROUGH.

> Dylan Roof on the far right [who] killed several people in an attempt to start a race riot. We have those two guys [President Donald Trump and Vice President Mike Pence]. You already know their story. Then we kind of have the forces of heterodoxy at the bottom challenging these forces of white supremacy and reaching for a common liberation beyond the basis of race, gender or class. So Black Lives Matter protests. . . . Look at the top section. [There] we kind of interrogate white supremacy as a force that is attacking Blackness in other aspects of society.

Henry's collage also contained visual depictions of violence against Black people but focused on the symbolic. Henry showed

> a picture. It's the hands and arms of a Black person and it's chained here. Then it's Black men. So, it's violence. . . . [It] kind of signifies the struggle that Black people have had to go through in this country. . . . This is still happening. And I have privilege because of my whiteness.

Although flat with regard to knowledge of Blackness, white students' visual representations of Black struggle supplemented their critiques of whiteness and white supremacy. Connor, for example, expressed his intent to "kind of interrogate white supremacy as a force that is attacking Blackness in other aspects of society," and spoke of "the forces of heterodoxy . . . challenging these forces of white supremacy and reaching for a common liberation beyond the basis of race, gender or class." Despite such well-meaning intentions, most white students seemed unable to unmoor (their) whiteness from Blackness, and/or make meaning of Blackness as more than a dangerous(ly) fixed thing rife with wanton violence.

Blackness in and beyond the Break. Isabelle's collage, however, was breathtaking; several of her peers gasped loudly when she unveiled it to the class. It was extraordinary not only for its aesthetic appeal but also because it made a clean break from most white students' conceptualizations of Blackness as misery; it was *beyond* the ordinary white knowledge of Blackness. Isabelle incorporated resilience and strength as themes in her visual depiction of Blackness (see Figure 1), explaining that

> I wanted to focus on strength . . . because I've heard from a couple of people that of course slavery was a huge piece of Blackness. But it was like a roadblock in Black culture. So, I wanted to focus on the pieces that [are] created [from] strength and perseverance.

Isabelle's theorizing of Blackness as made of "strength and perseverance" deviated from the knowledge displayed by her white peers. In Isabelle's collage, Blackness is something with a Black nucleus, not nothing. In fact, for Isabelle, Blackness is *someone* personified in her collage as an Afro-crowned, big booty-ed, brown-skinned Black woman (see Figure 1). The exceptionality of Isabelle's essay raises questions regarding where her comprehension of Blackness as someone-ness sprouted. Considering white students' normative deficit knowledges of Blackness—and comprehending that curriculum is anything from which a learner acquires knowledge and skills—I ask: What curricula buttressed Isabelle's knowledge of Blackness as abundance? How did she gain knowledge of Blackness as fullness of seemingly *everything*, from hair to lips to (in Black lingo) booty? What curricular and pedagogical experiences imbued her with the knowledge that a world in which Blackness became a thing without whiteness was possible? Moreover, which curricula and pedagogies may texturize the nuances of Isabelle's knowledge of Blackness? How do her learning needs differ from those of Henry, whose multimodal essay composition turned the spotlight away from Blackness and back toward white privilege (see Figure 8)? Additionally, how are Isabelle's and Henry's curricular and pedagogic needs similar to or different from those of Black students like Phoebe and Miracle, who entered the tertiary classroom already empowered with sophisticated knowledges of Blackness as something (more and less than human)? Most importantly, how might Blackness be *knowable* to both Black and white students?

Multimodal Essay Composition as Fugitive Flight (of Fancy)

Ages ago, in a land far away from the small liberal arts college in central Ohio where my students and I disrupted whiteness and dissected Blackness using multimodal essay composition as a tool for teaching and learning, I had some certainty about certainty. It was then that I published my most cited work to date: an article about my pedagogic use of discomfort with white students who comprised the majority segment of an interracial classroom (Ohito, 2016). At present, I am tormented by regret about my simple (in retrospect) interpretation of complex data. My data analysis travelled the narrative arc of a feel-good text, flowing smoothly and linearly from problem to (re)solution. The glaring problem, however, is that teaching and learning that incite a "necessary disruption" (Kinloch, 2018) to whiteness and anti-Blackness are infinitely more gnarly than that article suggests. The politics of an interracial classroom further exacerbate the inherent knottiness of those processes. Consider, for instance—in the context of this article—Phoebe's inclusion of the Kehinde Wiley portrait of a Black woman holding a white woman's decapitated head. Despite a display of mild physical discomfort, Phoebe was unapologetic when stating that the image was "not meant maliciously, but it's just to show that if anything is going to change it needs to be through violence." I am *almost* certain that Phoebe's assertion was not metaphorical; therefore, I wonder, what molds such violence might make in English teacher education. How might that violence manifest in curriculum and pedagogy, and at what (epistemic, ideological, material, and spiritual) cost, and to whom? In other words, what might be the curricular and pedagogical consequences of this possibly chaotic social change-driven violence? Phoebe's insight reflects that of Picasso, who remarked that "every act of creation is first an act of destruction" (quoted in Hallock, 2014). Both Phoebe and Picasso theorize creation and destruction as interdependent; moreover, Phoebe's knowledge signals that the making of a *new* world devoid of whiteness and anti-Blackness necessitates the annihilation of naturalized habitus (Asimaki & Koustourakis, 2014).

In the wake that is *this* world, efforts to escape whiteness and anti-Blackness are complicated by treacherous conditions—I am certain of this; however, I am also certain that my use of multimodal essay composition as a fugitive literacy practice created one path through which the disruption of whiteness and anti-Blackness occurred in a tertiary classroom that was as oriented to seeking freedom as to strengthening students' skills in reading and writing the word and the world (Freire & Macedo, 2005). Students' engagement with linguistic, visual, and aural modes of communication provoked corporeal awakenings within them (and me) and stirred awake the social consciousness of some. The brilliance of Rick's reflective admission that "the creative aspect of the collage woke me up" is encapsulated in its concise capturing of the pedagogical power of creativity harnessed by this curricular assignment. Rick's words show that creativity is a force full enough to evoke a wealth of embodied feelings, and powerful enough to spark social awareness about issues of (whiteness and anti-Black) injustice.

This assignment also caused an epistemic disruption to whiteness in the classroom by creating a portal through which Black students could escape the deadening violence of anti-Blackness (albeit temporarily) and engage (their) Blackness as "alive and vibrant" (Kellaway & Rankine, 2015, para. 10). Being interpellated (Althusser, 1971) as artists and composers helped learners such as Miracle confidently theorize Blackness as royal—and therefore desirable—and (pro)claim that "all Black people are all kings and queens." Rather than accepting the passive consumption of academics' extant (and sometimes deficit) theories of Blackness, the assignment asked that students access *their* critical thought(s), thereby positioning them as theorists, and both demanding and rewarding their active intellectual engagement with knowledge-making.

Further, the assignment irradiated (dis)similarities in how Black and white students acquired knowledge of Blackness. Both sets of students sourced their knowledges of Blackness from families and friends, lived experiences, and/or cultural artifacts such as rap music; however, there were stark racial differences in contents of those knowledges. Most white students' compositions revealed that Blackness was known to them as brimful of problems. This illuminates not only the curricular perniciousness of whiteness and anti-Blackness but also how embedded these entities are in the white imagination. The mooring of Blackness to bleakness is materially and direly consequential for Black people; "[b]ecause white men [and women] can't/ police their imagination/ black men [and women] are dying" (Rankine, 2014, p. 135). In contrast, Black students' multimodal essay compositions problematized Blackness. The artifacts created by Black students showcase their knowledges of Blackness as fraught *and* full of energy, indicating that generally, for this group, "'blackness' figures as a cosmological a priori, never fixed but ever shifting and creating new terrains of beings and becomings" (Braziel, 2009, p. 22). For Black students, Blackness not only matters, but *is* matter.

According to Baldwin (1962), "whatever white people do not know about Negroes reveals, precisely and inexorably, what they do not know about themselves" (para. 18). My white students did not know of the vitality of Blackness; what did they did not know about themselves and (their) whiteness? Moreover, what curricula and pedagogies would enrich their knowledge of Blackness as full of vim and vigor? What could anomalous white students like Isabelle—who "wanted to accentuate on the naturality and beauty of the Black body"—teach English teacher educators? Conversely, what curricula and pedagogies are necessary to affirm Black students' knowledges of Blackness as ebullient? What curricula and pedagogies could account for students like Sarahi, whose white/Latina racial identity blurs the white/Black binary? These questions emerge from my uncertainty as to how to reconcile the racialized variance in students' theories of Blackness. However, having (been) abandoned (by) naiveté, I am comfortable with this uncertainty. In fact, I am provoked by what remained unresolved at the conclusion of my self-study.

Phoebe's provocative insight regarding the relationship between change and violence—or rather, the idea that violence is a requisite for (social) change—continues to stimulate my thoughts. Phoebe's theorizing challenges scholars to grapple with the idea that creating a new world that is expansive enough to contain the pluralities of Blackness requires pivoting from *disruption* to *destruction* of whiteness and anti-Blackness as a goal. Semantics are important; the former term denotes interference and interruption, and the latter, obliteration and eradication. Whiteness does nothing more than cause damage, and there is exiguous evidence proving that it is possible "for white people to do whiteness well, and, in doing so, aid Black people in getting free" (Rigby & Zayid, 2016, para. 3). Why not abolish that which is irredeemable? This opens numerous lines of inquiry regarding what the curricular and pedagogical destruction of whiteness and anti-Blackness would resemble, and how that obliteration would impinge upon learning across racial categories, particularly if one accepts that schooling may provide "contingent possibilities for well-being for some and unmitigated safety for others" (Patel, 2016, p. 397). For example, I wonder if my pedagogical decision *not* to censure Phoebe's explanation of the aforementioned image affected my white students' sense of safety. If so, then I inadvertently reified a Western culture of education that denies *all* students "possibilities for well-being." Yet I am uncomfortable with the thought that I should placate white (students') frailty and feelings of alienation when the threat of material and social death looms ominously over the day-to-day lives of Black students (DiAngelo, 2016, 2018; Rigby & Zayid, 2016; Sexton, 2011). I am also cognizant that on a predominantly white college campus, classrooms like mine that are anchored to "vision driven justice" (Lyiscott, this issue) are atypical; therefore, there are few places available for Black students to aerate their unfiltered perspectives and feelings about whiteness and anti-Blackness, which may rightfully include rage and anger (hooks, 1995; Thomson, 2017). The crux of the tension described here is the *im*possibility of Black and white cohabitation in an interracial classroom designed to propel flight from whiteness and anti-Blackness, and the (ethical?) dilemmas of constructing curricular and pedagogical spaces that promise *all* students sanctuary and well-being when only *some* (i.e., Black students) are most adversely affected by inhaling the noxious airs of whiteness and anti-Blackness.

Multimodal essay composition is a fugitive literacy practice that performs "wake work" (Sharpe, 2016, p. 17); "[t]o perform 'wake work' is to labor within the space of paradoxes surrounding black citizenship, identity, and civil rights" (Horton, 2018, para. 3). If lovers of literacy are to awaken from whiteness and anti-Blackness in English teacher education, then we must create more such tools with which to toil for a world in which education is a practice of freedom capacious enough to allow Blackness to unmoor from whiteness and fly free. As this study shows, another world is more than a phantasmagoria; an abundance of Black students have already awakened to its existence; they know that Black ~~human~~ being animates, enlivens, and endarkens (Dillard, 2010) that just world's ample landscapes.

Romantic Dreams of Blackness after the End of This World

> **[B]lackness is like "darkness over the surface of the deep" as in the biblical myth from Genesis. It is primordial, yet unformed; formless, yet formable; a fecund materiality, yet also creative movement and kinetic potency.**
>
> —BRAZIEL, 2009, P. 22

> **The world is all about creation, and Black people are often the creators.**
>
> —MIRACLE, BLACK STUDENT, THIS STUDY

The United States is a dystopian world for Black people. If most apocalyptic movies are to be believed, then, at the end of the world, nothing survives. Yet if Blackness is nothingness in the white world, and my student, Miracle, is to be believed, then Blackness will survive the destruction of whiteness, and Black people will not only live in futurity, but will also create interminable futures well into infinity. If Blackness precedes being, then considerations of a world after whiteness warrant "conceptualizations of 'blackness' as genesis (or as generative)" (Braziel, 2009, p. 22). Besides pain, what does whiteness produce? Blackness, on the other hand, gives life; "Blackness is our everyday romance" (Moten, 2017, p. 279). In another world, Blackness is someone-ness, which means Blackness is something-ness. Something-~~ness~~ multiplied by a second something is double the number of somethings, which is greater than or equal to everything. This means that a double dose of something is, at least, everything. This must also mean that Blackness is, if nothing else, everything. In this calculus:

1. Blackness is Someone-ness (i.e., Something-ness, i.e., Something-ness)
2. Blackness (i.e., Something) x Something = Double Somethings
3. Double Somethings $\geq$ Everything
4. $\therefore$ Blackness $\geq$ Everything
5. $\therefore$ Blackness is, at a bare minimum, Everything

I am, quite unabashedly, a hopeless romantic. In the fantasies that I dream to escape the anti-Black dysmorphia of this dystopia, I, too, create another world where, at a bare minimum, *Blackness is everything*—ya dig?

TEACHING TIPS

Ohito and the Fugitive Literacies Collective issue a call to action and invite us to focus our collective work on the destruction of Whiteness and anti-Blackness. Ohito shares the how multimodal composition created opportunities for her students to theorize Blackness. To begin this process with your students, ask them to create a one-pager in response to the question, "What is Blackness?" Invite students to share their artifacts and discuss themes, questions, and tensions they notice. Keep track of these observations and revisit over time, perhaps alongside texts that you read in class.

NOTE

1. Recognizing the entanglement of language "rules" (e.g., capitalization), anti-Blackness, culture, identity, and power, I choose to capitalize *Black* in this article and do not do the same with *white* (see Perlman, 2015). I defer to the authors' capitalization choices in works referenced.

REFERENCES

Althusser, L. (1971). Ideology and ideological state apparatuses. In L. Althusser (Ed.), *Lenin and philosophy and other essays*. New York: Monthly Review Press.

artscanada. (1967, October). *Black*, 113.

Asimaki, A., & Koustourakis, G. (2014). Habitus: An attempt at a thorough analysis of a controversial concept in Pierre Bourdieu's theory of practice. *Social Sciences*, 3(4), 121–131.

Bailey, M., & Trudy. (2018). On misogynoir: Citation, erasure, and plagiarism. *Feminist Media Studies*, 18(4), 762–768.

Baker-Bell, A., Butler, T. T., & Johnson, L. L. (2017). The pain and the wounds: A call for critical race English education in the wake of racial violence. *English Education*, 49(2), 116–129.

Baldwin, J. (1962, November 17). Letter from a region of my mind. *The New Yorker*, 5.

Baldwin, J. (1973). The Black Scholar Interviews: James Baldwin. *The Black Scholar*, 5(4), 33–42.

Berchini, C. (2019). Reconceptualizing whiteness in English education: Failure, fraughtness, and accounting for context. *English Education*, 51(2), 151–181.

Berchini, C., & Tanner, S. J. (2019). Working through whiteness and white supremacy in English education [Editorial]. *English Education*, 51(2), 151–181.

Borsheim-Black, C. (2015). "It's pretty much white": Challenges and opportunities of an antiracist approach to literature instruction in a multilayered white context. *Research in the Teaching of English*, 49(4), 407–429.

Borsheim-Black, C., & Sarigianides. S. T. (2019). *Letting go of literary whiteness: Antiracist literature instruction for white students*. New York and London: Teachers College Press.

Braziel, J. E. (2009). *Caribbean genesis: Jamaica Kincaid and the writing of new worlds*. Albany, NY: State University of New York Press.

Campt, T. (2014, Oct. 7). *Black feminist futures and the practice of fugitivity*. Lecture presented at the Helen Pond McIntyre '48 Lecture at the Barnard Center for Research on Women, New York. Retrieved from http://bcrw.barnard.edu/videos/tina-campt-black-feminist-futures-and-the-practice-of-fugitivity/

Chandler, N. D. (2014). X—*The problem of the Negro as a problem for thought*. New York: Fordham University Press.

Coles, J. A., & Powell, T. (2019). A BlackCrit analysis on black urban youth and suspension disproportionately as anti-black symbolic violence. *Race Ethnicity and Education*, 1–21. doi:10.1080/13613324.2019.1631778

Conyers, J. L., Jr. (2016). Pedagogy, intersection, and research: A case study of teaching qualitative research methods in Africana studies. In J. L. Conyers Jr. (Ed.), *Qualitative methods in Africana studies: An interdisciplinary approach to examining Africana phenomena* (pp. 379–390). Lanham, MD: University Press of America.

Culler, J. (2011). *Literary theory: A very short introduction* (2nd ed.). Oxford: Oxford University Press.

Curriculum Inquiry. (n.d.). Curricular confrontations in the wake of anti-Blackness and in the break of Black possibilities [Call for papers]. Retrieved from http://www.curriculuminquiry.org/anti-blackness/

Davis, M. (2017, December 12). The work of examining and disrupting whiteness and privilege is unambiguously urgent. Retrieved from https://www2.ncte.org/blog/2017/12/work-examining-disrupting-whiteness-privilege-unambiguously-urgent/

Dei, G. J. S. (2017). *Reframing Blackness and Black solidarities through anti-colonial and decolonial prisms* (Vol. 4). New York: Springer.

Denzin, N. K., & Lincoln, Y. S. (Eds.). (1999). *The SAGE handbook of qualitative research* (3rd ed.). Thousand Oaks, CA: Sage.

DiAngelo, R. (2016). *What does it mean to be white?: Developing white racial literacy* (Vol. 497, 2nd ed.). New York: Peter Lang.

DiAngelo, R. (2018). *White fragility: Why it's so hard for white people to talk about racism*. Boston, MA: Beacon Press.

Dillard, C. B. (2010). The substance of things hoped for, the evidence of things not seen: Examining an endarkened feminist epistemology in educational research and leadership. *International Journal of Qualitative Studies in Education*, 13(6), 661–681.

Emdin, C. (2017). *For white folks who teach in the hood . . . and the rest of y'all too: Reality pedagogy and urban education*. Boston, MA: Beacon Press.

Fanon, F. (2008). *Black skin, white masks*. (R. Philcox, Trans.). New York: Grove Press. (Original work published 1967)

Ferreira da Silva, D. (2015). Toward a Black feminist poethics. *The Black Scholar: Journal of Black Studies and Research*, 44(2), 81–97. doi.org/10.1080/00064246.2014.11413690

Ferreira da Silva, D. (2017, February). 1 (life) ÷ 0 (blackness) = ∞ − ∞ or ∞ / ∞: On matter beyond the equation of value. *e-flux*, 79. Retrieved from https://www.e-flux.com/journal/79/94686/1-life-0-blackness-or-on-matter-beyond-the-equation-of-value/

Ferreira da Silva, D. (2018, September). In the raw. *e-flux*, 93. Retrieved from https://www.e-flux.com/journal/93/215795/in-the-raw/

Frankel, K. K., Becker, B. L. C., Rowe, M. W., & Pearson, P. D. (2016). From "what is reading?" to what is literacy? *Journal of Education*, 196(3), 7–17.

Freire, P., & Macedo, D. (2005). *Literacy: Reading in the word and the world*. London: Routledge.

Fuentes, M. J. (2016). *Dispossessed lives: Enslaved women, violence, and the archive*. Philadelphia, PA: University of Philadelphia Press.

Gramsci, A. (1989). *Selections from the prison notebooks*. New York: International Publishers. (Original work published 1971)

Grinage, J. (2019). Reopening racial wounds: Whiteness, melancholia, and affect in the English classroom. *English Education*, 51(2), 126–150.

Hallock, D. (2014, October 1). Every act of creation is first an act of destruction. Retrieved from https://duanehallock.com/2014/10/01/destroy-and-create/

Hamilton, M. L., & Pinnegar, S. (1998). The value and the promise of self-study. In M. L. Hamilton, S. Pinnegar, T. Russell, J. J. Loughran, & V. LaBoskey (Eds.), *Reconceptualizing teaching practice: Self-study in teacher education* (pp. 235–246). London: Farmer.

Hamilton, M. L., & Pinnegar, S. (2010). Re-visionist self-study: If we knew then what we know now. In L. B. Erickson, J. R. Young, & S. Pinnegar (Eds.), *Navigating the public and the private: Negotiating the diverse landscape of teacher education* (pp. 101–104). Provo, UT: Brigham Young University.

Hartman, S. (2016). The belly of the world: A note on Black women's labors. *Souls*, 18(1), 163–173.

hooks, b. (1991). Theory as liberatory practice. *Yale Journal of Law and Feminism*, 4(1), 1–12.

hooks, b. (1995). *Killing rage: Ending racism*. New York: Henry Holt and Company.

Hopkinson, D. (1995). *Sweet Clara and the freedom quilt*. Decorah, IL: Dragonfly Books.

Horton, D. (2018). Review of "In the wake: On Blackness and being" by Christina Sharpe (Duke University Press). *Lateral*, 7(1). Retrieved from https://csalateral .org/reviews/in-the-wake-blackness-being-sharpe-horton/

Hunt, E., & Martin, D. L. (Eds.). (2018). *Letters to the future: Black women/radical writing*. Tuscon, AZ: Kore Press.

Hurston, Z. N. (2015). *How it feels to be colored me*. Carlisle, MA: Applewood. (Original work published 1928)

Jacobs, H. (2001). *Incidents in the life of a slave girl*. Dover Thrift Editions. J. T. Pine (Ed.). New York: Dover Publications. (Original work published 1861)

Johnson, L. L. (2017). The racial hauntings of one Black male professor and the disturbance of the self(ves): Self-actualization and racial storytelling as pedagogical practices. *Journal of Literacy Research*, 49(4), 476–502.

Johnson, L. L., Jackson, J., Stovall, D., & Baszile, D. T. (2017). "Loving Blackness to death": (Re)imagining ELA classrooms in a time of racial chaos. *English Journal*, 106(4), 60–66.

Jones-Rogers, S. E. (2019). *They were her property: White women as slave owners in the American South*. London: Yale University Press.

Kellaway, K. (Interviewer), & Rankine, C. (Interviewee). (2015, December 27). *Claudia Rankine: "Blackness in the white imagination has nothing to do with black people"* [Interview transcript]. Retrieved from https://www.theguardian.com /books/2015/dec/27/claudia-rankine-poet-citizen-american-lyric-feature

Kincheloe, J. L., & Steinberg, S. R. (1998). Addressing the crisis of whiteness: Reconfiguring white identity in a pedagogy of whiteness. In J. L. Kincheloe, S. R. Steinberg, N. M. Rodriguez, and R. E. Chennault (Eds.), *White reign: Deploying whiteness in America* (pp. 3–30). New York: St. Martin's Griffin.

Kinloch, V. (2018). Necessary disruptions: Examining justice, engagement, and humanizing approaches to teaching and teacher education (TeachingWorks working paper). Ann Arbor, MI: University of Michigan. Retrieved from http://www.teaching works.org/images/files/TeachingWorks_Kinloch.pdf

Kinloch, V., & Lensmire, T. J. (2019). A dialogue on race, racism, white privilege, and white supremacy in English education [Editorial]. *English Education*, 51(2), 116–125.

Lambert, L. (2017, November–December). Antiblack weather vs. black microclimates: A conversation with Christina Sharpe. *Funambulist*, 14, 48–53.

Levine, J. (2018, February 12). Obama portrait artist Kehinde Wiley once painted black women decapitating white women. Retrieved from https://www.the wrap.com/obama-portrait-artist-kehinde-wiley-black-women-decapitating-white-women/

Loughran, J. (2007). Researching teacher education practices: Responding to the challenges, demands, and expectations of self-study. *Journal of Teacher Education*, 58(1), 12–20.

Love, B. (2019). *We want to do more than survive: Abolitionist teaching and the pursuit of educational freedom*. Boston, MA: Beacon Press.

Luttrell, W. (2010). Reflexive writing exercises. In W. Luttrell (Ed.), *Qualitative educational research: Readings in reflexive methodology and transformative practice* (pp. 469–480). New York: Routledge.

Lyiscott, J. (2019). *Black appetite. White food: Issues of race, voice, and justice within and beyond the classroom*. New York: Routledge.

McKay, D., Cunningham, S. J., & Thomson, K. (2006). Exploring the user experience through collage. In M. Billinghurst (Ed.), *Proceedings of the 7th ACM SIGCHI New Zealand chapter's international conference on computer-human interaction* (pp. 109–115). Christchurch, New Zealand: HCI.

McKittrick, K. (2014). Mathematics black life. *Journal of Black Studies and Research*, 44(2), 16–28.

Meek, M. (2005). Foreword. In P. Freire & D. Macedo (Eds.), *Literacy: Reading the word and the world* (pp. vi–ix). London: Routledge.

Menakem, R. (2017). *My grandmother's hands: Racialized trauma and the pathway to mending our hearts and bodies*. Las Vegas, NV: Central Recovery Press.

Morgan, P. D. (Ed.). (2012). *Maritime slavery*. London: Routledge.

Moten, F. (2013). Blackness and nothingness (mysticism in the flesh). *South Atlantic Quarterly*, 112(4), 737–780.

Moten, F. (2017). *Black and blur (consent not to be a single being)*. Durham, NC: Duke University Press.

Muhammad, G. E., & Haddix, M. (2016). Centering Black girls' literacies: A review of literature of the multiple ways of knowing Black girls. *English Education*, 48(4), 299–336.

Mullen, H. (1994). Optic white: Blackness and the production of whiteness. *Diacritics*, 24(2/3), 71–89.

Mustakeem, S. M. (2016). *Slavery at sea: Terror, sex, and sickness in the Middle Passage*. The New Black Studies Series. Chicago: University of Illinois Press.

Nowell, L. S., Norris, J. M., White, D. E., & Moules, N. J. (2017). Thematic analysis: Striving to meet the trustworthiness criteria. *International Journal of Qualitative Methods*, 16(1), 1–13.

Ohito, E. O. (2016). Making the emperor's new clothes visible in anti-racist teacher education:

Enacting a pedagogy of discomfort with white preservice teachers, *Equity & Excellence in Education*, 49(4), 454–467.

Ohito, E. O., & Loury, A. (forthcoming). "I write with intent": Writing as a Black feminist method of inquiry.

Oyler, C. (2011). *An examination of urban teacher education and the public good: Which public? What good? The missing curriculum of racial literacies*. Paper presented at the American Education Research Association Conference, April 8–12, New Orleans, LA.

Painter, N. I. (2015, June 20). What is whiteness? Retrieved from https://www.ny times.com/2015/06/21/opinion/sunday/what-is-whiteness.html

Patel, L. (2016). Pedagogies of resistance and survivance: Learning as marronage. *Equity & Excellence in Education*, 49(4), 397–401.

Perlman, M. (2015, June 23). Black and white: Why capitalization matters. Retrieved from https://www.cjr.org/analysis/language_corner_1.php

Price-Dennis, D., Muhammad, G. E., Womack, E., McArthur, S. A., & Haddix, M. (2017). The multiple identities and literacies of black girlhood: A conversation about creating spaces for black girl voices. *Journal of Language and Literacy Education*, 13(3), 1–18.

R. L. (2013). Wanderings of the slave: Black life and social death. *Mute*. Retrieved from https://www.metamute.org/editorial/articles/wanderings-slave-black-life-and-social-death

Rankine, C. (2014). *Citizen: An American lyric*. Minneapolis, MN: Graywolf Press.

Richardson, E. (2002). "To protect and serve": African American female literacies. *College Composition and Communication*, 53(4), 675–704.

Richardson, E. (2003). *African American literacies* (Vol. 8). London: Routledge.

Richardson, E. (2007). "She was workin like foreal": Critical literacy and discourse practices of African American females in the age of hip hop. *Discourse & Society*, 18(6), 789–80.

Rigby, K., Jr., & Zayid, H. (2016, March 31). White people have no place in Black liberation. Retrieved from https://racebaitr.com/2016/03/31/white-people-no-place-black-liberation/

Riggs, M. (Director). (1994). *Black is . . . Black ain't* [Motion picture]. San Francisco: California Newsreal.

Rogers, M. (2012). Contextualizing theories and practices of bricolage research. *The Qualitative Report*, 17(48), 1–17. Retrieved from https://nsuworks.nova.edu/tqr/vol17/iss48/3

Schieble, M. (2012). Critical conversations on whiteness with young adult literature. *Journal of Adolescent & Adult Literacy*, 56(3), 212–221.

Sealey-Ruiz, Y. (2016). Why Black girls' literacies matter: New literacies for a new era. *English Education*, 48(4), 290–298.

Sexton, J. (2011). The social life of social death: On Afro-pessimism and Black optimism. *InTensions*, 5. Retrieved from https://www.yorku.ca/intent/issue5/articles/pdfs/jared sextonarticle.pdf

Sharpe, C. (2012). Response to "ante-anti-blackness." *Lateral*, 1. Retrieved from https://csalateral.org/section/theory/ante-anti-blackness-response-sharpe/

Sharpe, C. (2016). *In the wake: On Blackness and being*. Durham, NC: Duke University Press.

Sleeter, C. E. (2001). Preparing teachers for culturally diverse schools: Research and the overwhelming presence of Whiteness. *Journal of Teacher Education*, 52, 94–106.

Souto-Manning, M. (2019). Toward praxically-just transformations: interrupting racism in teacher education, *Journal of Education for Teaching*, 45(1), 97–113. doi:10.1080/02607476.2019.1550608

Spillers, H. (1987). Mama's baby papa's maybe: An American grammar book. *Diacritics*, 17(2), 65–81.

Stella Adler Studio of Acting. (2016, June 16). *Toni Morrison's Final Thoughts at "Art and Social Justice"* [Video file]. Retrieved from https://www.youtube.com/watch?v=h3hhoyTbP6A

Street, B. (2003). What's "new" in New Literacy Studies? Critical approaches to literacy in theory and practice. *Current Issues in Comparative Education*, 5(2), 77–91.

Tanner, S. J. (2016). Accounting for whiteness through collaborative fiction. *Research in Drama Education: The Journal of Applied Theatre and Performance*, 21, 183–195.

Tanner, S. J. (2019). Whiteness is a white problem: Whiteness in English education. *English Education*, 51(2), 182–199.

Thomson, D. (2017). An exoneration of Black rage. *South Atlantic Quarterly*, 116(3), 457–481.

Wallace, D. (2018, April 30). Fred Moten's radical critique of the present. Retrieved from https://www.newyorker.com/culture/persons-of-interest/fred-motens-radical-critique-of-the-present

Warren, J. T., & Fassett, D. L. (2004). Subverting whiteness: Pedagogy at the crossroads of performance, culture, and politics. *Theatre Topics*, 14(2), 411–430.

Wilderson, F. B., III. (2015). *Incognegro: A memoir of exile and apartheid*. Boston, MA: South End Press.

Williams, H. A. (2005). *Self-taught: African American education in slavery and freedom*. Chapel Hill, NC: University of North Carolina Press.

Woodson, J. (2005). *Show way*. New York: G. P. Putnam's Sons Books for Young Readers.

Wright, M. M. (2015). *Physics of Blackness: Beyond the Middle Passage epistemology*. Minneapolis: University of Minnesota Press.

ESTHER O. OHITO is an assistant professor of English/literacy education at the New Brunswick campus of Rutgers, The State University of New Jersey; the Toni Morrison Faculty Fellow at the University of Massachusetts Amherst's Center of Racial Justice and Youth Engaged Research; and the Carnegie African Diaspora Fellowship Program Fellow at Maseno University in western Kenya. Ohito's research explores the poetics and aesthetics of Black knowledge and cultural production, the gendered geographies of Black girlhoods, and the gendered pedagogies of Black critical educators.

This article originally appeared in *Voices from the Middle 28.4*

(W)RITES OF PASSAGE: Black Girls' Journaling and Podcast Script Writing as Counternarratives

DELICIA TIERA GREENE

Introduction

"I don't always feel good about myself. I try to focus on all the good qualities I have, even though the Internet doesn't seem to think I have any. The world HATES Black girls. I struggle with how I see myself and the things the Internet say about us. I'm always targeted with hateful, racist comments about my kinky hair, facial features, and my body type."

This was Kenya's weekly journal entry in response to the prompt, "How does the world see you? Who are you to the world?" Kenya is a Black adolescent girl who participated in Dark Girls, a program designed to bridge Black girls' out-of-school and in-school literacies. Kenya's sentiment illustrates how the world sees her and her place in it and how she sees herself. Kenya's experiences also illustrate how she is regularly confronted with anti-Black rhetoric and images online that negatively impact her self-perception. Anti-Black rhetoric is discourse designed to dehumanize by stripping Blackness of value, and systematically marginalizing Black people. Kenya is a poet, a photographer, and an avid user of Facebook and TikTok. In further conversations, Kenya reveals how having access to digital tools affords her the opportunity to share so much of what she loves and who she is, including her verses as a spoken word poet, her images as a photographer, and her vocals as a singer.

ANTI-BLACK RHETORIC IS DISCOURSE DESIGNED TO DEHUMANIZE BY STRIPPING BLACKNESS OF VALUE, AND SYSTEMATICALLY MARGINALIZE BLACK PEOPLE.

Jalisa, a Black girl who also participated in Dark Girls, shared her weekly journal entry in response to the prompt. Jalisa writes,

> It's a cruel world out there. I'm always reminded of how the world doesn't have love for a Black girl!! I have a lifestyle WordPress blog on music, fashion, and hair and there are always racists comments about how "angry" my hair looks, how broad my nose is, and how full my lips are. I can't expect to see the good in myself if all I hear are negative comments from the world.

Jalisa is a blogger and YouTuber who finds comfort and solace in digital writing and performance despite her negative experiences online. Both Kenya and Jalisa's journal entries illustrate how Black girls as content creators are confronted with anti-Black racism in the digital sphere. This article focuses on how Black girls' "rites of passage" serve as opportunities to engage in "writes of passage" by rewriting their lives, humanizing their experiences, and countering dominant narratives about Black girlhood. In this article, Kenya and Jalisa's rites of passage entail recalling their personal Black girlhood experiences. The girls' writes of passage entail (1) connecting their collective experiences to broader social issues impacting Black girls and (2) collaborating on podcast script writing.

Black Girls' Rites of Passage

Black girls have varied lived experiences, however, there is also a shared experience based on their intersecting identities. Historically, Black girls' intersecting gendered and raced identities have positioned them at the margins within society. In current day, Kenya and Jalisa's experiences ("rites of passage") highlight how media-rich environments are spaces steeped in anti-Blackness toward Black girls. This is evident in how media outlets, specifically advertisements, commercials, movies/television, billboards, magazines, and social media sites/search engine algorithms portray Black girls and perpetuate anti-Black racism against them (Muhammad & McArthur, 2015). For example, algorithms are a sequence of computer instructions embedded in search engines; in Noble's (2018) study, a series of Google searches using the term "Black girls" yielded websites and images of porn with Black girls. This highlights how search engine algorithms perpetuate racism and sexualize Black girls' bodies.

Rites of passages are typically ceremonies that mark important, traditional periods in a person's life, such as the confirmation of an individual within a religious community, becoming a legally significant age, experiencing an epiphany in a moment in which a decision needs to be made, or taking responsibility for oneself and one's personal worldview or choices. These coming-of-age experiences represent a significant change of status in society and are usually celebratory in nature. For Black girls like Kenya and Jalisa, their "rites of passage" in a media-rich environment are not often celebratory in nature, but instead are often fraught with anti-Black comments and imagery that negatively represent Black girls and impact how they see themselves. Kenya and Jalisa's journal entries illustrate how the outside-of-school context allowed them to center and speak to their "rites of passage" and its impact on their socioemotional wellness and self-identity.

RITES OF PASSAGES ARE TYPICALLY CEREMONIES THAT MARK IMPORTANT, TRADITIONAL PERIODS IN A PERSON'S LIFE, SUCH AS THE CONFIRMATION OF AN INDIVIDUAL WITHIN A RELIGIOUS COMMUNITY, BECOMING A LEGALLY SIGNIFICANT AGE, EXPERIENCING AN EPIPHANY IN A MOMENT IN WHICH A DECISION NEEDS TO BE MADE, OR TAKING RESPONSIBILITY FOR ONESELF AND ONE'S PERSONAL WORLDVIEW OR CHOICES.

Black Girls' Digital Literacies In and Out of Schools

In many instances, schools are often sites of contention for Black girls because they do not account for the lived experiences, literacy traditions, and cultural identities that they bring with them into the literacy classroom (Greene, 2016). Oftentimes, literacy classrooms do not serve as socioemotional supports allowing Black girls to use writing to construct identities, make meaning, or engage in agency, since writing in schools traditionally adheres to narrow conceptions of literacy and tends to be viewed solely as a skills-based practice. This is further compounded given that the teaching force is comprised of 84 percent white women, resulting in instances in which white teachers are teaching Black children while often lacking an understanding of the cultural histories, linguistic nuances, and out-of-school digital literacy traditions of historically marginalized youth (Ellison, 2014; Haddix & Sealey-Ruiz, 2012; US Department of Education, 2016).

Black Girls' Digital Literacies centers Black girls' racialized and gendered identities to engage them in multimodal, equity-based pedagogies (Greene, 2016; Muhammad & Haddix, 2016; Muhammad & Womack, 2015; Price-Dennis, 2016; Richardson, 2003). This entails Black girls' "cultural identities, social location, and practices influencing how they make meaning and assert themselves socio-politically in and out-of-school contexts" (Richardson, 2003, p. 329). Digital literacies are emancipatory in nature allowing Black girls the freedom, creative control, autonomy, and agency to author their lives by "speaking out on misrepresentations of who they are and negotiating their identities" (Price-Dennis et al., 2017, p. 4). Digital literacies also serve as counternarratives and create opportunities for Black girls to clear space and speak back to racist ideologies that negatively impact their lives.

Black Girls' Writes of Passage

BLACK GIRLS' COLLECTIVE EXPERIENCES

Kenya and Jalisa revisited their journal entries and recalled their individual experiences as Black girls, how the world perceives them, and the broader societal issues impacting Black girls. In the conversation that ensued, I asked prompting questions such as: *What are your individual experiences as Black girls? Based on the sharing of your individual experiences with each other, what seems to be common experiences as Black girls? When you think about your common experiences as Black girls, what issues in society seem to be connected to them?* Kenya and

Jalisa highlighted how their individual experiences focused on their physical attributes, such as facial features and skin complexion. This led to conversations about their shared experiences focusing on standards of beauty. Kenya mentioned how "white women who are slim with blonde hair and blue eyes set the standards of beauty for everyone else. I think that is like the measurement forced on Black girls because we don't fit into that standard; we are either insulted or plain invisible."

Kenya and Jalisa then jotted down social issues that Black girls often experience, focusing on standards of beauty, including colorism, natural hair shaming, and facial and body features. They brainstormed how standards of beauty were tied to broader social issues negatively impacting Black girls, including schools' discriminatory policies on natural hair. This activity highlighted for them that their individual experiences were not isolated instances, but instead part of broader systemic issues in society that shape Black girls' collective experiences. This activity also entailed documenting elements of standards of beauty on a brainstorm poster, which laid the groundwork for their Black girls' podcast series, entitled *Hair Me!*

CONVERSATIONS ON PODCAST SCRIPT WRITING

I introduced Kenya and Jalisa to elements of script writing as they began to think about their collaborative podcast project, *Hair Me!: Black Girls' Chronicles* (see Table 1). They decided to sketch out elements of their 30-minute podcast (Haddix & Sealey-Ruiz,

TABLE 1

Hair Me! Black Girls' Chronicles Podcast Script Outline

Element of Podcast	Description
Intro audio and musical jingle *(throughout)*	Solange Knowles' *Don't Touch My Hair* (Instrumental)
Intro monologue	Introductions: Who are we? What are our individual interests? What are our shared interests? Personal experiences that led to podcast topic
Podcast content/topic	What are we going to talk about? • Schools banning Black girls' natural hair styles • Banning natural hair styles and the emotional pain it causes Black girls • Updating a school district's dress/hair code to include Black girls' culture How will content be delivered to our audience? • "Just kickin' it" model—Laid back, backyard barbeque conversation Main talking points of Hair Me! podcast: 1. Black girls suspended because of their natural hairstyles • Tiana Parker, age 7, switched schools after being forbidden from wearing braids • Louisville H.S. banned dreadlocks and cornrows • Black girl natural hairstyles considered "out of control" and "inappropriate" 2. Supporting quotes • "My principal wanted to embarrass me, like my natural hair was ugly" • "I don't see what the issue is since my hair wasn't bothering anyone!" 3. Call to action • Discuss cultural importance of Black girls' natural hairstyles • Updating district's dress/hair code • Suggest tips to create school spaces that value Black girls' culture
Closing remarks	Thank audience. Share info on how audience can learn more about the podcast series and contact you.
Outro audio	Beyonce Carter's *Brown Skin Girl*

2012). This collaborative project highlighted the creative decisions made to amplify their collective voices on schools' discriminatory policies on Black girls' natural hairstyles. Steeped in resistance and activism, they used their literacy practices as tools of survival and resistance in a society designed to oppress them (Collins, 2000).

In this activity, I prompted discussion by asking, "What supporting data might provide insight on schools' discriminatory practices on Black girls' natural hairstyles?" Kenya and Jalisa conducted an online search and evaluated websites based on currency, accuracy, authority, objectivity, and relevance. They found multiple instances of Black girls suspended from school due to their natural hairstyles. In one finding, a Black girl named Tianna Parker, age 7, switched schools after being forbidden to wear dreads. In another instance, a Black girl was banned from her senior prom for wearing braids. I asked, "What can we conclude about how schools view Black girls and their bodies?" Jalisa mentioned, "That schools feel entitled to control parts of who we are that are natural to us. Our hair grows out of our heads this way and yet it isn't seen as acceptable!" Kenya mentioned, "Society views dreadlocks, afros, mohawks, cornrows as unacceptable. Society considers them 'untidy,' 'inappropriate,' and 'out of control.'" In a subsequent online search, they found first-person quotes to support their points like: "My principal wanted to embarrass me, like my natural hair was ugly!"

AT THE CENTER OF THIS WORK IS THE NEED TO CREATE SPACES FOR BLACK GIRLS TO ENGAGE IN CRITICAL CONVERSATIONS AS THEY NEGOTIATE THEIR IDENTITIES AS BOTH DIGITAL USERS AND CONTENT CREATORS.

Next, Kenya and Jalisa thought about how school policies promote anti-Blackness. They discussed how they planned to address the discriminatory practices against Black girl's natural hair styles by reviewing their local school district's dress code policy. They highlighted the sections in the policy that were ambiguous, leaving decisions up to the discretion of leadership, and revised them to make it more inclusive for all hairstyles and hair types. Their plan was to finalize the revisions of the policy and address them at the next community school board meeting. Jalisa reiterated how important it is to be part of the school community, "to be seen and heard fully without having to change. What has to change are the policies!"

Then, I discussed the concept of layering audio into their podcast. I mentioned the "power of including media that connects to your topic and your overall message." Kenya wanted a resistance anthem for Black girls, so she suggested singer Solange Knowles' *Don't Touch My Hair*. Jalisa agreed, but suggested that they use the instrumental version of the song as both an intro and the background throughout the podcast. Kenya then suggested that they add an outro song as well and mentioned neo-soul singer Indie Arie's *Black Skin*. Jalisa agreed with the idea of adding an outro, but suggested Beyonce Carter's *Brown Skin Girl*, since it was more current, and their audience of young Black girls would be more familiar with her. While conversing, they drafted each element of their podcast script and expanded their talking points. Over the course of two weeks, they detailed their journal experiences, connected them to their collective experiences, researched the prominent relevant social issue, addressed that social issue by drafting a more inclusive school dress/hair policy, and then drafted a podcast script that centered Black girls by disrupting anti-Black discriminatory practices against Black girls' natural hairstyles.

Conclusion

Black girls out-of-school multimodal writings served as fertile ground to disrupt dominant narratives of who they are and how they see themselves. At the center of this work is the need to create spaces for Black girls to engage in critical conversations as they negotiate their identities as both digital users and content creators. Doing so entailed opportunities to brainstorm and organize their ideas both individually and collectively. For Black girls, to thrive in society is a political act. Black girls engaging in literacy both in print and digitally serve as tools of activism and resistance as they document their journey both through their "rites of passage" (journaling) and "writes of passage" (podcast scriptwriting).

To engage in this work authentically, literacy teachers must acknowledge and address their own biases and stereotypes against Black girls. Black girls must matter to literacy teachers outside of the classroom before they can matter in the classroom. Literacy teachers must shift their mindsets and genuinely view literacy broadly—beyond a skills-based practice and instead as one designed to encourage Black girls to engage in autonomy, agency, and social exploration. Literacy teachers must also view writing as a tool that can be used to support Black girls'

TEACHING TIPS

Greene's article makes visible the ways Black girls create connection between their lives and social issues. With this article, we have a front-row seat to watch their podcast development process. Building on Greene's work with these students, you can also invite students to create a collage that represents their "rites of passage." To begin, ask students to share their collages with a partner and begin to look for similarities and differences in their experiences. As students are engaged in this discussion ask them to identify three to four questions that could anchor a podcast or one-minute video about their rites of passage. Then offer them the option to create a script, record their podcast or video, and share with the community. After they share you can discuss the benefits of engaging in writing and multimodal production as "tools of freedom."

socioemotional needs and to rewrite and author their individual and collective lives in order to center and honor their self-development and self-perception (Greene, 2020; Muhammad, 2015). Literacy teachers must develop instruction that is limitless, without boundaries, and free-flowing in order to realize the potential and possibilities out-of-school writing spaces offer Black girls to honor their digital literacy practices, lived experiences, and counternarratives. Writing must be incorporated into instruction as a tool of freedom and not a tool of constraint.

REFERENCES

Collins, P. H. (2000). *Black feminist thought: Knowledge, consciousness, and the politics of empowerment* (2nd ed.). Routledge.

Ellison, T. (2014). Digital ontologies of self: Two African-American adolescents co-construct and negotiate identities through the Sims 2. *Digital Culture and Education*, 6(4), 334–57.

Greene, D. T. (2016). We need more "us" in schools: Centering Black adolescent girls' literacy and language practices in online school spaces. *The Journal of Negro Education*, 85(3), 274–89.

Greene, D.T. (2020). "Black female teachers are our school parents!!": Academic othermothering depicted in multicultural young adult literature texts. *Journal of Literacy and Language Education*, 16(1).

Haddix, M., & Sealey-Ruiz, Y. (2012). Cultivating digital and popular literacies as empowering and emancipatory acts among urban youth. *Journal of Adolescent & Adult Literacy*, 56(3), 189–92.

Muhammad, G. E. (2015). Searching for full vision: Writing representations of African American adolescent girls. *Research in the Teaching of English*, 49(3), 224–47.

Muhammad, G. E., & Haddix, M. (2016). Centering Black girls' literacies: A review of literature on the multiple ways of knowing of black girls. *English Education*, 48(4), 299.

Muhammad, G. E., & McArthur, S. A. (2015). "Styled by their perceptions": Adolescents girls' interpretations of Black girlhood in the media. *Multicultural Perspectives*, 17, 133–40.

Muhammad, G. E., & Womack, E. (2015). From pen to pin: The multimodality of black girls (re)writing their lives. *Ubiquity: The Journal of Literature, Literacy, and the Arts*, 2(2).

Noble, S. (2018). *Algorithms of oppression: How search engines reinforce racism*. New York University Press.

Price-Dennis, D., Muhmmad, G., Womack, E., McArthur, S., & Haddix, M. (2017). The multiple identities of Black girlhood: A conversation about creating spaces for Black girl voices. *Journal of Language and Literacy Education*, 13(2), 1–18.

Price-Dennis, D. (2016). Developing curriculum to support black girls' literacies in digital spaces. *English Education*, 48(4), 334.

Richardson, E. (2003). *African American literacies*. Routledge.

United States Department of Education (2016). *The state of racial diversity in the educator workforce*. www2.ed.gov/rschstat/eval/highered/racial-diversity/state-racial-diversity-workforce.pdf

MEDIA CITED

Arie, I. (2001). Black skin [Song]. *Acoustic soul* [Album]. Motown Records.

Knowles-Carter, B. (2019). Brown skin girl [Song]. *The lion king: The gift* [Album]. Columbia Records.

Knowles, S. (2016). Don't touch my hair [Song]. *A seat at the table* [Album]. Columbia Records.

DELICIA TIERA GREENE is an assistant professor in the Department of Literacy Teaching and Learning in the School of Education at the University at Albany, SUNY. Her research focuses on Black adolescent girls' literacy and language practices across spheres. Greene's work also focuses on literacy teachers' practices designed to support culturally relevant instruction for Black adolescent girls in urban secondary contexts. Contact the author at dgreene@albany.edu.

This article originally appeared
in *Research in the Teaching of English 55.2*

BROWN GIRLS DREAMING: Adolescent Black Girls' Futuremaking through Multimodal Representations of Race, Gender, and Career Aspirations

JENNIFER D. TURNER &
AUTUMN A. GRIFFIN

Inspired by Jacqueline Woodson's (2014) memoir, this article examines the ways Tamika and Malia, two African American adolescent girls and fraternal twins, act as Brown girl dreamers and articulate their career aspirations through multimodal compositions. Drawing on the psychological literature on youths' career aspirations, theories related to Black Girlhood and Black Girls' Literacies, and case study methodologies, we investigated two key questions: (1) In what ways do two Black adolescent girls represent their career dreams through drawings/sketches created in 2012 and digital dream boards designed in 2018? and (2) Across their 2018 digital career dream boards, what common visual images do two Black adolescent girls curate and interpret to imagine and/or (re)imagine their futures? We conclude with implications for how educators can (re)position Black adolescent girls as multiliterate futuremakers in secondary classrooms and center their career aspirations in English language arts curriculum.

"I WANT TO BE A WRITER." With those six simple words in *Brown Girl Dreaming* (2014), Jacqueline Woodson brought to light a childhood dream that would inspire her for years to come. At the age of 3, Woodson's passion for writing was ignited as she printed the letter J with her older sister's guiding hand. As a young girl, Woodson faced uncertainties and self-doubts about her writing; it was not until she read a library book filled with African American characters that she began to believe that her Black girl ideas, stories, and words were her "brilliance" (Woodson, 2014, p. 246). In *Brown Girl Dreaming*, Woodson envisioned, depicted, and situated herself as a futuremaker—a young Black girl who fought to define and fulfill her dreams of becoming a writer in order to pay homage to her family and resist the erasure of Black girls/women/people in literature. Through *Brown Girl Dreaming*, Woodson provides an opportunity to closely *listen* to the dreams of a young Black girl. In turn, we—two Black women literacy scholars and Jacqueline Woodson fangirls—have become interested in listening to other young Black girls who are dreaming, asking the questions: What types of professional work do young Black girls dream about doing? What career futures do they desire and why? If Woodson articulated and achieved her dreams of becoming a professional writer through literate practices (e.g., reading, writing), how might adolescent Black girls of the twenty-first century use their literacies to author their own professional and personal futures?

Inspired by these questions, we feature the career dreams and future goals articulated by two African American girls and fraternal twin sisters, Tamika and Malia,[1] in this article. Like many youths, Tamika and Malia are engaging with an essential task of adolescence: identifying their future professional goals and life aspirations (Andreassen, 2016; Watson & McMahon, 2005). However, as young Black girls, Tamika and Malia are striving to determine their own career dreams and assert their humanity in a society where "structural racism, sexism, and cultural hegemony . . . powerfully influences the lives and futures of Black females" (Richardson, 2002, p. 676). In seeking to understand and affirm Tamika and Malia as Brown girls dreaming in a broken world (Toliver, 2020), we pose the following research questions:

1. In what ways do two Black adolescent girls represent their career dreams through drawings/sketches created in 2012 and digital dream boards designed in 2018?
2. Across their 2018 digital career dream boards, what common visual images do two Black adolescent girls curate and interpret to imagine and/or (re)imagine their futures?

Theorizing Black Girls' Career Dreams

Career dreams are "an individual's point-in-time expressions of educational and occupational goals" (Andreassen, 2016, p. 16). Psychological research demonstrates that youths' career aspirations develop in early childhood and either change or are solidified throughout adolescence (Andreassen, 2016; Watson & McMahon, 2005). Adolescence is typically the developmental period when "idealistic aspirations are adapted through more realistic expectations of what is actually reachable" (Andreassen, 2016, p. 16) based on youths' identity characteristics (e.g., race, gender), academic experiences, life goals, personal interests, and perceptions of the workplace. While the psychological literature provides a foundational understanding of youths' career dreams as a developmental process, we were dismayed to find that the career aspirations and futuremaking experiences of Black girls are "often generalized with the experiences of Black males and White, Western, middle class girls, which continues to leave Black girls voiceless and their experiences invisible" (Greene, 2016, p. 274). In the few psychological studies where Black girls' career aspirations are examined, their Blackness and femaleness are framed as deficits to be overcome, suggesting that Black girls diminish themselves, their career aspirations, and their overall expectations for life success because society perceives their race and gender as cultural "disadvantages." S. P. Brown (1996) contends that as a result of "the *dual challenges* of race and gender" (emphasis added, p. 90), Black adolescent girls, regardless of socioeconomic status, "tend to set lower occupational goals and predict as well as expect lower occupational success" (p. 91). Relatedly, while narratives of Black women's success in predominantly White and male occupations exist, "there are *even more narratives* of complacency, defeat, and an inability to progress" (emphasis added, Farinde, 2012, p. 332), which may ultimately deter Black girls from pursuing those career fields.

We turned to Black Girlhood theories to conceptualize African American girls' career aspirations in more affirming ways. Rooted in Black Feminist Thought (Collins, 1991; hooks, 1993) and Intersectionality (Crenshaw, 1991), Black Girlhood theories acknowledge that Black girls' and women's experiences are unique based on their raced *and* gendered identities. These inseparable social identities function in tandem, creating intersecting and interlocking oppressions that are multiplicative rather than additive (Collins, 1991; Crenshaw, 1991). While Black girls and women are not a homogenous group, their intersectional epistemologies and experiences illuminate core themes—including the legacy of struggle, self-definition, resistance, political advocacy, and creativity—which profoundly shape their lives and futures (R. N. Brown, 2013; Collins, 1991; Halliday & Brown, 2018; hooks, 1993).

Black Girlhood theories offer a contextualized perspective on how race, gender, and age intersect to profoundly shape Black girls' career aspirations. Given that age is an undertheorized aspect of intersectionality (P. H. Collins, personal communication, October 19, 2018), we examined conceptions of Black girls' youthfulness advanced by Black women literacy scholars (Henry, 1998; Kinloch, 2010; Price-Dennis, Muhammad, Womack, McArthur, & Haddix, 2017) and prominent Black Girlhood theorists (R. N. Brown, 2013; Halliday & Brown, 2018). Moreover, Sealey-Ruiz's (2016) question, "What does it mean to be young, Black, and female in America?" (p. 290) called us to think more deeply about how young Black girls continually define their own futures while simultaneously navigating (mis)representations of Black girl/womanhood. Through a Black Girlhood lens, we theorized career dreams as creative spaces where young Black girls manifest their full humanity by naming and (re)claiming the future life aspirations that *they* desire. More specifically, our study illuminates Malia and Tamika's creative multimodal practices for designing images that express what their dreams for the future have become and are becoming. In doing so, we find it appropriate to deem Malia and Tamika both dreamers *and* visionaries, recognizing the criticality, creativity, and multimodal literacy skills that Black adolescent girls must have to make futures that resist deficit images of Black women and girls.

Black Adolescent Girls as (Career) Dreamers: Futuremaking with Black Girls' Literacies

We assert that Black adolescent girls' creative potential for dreaming and futuremaking is inextricably connected to their Black Girls' Literacies. Black Girls' Literacies are "multiple, tied to identities, historical, collaborative, intellectual, and political/critical "(Muhammad & Haddix, 2016, p. 325), meaning that Black girls affirm their intersectional identities by engaging and enacting varying modes of literacies rooted in the historical, collective, and liberatory literacy practices of their foremothers. Importantly, Black Girls' Literacies function as "ways of knowing and acting and the development of skills, vernacular expressive arts and crafts that help females to advance and protect themselves and their loved ones in society" (Richardson, 2002, p. 680). The protective role that Black Girls' Literacies play for African American girls is crucial, especially as they seek to make or articulate futures that counter controlling images (Collins, 1991) proliferating in schools (and other social institutions). In English classrooms, Black girls are rendered invisible in canonical texts and Eurocentric curricula (Griffin & James, 2018), erased by the silencing of their voices, dreams, knowledge, and textual interpretations (Carter, 2006). Distorted images of Black girls as illiterate, loud, aggressive, and disrespectful permeate English classrooms (Henry, 1998; Kinloch, 2010; Price-Dennis et al., 2017; Sealey-Ruiz, 2016), which ultimately minimize Black girls' literate potential, marginalize their intersectional identities, and perpetuate society's visions of fractured and tragic futures for Black girls and women.

Despite pervasive controlling images in schools and society, Black girls continue to dream about the futures they want to see for themselves. Research demonstrates how Black girls have countered deficit views of their future lives through written literacies, using "their pens to make sense of their identities for their personal development" (Muhammad & Womack, 2015, p. 8) and to determine their own destinies. For example, the urban Black girls in Schultz's (1996) study composed their own futures in journals and senior-year writing projects outlining their career goals (e.g., nursing, cosmetology), their future plans, and their struggles to achieve their visions. More recently, scholars have begun to examine how Black adolescent girls engage *multiliteracies* to imagine their own social futures (New London Group, 1996). Muhammad and Womack (2015) found that Black adolescent girls' multimodal compositions (created using Pinterest or Prezi) challenged stereotypical images of Black girlhood and reaffirmed more optimistic representations of their own life trajectories. Dunn, Neville, and Vellanki (2018) demonstrate how Black teen girls, in collaboration with other youth of Color, (re)imagined possibilities for more socially just futures with/in multimodal texts (e.g., posters/visual images, sculptures) that disrupted the school-to-prison pipeline, racial violence, and high-stakes testing. Along similar lines, 18-year-old Sara, an African American Muslim woman, collaborated with a friend to produce a short documentary that critiqued the religious oppression that Muslims experience in America and imagined hopeful and equitable futures for all (Stornaiuolo & Thomas, 2018). Taken together, these findings suggest a continued need to investigate how Black adolescent girls employ Black Girls' Literacies within multimodal spaces to author their own futures and imagine life possibilities in years to come.

Methods

Our positionalities as Black women literacy scholars have profoundly shaped the main premise of our study—that Black girls' *futures* matter. Thus, we openly shared our own positionalities, as Black women *and* dreamers, with Malia and Tamika. Jennifer shared how her dreams of becoming an endowed university professor and directing an interdisciplinary research center on Black futurity have emanated from her experiences as a professor at a predominantly White university; as a former college access counselor in a large urban secondary school; and as the mother of two Black teenage boys. Autumn, a former secondary English educator and doctoral student at the time, shared her own dreams of becoming a tenured professor at a research university, highlighting her desire to use her scholarship to change classroom approaches to literacy learning to center the needs and interests of Black students. As Black women researchers, we share common interests, cultural beliefs, and racial perspectives that connect us through "collective Black Girl [experiences]" (Greene, 2016, p. 294), yet we also acknowledge that our personal histories, trajectories, and backgrounds vary. Together, we conducted this inquiry by drawing upon a rich panoply of experiences anchored by our professional and personal lives, a shared commitment to conducting humanizing research (Paris, 2011), and our determination to help Black girls articulate and achieve the futures they desire.

Case Study Participants and Data Sources

Our case study participants were Tamika and Malia, fraternal twin sisters who identified as African American girls. Born in 2002, the girls lived in a predominantly African American community with their mother, a faculty member at a predominantly White public university, and their father, a dentist at a local Historically Black College and University (HBCU). As young girls, Tamika and Malia attended a private elementary school, and both girls enjoyed reading, sports, and spending time with friends. As teens, Tamika and Malia were enrolled in a private Catholic co-ed high school serving nearly 900 students. In their freshman year (2017–2018), Tamika and Malia completed college preparatory coursework, including English Literature and Composition, algebra, and physics, and both girls reported positive perceptions of their teachers and classes.

Drawing on case study methodologies (Barone, 2011), we marshaled rich visual and verbal data derived from studies conducted in 2012 and 2018, including (a) the girls' career dream drawings; (b) the girls' digital career dream boards; (c) transcripts from individual interviews with the girls; (d) transcripts from a focus group interview with the girls and the researchers; and (e) researcher field notes. The girls' visual images, created in 2012 and 2018, were especially pertinent for our descriptive case studies of the girls' career aspirations. Tamika and Malia created the 2012 career dream drawings as participants in a qualitative study conducted in a university-sponsored reading program. During a 1-hour "design session" (Turner, 2016) with Jennifer and three other children of color, nine-year-old Tamika and Malia created their career dream drawings and were informally interviewed about their visual images. Jennifer's field notes from the design session indicated that Tamika and Malia were "leaders in the group" who were "energetic, friendly, and helpful—they even insisted on cleaning up the papers, crayons, and markers."

Our case studies also featured the digital career dream boards that Tamika and Malia created during a June 2018 design session. Sitting around a large conference table with a spread of fruit, juices, and bagels, we invited 15-year-old Tamika and Malia to use Padlet, a free digital bulletin-boarding tool, to create a career dream board. We asked that their career dream boards include five to ten images, videos, or songs that represented their career aspirations and imagined professional identities. We remained in the room with the girls; however, we wrote field notes after the session to ensure that they didn't feel as if they were being "watched." We played popular songs by SZA, Kendrick Lamar, Ella Mai, and Drake, and encouraged the girls to eat and talk while they worked. The girls seemed comfortable during the design process, often singing along with the artists as they composed on their iPads, and at times laughing while pointing to images on their screens. Both girls completed their digital dream boards in about 30 minutes.

Additionally, we integrated individual and focus group interview data from the 2018 design session into our case studies. After the girls completed their digital career dream boards, Jennifer interviewed Tamika and Autumn interviewed Malia for 30–40 minutes. The interview protocol probed the girls' interpretations of their 2012 career dream drawings and 2018 digital career dream boards, providing space for the girls to reflect on their career aspirations and to discuss the meanings and memories their work evoked. During the 60-minute focus-group interview, each girl individually created a five-song playlist (including song titles and artists) that represented their future aspirations, and then they discussed their rationales with us. Next, we (the researchers) shared our own career dream boards with the girls, because we wanted our focus group to resemble a gathering around the kitchen table where "Black girls and women . . . come together, to be seen, to be heard, and to just be" (Haddix, McArthur, Muhammad, Price-Dennis, & Sealey-Ruiz, 2016, p. 380). Indeed, rich conversational spaces opened as we talked about our respective career dreams and our pathways toward achieving those goals, with the girls raising questions (e.g., "Why did you choose to join your sorority?") and making connections (e.g., "You saw [the movie] *The Hate U Give*? I want to see that!"). Finally, we discussed Sealey-Ruiz's (2016) question, "What does it mean to be young, Black, and female in America?" (p. 290), in a free-flowing conversation related to intersectionality, identity, and the digital tools that the girls perceived to be important for their futures.

Data Analysis

To understand the girls' career dreams and multimodal futuremaking, we critically analyzed the multimodal images that Tamika and Malia individually composed in 2012 and 2018 (within-case analysis) and examined the common visual images across their 2018 digital career dream boards (cross-case analysis). We adapted Serafini's (2014) framework to develop a coding sheet that we completed for each visual image (see Figure 1).

In Phase 1, we used the coding sheets to analyze each girl's image by carefully recording the characters, objects, and behaviors/actions (perceptual dimension); the relationships among the visual elements rendered through layout, salience, perspective, color, and other design choices (structural dimension); and the ways images visually represented intersectionality (i.e., race, gender, age) and Black Girls' Literacy practices (ideological dimension). We strengthened the trustworthiness of our interpretations by closely attending to the girls' explanations of their visual images derived from the individual and focus-group interview transcripts (Kress & van Leeuwen, 2006).

In Phase 2, we conducted our cross-case analysis. We first identified visual images appearing across the girls' 2018 digital career dream boards, using our completed coding sheets to reexamine *what* was visually represented (e.g., the image itself), *how* it was visually represented (e.g., visual grammar), and *where* it was situated (e.g., intersectional identities and literacies). Next, we determined common themes—such as *music*, *family*, and *language* —from the coding sheets, and looked for extended discourse related to these codes in the interview transcripts. Through these analyses, broader themes related to Black girls' multiliteracies and the (under)representations of Black career women emerged.

	Tamika	Malia
Image		AI NI YA
Perceptual Dimension	This image features a white woman with a young white girl. The white woman is wearing a white uniform and has a clipboard in front of her on a table. The girl has her hand on her forehead and looks upset. The woman's hand is placed gently on the girls' shoulder in what looks like a consoling gesture.	This is an image of a white woman standing in a maroon pant suit. The woman is wearing heels and has her hands in her pockets. The picture seems to be an ad for a clothing company.
Structural Dimension	This image is placed in the center of Tamika's dream board and is also the largest of all the images. She selected it because she thought it represented a child psychologist or counselor working with a child.	This image is placed in the third row to the right. It is the only one on Malia's career board that includes a human character. She selected this image explaining that people take women in pant suits "seriously."
Ideological Dimension	This image is the only one that features two white people on Tamika's dream board. Tamika mentioned that psychology is not a field where she sees many Black people represented and that her Google search did not yield many images of Black psychologists.	This image features a white woman and is the only picture on Malia's dream board that does so. This image is also the only one with a representation of Malia's future career that features a human character.
Participant Interpretation	It was difficult for me to find a Black psychologist…I feel Google says that Black people are usually working at restaurants…and not teaching and doing all of this. Like at my mom's conference that we went to it was a lot of white people…and then some Black people.	So, there's not a lot of women in STEM. That's what I've learned in the past year…So I don't see a lot of African American architects. I've only met one, and for engineers, I've met a few women…

FIGURE 1

Example of critical visual analysis coding sheet

Case Study Findings

The two case studies in this section highlight the career futures that Tamika and Malia composed as young adolescents (9 years old) in 2012 and as teenagers (15 years old) in 2018. We focus on the multimodal futuremaking practices that Tamika and Malia engaged to articulate their professional and personal aspirations while protecting and affirming their intersectional identities, experiences, and future possibilities as Black girls.

Tamika: Mapping Race and Gender in Future Career Spaces

Across her 2012 and 2018 multimodal compositions, Tamika creatively engaged the "politics of spatiality" (Dotson, as cited in Butler, 2018, p. 39) by purposefully mapping her career and personal goals "through the lenses of place, race, gender, and age" (Butler, 2018, p. 39). In 2012, 9-year-old Tamika aspired to be a gymnast (Figure 2).

As Tamika sketched, she chatted about Gabby Douglas, the young African American woman who became Olympic all-around champion that year. Tamika's image featured a gymnastics school as an imagined place that resembled the dance studios she and her sister had

FIGURE 2
Tamika's 2012 career dream drawing

attended since the age of 3. In bringing together prior gymnastics experiences with future visions, Tamika's sketch functioned as a map, designating areas for skills practice and movement that were important to her via multiple design devices (e.g., labels, arrows) and various shapes (e.g., circles, rectangles). As a young Black girl who had attended predominantly Black gymnastics schools, Tamika mapped the social geographies of mobility (e.g., doorways, arrows) and inclusivity (e.g., the welcome sign) that Black students navigated within the physical spaces of the gymnastics school. Relatedly, Tamika reported that she "liked being able to dance on [her current] team" and that she "really liked that kind of interaction" with the other girls. Anchored by these positive dance experiences, Tamika's map outlined the physical and socioemotional contours of a gymnastics school where young Black girls like her would be invited to develop their skills and experience success as future competitive gymnasts.

In 2018, 15-year-old Tamika's multimodal futuremaking shifted from mapping a career site (i.e., the gymnastics school) to charting race, gender, and youthfulness within her professional and personal futures (Figure 3).

Consistent with her 2012 map, Tamika's 2018 map located significance among the eight images representing her future goals and aspirations through salience (e.g., images' positioning and size) and visual devices (e.g., thin black arrows and labels). In the first row, Tamika's arrows directed movement from left to right. The first image depicted a Black ballet teacher working with young girls, including several Black ballerinas, and represented Tamika's dreams of becoming a dance teacher or choreographer. Although Tamika acknowledged that this image was "hard to find," she persisted in finding a Black woman dance teacher because she wanted to include an image that mirrored her own intersectional identities on her map.

FIGURE 3
Tamika's 2018 digital career dream board

Tamika selected images of a musical note and a Grammy award as visual renderings of her musical aspirations: "I want to be a singer after college. . . . I'm gonna try to win a Grammy . . . and . . . put my music out there." Envisioning her music career, Tamika curated a playlist that included inspirational songs connected to Black cultural genres such as contemporary rhythm and blues (R&B), gospel, and hip-hop:

- Best Part (H.E.R. & Daniel Caesar)
- Man in the Mirror (Keke Palmer)
- Tremors (SOHN)
- Bad and Boujee (Migos, featuring Lil Uzi Vert)
- Made to Love (John Legend)
- Take Me to the King (Tamela Mann)

On the second row, Tamika represented the languages she desired to learn via an image of multicolored speech bubbles, explaining, "I wanna learn different languages. I'm learning sign language next year and then I wanna learn Spanish . . . and then some type of African language." Although Tamika didn't specify an African language that she wanted to learn, it was clear that she was charting a future connected with African peoples and communities. In reading this future "map," Tamika then did something unexpected: she skipped the middle image and moved directly to the last image on the row. Using the arrow, Tamika linked the first image (language bubbles) to the third image, which depicted a globe with iconic landmarks on each continent (e.g., the Statue of Liberty, the Eiffel Tower) and airplanes flying in all directions, asserting that "for traveling the world, I'd have to learn a lot of different languages."

The final images on the third row were connected to Tamika's dreams for a marriage and family. The first image of a mansion represented Tamika's desires to have a "big house. . . . And everything I'm not getting as a kid I'm gonna get as an adult . . . like a bathroom and a TV in my room." With a black arrow signifying the image's importance, Tamika related her hopes for a marriage and family through an image of an African American mother, father, son, and daughter:

> I really want to have a family . . . [and] for my family idea, it's gonna be like this, where the husband does the cooking, and . . . goes grocery shopping. And my mom [said], "Have fun with that. I've never heard any husband wanting to go grocery shopping." And I [said], "No, he's gonna do that while I stay home, and if he goes to the grocery store, then I'll cook and make dinner for the kids."

Clearly, this image reflected the ways Tamika hoped to navigate marriage, partnership, and family in the future, mirroring the significance that many Black working women place on issues of work-life balance (A. Brown, 2018).

Finally, the image in the middle of the second row seemed to represent "uncharted territory" for Tamika. Prominently located in the center of the composition, the image depicted a White woman in a white uniform, seated next to a young White girl whose head was resting in her hand. This was the only image in Tamika's multimodal composition that included White people; all the other images depicted Black women, men, and children. When asked about this image, Tamika explained that it represented a "back up" career plan:

> I want to do singing and dance, and my mom [said], "Just make sure you know that singing and dancing are hard, and a lot of people don't make it." And I [thought], "If I don't do singing and dancing, I have to find something else that I like. . . ." At first, my mom wanted me to be a teacher. But I [thought], "Teachers [teach], but they don't get to actually . . . talk to the kids about how they're feeling." So I [said], 'I think I wanna change to a psychologist."

Here, Tamika's words "find something else" signaled how she was navigating this unknown career space, trying to make a way toward another occupation that would fulfill her. On Tamika's map, the middle image represented her exploration of child psychology as a professional site for socioemotional work with youth. Visibly frustrated, Tamika explained that it was "hard to find an image of a Black psychologist" in her online search, so she ultimately selected the image of the White woman and girl to represent this career. In working to digitally locate Black women in varying career fields, traversing unmapped terrain (i.e., child psychology), and excavating sites of passion (e.g., the arts, family, travel), Tamika was charting her own course toward a future that she asserted was "held in my own hand."

Malia: Building Black Girl Confidence for Successful STEM Futures

While the underrepresentation of Black women in science, technology, engineering, and math (STEM) may deter some young Black girls from pursuing science and math careers (Ireland et al., 2018), Malia had been dreaming of a future in STEM since she was 9 years old. In 2012, Malia aspired to be a veterinarian, and in her career dream drawing, she depicted herself smiling widely and standing next to a dog on an examination table (Figure 4). Malia wanted to be a veterinarian because she "loved animals and she wanted to help them when they were sick." At the time, her family had a dog, and she explained that when she "took my dog to the vet, it was pretty cool to see what they did."

Malia's drawing was simple but bold; the deeply saturated color of the blue marker, the character's direct gaze, and the thick, solid lines demand viewers' attention. Noting that blue was her favorite color, Malia carefully made several overlapping lines as strands of hair, bringing attention to her feminine identity. Though she never said if her dog's veterinarian was Black or female, Malia seemed to know that veterinary medicine was the kind of work she wanted to do; perhaps some of this confidence emanated from the books Malia reported reading, because she stated, "I like reading about animals and I know a lot about how animals grow and how to take care of them." This type of confidence in and affiliation with STEM work (e.g., veterinary medicine) nurtures Black girls' STEM identity development (Ireland et al., 2018).

Similarly, Malia's 2018 career dream board, entitled "Visions of the Future," communicated strength, stability, and vibrancy in the architectural field (Figure 5).

Malia stated that she didn't "know a lot of people [who] want to be architects; a lot of my friends want to be doctors and stuff. So I think I want to be different from everybody else. I want people to look at me and [say], 'Wow, she actually did that!'" Anchored

FIGURE 4

Malia's 2012 career dream drawing. Previously published in "Career Dream Drawings: Children's Visions of Professions in Future Workplaces," by J. D. Turner, 2016, Language Arts, 93, pp. 174. Copyright 2016 by the National Council of Teachers of English. Reprinted with permission.

FIGURE 5

Malia's 2018 career dream board

by this confidence, Malia designed her future world, including representations of spiritual, physical, mental, and familial domains. The background of her board was a city skyline in grayscale, suggesting that as an architect she had "built" her career dreams on an urban landscape. Malia composed her career dream board from 12 digital images in the shape of a diamond; she purposefully placed the images in chronological order and used her architectural imagination to build a vision for her future.

At the top, Malia placed an image of a large church with a tall cross that stood proudly atop the building. "This isn't *my* church," Malia explained, "but this is *a* church because I think that God is above everything, and we should put God first." For Malia, representing her faith as the starting point of her career dreams was vital. Grounded in Black spiritual practices, Malia included the image as a representation of how she interpreted the importance of her faith in her life, as it stood "above everything."

Below the image of the church, Malia included a colorful eighth note, explaining, that "music is a big part in . . . a lot of people's lives because it gets you through things and it's actually fun to listen to." Malia's playlist included:

- Encourage Yourself (Donald Lawrence)
- Jump (Cynthia Erivo)
- In the Middle (Isaac Carree)
- Never Needed No Help (Lil Baby)
- Teenage Fever (Drake)
- Help Us to Love (Tori Kelly)

Given Malia's strong spirituality, it is not surprising that three of the six songs on her playlist were gospel, and one other was heavily influenced by gospel music (e.g., a gospel chorus). Malia's playlist also included genres grounded in Black musical traditions, such as hip-hop and contemporary R&B.

To the right of the music note, Malia represented her love of soccer through an image of a soccer stadium; although there was no one on the field, the stadium seats appeared to be filled and the lights were shining brightly. Malia not only played soccer as a high school student, but she also aspired to play in college: "It's not a potential career, but I want to have it on the side [in college] and while I am an architect, I want to be able to play soccer." For Malia, soccer was a recreational activity that would allow her a physical and mental release from her job.

Malia then explained how the next visual, a clip-art image of a college, represented both others' postsecondary aspirations for her *and* her own collegiate dreams:

> Well, my mom wants me to go to [public university] because I can go there for free, but she said if I get a scholarship somewhere else, then I could go. So I am going to work really hard because I don't know if I want to go to [public university].

Although this opportunity existed for Malia, she recognized that it might not be the best choice for *her*. When asked about her dream school, Malia responded, "At first it was Duke. . . . Then it was Spelman. But now I am looking at University of Pennsylvania and schools in upper Massachusetts, like Amherst College, even though those are far away and those are small." Like other Black high school girls, Malia was considering a range of predominantly White institutions and a prestigious all-women's HBCU in her college search process. Race-related variables, such as a strong cultural affiliation and the opportunity for active racial self-development (Van Camp, Barden, Sloane, & Clarke, 2009) might become more integral to her college decision-making processes in the next few years.

Moving down the board, Malia described several images representing her architectural aspirations, asserting that she had intentionally designed these images to be read "in order." Based on her explanation, Malia planned to travel to Germany and Russia because she was interested in learning new languages: "This [image] is Germany because I want to learn German. I like that language. I don't know any German, I just want to learn German. And that [image] is Russia because I want to study abroad in Russia." Perhaps Malia envisioned traveling and learning about German and Russian architecture, because the buildings in the images had unique architectural styles (e.g., exceptionally tall buildings with rounded and colorful tops). To describe the next image, a White woman in a magenta pantsuit and high heels, Malia pointed to the pantsuit and exclaimed, "And that's a pantsuit [and] I really like that pantsuit and then that [image of the house] is supposed to represent me as an architect." While glancing at the White woman in the suit, Malia explained that she was aware there were very few Black women architects, but that she planned to advocate for other Black women once she became an architect. With the confidence that she could open doors for other Black women architects, Malia imagined herself as an architect, dressing for the job by wearing a pantsuit because she believed that people take women in pantsuits "seriously." Although Malia mentioned Hillary Clinton as a woman who wore pantsuits and was taken seriously, she quickly added, "but I don't know if I would really look up to her." Further, Malia was sure to clarify that it was the image of the house—a modern-style dwelling with large windows and a room jutting out from the rest of the house—and not the image of the White woman, that represented her future career. Thus, the pantsuit on Malia's board did not represent a desire to be a White woman; rather, Malia wanted to feel powerful in her pantsuit as a Black woman architect focused on the work of designing beautiful modern homes. Collectively, these images depicted Malia's interest in design, her future career as an architect, and her current positionality as a Black girl dreamer and visionary.

The next three images represented Malia's family and personal life outside of her architectural career. An image of two wedding bands above the word "marriage" reflected the kind of partnership she envisioned. An image of nine dogs reflected the love of animals she had as a young girl, and as she explained that she wanted dogs "a lot" in her future. The next image, a young Black girl with an afro puff hairstyle, represented the children that Malia wanted to have "after the dogs." We were especially intrigued by the image of this young girl, and by the notion that Malia didn't *just* see children in her family; she envisioned a young Black girl with natural hair. Her future child seemed to be a reflection of Malia's younger self and represented her own intersectional identities.

The final row of Malia's career dream board included a single image: an iceberg. Above the water, the word "success" was written; terms like "hard work," "late nights," "rejections," and "discipline" floated beneath the waterline. Malia understood that as a Black girl, she would have to work twice as hard to achieve her dreams. When she described her board at the end of the interview, she pointed to the images and noted, "This is success because that's my life planned out." Even in adolescence, Malia grasped the complexity of success and the often invisible or unnoticed labor it takes for Black women to create the beautiful ice sculpture on the surface.

Cross-Case Findings

In this section, we present findings from our cross-case analysis of Tamika's and Malia's 2018 multimodal compositions (see Figures 3 and 5). Specifically, we examine the girls' visual images related to two key themes: Black Girls' multiliteracies and (under)representations of Black career women.

Illuminating Black Girls' Multiliteracies for Future Success

Disrupting the illiterate futures projected onto Black girls in American society, both Tamika and Malia articulated the need for more opportunities to engage multiliteracies—in the form of professional, aspirational auditory (i.e., music), and African American Girls' Life Literacies—that would protect and advance (Richardson, 2002) their own future interests, goals, and aspirations.

Professional Literacies. Though Tamika and Malia had different career aspirations, the images they curated evoked shared understandings of professional literacies. In particular, the girls articulated the need for a shared language *of* work (i.e. dance, architecture) and a shared language *needed for* work (i.e., communicative language, Spanish) within their respective professions. For instance, in thinking of her future as a dance teacher, Tamika explained,

> For dancing, I would need to know . . . the names of the positions, and I would actually study the dance. But then, I just have to push myself more, and push my mom . . . to put me in dance places that actually make [dancers] do splits for like 15 minutes, and make us do leg lifts for 20 minutes. That type of place [where we] dance for three days a week [and] four hours of dance each day, because I feel that's what I would need to do.

Tamika understood that her future lay not solely in her raw talent, but in her ability to deeply understand the literacies in her field of interest; she knew that dancers have a shared language and understanding of how the body moves, and that in order to exist in that world, she must have that same understanding. Mirroring her sister's representation of the "success" iceberg, Tamika explicitly articulated the deep, often unacknowledged level of commitment it takes to be a successful professional dancer through a detailed description of the rigor and intensity of the classes/training.

Similarly, Malia explained that she would need to have "good writing skills" and "read blueprints" as an architect. When asked if understanding blueprints is a type of reading, Malia asserted, "Yeah, I guess blueprints could be like a type of language because you have to know what symbols represent and stuff. And . . . you have to know . . . what tools to use and measurements for architecture, too." Like Tamika, Malia acknowledged that she would need proficiency with languages related to architectural work (e.g., measuring, designing). Similar to other Black girls defining their career dreams (Griffin, 2020; Turner, 2020), both Malia and Tamika had already begun to articulate the critical role that professional discourses (e.g., career-oriented vocabulary, skills, and knowledge) would play in achieving future career success.

Furthermore, both girls expressed interest in learning another language as a means to successful work in international contexts through images on their digital career boards. Featuring images of foreign countries on her dream board, Malia explained how multilingualism would be beneficial to her as a future architect: "Well, if someone doesn't speak English and speaks Spanish, I'll be able to understand them and talk to them." Likewise, Tamika included an image of multicolored speech bubbles with "hello" in different languages on her dream board, explaining that this visual represented her desire to learn a variety of languages, including "sign language . . . Spanish, and some type of African language." Tamika further elaborated that as a dancer, she would have to travel the world and "learn . . . a lot of different languages to do that." Like other Black adolescent girls who have learned to speak multiple languages as a way to open doors for their futures (Griffin, 2020), Tamika and Malia realized that every "human encounter with another [is] a moment of response to the person in front of me on his or her terms, rather than based on my own comfort, convenience, or desires" (Case, 2015, p. 366). That is, Tamika and Malia employed their critical Black Girls' Literacies (Muhammad & Haddix, 2016) to question the power dynamics involved in traveling; rather than attempting to enact linguistic privilege as English-speaking Americans, Tamika and Malia acknowledged that they would be visitors in other countries, and they desired to use the communicative practices of the local people. Notably, both girls understood how language could function as a conduit to help them engage in business matters as they traveled for work.

Aspirational Auditory Literacies. In representing music using similar images (e.g., musical notes, a Grammy award) across their digital dream boards, Tamika and Malia enacted *aspirational auditory literacies*, or the intrinsic ability to select music that motivates or inspires aspirational achievement. Black women and girls engage music literacies for multiple purposes, including identity development (Gaunt, 2006) and political and personal empowerment (Halliday & Brown, 2018). In this case, Tamika and Malia carefully selected genres of music that reflected the complex intersectionalities salient to their future-making, including religious identities (e.g., Black gospel/spirituality), Black youth culture (e.g., hip-hop), and racial identities (e.g., R&B, hip-hop, gospel), which inspired and motivated them to pursue their career futures.

In her explanation of the songs she chose, Malia attended to the *content* of the songs. Importantly, Malia noted that several of the songs were favorites because they related to "taking risks," and she connected that idea to her own career aspirations: "I think if I were to be an architect, I'd be taking risks because there's not a lot of women in those fields." Malia selected "Encourage Yourself " and "Jump" because "I think everybody should encourage everybody and people should encourage others to do stuff." Similarly, Tamika's playlist was filled with songs that nurtured her artistic aspirations. She chose "Best Part" and "Man in the Mirror," two songs recorded with or by young Black female vocalists, because "I don't know what the word is, but when I sing these songs, they have the best vocals. It just sounds the best when I sing these songs." Contemplating her dance aspirations, Tamika continued, "'Made to Love' is a great song to dance to. . . . I thought at first it was instrumental, but there were words to it. . . . And then I like 'Bad and Boujee' because it's a hip-hop song and anyone dances to that." Importantly, Tamika selected songs that reflected her desires to sing and dance as a Black female artist—future careers that others had told her would be difficult to attain—and served as motivation to persist toward those goals.

African American Girls' Life Literacies. Lastly, Tamika and Malia included representations of African American Girls' Life Literacies on their dream boards.

We define *African American Girls' Life Literacies* as those non-scholastic, intersectional literacies that help African American girls to navigate the world in their Black female bodies (Richardson, 2002).

First, both girls included images related to future family goals on their dream boards (e.g., wedding rings, a young African American girl, an African American family). Envisioning her future family, Tamika explained, "I think, for my family idea . . . the husband does the cooking, and . . . goes grocery shopping." Clearly, she imagined a future where she would share responsibility with her partner, allowing her to pursue her career goals. Although Malia did not elaborate upon her hopes for a family, her images suggest that she did indeed hope to someday have a partner and raise a child. Despite literature suggesting that some Black girls lower their aspirations to balance work and family (S. P. Brown, 1996), Tamika and Malia imagined fulfilling family lives that would enable rather than constrain their career success.

The girls also explored personal and professional passions as integral aspects of their futures. For instance, Malia asserted that she intended to play soccer in her free time:

> It's not a potential career, but I want to have it on the side. . . . While I am an architect, I want to be able to play soccer [in] an adult league. I don't want to go professional because it's going to take up all my time.

Although soccer was not a career option, Malia was adamant about being able to play in her "free time." She realized what so many adults have forgotten: how we spend our free time is just as important to our quality of life as the careers we choose to pursue. Similarly, Tamika's desire to pursue artistic careers, rather than a more pragmatic career in child psychology, demonstrated that she believed her future work should incorporate both passion *and* necessity. Malia's and Tamika's ability to envision futures where they would make deliberate choices about how to spend their time resonates with the sentiments found in *Sisters of the Yam* (hooks, 1993), which details the ways Black women's work can and should allow us to "maintain a spirit of emotional well-being" by doing work that "makes life sweet" (p. 32). Like hooks (1993), Tamika and Malia understood that in order to live as Black women in "right livelihood" (p. 32), they must devote themselves to work they enjoyed and felt called to do.

Critiquing (Under)representations of Black Career Women

Across their digital dream boards, Tamika and Malia included images of professional women (e.g., the White woman working with the young girl; the White woman in a pantsuit; the Black dance teacher) that evoked thoughtful critiques about the underrepresentation of Black career women. Frustrated by the limited representations of Black women in STEM, Malia asserted:

> So, there's not a lot of women in STEM. That's what I've learned in the past year. . . . [And] I don't see a lot of African American architects, I've only met one. For engineers, I've met a few women, and people are amazed. . . . It's like, "You're actually an engineer, you actually make cars and stuff?" So, I was like, "Okay, you can do this," and as long as I focus and don't let other people's opinions get to me, then I think I could do it.

As a Black adolescent girl, Malia's comments highlighted her awareness of her own intersectional identities and revealed how she imagined negotiating (1) the lack of representation in the architecture profession, and (2) the probability of challenges and barriers to future professional success. Malia recognized that as a Black woman architect, she would be a "hidden figure" (Ireland et al., 2018, p. 227) in a field that privileges Whiteness and maleness. Through her words and images, Malia envisioned herself embodying the personal attributes (e.g., self-confidence, self-efficacy) that are critical to the success of Black women in STEM careers (Ireland et al., 2018).

In addition, Malia clearly anticipated future microaggressions, as her comments illustrated the disbelief she might encounter from people shocked that she was a successful Black woman architect. However, Malia decided to decenter "other people's opinions" and reimagine how the architecture profession might look if she served as a trailblazer for future Black women architects. When asked how she hoped to change representations of Black women in architecture, Malia replied,

> Well, I want to open it up. I want to encourage people, like young girls, to do it. I want to make my coworkers . . . know and realize that there's not a lot of people like me in that field and they need to make a change. I want to open their eyes to it because they might be in denial or they might not realize it.

Malia's critique of underrepresentation in the architecture profession transcended mere acknowledgement of the problem; she sought to be a part of the solution, imagining a future where she would use her status to "open up" the field and make it more inclusive and accessible to other Black women architects. In placing the responsibility for change squarely upon those responsible for upholding white supremacist patriarchy, Malia's digital career board redesigned the architecture profession in ways that made visible (Ireland et al., 2018) the contributions and success of Black women.

Relatedly, Tamika critiqued the underrepresentation of Black career women in digital spaces. She explained,

> It was hard finding a Black dancer [on Google]. I was like, "Are you serious?!" Because there's a lot of Black dancers out there. There's Debbie Allen who teaches dance, and there's Misty Copeland. There's a lot of Black dance figures out there. And I was like, "You guys should update Google for all these Black dancers."

Unfortunately, Tamika's critique is quite accurate. A quick Google search for images with the key term "dancers" produced the array of images represented in Figure 6, which renders Black dancers nearly invisible within the digisphere; the prominent Black dancers whom Tamika mentioned were not even yielded as results in the search.

Tamika's critique strongly resonates with Noble's (2018) book, *Algorithms of Oppression: How Search Engines Reinforce Racism*, which explains that Google's algorithms reflect the racialized and gendered biases of the programmers rather than providing a level playing field for all ideas, values, and identities. Thus, Tamika's assertion correctly places the responsibility for more inclusive representations of Black career women (i.e., professional dancers) on the programmers.

Notably, Tamika's critique of the lack of representation of Black career women in the digital realm also applied to the field of child psychology. After acknowledging that it was "hard to find an image of a Black psychologist on Google," Tamika explained,

> For psychology, I see how that happens because a lot of White people get all the big jobs. . . . And I feel like Google says, or people say, that Black people are usually working at restaurants and not teaching and doing all of this [waves her hand, perhaps indicating "work" in academia]. Like at my mom's [professional] conference that we went to, it was a *lot* of White people . . . and then some Black people.

Tamika's critique acknowledged the way mainstream media reinscribes white supremacist notions of anti-Blackness (Collins, 1991). She recognized that what "Google says" is merely a reflection of the inequities reproduced in many professional industries: "White people get all the big jobs," like those in psychology, while Black people are paid less, offered fewer opportunities for advancement, and may be relegated to supportive roles (e.g., service sector) rather than directive roles (e.g., executive positions) in the workplace (Noel, Pinder, Stewart, & Wright, 2019). Tamika identified the racist algorithms of major search engines like Google and took the observation a step further by pointing out how

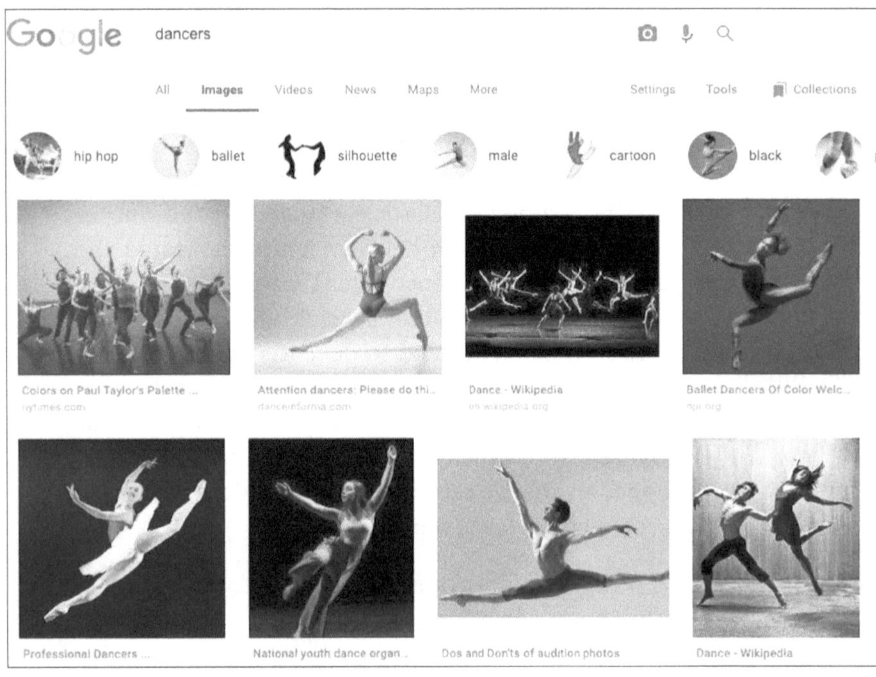

FIGURE 6
Screenshot of a search for "dancers" on Google

they affect our everyday lives. Given the racist algorithmic codes of the internet (Noble, 2018), it is quite possible that the girls were unable to find visual representations of their future selves as Black professional women that were satisfactory for inclusion, rendering their career dreams invisible to Google, a multimillion-dollar corporation cofounded by White men.

Call to Action

In light of research that has shown how Black girls are marginalized within traditional literacy spaces (Kinloch, 2010; Price-Dennis et al., 2017; Sealey-Ruiz, 2016), and because Malia's and Tamika's visions for their futures help us to see the liberatory possibilities available to Black girls when we acknowledge and engage their dreams, we see this study as a call to action. Specifically, we call on English teachers to move beyond traditional curriculum that erases and silences Black girls, and to reimagine literacy pedagogies by (1) seeing Black girls as learners *and* visionaries; and (2) centering Black girls' dreams and aspirations in the classroom.

To begin, Black girls, including Tamika and Malia, participate in literacy in ways that are tied to their racialized, gendered, and cultural identities. Black Girls' Literacies expand beyond the confines of the page and include such ways of knowing as dance, music, social media, and play—as exhibited by Tamika's and Malia's dreams for their futures. For teachers to acknowledge all the ways Black girls learn and communicate information, they must first come to understand these varied forms of literacy that exist outside of hegemonic narratives of who is literate and what constitutes literacy. To do so requires eliciting responses from Black girls about what they dream for their futures and what they desire to learn. Teachers can replicate the activities we implemented with Tamika and Malia, setting up a time for students to create multimodal representations and/or playlists to learn about their career interests and future goals. Then, using students' responses as a springboard, teachers can create a curriculum that prepares students for life beyond the walls of the school (Griffin & James, 2018). Enacting a similar model, Griffin (2020) co-created a digital literacy curriculum with nine adolescent Black girls. Together, they explored various aspects of their futures as Black women, including communication, healthy relationships with themselves and others, financial and civic literacy, future planning, and their imagined careers (e.g., photographer, beauty salon owner, lawyer, judge), while learning with, from, and about Black women and girls.

Likewise, we draw on the work of scholars who suggest teachers leverage Black girls' aspirational auditory literacies to critically analyze required texts and to decenter Eurocentric notions of literacy (Johnson, Jackson, Stovall, & Baszile, 2017). For instance, teachers could invite students to create playlists that mirror salient themes in classroom texts, which would allow Black girls to draw from their own musical interests and knowledge bases, while simultaneously thinking deeply and critically about the themes of a text. To be clear, we are not suggesting that teachers carelessly throw rap, hip-hop, or R&B songs into their curriculum, but rather that they work *alongside* Black girls to purposefully incorporate music in ways that humanize English curricula and classroom spaces. By shifting from curriculum transformation (e.g., choosing more "culturally diverse" books) toward curriculum co-creation, English teachers invite Black girls from the

TEACHING TIPS

Turner and Griffin investigate the dreams and aspirations of Black girls to better understand the place that future-making holds in their lives. To expand on the ideas shared in their article, you can invite your students to create a visual representation of the following questions:

- ***How does school support your career dreams and aspirations?***
- ***How does school get in the way of your career dreams and aspirations?***
- ***What is one practice in school that you would remove—or advocate for—to support the future you imagine for yourself?***

Curate a gallery walk for your students, using the visuals they create, and then ask them to use Post-it notes to record questions and comments for two to three visuals.

margins to the center, rendering both their present *and* future lives visible in schools.

Woodson's *Brown Girl Dreaming* reminds us that the dual oppressions of racism and sexism require Black girls to constantly live in multiple temporalities, not only remembering their pasts, but remaining present, and considering their futures. As they grow and shape their future careers, Malia, Tamika, and other Black girls navigate the tensions between enacting agency and resisting systemic oppression. Resisting the invisibility of Black girls in varying career fields (e.g., STEM fields, child psychology, dance), Malia and Tamika designed multimodal compositions where they acknowledged the fraught, sexist, and racist work history of Black women, (re) claimed their professional hopes and desires for the future, and sketched expansive life trajectories as they envisioned more equitable professional worlds for Black career women.

Given the ways adolescent Black girls must navigate these tensions as they progress through high school and toward their future careers, educators who work within and act as gatekeepers to anti-Black, patriarchal institutions have a responsibility to serve as agents of change. In doing so, educators must consider what it means to act as co-conspirators (Love, 2019) that assist Black girls in obtaining access to careers from which they might otherwise be barred. English educators, in particular, can help Black girls in the process of envisioning themselves in their futures, perhaps by assigning texts such as *Brown Girl Dreaming* and other memoirs by Black girls and women, to inspire new possibilities and worlds. Tamika and Malia, along with so many other Black adolescent girls, are making futures at a time when they are just becoming aware of how their intersectional identities will shape their professional careers and personal lives. As English educators and researchers, we must do all we can to support Black girls as they work toward the futures they have imagined for themselves.

NOTE

1. All names of people and places have been replaced with pseudonyms throughout this article.

ACKNOWLEDGMENTS

We would like to thank the editors, the reviewers, and Dr. Rossina Zamora Liu for their helpful feedback on earlier versions of this article. We are especially grateful to Tamika and Malia for sharing their dreams with us.

REFERENCES

Andreassen, I. H. (2016). Career aspirations and self-knowledge during adolescence. *Journal Plus Education*, 16(2), 15–23.

Barone, D. (2011). Case study research. In N. K. Duke & M. H. Mallette (Eds.), *Literacy research methodologies* (2nd ed., pp. 7–27). Guilford Press.

Brown, A. (2018, October 11). How some Black female professionals achieve the elusive work-life balance. *The Network Journal*. Retrieved from https://tnj.com/how-some-black-female-professionals-achieve-the-elusive-work-life-balance/

Brown, R. N. (2013). *Hear our truths: The create potential of Black girlhood*. University of Illinois Press.

Brown, S. P. (1996). Black female adolescents' career aspirations and expectations: Rising to the challenge of the American occupational structure. *The Western Journal of Black Studies*, 20 (2), 89–95.

Butler, T. (2018). Black girl cartography: Black girlhood and place-making in education research. *Review of Research in Education*, 42, 28–45.

Carter, S. P. (2006). "She would've still made that face expression": The use of multiple literacies by two African American young women. *Theory Into Practice*, 45, 352–358.

Case, A. (2015). Beyond the language barrier: Opening spaces for ELL/non-ELL interaction. *Research in the Teaching of English*, 49, 361–382.

Collins, P. H. (1991). *Black feminist thought: Knowledge, consciousness, and the politics of empowerment*. Routledge.

Crenshaw, K. (1991). Mapping the margins: Intersectionality, identity politics, and violence against women of color. *Stanford Law Review*, 43, 1241–1241.

Dunn, A. H., Neville, M. L., & Vellanki, V. (2018). #UrbanAndMakingIt: Urban youth's visual counternarratives of being #More ThanAStereotype. *Urban Education* . Advance online publication. Retrieved from https://journals.sagepub.com /home/uex

Farinde, A. A. (2012). The other gender: An examination of African American female students' career aspirations. *Journal of Modern Education Review*, 2(5), 330–342.

Gaunt, K. D. (2006). *The games Black girls play: Learning the ropes from double-dutch to hip-hop*. New York University Press.

Greene, D. T. (2016). "We need more 'US' in schools!" Centering Black adolescent girls' literacy and language practices in online school spaces. *The Journal of Negro Education*, 85, 274–289.

Griffin, A. A. (2020). *Finding love in a hopeless place: Black girls' twenty-first century self-love literacies* (Doctoral dissertation, University of Maryland–College Park). Retrieved from ProQuest Dissertations and Theses Database. (UMI No. 20700)

Griffin, A., & James, A. (2018). Humanities curricula as White property: Toward a reclamation of Black creative thought in social studies & literary curricula. *Multicultural Education*, 25(3/4), 10–17.

Haddix, M., McArthur, S. A., Muhammad, G. E., Price-Dennis, D., & Sealey-Ruiz, Y. (2016). At the kitchen table: Black women English educators speaking our truths. *English Education*, 48(4), 380–395.

Halliday, A. S., & Brown, N. E. (2018). The power of Black Girl Magic anthems: Nicki Minaj, Beyoncé, and "Feeling Myself" as political empowerment. *Souls*, 20, 222–238.

Henry, A. (1998). "Speaking up" and "speaking out": Examining "voice" in a reading/writing program with adolescent African Caribbean girls. *Journal of Literacy Research*, 30, 233–252.

hooks, b. (1993). *Sisters of the yam: Black women and self-recovery* (3rd ed.). Routledge.

Ireland, D. T., Freeman, K. E., Winston-Proctor, C. E., Delaine, K. D., Lowe, M., & Woodson, K. M. (2018). (Un)hidden figures: A synthesis of research examining the intersectional experience of Black women and girls in STEM. *Review of Research in Education*, 42, 226–254.

Johnson, L., Jackson, J., Stovall, D., & Baszile, D. (2017). "Loving Blackness to death": (Re)imagining ELA classrooms in a time of racial chaos. *English Journal*, 106(4), 60–66.

Kinloch, V. (2010). *Harlem on our minds: Place, race, and the literacies of urban youth* . Teachers College Press.

Kress, G., & van Leeuwen, T. (2006). *Reading images: The grammar of visual design* (2nd ed.). Routledge.

Love, B. (2019). *We want to do more than survive: Abolitionist teaching and the pursuit of educational freedom*. Beacon Press.

Muhammad, G. E., & Haddix, M. (2016). Centering Black girls' literacies: A review of literature on the multiple ways of knowing Black girls. *English Education*, 48, 299–336.

Muhammad, G. E., & Womack, E. (2015). From pen to pin: The multimodality of Black girls (re)writing their lives. *Ubiquity: The Journal of Literature, Literacy, and the Arts, Research Strand*, 2 (2), 6–45.

New London Group. (1996). A pedagogy of multiliteracies: Designing social futures. *Harvard Educational Review*, 66, 60–92.

Noble, S. U. (2018). *Algorithms of oppression: How search engines reinforce racism*. New York University Press.

Noel, N. Pinder, D., Stewart, S., & Wright, J. (2019, August). *The economic impact of closing the racial wealth gap*. Washington, DC: McKinsey & Company.

Paris, D. (2011). "A friend who understands fully": Notes on humanizing research in a multiethnic youth community. *International Journal of Qualitative Studies in Education*, 24, 137–149.

Price-Dennis, D., Muhammad, G. E., Womack, E., McArthur, S. E., & Haddix, M. (2017). The multiple identities and literacies of Black girlhood: A conversation about creating spaces for Black girls' voices. *Journal of Language and Literacy Education*, 13 (2), 1–18.

Richardson, E. (2002). "To protect and to serve": African American female literacies. *College Composition and Communication*, 53, 675–704.

Schultz, K. (1996). Between work and school: The literacies of urban adolescent females. *Anthropology & Education Quarterly*, 27, 517–544.

Sealey-Ruiz, Y. (2016). Why Black girls' literacies matter: New literacies for a new era. *English Education*, 48, 290–298.

Serafini, F. (2014). *Reading the visual: An introduction to teaching multimodal literacy*. New York: Teachers College Press.

Stornaiuolo, A., & Thomas, E. E. (2018). Restorying as political action: Authoring resistance through youth media arts. *Learning, Media and Technology*, 43, 345–358.

Toliver, S. R. (2020, April 21). *When you're dreaming in a broken world: Speculative fiction in a traditional field*. Keynote speech presented at the Speculative Education Colloquium.

Turner, J. D. (2016). Career dream drawings: Children's visions of professional identities, tools, and literacies on future workscapes. *Language Arts*, 93, 168–184.

Turner, J. D. (2020). Freedom to aspire: Black children's career dreams, perceived aspirational supports, and Africentric values. *Race, Ethnicity, and Education*. Advance online publication. Retrieved from https://www.tandfonline.com/toc/cree20/current

Van Camp, D., Barden, J., Sloane, L. R., & Clarke, R. P. (2009). Choosing an HBCU: An opportunity to pursue racial self-development. *The Journal of Negro Education*, 78, 457–468.

Watson, M., & McMahon, M. (2005). Children's career development: A research review from a learning perspective. *Journal of Vocational Behavior*, 67, 119–132.

Woodson, J. (2014). *Brown girl dreaming*. New York: Penguin Books.

JENNIFER TURNER is an associate professor in reading education at the University of Maryland.

AUTUMN A. GRIFFIN is a postdoctoral research fellow in the Graduate School of Education at the University of Pennsylvania.

This article originally appeared
in *Research in the Teaching of English* 55.3

"MY COLOR OF MY NAME": Composing Critical Self-Celebration with Girls of Color through a Feminist of Color Writing Pedagogy

This article will explore what I have conceptualized as critical celebration within an afterschool writing club for and with Girls of Color (GOC). Using a feminist of color theoretical framework and building upon existing literature about GOC and their writing practices, I will define critical celebration. I will then describe the ways the feminist of color writing pedagogy engaged in this group made space for critical celebration of and by GOC, thereby offering important implications for justice-oriented literacy education, not only for GOC, but for all students.

GRACE D. PLAYER

Introduction

This article is written in critical celebration of a group of Black and Asian American middle school girls who named themselves "The Unnormal Sisterhood." The Unnormal Sisterhood was a collective of seven Girls of Color (GOC) who met after school to write and read multimodal texts, talk, sing, and dance, while centering solidarity, their hopes, and their desires. This space was created for and with GOC facing intersecting forces of racism, sexism, classism, and other forms of oppressions.

The Unnormal Sisterhood became a place where GOC like 13-year-old Seraphina could proudly proclaim among their sisters, "I'm awesome." In a concise description of herself, Seraphina once stated, "I'm an awesome 13-year-old from Philadelphia. Girl. African American. Yeah, that's about it." With these words, she put forth her age, her city, her gender, her race, and her awesomeness as her primary descriptors, demonstrating the prioritization of her self-appreciation and her intersectional identity. This was the type of confidence, the celebration of self, that I wanted to erupt in The Unnormal Sisterhood. It is not that Seraphina's self-love was a product of The Unnormal Sisterhood—she came with it from the start. However, The Unnormal Sisterhood was a place where this GOC self-love was put to good use, where we attempted to eliminate the often societally imposed shame of loving oneself, of shouting out praise for one's own beauty, brilliance, and awesomeness, especially when you are female and of color. Importantly, it was also a place where, when self-love wavered or struggled to make itself visible, we could work toward it, critically delving into the ways the girls' worlds too often made self-love difficult.

This article will explore critical celebration within The Unnormal Sisterhood, which was the focus of a practitioner research study investigating GOC and their literacies. Building with the existing literature on GOC literacies, I will define *critical celebration* using a feminist of color theoretical framework. Using this definition, I will then describe the ways the pedagogy of The Unnormal Sisterhood made space for critical celebration of and by GOC, thereby offering implications for more justice-oriented literacy education for GOC. Cumulatively, this article argues for the necessity of curriculum and spaces in which GOC write for self-care and care of one another. This exploration of The Unnormal Sisterhood highlights literacy pedagogy that simultaneously centers the identity and experience of GOC while opening opportunity for critical exploration of their worlds and the ideologies that percolate within those worlds. The kind of sustained and ever-deepening work described here—work that is joyous and that requires real critical engagement—suggests that pedagogies that acknowledge the beauty, complexity, labor, and potentiality of GOC hold important possibilities for the envisioning of and creation of pathways toward collective freedom.

Literature Review

This piece stands shoulder-to-shoulder with, and in gratitude to, the work of other Women of Color (WOC) scholars researching the literacies of GOC and WOC. Though WOC have long theorized the revolutionary, healing, connective importance of writing for WOC (Anzaldúa, 1983; Bambara, 1980; Christian, 1988), only in recent years has empirical work on GOC literacies and writing, specifically, emerged more substantially. This is research that builds on WOC theories of writing, as well as the foundations laid by scholars like Fordham (1993), Powers-Carter (2006), and Henry (1998), who have helped the research community understand Black girl knowledges as well as the vulnerabilities Black girls face in schools.

The selection of literature reviewed brings to light the ways that scholars are already exploring the complexities of GOC and their writing practices. This matters because, as Muhammad and Haddix (2016) explain, "literacy educators must understand a more complete vision of the identities girls create for themselves, and the literacies and practices needed to best teach them" (p. 301). This work centers the ways that girls leverage their genius, agency, and literacy practices in the face of various intersecting vulnerabilities.

This body of research provides robust examples of how writing rooted in GOC identities and experiences can serve as a political tool. Through writing, GOC can create counternarratives that explore their brilliance and intellect and, in turn, construct critiques of intersecting racial and gendered injustices. Henry's (2001) foundational work explored the ways Black Caribbean girls used a Black girl reading/writing/discussion group to voice themselves in transgressive ways often silenced or punishable in dominant classrooms. Winn (2011) explored playwriting with incarcerated and formerly incarcerated girls who were able to fictionalize and perform some of their real-life experiences and, in turn, analyze and express their lives, their sense of deservingness, and their hopes. Muhammad (2015) examined the ways that Black Muslim girls used writing within a three-week writing course based on Qur'anic principles. She found that the girls, when invited to engage cultural traditions of writing about social issues, used writing as a source of agency to speak out against racialized and gendered oppression. McArthur and Muhammad (2017) also explored the ways that Black Muslim girls used writing that engaged Islamic principles and their experiences as Black American girls to enact an activist stance toward establishing Black Muslim sisterhood. González Ybarra (2020) found that Latina girls in an ethnic studies course leveraged *mujerista literacies* through culturally rooted practices like *testimonio* to engage shifts in consciousness and to reflect on their raced-gendered experiences. Flores (2018) created a collaborative space with Latina adolescent girls and their parents in which participants "disrupt[ed] the oppressive apolitical contexts and the silencing and controlling of bodies and narratives through the act of speaking one's truth orally, in writing, and through drawing" (p. 23). In this space, the girls and their parents used writing and storytelling to share strategies to navigate their lives, to build understandings between generations, and to build connections to their families, language, and culture.

This scholarship calls attention to the important ways that girls are using their identities and experiences to develop critical understandings of this world. My own scholarship proposes an extension of this work by highlighting the ways that GOC can work together across ethnic and cultural differences. The scholarship cited here emphasizes the dynamic nature of Black and Latina girls. However, few studies have taken up a feminist of color lens to explore multiracial groups of GOC, especially those including Asian American girls. Works of scholars like Lee and De Finney (2005) highlight the importance of writing coalitions for GOC in urban settings. The GOC in their project reported that the space allowed them to overcome a feeling of aloneness resulting from their racialized experiences, and to engage in critical learning about those experiences with other GOC. Stacey Lee's (2009) work also helps to illuminate the intersections of race and gender, particularly for non-East Asian girls. Though not literacy-specific, her research highlights how Hmong girls' school experiences are affected by pressures to simultaneously assimilate to white culture and adhere to culturally important domestic duties. Lee's work is one of the few empirical studies that provide critical insights into the complex relationship between Asian identity and gender, and the ways these interact to shape Asian girls' experiences in schools. A view into The Unnormal Sisterhood adds to the existing literature by exploring how GOC living in ever-diversifying neighborhoods and schools can engage with themselves and each other to envision and build toward better worlds for themselves and each other.

Tenets of Critical Celebration

Drawing from the foundational work by WOC reviewed in the previous section, I offer *critical celebration* as a lens through which to understand GOC literacies with an eye toward the complexity, the relationality, and the constantly evolving nature of GOC knowledge. The lens of critical celebration that will be unpacked in this section is rooted in the existing literature, as well as in WOC feminisms. However, this lens became more clearly defined during the collaborative work taken on by The Unnormal Sisterhood. The following four tenets are what emerged in our efforts to unseat superficial and false dominant narratives about GOC through our writing collaborative:

> Tenet 1: GOC knowledge, ways of knowing, and ways of being must be centered in understandings of girlhood.
>
> Tenet 2: GOC joys and vulnerabilities must be simultaneously acknowledged.
>
> Tenet 3: Critical sisterhood is established across difference.
>
> Tenet 4: Critical celebration is a journey.

The first tenet, the valuing of GOC knowledge, ways of knowing, and ways of being, is inspired by Ruth Nicole Brown (2009, 2013), who theorizes celebration, highlighting the need to listen to and trust in the dynamism of Black girls. She rejects simplification of Black girls to one flattened category and instead looks to their realities and complexities, illuminating the creative ways girls enact resistance, develop solidarity with one another, and create and use tools to navigate and understand their worlds.

To understand the brilliances of GOC, we must break with normative interpretations of "genius" and, instead, turn to WOC-created theories, recognizing that girls are possessors of complex knowledges born of intellectual, artistic, and activist lineages; of their positioning at the margins; of their bodies; of their relationships; of their experiences (Delgado-Bernal, 1999; hooks, 1990). When girls are seen as theorizers of their own experiences, we can forge pathways toward research and pedagogies where girls are given the opportunity to story their value on their own terms.

Tenet 2 requires a complex view of GOC that simultaneously acknowledges girls' joys and their vulnerabilities (Tuck, 2009). Communities of color have always created joy, even in the face of massive violence, marginalization, and oppression (Love, 2019). To form better critiques of raced-gendered oppression and better routes toward change, we must be privy to the beauty that GOC create even as they are oppressed. The fact is, GOC resist raced-gendered violence regularly, and we have much to learn about their sophisticated resistances. By celebrating their joy, we can better understand how and why we must join their joyful and critical resistance. I emphasize that critical celebration is not a naïve form of congratulation that ignores the current and historical contexts in which GOC exist. Rather, critical celebration gives room to GOC to create narratives of "awesomeness" as coexisting with and offering theories of change to the intersections of racism and sexism.

Tenet 3 highlights the importance of connecting across difference. As established by Tenets 1 and 2, GOC as a group are dynamic and face myriad experiences at the intersections of race, gender, and other identities. White supremacy has falsely constructed differences across racial and cultural lines as obstacles to solidarity against oppression (Bambara, 1983; Lorde, 2007). In turn, solidarity among nondominant women and girls can be, and often is, fractured. A failure to celebrate difference can be rooted in desires to erase one's own accountability to others. In particular, the centrality of anti-Blackness in white supremacist and heteropatriarchal projects (Sexton, 2010) creates fissures and blockages to potential sisterhoods across racial identities. Too often, anti-Blackness is ignored in "solidarity" efforts and, thus, white supremacy is reiterated and the silencing of Black voices is compounded. However, when we centralize difference, we realize the strengths accumulated in solidarity and develop strategies to support our sisters in facing vulnerabilities we do not face ourselves (Lorde, 2007).

Finally, Tenet 4 helps us to understand that critical celebration is a journey—a nonlinear journey that requires diligence. In GOC efforts to gain control over their representation, at times, the internalization of white heteropatriarchal beliefs can reveal itself. With a critical celebratory stance, we can work to better understand where these ideologies arise from and, in turn, collaborate with GOC across difference on moving toward justice. We must understand that part of critical celebration is seeing girls not only for the brilliance they possess, but also for their potential for continuous growth, their ongoing awakening, and their ability to push those engaged in critical celebration of GOC toward simultaneous growth and awakening. When establishing critical celebration across difference, opportunities to explore and share oneself in contexts that allow for active listening are crucial. Sisterhood and celebration are not automatic (Bambara, 1983), and so we must invite GOC to undertake a journey toward critical celebration of their sisters, knowing there will be misunderstandings and they may falter along the way, but that staying alert to and addressing missteps will propel us toward justice.

GOC literacies, and feminist of color writing practices in particular, can be mobilized to engage critical celebration, helping GOC become "more intimate with [themselves] and [each other]" (Anzaldúa, 1983, p. 169). This intimacy is one that builds on GOC knowledges, ways of knowing, and ways of being to bring light to the ways that girls are connected and different in both their joys and vulnerabilities. GOC literacies can provide guidance on the journey of critical celebration, making space not just for passive listening or even the practice of testifying and receiving stories, but also for the iterative introduction of new stories, terminologies, and theories to help put names to the experiences and ideas GOC form, to lovingly challenge one another's previously held misconceptions, and to collectively rethink assumptions. For the purposes of this article, I will specifically trace the ways The Unnormal Sisterhood *self*-celebrated in order to create ever-evolving self-portraits, providing opportunities for them to explore both their own place within systems of power, and also the places of their sisters.

Methodologies and Methods

This paper uses data collected over the course of 5 months from a practitioner research study utilizing ethnographic and feminist of color methodologies to explore how GOC leverage literacies to make sense of their identities, relationships, and world, and how literacy pedagogy can make space for these opportunities. This work was guided by the following questions:

- What happens when GOC are invited to think deeply about their identities, their relationships, and the issues that matter most to them using multimodal means of expression and exploration within a feminist writing pedagogy?
- What does a feminist pedagogy that is celebratory of GOC look like, and what is my role as the teacher-learner in this space?

Through this project, my conceptualization of critical celebration arose and became central to my approaches to data collection and analysis.

To critically celebrate GOC through research, it was necessary to enact methods that resist traditional research, which is frequently deficitizing, flattening, overly fixated on trauma and damage, and/or riddled with misinterpretations rooted in a white gaze (Evans-Winters & Esposito, 2010). A critically celebratory stance reflects what Eve Tuck (2009) describes as *desire-based* research. Tuck calls upon researchers working with minoritized communities to reject pathologization and to instead "document not only the painful elements of social realities, but also the wisdom and hope" (2009, p. 416). My approach to this project put desire at its core, engaging an iterative process that explored how The Unnormal Sisterhood moved toward criticality by mobilizing their genius, often joyfully, while simultaneously acknowledging the often oppressive contexts in which they existed.

POSITIONALITY

To engage critical celebration through research, one must acknowledge one's positionality, recognizing one's own journey toward understanding. I am a middle-class, straight, cisgender, mixed-race Japanese woman with familial roots in Brazil. My work is situated in relationship to my political identity as a WOC, following the lead of Morales, who claimed, "This tribe called 'woman of color' is not an ethnicity. It is one of the inventions of solidarity, an alliance, a political necessity that is not the given name of every female with dark skin and a colonized tongue, but rather a choice about how to resist and with whom" (Latina Feminist Group, 2001, pp. 102–103). With these identities, I am simultaneously inside and outside of community with the girls of The Unnormal Sisterhood. I am connected with them through the intersections of my gender and my nonwhite identity, which provide me with a certain amount of cultural intuition (Delgado-Bernal, 1999). However, I am also in many ways distanced and unable to completely understand their experiences. Through my methods, then, I proceeded with care to work in partnership with the girls in knowledge production, rather than overemphasizing my own expertise.

RESEARCH PARTNERS

The eight girls of The Unnormal Sisterhood were partners in knowledge construction, as will be explored in my explanation of my ethical stance. All these research partners attended or had graduated from a Catholic school in a working-class, low-income neighborhood in Philadelphia. For two and a half years prior to the launching of The Unnormal Sisterhood, I worked with youth and families in community-based research projects in a community center that shared a parking lot with the school. These projects, led by Gerald Campano and María Paula Ghiso, were highly relational, thus providing me with insights into the brilliances, hopes, and struggles of the community surrounding the school. It was through this work that I observed the need and desire for a GOC space that would provide not only sanctuary for GOC facing a variety of intersecting oppressions in school and beyond, but also academic supports through a critical writing pedagogy. After I proposed a GOC writing club to the principal, he gave me permission to recruit for the club, which would become part of the school's afterschool programming. Girls, some of whom I had worked with before in other projects, opted into the club after responding to a flyer I distributed to all middle school girls. Table 1 provides an overview of these research partners, including the ways they racially and/or ethnically self-identified. (All names are pseudonyms.)

TABLE 1
Identifications of the Girls of The Unnormal Sisterhood

Name	Grade	Race/Ethnic Identification
Ciara	6	Black
Diamond	6	Black/African American, Dominican, and Jamaican
Emily	6	Asian American/Vietnamese, white, Cambodian, and "a little bit Black"
Giselle	7	Asian American/Filipina
Halsey	7	Asian American/Vietnamese
Kathleen	7	Black/mixed
Seraphina	7	Black
Ash	10	Asian American/Indonesian

METHODOLOGICAL CONSIDERATIONS

Ethical and Humanizing Research. Core to critically celebrating the girls was the enactment of humanizing (Paris & Winn, 2014) and ethical (Campano et al., 2016) methods. I chose to reject traditional notions of research that frame the researcher as all-knowing and participants as objects of study—that fail to celebrate the full complexity of GOC. I elected, instead, to use a model of research done *with* community members. It remains my goal to delink my research from imperialistic ideologies (Tuhiwai Smith, 1999) and, instead, to move toward research that centers and celebrates the knowledges, traditions, and histories of marginalized peoples (Paris & Winn, 2014).

I attempted to stay attuned to the injustices the girls named, but also to the ways that they remained beautiful, creative, knowledgeable, and capable of imagining better worlds for themselves. I strove to "celebrate survival" (Tuhiwai Smith, 1999, p. 146), focusing on the ways that GOC transcend and seek to transcend the realities of intersecting racism, sexism, and other structural oppressions. Knowing the girls at a personal level helped me understand them in ways that defied dominant conceptions of GOC, and instead framed them as having inherent genius. Further, it meant bringing my own full humanity—as a learner, as fallible, as in many ways an outsider to their worlds—to position myself with humility to co-create knowledge with the girls of The Unnormal Sisterhood. As partners in knowledge creation, the girls were invited to engage in multiple aspects of my research, including having their voices and stories centered, driving the course of the project, participating in analysis, and presenting to the community. In all, this humanizing and ethical stance toward research enabled me to enact critical celebration of the girls, highlighting the dynamic ways they leveraged their knowledge and ways of knowing toward enacting resistance and navigating and understanding their worlds.

Practitioner Research. To engage a critically celebratory stance through my inquiry, practitioner research (Campano, 2007; Cochran-Smith & Lytle, 2009) seemed an optimal methodology. This framework allowed me to observe patterns that arose in the context of The Unnormal Sisterhood, and to engage in critical interventions as I made reflexive observations. I intentionally blurred the lines between research and practice to best understand GOC, their literacies, and my own teaching by intimately involving myself in the everyday aspects of my research. Practitioner research allowed me to work in alliance with the girls to produce new knowledge with social justice goals (Cochran-Smith & Lytle, 2009), viewing them as best positioned to understand and resist the sexist, classist, and racist forces that affect their lives (Collins, 2000; Mohanty, 2000; Moya, 2000). Practitioner research allowed me to celebrate the girls' knowledge, authentically and diligently noting the sometimes nonlinear pathways to consciousness that the girls embarked upon.

DATA COLLECTION AND ANALYSIS

To iteratively exercise critical celebration in my sense-making, I gathered data that centered the girls' voices. The data that informed this paper were collected over the course of 5 months, during which the girls met two times a week for one and a half hours. The data comprised artifacts, including the girls' writing, art, digital communications, and postings on our shared Instagram site; rigorous observational field notes derived from jottings taken during every session; transcriptions of select group meetings, semistructured interviews, and focus groups; and my lesson plans, created weekly before the club meetings.

Coding and Writing to Discover. I used ATLAS.ti software as I engaged in multiple rounds of analytic and in vivo coding to focus on the data closely and to prepare myself for some written analysis. Coding was conducted with the aim of "breaking down qualitative data into discreet parts, closely examining them, and comparing them for similarities and differences" (Saldaña, 2013, p. 100). After an initial read of my data, I had accumulated about 15 codes, which I was able to categorize into more overarching codes—*self-love, sisterhood*, and *critiques of schooling*—to notice larger patterns as well as connectivity between codes (See Table 2). The smaller codes did not neatly fit into just one category or another, displaying how the girls' lives and the issues they faced intersected and implicated one another; self-love, sisterhood, and their critiques were intertwined. The codes allowed me to track the themes that emerged in the girls' work, as well as my own pedagogical moves across texts and across time.

After I had categorized the data into codes, I went through a process of analytic memoing, seeking to use writing to crystalize meaning (Richardson & St. Pierre, 2008) and to better and more thoroughly celebrate the girls' knowledge. I wrote memos to summarize and connect my ideas with data over time, noting the ways that ongoing shifts in conversations reflected how the girls were entering a long-term dialogic spiral (Kinloch & San Pedro, 2014), a journeying toward consciousness. An overreliance on mechanistic coding can serve to reify colonialist ideologies and erase more organic knowledge creation (Tuck & Yang, 2014). So, though coding created discrete units of meaning and illuminated certain patterns, writing across the multiple facets of data engendered meaning in a way that was more organic, and more true to my personal journeying to discovery (Richardson & St. Pierre, 2008).

I also wrote what I consider celebratory narrative "portraits" that attempted to capture the essence of the girls, developing a sustained focus on individuality as well as relationships (Lawrence-Lightfoot & Hoffman Davis, 2002). As Lawrence-Lightfoot and Davis (2002) noted,

> Portraiture resists this tradition-laden effort to document failure. It is an intentionally generous and eclectic process that begins by searching for what is good and healthy and assumes that the expression of goodness will always be laced with imperfections. The researcher who asks first "what is good here?" is likely to absorb a very different reality than the one who is on a mission to discover the sources of failure. (p. 9)

TABLE 2
Coding Chart

Self-Love	Sisterhood	Critiques of Schooling
• Unnormal • Gender • Race/racism • Identity (other) • Self-love • Growth • Self-definition	• Unnormal • Gender • Race/racism • Identity (other) • Growth • Solidarity and sisterhood • Social action • Tension between girls	• Unnormal • Gender • Race/racism • Identity (other) • Self-definition • Social action • Sexism and sexual harassment • Teachers' treatment of students

Portraits helped to frame my analysis of the sisters' writing and talk, bringing deeper understandings of each girl's literacies, ways of knowing, and ways of being.

Member Checks. Member checks helped to provide transparency to the sisters and to make sure that their voices were not filtered too strongly through my own preconceptions (Maxwell, 2013), shaped by my own understandings as a straight, East Asian, middle-class, adult woman. Further, member checks gave the girls more control over what was shared about them, as they knew they always had the option to tell me not to share aspects of my research or to shift the way I spoke about them. In this way, I made efforts to establish findings as a product of dialogue between me and the girls (Kinloch & San Pedro, 2014). As I analyzed and wrote about my data, I would share my ideas either during club meetings or through email to make sure what I was writing felt true to them and represented them in the ways they desired.

The Pedagogy

The Unnormal Sisterhood embarked on a trajectory of study that covered three units: identity, sisterhood, and social change. This trajectory opened opportunities for a deep exploration of the girls' identities aimed at better understanding their strengths, brilliances, and uniqueness, as well as the oppressive structures they faced and how they might fight them. These three units were porous, and issues of self-love, sisterhood, and social justice were deeply intertwined. The practitioner research nature of this project allowed me to iteratively shape the curriculum, responding thoughtfully to the girls' questions by incorporating texts, artwork, and projects that centered what mattered to them and provided opportunities to develop the heuristics needed to describe, understand, and critique the phenomena they observed.

The curriculum built on my own experiences of working with traditional workshop models (Calkins, 1994) but provided a critical intervention in order to adjust to the political and historical contexts of GOC, drawing on the work of scholars like Gholnecsar Muhammad (2015), Sherell McArthur (McArthur & Muhammad, 2017), and Tracey Flores (2018). Building on traditions of WOC writing collectives such as the Combahee River Collective, the writers of *This Bridge Called My Back*, and Black women's literary societies (Royster, 2000), in this work we strove to cultivate the girls' agency through a literary collective. Rejecting Eurocentric images of writers as solitary, we instead followed feminist of color traditions of writing for healing, writing for connecting, writing to legitimize experiences with whiteness and patriarchy, and writing to uplift (Anzaldúa, 1983; Bambara, 1980, 1983; Christian, 1988). The feminist writing traditions that inspired this work put forth the notion that writing could involve a dynamic coming together that focused on the humans involved—centering their health, their relationships, their intellectual growth, their development of agency and advocacy, their critical engagement, and their politics (Tuhiwai Smith, 1999). Establishing the conditions for this human and relational writing resulted in the creation of both physical products of writing and a GOC community that was tethered by these literary engagements.

For this community to emerge, it was important to invite the girls to investigate their own identities, to learn with and from one another, and to imagine worlds that they deserved. All this was done by taking on a critical stance to explore the myriad issues they reported facing as GOC. This meant that, although they wrote with their experiences at the center, they critiqued what they'd written as we layered feminist of color perspectives into our conversations. Everything the girls wrote wasn't inherently "perfect," but, instead, was part of a process of reflection and growth that emerged as they took note of both the beauty of their stories and the ways white supremacist and sexist ideologies sometimes seeped into their writing. By engaging with one another through writing, they could challenge and grow these ideas together.

Because the work was sensitive to the girls' needs, it was necessary to have structure, but also to be responsive and flexible, particularly as an antidote to their overly structured and controlled days (Brown, 2009, 2013; Saavedra & Marx, 2016). Though I provided materials, plans, and directions, I also gave the girls opportunities to choose what to do during our time together, enacting an ethos of GOC freedom and trusting the girls' intuitions about what they needed from the club. A typical day in the club started with a period of informal conversation about the goings-on of their lives, which usually lasted about 10 minutes but, when necessary, could last longer. Each meeting also gave the girls an opportunity to interact with WOC- and GOC-produced texts, including poems, quotes, essays, videos, paintings, music, and so on. These texts served both as mentor texts for the girls' own writing and as vehicles to teach them theories, vocabularies, histories, and contemporary issues related to our ongoing discussions. These texts framed WOC and GOC as their intellectual, activist, and artistic ancestors and contemporaries, and included theories, vocabulary, and stories often left out of dominant curriculum. Table 3 shows an example of how texts and subsequent writing responded to ongoing conversations among the girls.

The curriculum was centered on WOC theorizations of the importance of writing as resistance. Every day, we would write or otherwise produce texts in response to or inspired by our texts and conversations. During the time set aside for writing, I would provide minilessons, give feedback, and promote peer feedback. Minilessons used mentor texts as reference points for the girls, and were aimed at thinking about craft as well as content. As the girls wrote, I would float between girls, checking in with them and giving feedback as necessary. This feedback was aimed at celebration, helping girls to build on their strengths toward crafting pieces they were proud of. At least once a week, the girls were invited to share their writing with one another. In addition to the actual club meetings, the girls interacted via our co-owned Instagram account in between and sometimes during meetings.

Critical Celebration through Writing

Through a variety of multimodal literacy engagements, The Unnormal Sisterhood practiced critical celebration of themselves. By studying their writing and related conversations, we can see all four tenets of critical celebration: (1) GOC knowledge, ways of knowing, and ways of being were centered; (2) GOC joys and vulnerabilities were simultaneously acknowledged; (3) sisterhood was established across difference; and (4) critical celebration was undertaken as a journey. The girls' work on self-exploration demonstrates the importance of centering GOC as the storytellers of their lives in order to build coalitional and collective critical understandings over time.

"MY NAME IS IMPORTANT": INTRODUCING OURSELVES IN CRITICAL CELEBRATION

Sarah Ahmed, in reflection on the work of Audre Lorde, describes an important lesson she learned from the Black feminist writer:

> Introducing ourselves matters; naming yourself, saying who you are, making clear your values, cares, concerns, and commitments, matters. Each time you write or you speak you are putting yourself into a world that is shared. . . . Lorde always took the risk of naming herself and of asserting her existence in a world that made her existence difficult. (Lorde, 2017, introduction by Ahmed, p. v)

It was with this spirit of Lordeian introduction that I invited the girls to write, putting themselves into the world on their own terms. This did not escape the girls. During a one-on-one writing conference, Seraphina shared that things were different in the club than in her seventh-grade classroom. She told me about the dehumanization she felt in her classroom as compared with what it felt like to be respected by her teacher in the club. I encouraged her to write it out. In the remaining minutes of the workshop, Seraphina

TABLE 3
Example of Creating GOC Responsive Pedagogy

Critical Incident(s)	Author	Mentor Text	Invitation to Write and Activities
Ongoing conversations about Black Lives Matter vs. Asian activism; discussion of tensions between Asian and Black community members	Niki Magtoto	Essay: "Why Grace Lee Boggs, Yuri Kochiyama, and Richard Aoki have given me #SquadGoals"	1. Oral discussion: What did you learn from this piece? 2. Writing Part 1: What did you learn from this piece and your sisters' reflections? 3. Writing Part 2: Minilesson on writing interview questions 4. Skype interview with the author using questions

wrote a brief journal entry recounting the dehumanizing experience of being called "inmates" and "animals" by her teacher (Figure 1).

Later, when she shared her entry with her sisters, she proclaimed, as if speaking to her teachers, "You have no right to deprive me of my name." This statement echoes what so many WOC theorists have asserted: that naming ourselves for ourselves matters in a world that too often tries to distort our realities to fit the white male gaze (Anzaldúa, 1983; Lorde, 2007).

As an introduction to self-naming, one of our first engagements with literature was a reading of Mexican American writer Sandra Cisneros's (1991) short story "My Name." "My Name" is a lyrical narration of a young Mexican American girl's relationship to her name, Esperanza. Through the story, she traces her name's history, its meaning, and its effect on her self-understanding and her connection and disconnections to her family and the world. Cisneros's prose points to the cultural and affective importance of naming and explores how one young girl both resists patriarchal histories and attempts to reclaim herself.

After reading the story and discussing it, the girls wrote short jottings about their own names in their notebooks. This was an opportunity for the girls to reflect on the essences of their own names, and share with the rest of the group what they, in that moment, distilled from their names. As they wrote, some girls went online to look up the meanings of their names, some chatted with one another in between jottings, and others simply wrote. The writings that the sisters engaged in, though brief, unearthed and expressed their nuanced personalities, cultural identities, and relationships to others and the world around them. In other words, the girls, as they explored their names, engaged in a process of critical celebration. Through the following examples, some of the functions of critical celebration will be unearthed: how for Diamond, thoughtful critiques of the misperceptions of Black girls emerged; how for Halsey, explorations of her intersectional identity came forth; how for Seraphina and Giselle, powerful claims of uniqueness and strength were made; and how for the group as a whole, a sense of complex sisterhood was engendered.

DIAMOND'S SPIRITED NAMING

Diamond, a Black sixth grader who eventually came to identify as a lesbian, produced lines of poetry to describe her understandings of her name, including what she calls, "my color of my name" (Figure 2).

Although brief, Diamond's six-line reflection asserted her values, her commitments, her cares. Economically choosing her words, she painted a rich, multilayered vision of who she was. She provided an image of the potentiality for GOC to be many things at once.

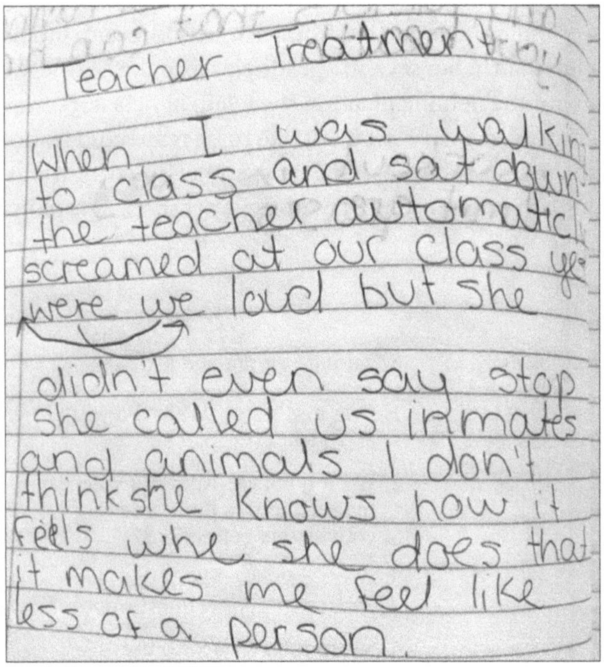

Teacher Treatment
When I was walkin
to class and sat down
the teacher automaticl
screamed at our class yes
were we loud but she
didn't even say stop
she called us inmates
and animals I don't
think she knows how it
feels whe she does that
it makes me feel like
less of a person.

FIGURE 1
Seraphina's journal entry

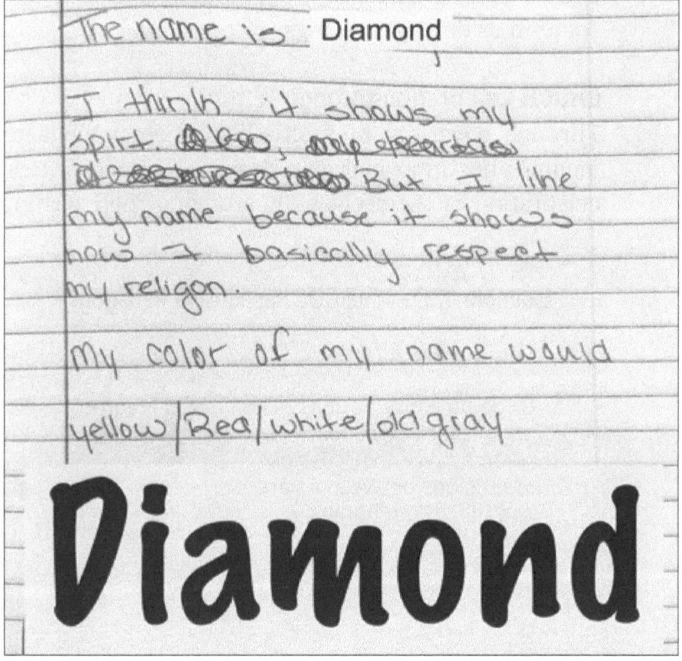
The name is Diamond
I think it shows my
spirt. But I like
my name because it shows
how I basically respect
my religon.
My color of my name would
yellow/Red/white/old gray
Diamond

FIGURE 2
Diamond's poem

Diamond first addressed her spiritedness, a liveliness that is worth celebrating. Importantly, this statement pushed back on negative perceptions of Black girls, who are often framed by dominant ideologies as having bad attitudes and being aggressive and "unladylike" (Morris, 2016). This poem, in fact, struck a sharp contrast with how Diamond narrated her interactions with teachers, a conversation that was central to our exploration of GOC rights. As can be seen in the following excerpt from a transcript of a meeting, Diamond was critically aware of the ways she was being harshly and unfairly disciplined and how her actions and words were regularly misinterpreted by her teachers.

> I remember when the counselor came in. It's like a new counselor who comes in every Monday, and we were talking and, um, she was like, what else makes you mad, and I raised my hand and I had said, "Teachers," and Ms. X started staring at me, was like, "Why did, why did she say that?" . . . and the counselor said, "Why, what makes you mad, why the teachers make you mad?" . . . I said, "They say things that aren't true and they always believe, and they always take the other side." And Ms. X was like, "Well you never talk to me." And I said, "Ms. X, I wasn't talking about you specifically. I'm talking about teachers." And she said, "Do not get smart, Diamond. Do not get smart, Diamond. You need to take a walk."

She was, at that point, kicked out of her class and made to miss what could have been valuable instructional time.

This story illustrates an incident of a Black girl being unjustly punished for expressing an opinion. Diamond attempted to express her frustrations and perhaps even open up conversations about how schools could transform to better serve students. Yet, rather than taking this opportunity, her teacher immediately punished Diamond, kicking her out of class, and labeling her as "smart"—meaning disobedient, not intellectual. This seems to reflect that oftentimes, the qualities that white male students are rewarded for—outspokenness, assertiveness, a sense of deservedness—when present in Black girls, are seen as punishable (Morris, 2016). However, through critical celebratory acts—recounting this narrative among her sisters and writing in self-adulation—Diamond expressed thoughtful and sincere critiques in a straightforward and lively way, tapping into her understandings of her lived experiences and cultural means of communication. Diamond emphasized that her teacher misinterpreted her and then punished her. In her name description, though, Diamond was able to rebel by naming herself, thereby claiming self-love and professing her spiritedness. Critical celebratory pedagogy invited Diamond to, across time, share her experiences and her GOC interpretations of these experiences with her sisters, helping to resist and invite critical interpretations of teacher-centric (and Eurocentric) ideologies.

In her writing and subsequent discussions, Diamond also referred to her religion, an aspect of her identity that was both important and complicated. While her identity as Christian was core to her self-description, she was also grappling with the ways scripture had been interpreted in her family as she developed her lesbian identity. In various conversations, she brought up that her grandmother claimed homosexuality was a sin. This deeply troubled Diamond, as she was beginning to explore her sexual orientation. In my field notes, I recorded:

> Diamond brought up, again, the issue of being gay and asked whether it was good or bad. She continued to explain herself, a bit exasperated. She said that her grandmother tells her that being gay is bad. She added that she was more of a tomboy and liked "boy" things, but that her grandma said that God didn't like that. She said she wasn't gay, but she liked things that boys liked. . . . She looped back to the question of being gay and whether or not it was bad. She asked, "where did it start that being gay was bad?"

Like Esperanza of "My Name," Diamond demonstrated that cultural and familial ties are often far from simple. With critical celebration that refused simple answers and allowed for critique within one's communities, Diamond started to push open doors to more complete and intersectional appreciation of complex GOC identities. This highlights how, when GOC embrace their own experiences and understandings, they can critique both larger social structures and the ways that injustice can sometimes exist in their own communities.

Beautifully illustrating her complexity, Diamond also poetically colored her name in her writing, imagining its multiplicity—her multiplicity—in vibrant yellow and red, moving to subdued white, and finally "old gray." She emphasized that, while frequently bright and energetic, she could also, at times, be quiet and "dull," even, something that we should all have permission to do and that Black girls are often denied as they are labeled as overly aggressive and loud (Collins, 2000; Morris, 2016). This colorful naming challenged the notion that she could be reduced to anything simple, to any monolith. Over the lines of this poem, she gave herself permission to be so much more than Black girls are typically permitted to be.

HALSEY'S IMPORTANCE

Like Diamond, Halsey, a seventh-grade Vietnamese girl, displayed an ability to project herself into the world on her own terms. She wrote:

> My name means life like the way I am happy to live. It also means something very important. Shows the way my parents frantic. On what to call me. On what to represent them. My name is important. It means life, hazelnut, a great philosopher, a beautiful, even a little one too. Surprises me how one word describe me so well.[1]

In this poem, she tapped into celebratory language when describing herself and her name, stating that she was beautiful, philosophical, happy, and lively. She made the move of naming herself as important.

Similarly to Diamond, Halsey reflected her cultural heritage through the description of her name. She explained the importance of naming to her family—to her frantic parents, her name would not only represent her, but them as well. Looking across her writing, it was evident that her cultural and familial ties mattered to her. This was further reflected in a second poem in which she spoke back to dominant understandings of Asian American identity through a critique of Vietnamese erasure. In this poem, she wrote:

> Tet
> People get mistaken
> For a holiday that's already taken
> Tet
> My culture
> Vietnamese
> It's not Chinese New Year
> Is Vietnamese instead.

She expressed her frustrations with people conflating her Vietnamese culture with Chinese culture, naming herself and her community as important and worthy of attention.

Halsey, though, also voiced that she was more complex than what could be captured by the label *Vietnamese American*—she was also Philadelphian, teenaged, female, feminist, and so on. She claimed what might be considered a rhizomatic identity (Campano et al., 2020; Deleuze, 1994) as she developed a conception of herself tied both to her family and heritage, as well as to her unique personality. In another autobiographical text (Figure 3), she showed how she was not only connected to her parents but also to youth and popular culture. In this text, Halsey introduced herself as liking dogs; the TV series *The Walking Dead*; the group of teen internet idols known as Magcon; pop musician Shawn Mendes; and internet stars the Dolan Twins.

Across a variety of texts, she acknowledged the impact of her family on her identity, *and* projected that she was her own person. This illustrates the complex self-conception that immigrant students can adopt, showing that they can both be admiring of and respectful toward their parents, families, and cultures, and also uniquely construct their identities from a variety of cultural and community influences, including friends, pop culture, their neighborhoods, and so on. Halsey showed herself as multilayered, desiring, and important. Critical celebratory pedagogy opened space for her to explore and express these multiple identities that were, at times, in tension with one another, helping her not only to process critical approaches to her identity, but also to illuminate the complexity of Asian girlhood to her sisters.

SERAPHINA'S AND GISELLE'S RESISTANT NAMING

In rebellion against master narratives that serve to devalue GOC, in their writing, some of the girls did the sophisticated work of referring to negative ideologies about GOC while maintaining a celebratory stance.

FIGURE 3
Halsey's short autobiographical text

They asserted their importance in a world that did not always treat them kindly. Seraphina wrote:

> Seraphina
> Not Sarah or Sarfana[2]
> I am
> unique
> powerful
> and strong
> nor will I let
> Anyone
> get me down
> Lastly I am
> me.

Giselle, a Filipina seventh grader, wrote:

> My names unique. The way im different from others and how I be myself. My name means strong also. To be Proud and don't let people bring me down.

Both girls specifically highlighted their uniqueness and their strength. They underscored these ideas, paired with convictions of being oneself. Seraphina used her last lines to convey, "Lastly, I am / me," isolating the word "me" for emphasis. Giselle claimed her name's meaning as "strong" and asserted that she knew "how I be myself."

Interestingly, they both not only indicated that this mislabeling was something they had experienced, but also claimed they did not "let" others do this to them. Seraphina's poem noted the ways others had refused to learn her name, an experience all too common among WOC and GOC. However, she also proclaimed her power and strength in the face of these misnamings. Both Giselle and Seraphina showed an awareness of the negative perceptions that others had of them, a feeling confirmed by many WOC scholars citing the negative conceptions of WOC and GOC shaped by white supremacist heteropatriarchal myths (Collins, 2000; Lugones, 1987). However, by not "letting" anyone treat them this way, they performed agency in resisting those narratives in favor of self-love. They were demonstrating the active role they took in critically celebrating themselves, aware of the negative stereotypes cast on them, but also able to take charge of positioning themselves on their own terms, rather than on the terms of those stereotypes. Indeed, they asserted the notion proclaimed by Seraphina, that no one had the right to "deprive [them] of [their] name[s]."

Across these pieces of writing, it is evident that the girls brought strong senses of self to the table. In these brief introductions, they, as Audre Lorde did, staked a claim of who they were despite any other messages the world might project about them. They introduced themselves in rebellious manners that unearthed their strengths, their vulnerabilities, and, importantly, their appreciation for themselves.

THE GROUP NAMING: UNNORMAL SISTERHOOD

Naming was not just individualistic, but allowed the girls to also claim a group identity. We came to The Unnormal Sisterhood's name by discussing our goals and desires for the group and studying the names of some other GOC writing groups, including the Sistahs (Wissman, 2007) and the Sister Authors (Muhammad, 2015). Then, we brainstormed a list of possible names. From the list produced, the girls voted on a name and unanimously chose The Unnormal Sisterhood.

Unnormal and *sisterhood* play together to reveal the four tenets of critical celebration. First, the girls drew on a playful ingenuity with their creation of the word *unnormal*, which discarded the pejorative connotations of *abnormal* and instead pointed to a celebration of otherness. *Unnormal* illuminated their feelings, both as individuals and collectively, of being *other*, outside of the norm. Outsider status, Imani Perry (2004) explains, is often celebrated in hip hop culture, as nondominant people "centraliz[e] the position of otherness as a site of privileged knowledge and potential" (p. 107). This naming seemed to tap into cultural and gendered ways of knowing that understood GOC marginality as power. The concept of *unnormal* also pointed to the girls' ability to use an intersectional lens to self-define beyond the often monolithic definitions of GOC, again highlighting the importance of GOC knowledges in constructing understandings of GOC.

Importantly, the girls specifically chose to name themselves as a sisterhood, acknowledging the centrality of female connection across nondominant difference. The pairing of *unnormal* and *sisterhood* further signaled the possibilities for the composition of an alternative form of sociality that rejected the notion that being a collective *other* would be an antisocial stance for GOC. Rather, this naming suggested the importance of, in the words of Alice Walker (1983) in her definition of *womanist*, being "not separatist, except periodically, for health" (p. xi). Work toward a liberatory goal, done hand-in-hand with ones' sisters and separate from whiteness and masculinity, is necessary and healing critical work.

Reflections on Learnings

The girls' writing not only functioned as self-celebratory and individualistic, but it also had more expansive and communal effects. As the sisters reflected on the group, one of the major themes that emerged was the idea that they became better because they learned about one another. Ash, a 10th grader and immigrant from Indonesia who served as a sort of teaching assistant to me, spoke about her own coming to understandings of intersectional feminism and how, though she faced anti-Asian oppression, she also understood that she did not contend with the severity of anti-Blackness. She explained, "The girls at the club are so very inquisitive and smart, they definitely taught me some of these things."

Halsey, too, expressed that her perspectives had evolved as a result of learning about the other girls. In an interview, she said the following: "The thing that was important was that we learned each other's ethnicity and race and family background . . . like culture, and we learned about other people's culture are very important so you have more knowledge so you won't offend anyone else of that race." In another conversation, she commented, "I get to understand what other races go through, like such as discrimination and how it feels being an outsider. I know that I can help comfort people because I've been through the same things. And, I guess it is really empowering to me knowing that I can help the world." With these words, though she demonstrated a still-emerging ability to articulate her definition of justice, she showed that her engagement with the other girls and the opportunity to learn from their experiences had shifted her ways of acting more justly in the world. She explained that this knowledge of others' identities and heritages strengthened her ability to act in solidarity with her sisters, even if they didn't have exactly the same experiences as her.

Giselle emphasized her appreciation for knowing the other girls in the group. When asked about her favorite part of the group, she responded, "It was like, this is where we had a fun time being with these girls and knowing them more. . . . And [we] learn a lot about women's power." This reflected that Giselle took joy in being with the girls and that within that joyful space, she learned about them. What's more, she then mentioned that her other favorite part was learning about "women's power." The work of the group was not only to celebrate the girls as individuals and to teach one another about their experiences, but to do this side-by-side and with a theoretical stance that equated what they were learning about one another with power. Ash, Halsey, and Giselle all provided insight into the ways that, as girls shared parts of themselves with each other, the whole group benefited as their critical stances and feelings of empowerment evolved.

Discussion

As the sisters strove to understand themselves as transcendent of narrow and often negative views of GOC, as powerful in spite of and perhaps as a result of their marginalized positions, literary experiences that promoted the loving exploration of self were a key tool of critical celebration. The sisters created texts that both expressed and further developed their theorizations of their lived experiences, their own brilliances, and the ways they navigated the world both as holders of unique identities and as members of sisterhoods. The girls' work exposed the many ways that they were resilient to the negative stereotypes and deficitizing discourses that surrounded their intersectional identities. Further, by centering these literary engagements within The Unnormal Sisterhood, the girls were able to produce counternarratives that brought to light their complex and nuanced understandings of themselves and their relationships to the world around them. These counternarratives also served as a political move against dominant ideologies about GOC, projecting more accurate GOC-produced understandings.

What's more, the girls' sense of self-love was not solely self-serving. Rather, they enacted self-love in a collectivity with their sisters in a way that resulted in an enhanced community. The sisters cited the process of learning about one another's identities and experiences as core to their work toward collective resistance. As they partook in self-celebration, they not only analyzed their sense of self-worth, but also introduced their sisters to aspects of themselves that were perhaps obscured by dominant discourses. This, in turn, allowed the girls to better understand how to support one another and work with one another.

As the popularity of the "self-care" movement erupts, especially among women claiming their right to treat themselves with kindness, it is important to be mindful of how critical celebration plays an active role in justice-oriented self-care for WOC and GOC. Many WOC describe the origins of the self-care movement as specifically inspired by WOC like Audre Lorde (1988), who declared that "caring for myself is not self-indulgence, it is self-preservation and that is an act of political warfare" (p. 132). Through Lorde's lens, self-care is more than self-centered luxuriating. It is, instead, a commitment to oneself in the face of white supremacy—a commitment that serves not just the self, but extends to other oppressed people. Writing for oneself and for one's sisters, caring for oneself through the healing process of writing, can do this political work, giving shape to a robust and resistant consciousness among GOC.

Implications

Though it is certainly not a panacea for the multitude of issues GOC face at the intersections of race, gender, class, and other identities, critical celebration in writing curriculum offers a stance that allows teachers, researchers, and GOC themselves to understand GOC for their inherent worth, their brilliance, their deservingness. This work highlights the necessity for curriculum and spaces in which GOC write for self-care and care of one another. Critical celebration highlights GOC identity and experience as core to the curriculum while also affording GOC opportunities to think critically about their worlds and the ways that white supremacist ideologies can interrupt their ability to love themselves and each other as GOC.

This is especially important within a global and local social and educational context that fails to see GOC for their dynamism and continually ignores their vulnerabilities in schools and beyond. Black girls in particular are faced with corporal punishment, expulsion, and suspensions at staggering rates, while their needs and desires are ignored (African American Policy Forum & Center for Intersectionality and Social Policy Studies, 2015; Morris, 2016). Southeast Asian girls are largely ignored in research, and their vulnerabilities are obscured by aggregate statistics that portray Asian Americans as successful while disregarding the ways the United States education, housing, immigration, and economic systems fail certain groups of Asian Americans (Goodwin, 2010; Lee, 2009).

The work of The Unnormal Sisterhood suggests that literacy curriculum in and out of schools should be reshaped to simultaneously center GOC and other minoritized identities and knowledges, while also providing space for those knowledges to be used toward critical work. One step forward would be to invite a variety of genres, thereby providing opportunities for girls to write from personal experience, with emotion, and without the constraints of the over-structured five-paragraph essays that are so predominant in schools, and particularly schools that serve youth of color. As so many WOC writers have explored, writing can provide opportunities for GOC to name their lives and understandings, center these as worthwhile, and challenge the white supremacist, sexist logics with which they are confronted (Anzaldúa, 1983; Bambara, 1980; Christian, 1988). Writing in ways that are based on WOC and GOC knowledge and ways of knowing, then, can provide routes toward more complete understandings of GOC strengths and vulnerabilities, understandings youth in classrooms as well as teachers would do well to grapple with. As demonstrated by the girls' writing, this isn't a one-shot deal. Rather, the complexities of the girls' identities required multiple pieces placed in conversation with one another and paired with ongoing conversations about self to truly unearth the ways girls are and strive to be. Thus, in a critical celebratory classroom, this work must be constant and rigorous, and not merely symbolic.

Of significance is the observation that, oftentimes, interacting with texts by other WOC and GOC served to prompt deeper writing. Minoritized voices, and in particular the voices of WOC, should be centralized in literacy classrooms, thereby bringing WOC knowledge, ways of knowing, and ways of being to bear. WOC written texts can be used as mentor pieces, providing examples of multimodal creation as well as aspirational images of what it means to be an intellectual and a creator. Additionally, these pieces add necessary critical perspectives that Eurocentric curriculum lacks. All students deserve a curriculum that frames WOC as skilled holders and creators of knowledge necessary to building a robust understanding of our world.

Furthermore, it is critical that teachers allow students to share their writing with one another, not only for surface purposes like peer editing, but to provide opportunities for students to teach and learn with and from one another as they build the intimacy that arises from sharing stories (Anzaldúa, 1983). Critical celebration demands the establishment of

TEACHING TIPS

Player draws from feminists of color to guide her planning and writing pedagogy with girls of color. After reading and viewing texts with your students that explore experiences girls of color (GOC) have in our society, engage students in a discussion about what they learned. Next, ask students to create a one-minute media post about one or two issues they notice disproportionately impacting GOC in their school or home communities. Share the video and discuss reasons why these issues impact GOC. Then brainstorm ideas that the class can implement to address these issues in their school community.

understandings across difference, and the sharing of stories and voices is one way to accomplish this. When minoritized student voices are centered as important, new and vital understandings on which to build justice-oriented work can be established. In turn, they may come to critique and challenge dominant ideologies with their own *and* each other's freedom in mind, a goal that transcends the narrow conceptions of academic achievement too often forwarded in dominant schooling.

Teachers of literacy in and out of school have a responsibility to their students, and in particular, to their most marginalized students, including GOC. By engaging critical celebratory pedagogies in the classroom, they can play a role in creating environments that promote students' authority over their own self-expression, the building of understandings across difference, and the journey toward critical understandings rooted in GOC knowledge. Of course, literacy instruction, in and of itself, cannot create revolution, but it can be one tool that can be used in schools and other educational contexts to provide GOC and other marginalized students with opportunities to leverage their brilliance to help forge a path toward freedom.

NOTES

1. The meanings behind Halsey's name are not reflected by her pseudonym.
2. Words are changed slightly to reflect Seraphina's pseudonym. The original poem referenced mispronunciation of Seraphina's real name.

REFERENCES

African American Policy Forum & Center for Intersectionality and Social Policy Studies. (2015). *Black girls matter: Pushed out, overpoliced and underprotected.* Kimberlé Williams Crenshaw.

Anzaldúa, G. (1983). Speaking in tongues: A letter to third world women writers. In C. Moraga & G. Anzaldúa (Eds.), *This bridge called my back: Writings of radical women of color* (2nd ed., pp. 165–174). Kitchen Table: Women of Color Press.

Bambara, T. C. (1983). Foreword. In C. Moraga & G. Anzaldúa (Eds.), *This bridge called my back: Writings of radical women of color* (2nd ed., pp. vi–viii). Kitchen Table: Women of Color Press.

Bambara, T. C. (1980). What it is I think I'm doing anyhow. In J. Sternburg (Ed.), *The writer on her work* (Vol. 1, pp. 153-168). Norton.

Brown, R. N. (2009). *Black girlhood celebration: Toward a hip-hop feminist pedagogy.* Peter Lang.

Brown, R. N. (2013). *Hear our truths: The creative potential of Black girlhood.* University of Illinois Press.

Calkins, L. M. (1994). *The art of teaching writing.* Heinemann.

Campano, G. (2007). *Immigrant students and literacies: Reading, writing, and remembering.* Teachers College Press.

Campano, G., Ghiso, M. P., & Welch, B. J. (2016). *Partnering with immigrant communities: Action through literacy.* Teachers College Press.

Campano, G., Nichols, T. P., & Player, G. D. (2020). Multimodal critical inquiry: Nurturing decolonial imaginaries. In E. B. Moje, P. P. Afflerbach, P. Enciso, & N. K. Lesaux (Eds.), *Handbook of reading research* (Vol. 5, pp. 137–152). Routledge.

Christian, B. (1988). The race for theory. *Feminist Studies*, 14(1), 67–79.

Cisneros, S. (1991). *The house on Mango Street.* Vintage Books.

Cochran-Smith, M., & Lytle, S. L. (2009). *Inquiry as stance: Practitioner research for the next generation.* Teachers College Press.

Collins, P. H. (2000). *Black feminist thought: Knowledge, consciousness, and the politics of empowerment.* Routledge.

Deleuze, G. (1994). *Difference and repetition.* Columbia University Press.

Delgado-Bernal, D. (1999). Using a Chicana feminist epistemology in educational research. *Harvard Educational Review*, 68(4), 555–579.

Evans-Winters, V., & Esposito, J. (2010). Other people's daughters: Critical race feminism and Black girls' education. *Educational Foundations*, 24(1), 11–24.

Flores, T. (2018). Breaking stereotypes and boundaries: Latina adolescent girls and their parents writing their worlds. *Voices from the Middle*, 25(3), 22–25.

Fordham, S. (1993). "Those loud Black girls": Women, silence, and gender "passing" in the academy. *Anthropology and Education Quarterly*, 24(1), 3–32.

González Ybarra, M. (2020). "We have a strong way of thinking . . . and it shows through our words": Exploring mujerista literacies with Chicana/Latina youth in a community ethnic studies course. *Research in the Teaching of English*, 54(3), 231–253.

Goodwin, A. L. (2010). The laundromat as the transnational local: Young children's literacies of interdependence. *Teachers College Record*, 118, 1–46.

Henry, A. (1998). "Invisible" and "womanish": Black girls negotiating their lives in an African-centered school in the USA. *Race Ethnicity and Education*, 1(2), 151–170.

Henry, A. (2001). The politics of unpredictability in a reading/writing/discussion group with girls from the Caribbean. *Theory into Practice*, 40(3), 184–189.

hooks, b. (1990). *Yearning: Race, gender, and cultural politics*. South End Press.

Kinloch, V., & San Pedro, T. (2014). The space between listening and storying: Foundations for projects in humanization. In D. Paris & M. T. Winn (Eds.), *Humanizing research: Decolonizing qualitative inquiry with youth and communities*. Sage Publications.

Latina Feminist Group. (2001). *Telling to live: Latina feminist testimonios*. Duke University Press.

Lawrence-Lightfoot, S., & Hoffman Davis, J. (2002). *The art and science of portraiture*. Jossey-Bass.

Lee, J.-A., & De Finney, S. (2005). Using popular theatre for engaging racialized minority girls in exploring questions of identity and belonging. *Child & Youth Services*, 26(2), 95–118.

Lee, S. J. (2009). *Up against whiteness: Race, school, and immigrant youth*. Teachers College Press.

Lorde, A. (1988). *A burst of light: Essays*. Firebrand Books.

Lorde, A. (2007). *Sister outsider: Essays and speeches*. Crossing Press.

Lorde, A. (with Eddo-Lodge, R., & Ahmed, S.). (2017). *Your silence will not protect you*. Silver Press.

Love, B. (2019). *We want to do more than survive: Abolitionist teaching and the pursuit of educational freedom*. Beacon Press.

Lugones, M. (1987). Playfulness, "world"-travelling, and loving perception. *Hypatia*, 2(2), 3–19.

Maxwell, J. A. (2013). *Qualitative research design: An interactive approach* (3rd ed.). Sage.

McArthur, S. A., & Muhammad, G. E. (2017). Black Muslim girls navigating multiple oppositional binaries through literacy and letter writing. *Educational Studies*, 53(1), 63–77.

Mohanty, S. P. (2000). The epistemic status of cultural identity: On *Beloved* and the postcolonial condition. In M. Moya & M. R. Hames-García (Eds.), *Reclaiming identity: Realist theory and the predicament of postmodernism* (pp. 29–66). University of California Press.

Morris, M. W. (2016). *Pushout: The criminalization of Black girls in schools*. The New Press.

Moya, P. (2000). Introduction: Reclaiming identity. In P. Moya & M. R. Hames-García (Eds.), *Reclaiming identity: Realist theory and the predicament of postmodernism* (pp. 1–23). University of California Press.

Muhammad, G. E. (2015). Iqra: African American Muslim girls reading and writing for social change. *Written Communication*, 32(3), 1–31.

Muhammad, G. E., & Haddix, M. (2016). Centering Black girls' literacies: A review of literature on the multiple ways of knowing of Black girls. *English Education*, 48(4), 299–336.

Paris, D., & Winn, M. T. (Eds.). (2014). *Humanizing research: Decolonizing qualitative inquiry with youth and communities*. Sage Publications.

Perry, I. (2004). *Prophets of the hood: Politics and poetics in hip hop*. Duke University Press.

Powers-Carter, S. (2006). "She would've still made that face expression": The uses of multiple literacies by two African American young women. *Theory Into Practice*, 45(4), 352–358.

Richardson, L., & St. Pierre, E. A. (2008). Writing: A method of inquiry. In N. K. Denzin & Y. S. Lincoln (Eds.), *Collecting and interpreting qualitative materials* (pp. 473–500). Sage Publications.

Royster, J. J. (2000). *Traces of a stream: Literacy and social change among African American women*. University of Pittsburgh Press.

Saavedra, C. & Marx, S. (2016). Schooling as taming wild tongues and bodies. *Global Studies of Childhood*, 6(1), 42–52.

Saldaña, J. (2013). *The coding manual for qualitative researchers* (2nd ed.). SAGE Publications.

Sexton, J. (2010). Proprieties of coalition: Blacks, Asians, and the politics of policing. *Critical Sociology*, 36(1), 87–108.

Tuck, E. (2009). Suspending damage: A letter to communities. *Harvard Education Review*, 79(3), 409–427.

Tuck, E., & Yang, W. (2014). Unbecoming claims: Pedagogies of refusal in qualitative research. *Qualitative Inquiry*, 20(6), 811–818.

Tuhiwai Smith, L. (1999). *Decolonizing methodologies: Research and indigenous peoples*. Zed Books.

Walker, A. (1983). *In search of our mothers' gardens: Womanist prose*. The Women's Press.

Winn, M. (2011). *Girl time: Literacy, justice, and the school-to-prison pipeline*. Teachers College Press.

Wissman, K. (2007). "Making a way": Young women using literacy and language to resist the politics of silencing. *Journal of Adolescent & Adult Literacy*, 51(4), 340–349.

GRACE D. PLAYER is an assistant professor of literacy at the University of Connecticut Neag School of Education. She is an Asian American daughter, sister, educator, researcher, writer, and artist.

This article originally appeared in *Language Arts* 97.5

DISRUPTING RACE-EVASIVE PRACTICES IN LITERACY TEACHER EDUCATION: Reflections on Research and Implications for Policy

This column addresses why race matters in literacy teacher preparation and how teacher-educators and researchers might disrupt pervasive, long-standing race-evasive practices.

MELISSA MOSLEY WETZEL

AS THE 2019 SCHOOL YEAR approached, my social media feeds began to reflect the efforts of educational activists to bring race and racism to the attention of families, policymakers, and teachers. In Cobb County, Georgia, an Atlanta news journal featured the group Stronger Together that sought to "implement training for teachers and staff on how to identify and correct 'implicit bias,' which refers to stereotypes or attitudes that can affect actions unconsciously" (Dixon, 2019). Locally, where I prepare teachers, a group called Educators in Solidarity were getting ready to attend their sixth Round Rock Independent School District board meeting to give anonymous testimony of teachers and families regarding racial inequities in the district. These two groups stand on the shoulders of activists and community organizers who have long fought for racial equity in the United States. Social-justice educators now, across the United States, ask for the public's attention as they act to confront racial bias and inequities in school.

In this Research and Policy column, I argue that educators should attend to race in literacy teacher education. Then, I discuss what we know about race, racism, and racial identity in literacy teacher education by sharing some findings of a literature review. That section is followed by a review of how teacher-educators might disrupt race-evasive practices in literacy education. Finally, I argue for a set of recommendations for teacher-education policy and practice based on what we can learn from this literature.

Why Attend to Race, Racism, and Racial Identities in Literacy Teacher Education?

Although structural and institutional racism is prevalent in US schools, racial bias and inequities are often upheld when teachers evade race and racism as a framework for understanding students' educational experiences and opportunities. In 1999, Larson and Irvine proposed that a core concern of the time was the "cultural mismatch" of students and their teachers. Since then, an even wider disparity has grown between the racial demographics of teachers and students in the United States. Researchers in the field of literacy have been interested in and explored this demographic imperative as well as how we can better prepare teachers of literacy within this context. Two decades later, Harper (2018) reaffirmed that the racial mismatch of students and teachers was the most pertinent issue for educators (Mosley Wetzel et al., 2019), and Haddix (2017) asked that literacy researchers continue to consider what it will take to build a teaching force that guides us to racial equity. Haddix contended that in literacy classrooms, a diverse teaching field is critical to diversify the perspectives and knowledge that students encounter in school: "All teachers are teachers of literacy. Any goal to improve literacy education for all students must involve a close look at the educators charged with delivering literacy curriculum with equity-minded, culturally relevant, and anti-racist pedagogies" (p. 142). Race is "on the table" in public discourse, and literacy teachers are called upon to transform spaces to be more equitable for racially diverse students. As we continue to work on diversifying the teaching force in this country, we must simultaneously continue to confront racism and consider what it means to prepare teachers to confront racism in schools as well as to actively resist participating in and perpetuating racist teaching practices.

The racial and linguistic mismatch between the teaching force and the students in US schools often leads to teachers neglecting students' interests, culture, and resources as opposed to having the sociocultural knowledge to recognize and draw on these strengths. Brown (2013) proposed the concept of critical sociocultural knowledge, the knowledge that might support them in being transformative when teaching linguistically and culturally diverse students. This knowledge is associated with pedagogical tools used to identify young people in terms of their assets, the structures and processes of oppression that students experience, and advocacy for students across educational settings. This knowledge is important to all teachers because a teacher's racial identity influences what resources they see and value. Because of the racial inequities of significance within educational contexts, researchers like Brown (2013) have been interested in how preservice teachers come to understand their own formative experiences as well as how they learn critical sociocultural knowledge, in particular regarding race, racism, and racial identity.

How has literacy-teacher education engaged with the complexities of preparing predominately White females to work in increasingly diverse sociocultural contexts? Literacy researchers often cite the impetus of the racial mismatch between teachers and students. Drawing on scholars such as Banks and Banks (2009), researchers argue that the pedagogical decisions of a teacher matter concerning the roles and worlds they inhabit. In US schools today, children and youth are under increased stress and insecurity because of policies for immigration and the prevalence of racial violence and police brutality. Since the 2016 US presidential election, in which candidate Trump appealed to his voters with racist rhetoric, hate crimes have increased and the stakes have risen for students of Color who are visible targets of racial violence in school and their communities (Pollock, 2017). Teaching Tolerance, ReadWriteThink, Rethinking Schools, and the Anti-Defamation League, among other organizations, have created and collected resources for educators to address racial violence in the curriculum, and researchers have argued for increased curricular attention to the social, political, and cultural context of education in the United States (Darling-Hammond, 2017; Justice & Stanley, 2016).

Since the election of Trump, and in response to the #BlackLivesMatter movement, teacher-educators have innovated with such curriculum in their courses, drawing on a long tradition of teacher-educators working for social justice. Literacy teachers do not have the option to be neutral; to read these texts requires recognizing the partiality of representations and misrepresentations in the media regarding immigration and other political issues. However, teacher-educators have identified the fears of preservice teachers in doing so. Using an Obama political speech as text, Dávila and Barnes (2017) explored what happens when preservice teachers imagine teaching with such a text. Although their teacher-educators supported them in thinking about how such a document might be an entry into discussing equity and justice, preservice teachers in this study were attracted to teaching methods that would allow them to assume "positions of neutral impartiality and withholding their opinions" (p. 315). As teacher-educators ask preservice teachers to think about racial violence and equity as part of their work as literacy teachers, they will confront long-standing norms of neutrality and curricular choices that do not actively engage in anti-racism.

RACE IS "ON THE TABLE" IN PUBLIC DISCOURSE, AND LITERACY TEACHERS ARE CALLED UPON TO TRANSFORM SPACES TO BE MORE EQUITABLE FOR RACIALLY DIVERSE STUDENTS.

Whiteness is the ability to move within many spaces without engaging with race, racism, and inequity. This unexamined access is another key reason that teacher-educators must attend to race, racism, and racial identities in literacy-teacher education. When working in schools that are culturally and linguistically diverse, Whiteness is salient because of the layers of institutional identities and privileges that teachers hold (Ladson-Billings, 1999). Schools and society continually recenter Whiteness, making it difficult for many teachers to examine the racial identities they bring to the classroom and their own relationship to Whiteness (Picower, 2009). Oyler (2017) draws on the research of critical scholar Stetsenko (2014) to argue that a teacher's work today is to commit to actions that resist and re-envision new possibilities for communities. This action is curricular and involves identity work. Both literacy-teacher educators and literacy teachers have to consider how White privilege impacts our students. It is our duty as educators. There will be tensions in our work, but we can discover ways to learn within and through such tensions (Mosley Wetzel, Svrcek, Daly-Lesch & LeeKeenan, 2019). Critical Whiteness studies has moved the field beyond individualized notions of what it means to be racist or anti-racist and brought attention to the essential work of deconstructing or reading interactions through a lens that interrogates race and racism or reconstructing new, more anti-racist practices (e.g., Leonardo, 2002).

In multiracial, linguistically, and culturally rich spaces, experiences and encounters between teachers, teachers and students, interns and cooperating teachers, and others are highly racialized. As a field, we must reflect on how we engage in these moments and whether to keep going with business as usual. We also need to understand more about how and why it is difficult in literacy-teacher education to engage preservice teachers in teaching and learning with a framework of race and racism. What will compel preservice teachers—many of whom are White and female and often not engaging with frameworks of race and racism—to read their own racial identities within the contexts where they work and to analyze interactions using critical sociocultural knowledge (Brown, 2013)? Beyond exploration, how are preservice teachers supported to build new, brave practices that lead to more socially just classrooms and schools, and in what ways is Whiteness and its invisibility a barrier to such work?

IN MULTIRACIAL, LINGUISTICALLY, AND CULTURALLY RICH SPACES, EXPERIENCES AND ENCOUNTERS BETWEEN TEACHERS, TEACHERS AND STUDENTS, INTERNS AND COOPERATING TEACHERS, AND OTHERS ARE HIGHLY RACIALIZED.

What Do We Know about Race in Literacy Teacher Education?

To answer this question, our racially, linguistically, and culturally diverse research team conducted a review of articles published in English from 2001 to 2018 (Mosley Wetzel et al., 2019). We asked, what do we know about how to prepare teacher candidates in literacy for the work of taking sociocultural knowledge into account when preparing to be a literacy teacher? Our team defined sociocultural knowledge broadly to include knowledge of race, culture, language, sexuality, gender, and other identities, as well as the reasons these identities matter in educational contexts. We started with a database called CITE-ITEL (2016) (https://cite.edb.utexas.edu/), a joint project of the University of Texas at Austin and the Literacy Research Association that focuses on peer-reviewed international journals published in English focused on initial preparation of literacy teachers. Through a search of 650 articles, we found 107 articles that focused on sociocultural knowledge of teachers. It was a comprehensive review; our team included all articles that related to the literature review topic. In this section, I describe studies that show how teacher-educators have endeavored, with barriers, to engage preservice teachers in exploring their racial identities as well as the resources of students of Color.

EXPLORING RACIAL IDENTITIES

Exploring racial identities is one way teacher-educators have considered through research how teachers bring particular positions and racial identities to classrooms and how they can explore and expand them (e.g., Marx & Pennington, 2003; Ohito, 2016; Simon, 2015). Researchers and educators have drawn on a number of frameworks, from McIntosh's (1991) metaphor of the "invisible knapsack" to describe the unearned privileges that Whiteness affords to more recent metaphors such as "White fragility" (DiAngelo, 2018) that bring attention to how perspectives, discourse, and actions uphold such privileges. Just over a quarter of the 107 articles our team reviewed in literacy-teacher education were focused on how preservice teachers are prepared to teach literacy by focusing on their own identities and experiences in and out of school. Across these articles, more than half of the participants identified as White. Across many of the studies, literature written for young people was a tool to begin to explore the stories and experiences of others next to their own in preparation for teaching in diverse classrooms (e.g., Voelker, 2013). In many of the studies, preservice teachers engaged in autobiographical work to identify their identities and cultures without exploring literature.

In these studies, preservice teachers commonly drew on "universality," which Glenn (2012) defines as "not the same lived realities among people everywhere but intimates instead the shared elements of existence that draws us together as a human species" (p. 335). When reading a novel about a character who is a person of Color, the preservice teacher might connect the experience of that character and her own experience. Some argue these kinds of connections allow for empathy and deeper understanding of the experiences of people of Color, but Glenn warns that these kinds of connections often lead to the "intimation that race doesn't really matter" (p. 336) or provided a context for preservice teachers to "other" people with different racial or cultural experiences (Hammett & Bainbridge, 2009). In these instances of discussing or focusing on universality, preservice teachers were often unable to recognize the impact of race and racism in the characters' lives. It was difficult for preservice teachers in the study to identify differences between their own lives and their students' without drawing on deficit perspectives (e.g., Monroe & Ruan, 2018; Xu, 2000), perhaps because of the pervasive tendency to identify universality in US culture and schooling.

Also in the articles, researchers focused on the nuanced ways that preservice teachers can engage in broadening their understanding of the experiences of students of Color through such self-exploration. For example, preservice teachers participated in writing autobiographies alongside a biography of a student of Color they were working with in a practicum or classroom (Murillo, 2010). They then identified the deficit discourses that often come to the surface in this kind of writing. Also, completing equity audits (Miller, 2014) allowed preservice teachers to more deeply understand the experiences of students in schools that are linguistically and culturally complex (Ball, 2009). One researcher focused on preservice teachers of Color, who worked on examining their own cultural identities, and finding deepened understandings about the ways cultural and linguistic identities "matter" in teaching (Haddix, 2010). In another study, preservice teachers wrote scenarios in which a teachers' identity or culture would be relevant in literacy teaching (Mendelowitz, 2017). The teacher-educator's intent was to build critical consciousness of one's positionality, moving beyond the preservice teacher's exploration of personal cultural or linguistic background to where their deficit perspectives come from—their participation in systemic racism and gaps in their knowledge about structural inequities. Telling narratives of their experiences through a lens of race and injustice helped to move the preservice teachers forward in examining race, racism, and racial identities.

EXPLORING RESOURCES OF STUDENTS OF COLOR

For inclusion in our review, we required that the author drew on a critical perspective in education, such as culturally responsive pedagogy (Ladson-Billings, 2009) or anti-racist teaching (Sefa Dei, 1999) in the context they studied. These perspectives bring attention to the resources that students bring to school that vary from those that have been traditionally valued, such as standard English, accurate decoding and fluency, or getting the meaning "right" (Aukerman, 2015). Over 40 percent of the 107 articles we reviewed centered student assets and what teachers do concerning these resources. Assets included students' linguistic resources (e.g., Souto-Manning & Price-Dennis, 2012), cultural histories (e.g., Simon, 2015), and lived experiences (e.g., Escamilla & Nathenson-Mejia, 2003). Preservice teachers learned about students by working with them in academic contexts such as after-school tutoring, in-school practicum, and other educational settings.

Teacher-educators often found that preservice teachers had trouble understanding and identifying the ways that *not seeing* a student's assets might hold broader structural inequities in place or be forms of racial violence. In the articles we reviewed, some preservice teachers embraced the idea that students' cultural and linguistic practices can be drawn upon when planning for instruction, whereas other preservice teachers persisted in their deficit views of the languages students speak (e.g., Lazar, 2007). Preservice teachers sometimes felt underprepared to address inequities in the classroom, deciding these issues were not relevant to the work of teaching (e.g., Dávila, 2013). They also explicitly resisted children's literature, young adult literature, or professional literature with critical perspectives that pushed them to identify the racial violence embedded in their perspectives (e.g., Souto-Manning & Price-Dennis, 2012). Few authors addressed White privilege in these studies, evading a discussion of how it might be so that within a space focused on equity and justice, the maintenance of such racial violence could occur. Amos (2016) suggests that in these spaces, preservice teachers may know about a students' resources for literacy when working closely with them but may still be limited by the "overwhelming presence of whiteness in education" (p. 1002). Understanding how and why schools keep inequities in place by undervaluing student resources is tough for teachers to embrace because of the very normalized ways that Whiteness is privileged in many societal spaces. Amos writes, "Because of its integral nature, whiteness is taken for granted and is invisible to whites. Therefore, it is normalized and naturalized. As a result, whiteness becomes a foundation of white racism" (p. 1003).

In a contrasting study, Falter and Kerkhoff (2018) used *All American Boys* by Reynolds and Kiely (2015) to engage preservice teachers in thinking about the inclusion of curriculum that directly engages with racism. Falter and Kerkhoff (2018) write that through the exploration of literature, the preservice teachers in their study did consider how politics would affect their decisions about curriculum and instruction in their future classrooms. Perhaps because the literature they chose presented two perspectives that were racially different, the students encountered the idea that neutrality is not possible, but every text holds a perspective.

A disappointingly small subset of the articles that were focused on student resources specifically used a framework of race to identify the importance of or analyze deficit perspectives of students. These authors focused on topics such as language variation, the origins of Black language, the reasons variation matters and persists, and language and power. This approach diverges from earlier work that centered on contact or relationships with culturally and linguistically diverse learners as a way to disrupt deficit perspectives. For example, in two studies, preservice teachers learned about multilingualism and their appreciation for those backgrounds grew into more nuanced understandings of language as part of culture (e.g., Mahalingappa, Hughes, & Polat, 2018; Murillo, 2010). In some of the studies we reviewed, critical sociocultural knowledge included pedagogical knowledge about how to leverage students' resources for teaching, such as Wall and Hurie (2017), who studied the post-conferences between bilingual preservice teachers and university facilitators that enabled three bilingual preservice teachers to draw on their linguistic resources in the conferences to think about how to teach in more inclusive ways. Finally, scholars focused on deepening preservice teachers' sociocultural knowledge by teaching institutional factors that reproduce racial inequalities (e.g., Dávila, 2011; Miller, 2014; Simon, 2015). Drawing on the philosophy of Wynter (1984), Brown (2013) contends Whiteness long been associated with what is right and just in Western conceptions of humanity; whereas Blackness is associated with "undesirability" (p. 324), and therefore, "black people have, and continue to exist in framing discourses that deny their humanity" (p. 325). In this small group of studies, authors focused more squarely on how preservice teachers learned how and why the deficit discourses are held in place, even when that work was sometimes painful. Indeed, when we address deficit perspectives, we call into question the ways we know and understand the world, and that is incredibly necessary and difficult work. We envisioned that in the future, more teacher-educators might center such critical sociocultural knowledge in their literacy methods courses as a way to empower preservice teachers to recognize diversity as an asset.

Disrupting Race-Evasive Literacy-Teacher Education

The team that reviewed the literature I have described in this column was racially, religiously, culturally, and linguistically diverse, and we were dismayed at the number of articles that did not engage with race and critical sociocultural knowledge when preparing teachers to be responsive to diversity in schools. We saw this absence in terms of who conducted the research studies (researchers were mostly White or did not racially identify) and in the racial demographics of the preservice teachers who were studied. Also, a few articles focused on learning with others within a racially diverse community. For the most part, teacher-educators tended to collect individual-level data and were more likely to provide in-depth case studies than close analyses of group processes and learning. Such a silence is significant because we know little of the collective engagement and learning that happens within literacy-teacher education spaces.

The percentage of researchers who identified as scholars of Color or identified racially at all increased when the area of research was race, racism, and language or multiliteracies/bilingual literacy instruction. Also, in 21 percent of the articles, the teacher candidates were not identified racially or in terms of positionality beyond gender, and in most, authors only named positionality; racial and other identities or intersectionality were not taken up as essential aspects of the work. Based on these silences, we can assume that more than half of the articles we reviewed included only preservice teachers who are White and that race was more often than not ignored when it came to the teachers and teacher-educators learning to teach literacy. As Lysaker and Handsfield (2019) comment, to name race or engage with race in literacy-teacher education represents a disruption in flow, the normalized, business-as-usual work of teacher education. In this area of research, the flow of engaging with race through a color-blind perspective or to intimate that race doesn't matter is deeply problematic. In other words, research in literacy teacher education in the area of sociocultural knowledge has mostly perpetuated the idea that race doesn't matter.

The alternative is to center race in the positionality statements of researchers and to embed reflexivity in the design and implementation of the study. For example, Skerrett and her colleagues align their positionality statements, theoretical frameworks, and study design with critical race and Black feminist perspectives (Skerrett, Pruitt, & Warrington, 2015). When focusing on the participation of two preservice teachers, one who identified as White and one who identified as Black, within online discussions around professional texts, the authors focused on the "specialist knowledge frameworks" each brought to analyze inequalities in society. They write, "The two preservice teachers employed these . . . to analyze and challenge racial, linguistic, and other forms of injustice in English education and suggest curricular and instructional approaches that would promote educational equity for diverse students" (p. 331). They also used their framework to analyze the ways their peers contested the specialist forms of knowledge that both of the preservice teachers brought to bear on the discussions. In summary, researchers can deeply engage in positioning themselves in terms of racial identities and also use their perspectives to illuminate how race operates in literacy teacher education classrooms.

In the aforementioned study, Skerrett and colleagues (2015) suggest that the specialist knowledge of a preservice teacher of Color was essential to the group's learning in online discussions. Jasmine, the preservice teacher, drew on her racial literacy in response to professional readings online as a Black woman to challenge discourses that diminished the impact of race in English education. Another exemplar study that includes a focus on collective learning was conducted by Heineke (2014), who used Little's (2002) framework for learning communities of teachers to analyze how preservice teachers developed knowledge of and practices for teaching English learners. Heineke used discourse analysis to find examples of conversations that illustrated learning about learners, about self, and future practices. Rogers and Mosley (2008) similarly shared how an African American preservice teacher challenged a White peer's interpretation of a book with a White protagonist working toward racial justice. Through a multimodal analysis, the authors propose that such close attention to interactions is needed to understand how preservice teachers learn racial literacy within teacher-education programs. These studies bring awareness to both the contributions of a diverse preservice teacher group in the learning of preservice teachers as well as the features of conversations that engage critical sociocultural knowledge as a tool for analysis (Brown, 2013).

RESEARCH IN LITERACY TEACHER EDUCATION IN THE AREA OF SOCIOCULTURAL KNOWLEDGE HAS MOSTLY PERPETUATED THE IDEA THAT RACE DOESN'T MATTER.

Attending to collective learning and group dynamics is essential if we are to move past the flow; to disrupt the intimation that race doesn't matter in literacy-teacher education. Amos (2016) draws on a framework of race evasiveness to analyze how preservice teachers of Color were impacted—negatively—by their White peers in the classroom in a discussion. In this article, Amos draws on interviews of preservice teachers and her reflective memos, attending carefully to her role and positionality in the study. She attends to the ways her positioning contributed to race evasiveness in the discussions and extrapolates her findings to reason about the failures of the literacy-teacher preparation program. Amos proposes that preservice teachers do not have adequate support for the work they do to interrupt Whiteness in teacher education (see also Haddix, 2017).

Reflecting on the literature, our research team often noted that there is no lack of studies that provide us with models of what it looks like and sounds like when preservice teachers, who are mostly White, are engaged in learning through experiences with multicultural literature or in teaching linguistically and culturally diverse children and youth. However, these engagements are not enough. Most of these studies have not attended to the rapidly shifting political, social, and cultural contexts of teaching, nor the importance of racial identities in literacy teacher education. The activist stance that Oyler (2017) suggests points us to further examine collective learning within teacher education programs, especially instances and models when the pervasive "overwhelming presence of whiteness" (Amos, 2016, p. 1002) is disrupted by teacher-educators or preservice teachers within a university course or experience. As teacher-educators, we must continue to work against persistent and pervasive race-evasive practices in teacher education to disrupt the flow of business as usual.

Recommendations for Policy and Practice

How might teacher-educators apply a race conscious lens and engage in resistance to the race-evasive policies that guide their programs? In this column, I have made a case for closer attention to race in literacy teacher education. I've drawn on a literature review to discuss what we are currently doing in literacy-teacher education. I conclude by asking, what might lead to widespread alignment within teacher education programs in literacy that directly engage, rather than evade race as a framework?

The first set of recommendations applies to how a program articulates how they wish to disrupt business as usual. Teacher-educators will have to recognize, value, and engage with tensions when working toward race-conscious and critical approaches to teacher preparation. For some time, my colleagues and I have been working on developing cross-cutting themes that reflect our core agreements about the teacher we want to emerge from our program. Responding to an initial draft, the graduate students who are responsible for teaching many of the teacher-education courses called for a more explicit recognition of the ways we are complicit in *and* work against oppression, racial inequities, and White privilege. Through the process of writing and revising this document, we found ourselves committing to providing widespread curricular changes in ways that supported those faculty who were already taking risks by disrupting flows. A widespread investment and alignment are powerful, but the danger is that an assumption that we have arrived at a collective understanding might hinder the growth of new ideas and practices. As a program, we have decided to form working groups in curriculum change to continue to examine our practices using a critical lens to grow our courses.

According to the research, our field has established a practice of self-exploration through autobiography or examining one's history concerning the stories of others (e.g., Emdin, 2016; Pollock, 2008; Singleton, 2014). We might center these texts to create assignments for preservice teachers to engage in self-exploration of their racial identity as they move through different contexts. We might expect that in some contexts, preservice teachers will draw on universality as a lens to position themselves with others, and in other settings, the same preservice teacher might need the support of critical frameworks to understand their positioning. We would expect that self-exploration would occur over time and across contexts and that a core set of beliefs or a vision would be a touchstone throughout the process. Disruption of business as usual would require that these explorations occur in groups that are multiracial and include people who see the world from different perspectives with guidance from teacher-educators to engage productively in tensions about the design and implementation of such practices. Such diversity might make it more likely that White preservice teachers and teacher-educators would be held accountable for reading these designs through a lens of Whiteness and race, but it would be critical to have knowledgeable facilitators who know how to support people who have deep-seated negative and racist beliefs to work through. Taking an inquiry approach to such work might support preservice teachers to later engage in this same autobiographical work with students, further expanding their understandings of students' resources and positioning within educational spaces.

The second area of change supports preservice teachers and their teacher-educators to engage in disrupting Whiteness in education. Support might occur within professional communities (Little, 2002) that include partners in teacher education, such as mentor teachers, teacher-educators from the university, supervisors who work in the field, and preservice teachers. To disrupt business as usual, these learning communities would be racially, linguistically, and institutionally diverse. Tensions such as those that emerge when we come face to face with extreme privilege would be facilitated by those knowledgeable about how Whiteness operates in such discussions. In order to avoid placing the burden on faculty of Color, professional development might be provided by a facilitator who is experienced in mediating learning in racially diverse spaces. Groups might do the work of developing joint efforts and tools to understand change inside of programs, indicators that things are going well, and ways to identify productive tensions. Such learning communities would also need to check themselves in terms of compliance and critical engagement, such as using tools to recognize the signs that the community is privileging compliance over innovation. They may do so by engaging in cycles of problem-posing and problem-solving, as both Simon (2015) and Picower (2007) illustrated in their studies of preservice-teacher learning.

Although disrupting race-evasive practices in literacy-teacher education at the level of a program or comprehensively in the field will take time, we cannot wait. I would encourage activist groups such as Stronger Together in Cobb County and Educators in Solidarity in Round Rock to demand of teacher preparation programs the same kinds of anti-racist pedagogies and practices they demand of school districts. As teacher-educators, we must review and revise much of what we do in literacy-teacher education to help preservice teachers recognize and disrupt Whiteness and implicit bias because they will need to continue this work throughout their careers. We know the schools we have now are not the schools we need to realize a more racially just and equitable world, and that is important to keep central.

ALTHOUGH DISRUPTING RACE-EVASIVE PRACTICES IN LITERACY-TEACHER EDUCATION AT THE LEVEL OF A PROGRAM OR COMPREHENSIVELY IN THE FIELD WILL TAKE TIME, WE CANNOT WAIT.

NOTE

The author would like to acknowledge the critical support of the department editors of this special issue, Theresa Rogers and Elizabeth Marshall, as well as members of the research team: Saba Khan Vlach, Natalie Sue Svrcek, Erica Holyoke, Lakeya Omogun, Cori Salmerón, Nathaly Batista-Morales, Laura A. Taylor, and Doris Villarreal.

TEACHING TIPS

In this policy column, Mosley Wetzel examines why race matters in teacher preparation and how to move beyond race-evasive practices that have created barriers for meaningfully engaging in racial literacy work. This essay provides an opportunity to explore your experiences with race and racism. Below are a few questions to guide your self-reflection in this work:

1. ***In what ways might you be complicit in perpetuating racial inequities, racial oppression, and/or White privilege?***
2. ***In what ways do you work against racial inequities, racial oppression, and/or White privilege?***
3. ***What tension/s do you notice?***
4. ***What steps can you take to align your actions and eventually teaching practices with the principles of racial literacy?***

Your responses to these questions can inform how you develop antiracist curriculum and pedagogies, as well as your relationships with your co-workers, students, and families of color.

REFERENCES

Amos, Y. T. (2016). Voices of teacher candidates of color on white race evasion: "I worried about my safety!" *International Journal of Qualitative Studies in Education*, 29(8), 1002–1015.

Aukerman, M. (2015). How should readers develop across time? Mapping change without a deficit perspective. *Language Arts*, 93(1), 57–64.

Ball, A. F. (2009). Toward a theory of generative change in culturally and linguistically complex classrooms. *American Educational Research Journal*, 46(1), 45–72.

Banks, J. A., & Banks, C. A. M. (Eds.). (2009). *Multicultural education: Issues and perspectives*. John Wiley & Sons.

Brown, K. D. (2013). Trouble on my mind: Toward a framework of humanizing critical sociocultural knowledge for teaching and teacher education. *Race Ethnicity and Education*, 16(3), 316–338.

CITE-ITEL (2016). A dialogical synthesis of research into initial literacy teacher preparation. https://cite.edb .utexas.edu.

Darling-Hammond, L. (2017). Teaching for social justice: Resources, relationships, and anti-racist practice. *Multicultural Perspectives*, 19(3), 133–138.

Dávila, D. (2011). "White people don't work at Mcdonald's" and other shadow stories from the field: Analyzing preservice teachers' use of Obama's race speech to teach for social justice. *English Education*, 44(1), 13–50.

Dávila, D. (2013). Cultural boundaries or geographic borders? Future teachers define "American" in response to *In my Family/En mi familia*. In P. J. Dunston, S. K. Fullerton, C. C. Bates, K. Headley, P. M. Stecker (Eds.), *The 61st yearbook of the literacy research association* (pp. 260–272). Literacy Research Association.

Dávila, D. & Barnes, M. E. (2017). Beyond censorship: Politics, teens, and ELA teacher candidates. *English Teaching: Practice & Critique*, 16(3), 303–318.

DiAngelo, R. (2018). *White fragility: Why it's so hard for white people to talk about racism*. Beacon Press.

Dixon, C. (2019, August 9). Group wants Cobb schools to address racism, bias in classroom. *Atlanta Journal Constitution*. https://www.ajc.com/news/local-education /group-wants-cobb-schools-address-racism-bias-classroom/atupmw3 rht0zdANv1sOGTJ/#

Escamilla, K., & Nathenson-Mejía, S. (2003). Preparing culturally responsive teachers: Using Latino children's literature in teacher education special issue: Partnering for equity. *Equity & Excellence in Education*, 36(3), 238–248.

Emdin, C. (2016). *For white folks who teach in the hood . . . and the rest of y'all too: Reality pedagogy and urban education*. Beacon Press.

Falter, M. M., & Kerkhoff, S. N. (2018). Slowly shifting out of neutral: Using young adult literature to discuss PSTs' beliefs about racial injustice and police brutality. *English Teaching: Practice & Critique*, 17(3), 257–276.

Glenn, W. J. (2012). Developing understandings of race: Preservice teachers' counter-narrative (re)constructions of people of color in young adult literature. *English Education*, 44(4), 326–353.

Haddix, M. (2010). No longer on the margins: Researching the hybrid literate identities of Black and Latina preservice teachers. *Research in the Teaching of English*, 45(2), 97–123.

Haddix, M. M. (2017). Diversifying teaching and teacher education: Beyond rhetoric and toward real change. *Journal of Literacy Research*, 49(1), 141–149.

Hammett, R., & Bainbridge, J. (2009). Pre-service teachers explore cultural identity and ideology through picture books. *Literacy*, 43(3), 152–159.

Harper, S. (2018, May24). Big ideas on equity, race, and inclusion in education. *71st EWA National Seminar*. Keynote address presented at the meeting of the Education Writers Assocation, Los Angeles, CA.

Heineke, A. J. (2014). Dialoguing about English learners: Preparing teachers through culturally relevant literature circles. *Action in Teacher Education*, 36(2), 117–140.

Justice, B., & Stanley, J. (2016). Teaching in the time of Trump. *Social Education*, 80(1), 36–41.

Ladson-Billings, G. (1999). Preparing teachers for diversity: Historical perspectives, current trends, and future directions. In L. Darling-Hammond & G. Sykes (Eds.) *Teaching as the learning profession: Handbook of policy and practice* (pp. 86–123). Jossey-Bass.

Ladson-Billings, G. (2009). *The dreamkeepers: Successful teachers of African American children*. John Wiley & Sons.

Larson, J., & Irvine, P. D. (1999). "We call him Dr. King": Reciprocal distancing in urban classrooms. *Language Arts*, 76(5), 393–400.

Lazar, A. M. (2007). It's not just about teaching kids to read: Helping preservice teachers acquire a mindset for teaching children in urban communities. *Journal of Literacy Research*, 39(4), 411–443.

Leonardo, Z. (2002). The souls of white folk: Critical pedagogy, whiteness studies, and globalization discourse. *Race, Ethnicity and Education*, 5(1), 29–50.

Little, J. W. (2002). Professional community and the problem of high school reform. *International Journal of Educational Research*, 37(8), 693–714.

Lysaker, J. T., & Handsfield, L. J. (2019). Integrative research syntheses as sites of disruption in literacy teacher education. *Journal of Literacy Research*, 5(2), 252–258.

Mahalingappa, L., Hughes, E. M., & Polat, N. (2018). Developing preservice teachers' self-efficacy and knowledge through online experiences with English language learners. *Language and Education*, 32(2), 127–146.

Marx, S., & Pennington, J. (2003). Pedagogies of critical race theory: Experimentations with white preservice teachers. *International Journal of Qualitative Studies in Education*, 16(1), 91–110.

McIntosh, P. (2007). White privilege: Unpacking the invisible knapsack. In P.S. Rothenberg (Ed.) *Race, class, and gender in the United States: An integrated study* (pp. 177–82). Worth Publishing.

Mendelowitz, B. (2017). Conceptualising and enacting the critical imagination through a critical writing pedagogy. *English Teaching: Practice & Critique*, 16(2), 178–193.

Miller, sj (2014). Cultivating a disposition for sociospatial justice in English teacher preparation. *Teacher Education and Practice*, 27(1), 44–74.

Monroe, L., & Ruan, J. (2018). Increasing early childhood preservice teachers' intercultural sensitivity through the ABCs. *Journal of Early Childhood Teacher Education*, 39(1), 1–15.

Mosley Wetzel, M., Svrcek, N. S., Daly-Lesch, A., & LeeKeenan, K. (2019). Coaching through the hard parts: Addressing tensions in teaching with one preservice teacher learning to teach literacy in a fifth-grade classroom. *Teaching and Teacher Education*, 82, 43–54.

Mosley Wetzel, M., Vlach, S. K., Svrcek, N. S., Steinitz, E., Omogun, L., Salmerón, C., . . . & Villarreal, D. (2019). Preparing teachers with sociocultural knowledge in literacy: A literature review. *Journal of Literacy Research*, 51(2), 138–157.

Murillo, L. A. (2010). Local literacies as counter-hegemonic practices: Deconstructing anti-Spanish ideologies in the Rio Grande Valley. In R. T. Jiménez, V. J. Risko, M. K. Hundley, & D. W. Rowe (Eds.), *59th yearbook of the National Reading Conference* (pp. 276–287). National Reading Conference.

Ohito, E. O. (2016). Making the emperor's new clothes visible in anti-racist teacher education: Enacting a pedagogy of discomfort with white preservice teachers. *Equity & Excellence in Education*, 49(4), 454–467.

Oyler, C.J. (2017). Constructive resistance: Activist repertoires for teachers. *Language Arts*, 95(1), 30–39.

Picower, B. (2007). Supporting new educators to teach for social justice: The critical inquiry project model. *Penn GSE Perspectives on Urban Education*, 5(1), 1–22.

Picower, B. (2009). The unexamined whiteness of teaching: How white teachers maintain and enact dominant racial ideologies. *Race, Ethnicity and Education*, 12(2), 197–215.

Pollock, M. (Ed.). (2008). *Everyday antiracism: Getting real about race in school.* The New Press.

Pollock, M. (2017). Three challenges for teachers in the era of Trump. *Educational Studies: Journal of the American Educational Studies Association*, 53(4), 426–427.

Reynolds, J., & Kiely, B. (2015). *All American boys.* Athenium Books.

Rogers, R., & Mosley, M. (2008). A critical discourse analysis of racial literacy in teacher education. *Linguistics and Education*, 19(2), 107–131.

Sefa Dei, G. J. (1999). The denial of difference: Refraining anti-racist praxis. *Race, Ethnicity and Education*, 2(1), 17–38.

Simon, R. (2015). "I'm fighting my fight, and I'm not alone anymore": The influence of communities of inquiry. *English Education*, 48(1), 41–71.

Singleton, G. E. (2014). *Courageous conversations about race: A field guide for achieving equity in schools.* Corwin Press.

Skerrett, A., Pruitt, A. A., & Warrington, A. S. (2015). Racial and related forms of specialist knowledge on English education blogs. *English Education*, 47(4), 314–346.

Souto-Manning, M., & Price-Dennis, D. (2012). Critically redefining and repositioning media texts in early childhood teacher education: What if? and why? *Journal of Early Childhood Teacher Education*, 33(4), 304–321.

Stetsenko, A. (2014). Transformative activist stance for education: The challenge of inventing the future in moving beyond the status quo. In T. Corcoran (Ed.) *Psychology in education: Critical theory-practice* (pp. 181–198). Rotterdam: Sense Publishers.

Voelker, A. N. (2013). Tomorrow's teachers engaging in unprotected text. *Journal of Children's Literature*, 39(2), 23–36.

Wall, D. J., & Hurie, A. H. (2017). Post-observation conferences with bilingual pre-service teachers: Revoicing and rehearsing. *Language and Education*, 31(6), 543–560.

Wynter, S. 1984. The ceremony must be found: After humanism. *Boundary*, 12(3), 19–70.

Xu, S. H. (2000). Preservice teachers in a literacy methods course consider issues of diversity. *Journal of Literacy Research*, 32(4), 505–531.

MELISSA MOSLEY WETZEL is a professor of Language and Literacy Studies in the Department of Curriculum and Instruction at the University of Texas at Austin, where she teaches courses in elementary reading and literacy, coaching and mentoring, and literacy leadership. Dr. Wetzel's research focuses on how teachers and students together design literacy practices that are transformative using anti-racist and critical literacy approaches.

This article originally appeared
in *English Education 52.4*

"I KNOW YOU DON'T LIVE IN DETROIT, RIGHT?" An Attempt at Racial Literacy in English Education

MARY L. NEVILLE

This essay begins with my memory of a provocation from a former student about my presence in Detroit as a white English teacher—a provocation invoking the intersections of race and space. The incident inspired the creation of an English education methods syllabus centered in racial literacy frameworks, analyses of space, and prioritizing youth voice for English teacher educators and preservice teachers. It is my hope that this essay offers space for English educators to respond meaningfully to student analyses of power and oppression through English curricula.

EXCEPT FOR THE LIGHT of the projector and the creaking of the furnace, our classroom was peacefully dim and relatively quiet. My 10th-grade English language arts students were diligently copying the definitions of tone and mood into their literature notes, with a few students glancing up at the painting displayed on the overhead projector. This brightly colored image featured two figures walking down a street on a rainy day, their bodies huddled together under one umbrella. On the whiteboard, an objective stated, Students will be able to apply the elements of tone and mood to the description of setting in The Kite Runner. I turned toward the class with a discussion prompt about the tone of the painting on my lips, but Richard instead broke the silence: "Miss, now I know you don't live in Detroit. Right?"

Deer-in-headlights, I managed, "Yes, Richard, I live in the city with my husband. Now, what type of tone do you think this image portrays?" In answering Richard's question in this way, I failed to answer his *real* question, paralyzed as I was by my inability to move with dexterity around the stated objective of the day. While I did not immediately grasp the impact on my life of this seemingly small moment, Richard's question stayed with me years later, eventually urging me toward graduate school to study how white teachers might better construct an antiracist ELA curriculum.

As I reconsider this moment now, I know that I approach Richard's intentions in asking this question with several assumptions. What I do know is that a white,[1] woman teacher standing at the front of a classroom of majority Black and Brown teenagers was a strikingly familiar scene for my students. Richard's experience as a Black young man having mainly white teachers is reflected across the city's and the nation's teaching workforce (Carter Andrews et al., 2019). Moreover, Michigan schools are the second-most segregated in the country, tying with Mississippi and just behind Washington, D.C. (Carmody & Wiowiecki, 2017). While developers/outsiders were and continually are gentrifying Detroit (Clement & Kanai, 2014), the area in which the school is located was an almost entirely Black and Brown community (Jackman, 2018). Thus, I had assumed that Richard was highlighting my presence as a white person in this classroom and the absence of white people who lived in his neighborhood.

In addition to my physical presence as a white person in this class, I likely performed whiteness in ways that may have prompted Richard to read me and my approach to teaching English as white. Whether it was the marking of my physical body as white or my "whit-ification" (Kinloch, 2010, p. 11) of this classroom space, Richard seemed to apply a racialized knowledge of his city and community to

*The term *provocateur* has its origin in then-NCTE President Sandy Hayes's welcome to the CEE 2013 Summer Conference, during which she shared her wish that she could swap the "troublemaker" label she had been given for her name badge at the International Society for Technology in Education conference the month before with then-NCTE Executive Director Kent Williamson's, who was fittingly labeled "provocateur." I can think of no better inspiration than Kent for this section. TSJ this moment. Richard's noting of this racialized pattern espoused much of what 10th-grade English language arts standards call for students to exhibit: a habit of critical thinking—a reading of both texts and the world to analyze systems of injustice and work toward change.

As I now reflect, I wonder if Richard's real question may have been: *Why are you here?* In this essay, I recenter Richard's provocation as I consider the ways that English teachers might enact racial literacies through an English methods curriculum centered in spatial analyses of race and geography (Guinier, 2004; Kinloch, 2010). While I might have constructed a secondary ELA curriculum in response to Richard's question, I instead chose to create an English teacher education course plan because I seek to work with new English teachers who, like myself in the moment of Richard's question, might more strongly situate racialized analyses of texts within the cities in which they teach. In offering this curriculum, I do not assume that such a course would necessarily prepare teachers to better respond to questions like Richard's. Instead, I argue that this curriculum may allow teachers to understand how to situate their antiracist English language arts courses within the spatial and temporal contexts within which they teach ELA students. As English education scholars have argued, the literacies and cities of youth in and out of secondary English classrooms are already-present texts through which teachers and students may learn from, engage, and sustain community (Baker-Bell, Stanbrough, & Everett, 2017; Kinloch, 2010; Paris & Alim, 2014; Watson & Beymer, 2019). The questions youth pose about their world may inform preservice teachers' construction of ELA curricula focused on racial justice and founded in analyses of space, youth voice, and the everyday as art (Kinloch, 2010). In what follows, I provide the theoretical underpinnings for a racial literacy English education methods syllabus centered in both Richard's question and the city of Detroit as text. To begin, I note my positionality within this work.

Reading Me before Reading Detroit, or: Why Are You Here?

> **White teachers do not have to contend with their own complicity in whiteness and do not have to stand in the discomfort that necessarily accompanies working against it.**
>
> —FRANKLIN-PHIPPS & RATH (2019, P. 146)

Why *was* I there? What had led me to be standing at the front of the classroom, deflecting any real discussions surrounding race and my role in maintaining whiteness as it played out in the spatial and literacy lives of my ELA students? In considering how youth in Harlem respond to and interrogate gentrification within their communities, Kinloch (2010) centered Freire's (1970/2000) notion of space: "People, as beings 'in a situation,' find themselves rooted in temporal-spatial conditions which mark them and which they also mark" (p. 90). As I construct a racially literate English teacher education syllabus, I focus on how teachers and youth both "mark and are marked by" the spaces in which they live, learn, and teach, and I begin with how I have similarly marked and been marked by such spaces. To do this, I turn to Morrison (1973), who asked, "How does a reader of any race situate herself or himself in order to approach the world of a black writer? Won't there always be apprehension about what may be revealed, exposed about the reader?" (p. xii). What does it mean for me to teach Black and Brown students within the city of Detroit, and what does it now mean that I approach teacher education through a lens of racial literacy within the context of Detroit? What do my approaches to this city "reveal" and "expose" about me?

I grew up in a medium-sized town an hour and a half from the classroom where Richard asked me his question, and I attended almost entirely white Catholic schools from grades 1 through 12. Growing up in these all-white spaces in Michigan, Detroit was lauded and hushed, praised and feared. Unless touting the skills of Barry Sanders's running game or the beauty of the old houses in the Boston Edison district, it was almost rude to bring up Detroit in the spaces in which I grew up. Despite being interested in teaching English since I was a child, it was not until after high school that I learned of the *Milliken v. Bradley* court case, legislation that had profound impacts for the current system of public schooling in Detroit. Even though I proudly wore the old English D baseball caps, I did not learn about the history of Detroit, racialized or otherwise; I did not visit iconic Belle Isle, and I observed no more than awkward glances when Detroit's 1967 race rebellion was mentioned. In sum, Detroit was admired, feared, and ignored in the spaces in which I was raised and was learning.

These (mis)representations of Detroit within my upbringing are important to consider alongside my experiences as a past ELA teacher and current English teacher educator. Some, if not many, of the preservice teachers with whom we work may have experiences with similar narratives about the cities in which they will one day teach. Kinloch (2010) writes that the grand narrative of danger and damage in Harlem (and Detroit) "tells contradictory stories about existing conditions within urban communities by ignoring the stories local residents have about their community" (p. 89). Youth and community members are often already analyzing the "relations of power and discipline" that are at play in the discursive and material realities of their cities (Soja, 1990). Thus, it is important for PSTs to be able to interrogate these broader societal narratives about race and space to more fully engage in and learn about the contexts in which they teach.

Richard's school was the first space in which, at the age of 25, I worked and existed where the vast majority of individuals with whom I interacted were people of Color. Having three years of teaching experience, I came to Detroit through a Catholic service program, teaching English at Richard's high school for ninth and tenth grade. Despite my lack of actual teaching experiences with predominantly Black and Brown students, I somehow still strongly considered myself at the time an antiracist teacher. The art, voices, and space of the city of Detroit agitated that notion within me. I worked to confront why I might think of myself as antiracist, how my whiteness offered undue and innumerable privileges in my life, and how the historical legacies of race and racism affect the neighborhoods within which my students lived and attended school. Teaching in Detroit made me aware of the contours of what I did not know about race, racism, and the city itself. Learning about the city, with its vast histories, art, and acts of resistance to oppression, helped me to confront the depth of my lack of understanding of race and my racialized positionality within this city's schools. Most saliently, Detroit taught me the importance of "learning rather than knowing" (Guinier, 2004) and the impossible, yet necessary, task of fully deconstructing my whiteness within a racialized society.

Guinier (2004) first offered the concept of racial literacy as a way to analyze how race is "conjugated by class and geography" (p. 116). Those attempting racially literate analyses will "discern the structural, political, and economic circumstances or antecedents that underlie racism and advantage" (p. 100). Racial literacy, then, notes the "complex interactions" between the choices of an individual and the institutional and environmental forces that shape these decisions (Guinier, 2004; Skerrett, 2011). The process of understanding racial inequities as interacting with both the individual and the institutional involves the rejection of an "either/or" binary. The system of schooling within which new teachers learn to teach is the result of continued and state-sanctioned racialized inequities that have dismantled schooling for Black and Brown children, and, simultaneously, this injustice is supported by our individual decisions, particularly as white teachers (Love, 2019; Muhammad, 2019).

The course offered here is designed for a full academic year (two semesters); however, I have included segments of texts in the syllabus in order to point educators toward the most salient aspects of the texts for a racial literacy framework. I encourage teacher educators to choose those texts that most challenge their preservice teachers to consider the historical and contemporary systems of oppression present in their teaching contexts. I organize this course through five interconnected approaches: Architecture and Space (living); Transportation (moving); Art (resisting); School (learning); and Media (reading) (see also Neville, 2019).

Conclusion

I invite us to return to the opening classroom scene from this provocation: the light of the projector, the creaking furnace, Richard's thoughtful question about my place within the city—"Miss, I know you don't live in Detroit. Right?" I had responded to Richard's question with a perfunctory, "Yes, Richard, I live in the city," before returning us to our planned objective. I see the syllabus presented here as an imperfect attempt to respond to Richard's questions, albeit years later. I do not claim that, had I engaged with this syllabus as a preservice teacher, I would have responded to Richard's inquiry with pedagogical perfection; racial literacy scholars argue that one can never "arrive" at an antiracist state of existence. Instead, one must continually sit in the uncomfortable, indeterminate process of becoming (Franklin-Phipps & Rath, 2019). This is true for my experiences in working toward racial literacy, and it will also be true for the preservice teachers in my courses. I'd like to think, though, that I would have at least responded in the moment by pausing our lesson and engaging in a dialogue about Richard's astute observation. In offering this framework, it is my hope that preservice teachers will tussle with the messy, uncertain, and inevitably incomplete process of becoming

Reading Ourselves and Reading Detroit: A Racial Literacy Methods Course for English Teacher Education[2]

Course Objectives	
Preservice teachers (PSTs) will be able to situate themselves within contemporary and historical conversations about Detroit across living spaces, transportation, schooling, art, and media.	
Course Final Assessment	
PSTs will create an ELA course plan for their classroom in Detroit, engaging an analysis of the self, space, youth voice, and art. This unit plan will include one lesson plan co-designed with youth.	
Approach 1: Space and Architecture (Living)	
Objective(s)	• PSTs will be able to correlate their understanding of national and local residential segregation to the physical buildings, architecture, and neighborhoods of Detroit. • PSTs will be able to situate themselves within the historical and contemporary contexts of Detroit.
Potential texts	**National narrative:** • Wilkerson (2011): *The warmth of other suns: The epic story of America's Great Migration.* Focus: "The Great Migration," Part Two. • Rothstein (2017): *The color of law: A forgotten history of how our government segregated America.* Focus: "Racial zoning," "Private agreements, government enforcement," "White flight," "State-sanctioned violence." • Kinloch (2010): *Harlem on our minds: Place, race, and the literacies of urban youth.* **Local narrative:** • (Methods course instructor)'s geographic autobiography, outlining her relationship to the city of Detroit. • Gentrification and schooling: Nikole Hannah-Jones (2015), Gentrification doesn't fix inner city schools; • Redlining and the closing of generational wealth for Detroit's Black families • "Why I Sit": East Lansing High School student Alex Hosey editorial in the *Lansing State Journal* • The 8-mile wall • The urban farming movement before and after white flight • Sugrue (2005): *The origins of the urban crisis* • New Day Films: Conversations along a postal route • Architecture of Detroit: The Detroit Institute of Art; houses, neighborhoods, and church structures in Detroit
Assessment(s)	• PSTs will create a product of their choice that shows the effects of residential segregation, gentrification, or other housing topic within the city of Detroit. Options include a research paper, 3D map of the city, oral history of a Detroit neighborhood from community members or elders, autobiography of Detroit, or another option of their choice. • PSTs will construct a geographic autobiography, outlining their relationship to their created map of Detroit. PSTs will focus on what it means for them, given each of their individual positionalities, to teach in Detroit, and what this may mean to the communities who live in the city given the historical legacies of power, resistance, and oppression in the city.
Approach 2: Transportation (Moving)	
Objective(s)	• PSTs will be able to analyze how transportation affects the education, economic opportunity, and physical layout of the city of Detroit, and will construct meaning about transportation with their students in mind. • PSTs will be able to prioritize youth voice, relying on the expertise of their students to construct a unit plan about Detroit transportation.

Potential texts

Local narrative:

- *Milliken v. Bradley*: Alvarez (2013), How court's bus ruling sealed differences in Detroit schools
- Significance of Detroit train depot
- James Robertson: Heart and sole: Detroiter walks 21 miles in work commute
- Streetcar over "real transit": How Detroit's streetcar overlooked real transit needs to satisfy a well-connected few
- Scooters and gentrification: Who gets access to transportation?
- Oakland and Macomb refusal of regional transportation system
- Cowen, Edwards, Sattin-Bajaj, & Cosby (2018): Motor city miles: Student travel to schools in and around Detroit

Assessment(s)

- PSTs will conduct some sort of communication (e.g., interview, focus group, survey) with one or more Detroit youth, learning from them about what is necessary to know about Detroit transportation.
- PSTs will create a unit plan and performance assessment for their secondary ELA students using the input from their students. This plan will focus on PSTs' and students' understanding of the effect of transportation for the ways Detroiters move, broadly defined. PSTs will connect their unit plan to at least one of the other approaches: housing, schooling, art, or media.

Approach 3: Art (Resisting)

Objective(s)

- PSTs will be able to illustrate their understanding of the impact of art as resistance and art as joy in the city of Detroit.
- PSTs will be able to prioritize youth voice, relying on the expertise of their students to construct a unit plan about Detroit art.

Potential texts

Local narrative:

- Motown music
- Current music from Detroit, including art from Dilla Youth Day and student expertise.
- The Detroit Public Library and, across Woodward, the Detroit Institute of Arts; Wright Museum.
- Statues of Detroit, in particular: Tower of Freedom/Underground Railroad Monument on Detroit Riverfront. A set of two statues, one on Detroit's Riverfront looking across the river toward Canada.
- Visiting or learning about Detroit places devoted to art: Detroit Techno Museum, Motown Museum, The Heidelberg Project, Dabls Mbad African Bead Museum, The Raven Lounge, the historic Blue Bird Inn, The Museum of Contemporary Art, Street art in Brightmoor neighborhood, Riverwise Magazine.
- Murals of Detroit: D. Fernandez, Mural honoring Yemeni Americans, Hamtramck, MI; D. Fernandez, Mural, *Mano de Obra Campesina (Hand of the Peasant Labor)*; S. G. James, The definitive list of everything that will keep you safe as a Black being in America; B. Perez, Southwest Detroit Mural; Murals on Detroit's 8-mile wall.

Assessment(s)

- PSTs will conduct some sort of communication (e.g., interview, lesson plan, survey, focus group, or letter) with one or more Detroit youth, gathering input around what is necessary to know about Detroit art. PSTs will create a lesson plan in response to this information.
- PSTs will construct an aesthetic product of their choice to illustrate their understanding of how Detroiters have used art as resistance and art as joy. Products may include a collage, visual illustration, book of original poems, timeline of historical events, geographical map, screenplay, songs/musical accompaniment, iMovie, intertextual response, or an option of your choice.

Approach 4: Schools (Learning)

Objective

- PSTs will be able to relate the national and local history of schooling to their own educational experiences and the educational experiences of youth in their classrooms.

Potential texts

National narrative:

- Muhammad (2019): *Cultivating genius: An equity model for culturally and historically responsive literacy.*
- Morris (2016): *Pushout: The criminalization of Black girls in schools.*
- Love (2019): *We want to do more than survive: Abolitionist teaching and the pursuit of educational freedom.* Focus: "We who are dark," "Educational survival," "Abolitionist teaching, freedom dreaming, and Black joy."

Local narrative:

- Southwestern and Western High School student walkouts
- *Riverwise Magazine*: Why Black Bottom matters
- We the People of Detroit Community Research Collective
- *Riverwise Magazine*: Young activists test for water safety
- A school district in crisis
- Homrich-Knieling (2018): What the numbers don't show
- The impact of Detroit's emergency managers for Detroit Public Schools
- Halvorsen (2012): African-centered curriculum in Detroit post-*Milliken vs. Bradley*
- Analysis of Grace Lee Boggs School, particularly its focus on place-based education
- Impact of charter schools in Michigan

Assessment

- PSTs will co-create a lesson plan with one or more students on the historical and contemporary contexts of Detroit schooling.
- Together with one or more peers and/or fellow teachers, PSTs will construct an action plan to interrupt the historical legacies of race and racism within educational organizations within their city. This will entail PSTs working with local educational stakeholders to somehow respond to an issue made evident in this "schooling" section of the syllabus.

Approach 5: Media (Reading)

Objective

- PSTs will be able to construct a unit plan about media narratives of Detroit and other urban contexts that is rooted in youth experiences and expertise.

Potential texts

National narrative:

- Kinloch (2010): *Harlem on our minds: Place, race, and the literacies of urban youth* (full text, from previous approach).
- Duvernay (2016): *13th* (full text).
- Kendi (2017): *Stamped from the beginning: The definitive history of racist ideas in America.* Suggested approach: Jigsawed chapters for each part.
- Thomas (2017): *The Hate U Give.*

Local narrative:

- The life and activism of Grace Lee Boggs (Documentary: American revolutionary; History of Detroit Summer)
- The history and impact of the Allied Media Project
- Counter-storytelling for LGBTQ+ youth at the Ruth Ellis Center

Assessment

- PSTs will analyze the local school district, city governance, and other local political entities for issues of racial injustice and construct an action plan to disrupt such injustices using community-based models as a guide. For example, PSTs might analyze the local school district's school suspension and expulsion rates for racial disparities and construct an action plan for how they, as an individual, might work to disrupt these injustices, always connected to broader community engaged efforts.
- PSTs will construct a unit or lesson plan for youth in their classes and construct a proposal to submit for the Allied Media Conference.

TEACHING TIPS

Neville's article explores an essential component of racial literacy: self-reflection. Sealey-Ruiz (2020) refers to a deeper dive in this work as the archaeology of self. To goal is to gain a better understanding of how our life experiences influence our capacity for racial literacy. To begin this deeper dive, ask each person in the classroom to create an artifact (beginning with the teacher) that represents the "complex interactions" they have as a person who is racialized when navigating systems in our society (e.g. healthcare, justice, finance, education). Discuss the themes and issues that emerge from the artifacts and how the class could collectively address those issues. Revisit these artifacts throughout the school year to think through the complexities of cultivating racial literacy as a path to racial equity.

(Franklin-Phipps & Rath, 2019) that is involved with attempting racially literate pedagogies, and I hope that I will do the same. By asking preservice teachers to engage in historical, spatial, and artistic analyses of the cities in which they teach, it is my aim to construct a complicated curriculum that is worthy of the students, like Richard, who exist within and beyond our classroom walls.

NOTES

1. I follow Johnson (2018) in purposely capitalizing Black, Brown, and people of Color and lowercasing white and whiteness. I do this to "disassemble white supremacy in my language" (p. 121).

2. I have included many citations for this course syllabus, some of which are websites with hyperlinks that won't be accessible in the print version of this piece. For further information and for the full citation of each text, please email me directly at marylneville@gmail.com.

REFERENCES

Baker-Bell, A., Stanbrough, R. J., & Everett, S. (2017). The stories they tell: Mainstream media, pedagogies of healing, and critical media literacy. *English Education*, 49(2), 130–152.

Carmody, S., & Winowiecki, E. (2017, December 4). Report: Michigan schools second-most segregated in the nation. *Michigan Radio*. Retrieved from https://www.michiganradio.org/post/report-michigan-schools-second-most-segregated-nation

Carter Andrews, D. J., Castro, E., Cho, C. L., Petchauer, E., Richmond, G., & Floden, R. (2019). Changing the narrative on diversifying the teacher workforce: A look at historical and contemporary factors that inform recruitment and retention of teachers of Color. *Journal of Teacher Education*, 70(1), 6–12.

Clement, D., & Kanai, M. (2014). The Detroit future city: How pervasive neoliberal urbanism exacerbates racialized spatial injustice. *American Behavioral Scientist*, 59(3), 369–385.

Franklin-Phipps, A., & Rath, C. L. (2019). Collage pedagogy: Toward a posthuman racial literacy. In C. R. Kuby, K. Spector, & J. J. Thiel (Eds.), *Posthumanism and literacy education: Knowing/becoming/doing literacies* (pp. 142–155). Routledge.

Freire, P. (1970/2000). *Pedagogy of the oppressed*. Continuum.

Guinier, L. (2004). From racial liberalism to racial literacy: *Brown v. Board of Education* and the interest-divergence dilemma. *The Journal of American History*, 91(1), 92–118.

Jackman, M. (2018, May 25). Report finds greater Detroit among most segregated U.S. metropolitan areas. *Detroit Metro Times*. Retrieved from https://www.metrotimes.com/news-hits/archives/2018/05/25/report-finds-greater-detroit-among-most-segregated-us-metropolitan-areas

Johnson, L. L. (2018). Where do we go from here? Toward a critical race English education. *Research in the Teaching of English*, 53(2), 102–124.

Love, B. L. (2019). We Want to Do More Than Survive: Abolitionist Teaching and the Pursuit of Educational Freedom. Boston: Beach Press.

Muhammad, G. E. (2019). Cultivating Genius: An Equity Framework for Culturally and Historically Responsive Literacy. New York: Scholastic.

Kinloch, V. (2010). *Harlem on our minds: Place, race, and the literacies of urban youth*. Teachers College Press.

Morrison, T. (1973). *Sula*. Plume.

Neville, M. L. (2019). "Racism is a God-damned thing": The implications of historical and contemporary Catholic racism for ELA classrooms. In M. M. Juzwik, J. C. Stone, K. J. Burke, & D. Davila (Eds.), *Legacies of Christian languaging and literacies in American education: Perspectives on English language arts curriculum, teaching, and learning*. Routledge.

Paris, D., & Alim, H. S. (2014). What are we seeking to sustain through culturally sustaining pedagogy? A loving critique forward. *Harvard Educational Review*, 84(1), 85–100.

Skerrett, A. (2011). English teachers' racial literacy knowledge and practice. *Race, Ethnicity, and Education*, 14(3), 313–330.

Soja, E. (1990). *Postmodern geographies: The reassertion of space in critical social theory*. Verso.

Watson, V. M., & Beymer, A. (2019). Praisesongs of place: Youth envisioning space and place in a literacy and songwriting initiative. *Research in the Teaching of English*, 53(4), 297–319.

MARY L. NEVILLE is an incoming assistant professor of K-12 Literacy at New Mexico State University. Her current research interests include antiracist English language arts pedagogies and English teacher education, emotion, and arts-based research. She has been a member of NCTE since 2015.

This article originally appeared
in *Research in the Teaching of English* 55.4

IN DIALOGUE: Solidarity

DANNY C. MARTINEZ,
APRIL BAKER-BELL,
ALAYNA EAGLE SHIELD
& CLIFFORD H. LEE

IN THE FALL OF 2020, I (Danny C. Martinez) had the privilege of being in conversation with April Baker-Bell, Alayna Eagle Shield, and Clifford Lee to discuss solidarity and what it means for us in our work toward justice in literacy research with our varied communities. Our conversation took place in the midst of the global COVID-19 pandemic, where in the United States, Black, Indigenous, and People of Color (BIPOC) continue to experience infection, displacement, and death at alarming and disproportionate rates. At the same time, the Black Lives Matter movement is needed more than ever as we have witnessed and experienced anti-Blackness and a thriving white supremacist movement in this country and beyond. Our discussion of solidarity brought us together to consider how we as scholars of color and our white co-conspirators (Love, 2019) must act courageously and collaboratively for BIPOC and other groups facing interlocking systems of domination (Combahee River Collective, 1979/1997). The following is an edited version of a conversation that lasted close to two hours. We have tried our best to present the threads of a beautiful, healing, and energizing conversation that left us with more questions, yet an appreciation for the stories that weave our collective experiences together as we work toward solidarities across all communities.

Danny: Thank you all for joining to discuss solidarity and what it means in our scholarship as literacy researchers who work with and alongside BIPOC communities. I was asked to contribute to In Dialogue in 2019, and solidarity was a theme that quickly came to mind as I was thinking about implicit moments of solidarity I had observed in my own research. I never imagined that our conversation about solidarity would happen in the midst of a global pandemic compounded by more racialized violence across BIPOC communities, Black communities in particular. I considered solidarity more closely in my own work thanks to April Baker-Bell's invitation to contribute to a special issue of *English Education* that centralized racialized violence and its implications for the English classroom (Baker-Bell et al., 2017). In my contribution I wanted to understand and imagine the language of solidarity that was already being used across racial and ethnic groups in Black and Latinx literacy learning spaces, ELA classrooms specifically (Martinez, 2017). I had been observing Black and Latinx youth in solidarity with one another for some time when I was a teacher in San Francisco and Los Angeles. After spending time in Chicago and now living and conducting research in Northern California, I consistently witness implicit solidarities across youth racial and ethnic groups.

Typically, we understand Black and Brown communities as being in tension with one another because of larger narratives that thrive and benefit from these imagined tension-filled interactions. In classrooms I observed, I saw and heard quite the opposite. Just as McDermott and Raley (2011) and Gutiérrez et al. (2017) asked us to rethink ingenuity not as an individual trait, but as a communal and collaborative trait. It is not one person that is ingenious, it's a community that facilitates ingenuity. We can see this only if we are willing to "look anew" (Gutiérrez et al., 2017). So, I think about ingenuity when I observe what Black and Latinx youth have been doing in classrooms and in their communities for some time. They are being in solidarity with one another, by using each other's language, by resisting white language being naturalized, and by reacting to and disrupting larger white supremacist narratives in their classrooms. So currently, I'm thinking about *how* we "look anew" at what Black and Brown youth are doing to be in solidarity with one another. And I want to know what teachers can learn from unearthing implicit solidarity practices. This may not be the solidarity celebrated in the news, but it is a solidarity that we can leverage for learning and sustaining in the classrooms.

April: In my own work, I think about the world we live in right now, from the perspective of someone who taught in Detroit, where I always taught 99% Black students. In that context, it was easy to look at violence in Indigenous and Latinx communities and think, "that's happening to them," and not to see it in relationship to what we, Black people, were experiencing in our own communities. Our relationship to white supremacy is not separate from what's happening in other communities. So, I think, what does solidarity look like? How do we help youth understand solidarity in homogenous spaces, in all-Black spaces? How do you get these youth to understand solidarity? In a recent piece (Baker-Bell, 2020b), I talk about Charlene Carruthers (2018), who states, "None of us are free unless all of us are free." This is a way of thinking through what solidarity means. We are not free if other communities of color are not free. We need to educate youth about these issues that seem distant from their own, but are really very connected to them.

I also ask, how are we, academics, in solidarity with our communities? Academia is a space that makes us feel that *we* are coming to academia to learn something to go improve *our* communities. And I see that as very separate. I didn't come to academia because my community needed something from *it* to become better. Academia needs to be better, and I think our communities force it to be that way. That's also a challenge. Navigating the tenure track and publishing felt like it was keeping me from doing the work that I could be doing in my community. But that changed when I heard from teachers all around the nation, telling me, "Thank you for writing this piece," and I saw writing as something that can be connected to the work that I'm doing in my community. It's not necessarily taking me away from community, but it's allowing me to connect with broader communities. So, I think about solidarity, I guess, in so many different ways. How are we in solidarity with our own community needs? And, I think, that's a question that we should always be thinking through in the field.

Clifford: I tried to come up with a definition of solidarity for myself. I think of it as working collaboratively in mutually beneficial relationships across false borders that separate us, as a result of white supremacist capitalist patriarchies. I started thinking, what are other ways that we connect? I was thinking about youth cultures, popular cultures, multiliterate practices, ancestral knowledges (particularly among communities of color), and the shared experiences of dealing with interlocking systems of domination. In that process of struggling, resisting, we have the opportunity for imagining and creating together. In the research that I have been doing, I seek opportunities to create, build, and imagine with young people. So, I ask: What does solidarity look like? Sound like?

I'm glad April brought it back to the teacher level. I started thinking back about my first experiences of teaching as a 23-year-old, teaching mostly 11th and 12th graders that I was only a few years older than. This was in East Oakland at a small public school. One of the first instances that stood out to me was hearing one of my students say something that included "ax" (in Black Language). I turned around and it was a Latinx student, and I thought, "Whoa, that's interesting." Prior to this, I had worked in a school that was 80% Black. I thought, "This is uniquely Oakland." What I came to realize was that many immigrants that came to Oakland were being acculturated not to white America, but to Black America. For these immigrant families, Black people were their neighbors, they were the people on their block. And, it was not just language, it was food, culture, and traditions. I was fortunate to work with Latinx, Black, Southeast Asian, Polynesian, and Yemeni students and observe how they connected across groups. Initially it may seem superficial. Black, Latinx, Southeast Asian, Polynesian, Yemeni kids would get banh mi sandwiches or tacos together. But over time, these small experiences led youth to develop stronger relationships and ties. They started seeing commonalities and their collective struggles and resilience against white supremacy, capitalism, patriarchy, and heteronormativity.

I talk about solidarity very honestly in my own home with my family and other Asian folks. I believe, until we surface our own issues, we can't discuss how we can genuinely be in solidarity with others if we don't do the hard work within ourselves. Sometimes that means having difficult conversations with your mom, your aunt, your grandma, or your cousin. And so, I think, this is one aspect of what I would emphasize is needed to be in solidarity with others.

Alayna: When I was in San Antonio at the American Educational Research Association conference in 2017, it was the first time I had been asked to speak at something so big! I felt out of place and I wasn't in academia at the time, but it was where I started to really think about what it means to be in solidarity. I grew up with a tribal college where our professors are like our aunties and uncles, and they don't have these big degrees. They've lived in our communities our whole lives. I didn't really know how crazy the academic world was until I was at AERA. I had previously met Rae Paris and Django Paris at Standing Rock. This was huge, because I got to meet them before their titles. They became relatives before I got to know their world of academia. I was stressed and nervous at AERA and asked Django, "Why am I going to be speaking?" He told me, "Be yourself. Just speak from your own experience." And for me, in that little moment, that was solidarity for me. I believe academia can try to make us be things that we're not, and that is not why I'm here.

I grew up with elders who had experiences with scholars, anthropologists coming in and extracting information. I remember being at a meeting with all my relatives where my dad was part of the Elders' Preservation Council. At this meeting, we were talking about the work we were trying to do within our community, and one of my uncles started making comments about people with PhDs. He said, "You know what? PhDs, they come in and they steal *our* knowledge. Your dad was talking about how we shouldn't trust them." I knew my dad's views had changed since I joined academia, so I took a breath and I started joking, "For real dad, you were talking about me?" For me to be who I am in a PhD program has shifted my dad's mind that scholarship and ideas can shift, but it takes a lot of work.

Being around academics, I sometimes feel anxious, and feel like I can't be myself. At the University of Washington, there are some Natives who never knew their community. But they have the language of academia down. And so, I've had to learn to be in good relation with them also. Initially I'd be really upset, thinking, "You don't even know!" But it's not their fault they don't know their histories or have never lived within their communities, and I'm only responsible for myself and my own actions. And so, when I think about solidarity, I really do think about what it means to look at each other as relatives.

Danny: The notion of being in relation is so important. I'm thinking of my earliest research in Los Angeles. I would often ask Black youth, "What do you think about your Latinx friends and classmates who speak Black English?" One student, Jerome, looked at me one day, making a face like, *Really? Of course, we speak like each other.* His actual words were, "We grew up in the same biosphere!" Jerome was like, *Why* *wouldn't we speak like one another? We live together in the same community. We're in the same schools.* And this was the sentiment I kept hearing from the youth.

Many Latinx students would make statements about how they needed to be in relation with their Black peers: "We are learning from them and they are learning from us, too." While many would talk about the words and phrases of language they would teach one another, others would point to being in relation. From these youth I learned that while adults assume that we must model relationship-building for youth, these youth were already doing it themselves. They were not waiting for us to be in solidarity with one another. Racial and ethnic tensions between the groups existed, but overwhelmingly so did everyday moments of shared collaboration and solidarity between Black and Latinx youth.

April: One of the things I think about is praxis. For example, solidarity is an action. It's not just what you say—like, "I'm in solidarity with . . . "—but, what is your praxis? That's the first thing I notice. How do we make people feel? What's the practice of solidarity? And how are we doing that with youth? In my book (Baker-Bell, 2020a), I talk about what I call a *Detroit Literacy*. When I enter into a space with youth in various schools and contexts in Detroit, just because I am from Detroit doesn't mean that I can work with different youth in every single school I go into, or that I have the authority to be in that space. And just because I'm Black, doesn't make me connected. The youth read me. They're like, "Where are *you* from? What side of town are *you* from? What high school did *you* go to?" And so, they ask me a series of questions. I don't get upset with the youth questioning me. This is what they should do. If I'm going to be in their space, they should be able to question me. And I shouldn't feel like they're reading me or they're disrespectful or something. And no matter if you look like them or not, this is what it means to be in community with your community.

We also have some types of beliefs that we've internalized about each other that are not helpful. We know we do have those uncles, we do have those dads, we have people in our family that say some messed-up stuff. And we sometimes internalize it, too. But how do we do the work on ourselves so we can speak back in our own communities with love, and show why this is not right? This is perpetuating the very oppression that you're talking about oppressing you. We're doing it to other people.

Clifford: I know some of us have done the work to connect our behaviors, actions, and ideologies to our own families and communities. I think, "That's from my mom or my grandma. Why does she say that? What did she experience? What types of intergenerational trauma is she passing down? And how can I interrupt that?" That is a lot! When working with teachers, I work with them to recognize our respective positionality and how to unlearn some of it as well. How to really recognize how we might be perpetuating certain things. With teachers, I say, "You need to do the self-work in order to examine what you're unintentionally doing to our young people."

Alayna: I want to comment on the idea of our own internal shame. I think about growing up on the Rez, and how we were taught ABCs, colors, animals—the simplest things that we're taught. There were a few of us who excelled in our language and who grew up traditionally because we had a fluent speaker at home. For me, it was my dad. However, many times Native youth equate our language and our culture with poverty because they see our grandparents struggling. They see it because it was by design that our grandparents were placed at the lowest of the low because of the Dawes Act, which gave the most traditional people the crappiest lands. I think about how shame is almost unconscious, when we equate our language and our culture with poverty. When we see white kids being praised for speaking our languages better . . . almost like it's cool or cute or something. But when it's our own people doing it, then it's not the same. Anyway.

April: Sometimes the white kid gets cool points for just sounding Black. We even see how Black Language gets capitalized on. This, despite how Black children and youth who speak Black Language go through school being corrected, being policed, and being mistreated. And then you have white Instagram celebrities, or folks creating clothes and pillows and mugs capitalizing on the language. But they don't go through what we go through using our language. It seems cool, but it's problematic because Black folks are often told that we can't use our language as a resource in schools to learn. Because people want to deny and denounce it, but someone else can take it and it's cool. There are so many communities of color who come into classrooms multilingual from the jump, and they are labeled as struggling language learners. It's just problematic, and we have to call that stuff out.

Clifford: I was born in Hong Kong when it was still a British colony. And I've seen this over time, not just in my own experience. There's this colonized superiority because we were colonized by the British; some Hong Kongers have this sense of, "We're more cultured and we're better than mainlanders." Things have shifted now, because mainland China's become such a huge superpower. But even now, we're talking about Chinese people hating on other Chinese people because of that mentality. And so, talk about shame. That's a powerful force in the human psyche in shifting actions and behaviors. Right?

Alayna: The thing for us is, there's a cultural significance to shaming that holds people accountable for their actions. For instance, if you stole somebody's woman or stole someone's horse or whatever, there's a certain way that you would be shamed. We tease and we shame. But we had an elder tell us at a recent elder's gathering that we don't shame the right way, like we used to. We do it to be mean. We do it, too, with our language, and things that strike us right in the heart when we're still so tender and trying to reclaim those things. And so, when we're in the process of reclaiming our languages, reclaiming our ceremonies, reclaiming our kinship, a lot of times we're shamed and not in a good way. In this day and age, we shame in a hurtful way.

April: As a Black Language speaker, I did not know there was a history until I was in graduate school. I knew Black Language was OK, and that it was valid just because this was the way my community spoke. But I didn't know the history and ties to enslavement. So, a lot of my work is about reclaiming those histories. It's not about code-switching or these technical differences between languages per se. It's about the history of it. How did it come about? It's about literacy, but also understanding how anti-Blackness is embedded.

When I was doing my dissertation research, I was talking to kids about the history of Black Language. There was a woman sitting in the room, listening to me. Afterwards, she pulled me aside and asked, "What are you doing? What are you doing with these kids? What are you talking about? Why are you teaching them about Ebonics?" I explained to her why it's important for them to know the history. We had to have a dialogue. Really, it was deep work that happened within 15 minutes, because she didn't understand the purpose. I told her, "It's important for them to know their language and what it comes from." She started talking about the reason she always shamed Black kids, because of how she was treated when she went to an all-white school in the '70s. She was teased and corrected, and she explained how much damage that did to her. And she's like, "So that's my perspective. That's where I come from, but I see what you're doing and I see why that's important." And she's like, "Keep doing what you're doing." Another Black teacher a few years prior asked me, "What are you trying to do? How are you arguing that a language that's not a language is a language?" And I was like, "Well, listening to your words, actually, is validating that it is a language because you're using it." So, it's really interesting what happens even in our own communities, that this notion of Ebonics or speaking Black is so horrible that we're denouncing it while speaking it.

And so, I think, we also must be in conversation with parents who've gone through experiences like that woman was telling me about. That's why I love listening to youth, because they tell you things. They will say, "It's happening at school, but it's happening at home, too.

My parents also will get on me." I'm not upset with the parents, because I understand what it means to go through school systems, and to navigate this world and constantly be policed and corrected. And they don't want their kids going through that, is their thinking. But not recognizing that whole line of thinking is not helping at all. It's like double damage that's happening on both sides. So I think about our work beyond schools. That's why Carmen Kynard and I came out with the Black Language Syllabus—a digital resource where people don't have to wait on schools to get it right.

Clifford: I just want to build on what April said. Kris Gutiérrez, who mentored me and Danny, told us, "You should leave your research site a better place than when you entered it." And that's one of the things I have never forgotten as a research scholar. We, as educators and researchers, had the opportunities, time, and privileges to study learning theories, multiliteracies, language research, ethnic studies, and curriculum and pedagogies that are culturally sustaining and community-responsive. If you're doing a self-study or you had a role in developing the curriculum, this is the time to show how you connect the dots for others. At the end of a study, I hope to share some of the things I've learned from being in community with students and/or with the teacher. So, if you go into a research site and you see some of these things happening, I think it's time to put aside nice politics or whatever. Maybe at the end of the research study, or even during the research study in some cases, you can have a conversation with the teacher. Educate them about why Black Language is a language and drop that knowledge on them. That's how I feel like the praxis is happening with the work that we do. And I feel like a critical part of it is integrating an ethnic studies approach within the curriculum standards. And it shouldn't even be a separate thing, but unfortunately, as of now, it still is.

April: I think it's just all super-important, especially now with the Trump administration and the recent attacks on critical race theory, ethnic studies, and antiracist work. This is why it's so important to think about solidarity in our work, and how we can't be limited just to school spaces. With the attacks that are happening—not saying that they're going to necessarily move forward, but there are some schools and districts that are happy to hear the attacks because they don't want to do the hard work anyway—what does this mean for us and our work? How does it shift what we're doing?

Alayna: When I think about our tribal schools, I think of youth in our communities who have grown up in tough home situations. My dad's mentality always used to be, "Well, it starts in the home. You learn traditions, language, ceremonies, and protocol in the home." And I used to be confused. I would say, "So what does that mean for the kids who don't have these things in their homes?" I was fortunate that I grew up with a dad who was a fluent speaker and knowledge keeper. He's the last chief in our community that was traditionally appointed by elders. I was fortunate to have that knowledge, but what about the kids who don't have that? Do they not deserve it, then? And my dad was speechless, which rarely happens. But it's true that we need to be creating spaces for our youth to learn about their history, about their culture, about where they come from, and the truth behind why the rest of society fears us really knowing who we truly are.

Danny: I'm thinking about teacher education, and how frustrated I have been by the limited views about what should be part of the curriculum. Anything that goes beyond traditional teacher education is seen as having to exist in the sole "diversity" course. We need to break out of the traditional. The work with the Black Language Syllabus and the *Educational Linguist* blog by Nelson Flores is so important for me as a teacher educator specifically, as we seek to share what we have access to as academics with a larger audience. I think some of the work around solidarity is imagining different and new learning spaces because the institutions that we rely on aren't set up to have us do this work.

April: I feel like I rely on the wisdom of my community to come and bring *it* into academic spaces. To transform what's happening there. But then also, what can I do with institutional resources to hold institutions accountable? They want to claim outreach and engagement? How then do I tap into resources to do things in our community? The *Hate U Give* series that I did at Michigan State was really about the community. Youth wanted to read *The Hate U Give* so that they could talk about police brutality, anti-Blackness, and all of that stuff. So how do I hold this institution accountable for making that happen? We need resources, we need books. Youth want to go to the movies. And this is what I need institutions to be able to do.

I believe we are building something that we haven't seen yet. I think that we have elders and ancestors that went ahead of us to make this space, where we can do our work. But what are we doing for those that are coming behind us? How are we clearing the space to make it where they're not even facing the type of things that we're facing? We also have to let them know they don't have to give up all of themselves, because that's actually a very dangerous thing. Don't give yourself up to be in this academic space, because it's not going to free you from anything. I appreciate this dialogue, because we're saying that you can do something different. You probably don't even see it yet, but you can work toward building that. That's important work to do. And solidarity work. How are we in solidarity with generations to come?

Alayna: Or how are we using the platforms and the spaces that we're in to bring our elders, youth, and community members in to be able to share their knowledge and expertise? How are we shielding them and bringing them in to share the knowledge? And using whatever resources and titles and letters are behind our names *for* them? That's what I've been thinking a lot about. It was really hard for me to decide that I was going to get my PhD, because I'm already in my community doing the work and I didn't want to create a hierarchy with my letters (PhD), above any elders or knowledge keepers. So I struggled a lot during my first year of my PhD program. I'm not glad the pandemic happened, but I'm glad I was able to come home during the pandemic. I was able to see that my community is still here. We're still doing the work. Everything's OK, all things considered. But it was really a shock for me to think about what I am giving up to be in this academic space and to ask myself, "Why am I doing it?"

When I first considered going to the University of Washington, Django would tease and say, "OK, we know you don't 'need' a PhD, but here are some ways it could be helpful for your community." And I'd be like, "OK, good, at least you know"—almost like I was trying to convince myself that I didn't need to be there and to assure people, mainly myself again, that I wasn't going to get lost in academia. I'm constantly thinking of how to bring community presence and voices into academic spaces.

April: I love that, because it also gets us to question, who are teacher educators? Who are knowledge holders? And it's not traditional for me. I think about my mom. . . . If I have anything going down in academia, I'm calling my mom to figure out what's the way forward. She has a lot of wisdom. I think about the people in my community that have so much wisdom. I think about activists who are not academics or teacher educators but are doing this type of educating work.

Clifford: In my courses, I've had organizer and activist friends come in to talk about systemic racism, complementing academic texts. We need to flip the whole understanding of who is a knowledge holder. I have also invited my former high school students, who are adults now, to come into my classroom as guest speakers, because who else would be better to share what is important to become a good urban educator than the students that went through urban K–12 schools? I think that is part of our work. And, I think, another part of our work is translating those types of things for the academic audience that doesn't even have access to the communities or to the activists, organizers, cultural workers, and elders in the communities. Because they don't understand, they don't even have the language to be able to communicate or the access to connect with them.

Additionally, often we talk about the importance of teaching teachers to learn about the students' cultures and communities. I push my students, telling them that not only do they have to learn about their students' culture and community and ways of being, but they have to know about it more deeply, in a more insightful and profound way. And what I mean by this is, for example, the social media digital literacies that young people are immersed in. Some teachers might do cool projects like, "Hey, we incorporate Twitter into the curriculum." But my push is, where's the criticality in that? What are these social media tools actually doing to take advantage of us? How do we have those conversations in addition to utilizing these popular literacy practices that our young people use?

One example I'm thinking about is facial recognition. This has become so ubiquitous nowadays in many smartphones, in addition to other technologies. We had a project with youth at YR Media where we were developing our understanding of how facial recognition operates. Young people then created tools using materials like construction paper and tape, to put on their faces to trick the facial recognition. We knew that facial recognition started for policing and surveillance, and not just to unlock phones. So, we wanted to teach other people about how this technology is actually impacting historically oppressed communities in awful ways. This work was also really fun. There was lots of laughter and joy when the young people were putting these things on their faces. And they were trying to build something as an alternative to it. So, talk about reimagining what these multinational, profit-generating tools are typically used for. They're trying to figure out, "Can we utilize these types of things for other ways?" And so that's what some of the work that we have ahead of us. We just published this project and I couldn't be prouder of what this group of youth and staff created. https://interactive.yr.media/erase-your-face/

April: What we see happening in classrooms and what younger teachers are thinking of is forming this superficial type of solidarity across groups of young people. Danny, I heard you saying that in your experience, young people were organically building these solidarities. How can we build on what they're already doing? Versus these presentations of cultures that teachers tend to represent in their classrooms as a way of understanding different communities—that just feels really superficial. One of the things that we need to do is encourage teachers to think about how this is happening already. Some of this is not something you need to create, because it's already there. And just thinking from a youth perspective, how unnatural it might feel when you're trying to put people in solidarity and community with each other, and it already exists. So, I think that is important. And that's our work, as language and literacy scholars and researchers, to continue to think through.

TEACHING TIPS

These authors examine the role that solidarity has in advancing their work for justice in literacy education and research. As a way to explore the ideas they discuss, you can host a community meeting for your class, grade level, or school. Some possible questions to discuss:

1. ***How are you "in relation" with the community in ways that honor the histories, identities, and voices of the people who live there?***
2. ***What practices do you engage in to disrupt hierarchies that further exclude the voices and physical presence of people from historically marginalized communities?***
3. ***What has this conversation taught you about yourself and your community?***
4. ***What do you plan to do with this new insight?***

REFERENCES

Baker-Bell, A. (2020a). *Linguistic justice: Black language, literacy, and pedagogy*. Routledge.

Baker-Bell, A. (2020b). "We been knowin": Toward an antiracist language and literacy education. *Journal of Language and Literacy Education*, 16(1), 1–12.

Baker-Bell, A., Butler, T., & Johnson, L. (2017). The pain and the wounds: A call for critical race English education in the wake of racial violence. *English Education*, 49(2): 116–129.

Carruthers, C. (2018). *Unapologetic: A Black, queer, and feminist mandate for radical movements*. Beacon Press.

Combahee River Collective. (1997). A Black feminist statement. In L. Nicholson (Ed.), *The second wave: A reader in feminist theory* (pp. 63–70). Routledge. (Reprinted from *Capitalist patriarchy and the case for socialist feminism*, pp. 362–372, by Z. Eisenstein, Ed., 1979, Monthly Review Press.)

Gutiérrez, K. D., Cortes, K., Cortez, A., DiGiacomo, D., Higgs, J., Johnson, P., Lizárraga, J. R., Mendoza, E., Tien, J., & Vakil, S. (2017). Replacing representation with imagination: Finding ingenuity in everyday practices. *Review of Research in Education*, 41(1), 30–60.

Love, B. L. (2019). *We want to do more than survive: Abolitionist teaching and the pursuit of educational freedom*. Beacon Press.

Martinez, D. C. (2017). Imagining a language of solidarity for Black and Latinx youth in English language arts classrooms. *English Education*, 49(2), 179–193.

McDermott, R., & Raley, J. (2011). Looking closely: Toward a natural history of human ingenuity. In E. Margolis & L. Pauwels (Eds.), *Handbook of visual research methods* (pp. 372–391). SAGE.

DANNY C. MARTINEZ is an associate professor of language, literacy and culture at the University of California, Davis. His research is inspired by his experiences as a middle and high school literacy teacher in San Francisco and Los Angeles. His scholarship explores the cultural and communicative practices of Black and Latinx youth in secondary literacy classrooms, and teacher learning as it relates to leveraging youths' rich communicative repertoires for learning. Martinez's future work will continue to grapple with notions of solidarity and ingenuity in the lives of Black and Latinx teachers and their students through the support of the Spencer Foundation.

APRIL BAKER-BELL is a transdisciplinary teacher-researcher-activist and associate professor of language, literacy, and English education in the Department of English and Department of African American and African Studies at Michigan State University. A national leader in conversations on Black Language education, her research interrogates the intersections of Black language and literacies, anti-Black racism, and antiracist pedagogies. Baker-Bell is the recipient of many awards and fellowships, including the 2021 Andrew W. Mellon Foundation's New Directions Fellowship, the 2021 Michigan State University's Community Engagement Scholarship Award, Michigan State University's 2021 Distinguished Partnership Award for Community-Engaged Creative Activity, and the 2020 NCTE George Orwell Award for Distinguished Contribution to Honesty and Clarity in Public Language for her recently published book, *Linguistic Justice: Black Language, Literacy, Identity, and Pedagogy.*

ALAYNA EAGLE SHIELD is Húŋkpapȟa Lakȟóta and is a citizen of the Standing Rock Sioux Tribe. She is also Dakȟóta and Sáhniš (Arikara). Alayna is a mother of three beautiful children and married. She holds a bachelors of science degree, is an eminent scholar in the Lakȟóta language, has her masters degree in public health, and is a doctoral student at the University of Washington. Alayna is currently the Co-Executive Director of the Mni Wiconi Clinic and Farm and the Co-Founder of the Mní Wičóni Nakíčižiŋ Wóuŋspe (Defenders of the Water School).

CLIFFORD H. LEE is the program director and associate professor in the Educators for Liberation, Justice, and Joy (ELJJ) teacher education program at Mills College. As a former public-school teacher in East Oakland, his interests and passions remain focused on transforming educational systems and spaces of urban youth of color. His research, teaching, and social justice advocacy examines and creates opportunities for youth to participate and engage in learning at the intersections of critical pedagogy, computational thinking, multiliteracies, and youth culture. He is currently the Scholar-in-Residence at YR Media, a national network of young journalists and artists.

CALL FOR MANUSCRIPTS

NCTE SPECIAL ISSUES SERIES

VOLUME 2, RACIAL LITERACIES

INFORMED BY THE SOCIOPOLITICAL AND SOCIOCULTURAL CONTEXTS FOR YOUTH

DEADLINE: JANUARY 10, 2022

EDITOR: AYANNA F. BROWN

The mesmerizing and disturbing lyrics of "Strange Fruit," a sobering and haunting melody written in 1930s by Abel Meerepool and famously performed by Billie Holiday, began as a poem penned in response and reaction to the incessant crimes against Black life. Specifically, Meerepool authored "Bitter Fruit," which later was performed and published as "Strange Fruit," to protest the lynching of two Black teenagers in Indiana. In the article "The Story behind Billie Holiday's 'Strange Fruit'" (2021), Liz Fields notes that "despite strong resistance, especially from radio stations in the South who refused to play 'Strange Fruit,' the song rose in the charts." The lyrics read, "Southern trees bear a strange fruit / Blood on the leaves and blood at the root / Black bodies swingin' in the Southern breeze / Strange fruit hangin' from the poplar trees."

This text situates this call to deepen the conceptualization of racial literacies, a heuristic for examining how the development of the study of race within K–college settings can be informed by the sociopolitical and sociocultural contexts of the United States. Much like Meerepool's terrifying inspiration during the 1930s, twenty-first century K–college youth have witnessed and been exposed to racially motivated domestic terrorism in the United States rooted in our nation's (a) unreconciled historical ideologies and (b) proliferation of curricular violence working to minimize and/or erase the significance of race in the study of social sciences at K–college levels. Today's youth are not protected from racism and its physical, psychological, and economic contexts any more than the two teens whose bodies swung in the midwest Indiana breeze in the 1930s. How are they invited to process 2019–2021 in the development of content knowledge as literate practices?

How do we conceptualize the intellectual investments necessary to cultivate the abilities of school-aged youth to think, reflect, respond, and react to the social, cultural, political, and economic contexts for race in school settings? In what ways do teachers utilize the everyday life experiences of youth as a means to develop the academic skills to enact change and survival skills to live? How do we create space in the development of youth to use the arts to speak to life?

This special issue seeks to curate both theoretical considerations and praxis for racial literacies in K–college classrooms. There are three areas for submission: (1) theory, (2) praxis, and (3) community.

THEORY

There will be a few select manuscripts chosen to support an effort to further the theorizing of racial literacy/ies. Guiding questions for these submissions might include, but are not limited to, the following: How do we situate racial literacy and literacies as necessary knowledges, skills, and pedagogies in a society organized by racialism? How might racial literacies be conceptualized as intellectual work that supports building conceptual knowledge and ideas? How can scholars explore racial literacies' plurality and what does this add to the study of diverse learning in schools?

PRAXIS

In what ways are teachers creating opportunities for racial literacies within and beyond the boundaries of state-sanctioned curriculum, including teacher education programs? How are teachers building racial literacies alongside culturally responsive pedagogy? What do racial literacies as planning for instruction consider when building equitable assessment practices? How do teachers use diverse texts to support developing interdisciplinary studies within racial literacies practices?

COMMUNITY

How are educators using racial literacies as a source for community building that interfaces with students' classroom learning? In what ways is collaboration with community organizations working to sustain student identities and family engagement in learning? What constitutes community and learning within a racial literacies framework?

Submission Guidelines

- Manuscripts should be double spaced throughout (including quotations and works cited pages) with standard margins.
- Theory manuscripts should be no more than 5,000 to 7,000 words (including citations).
- Praxis and community manuscripts should be no more than 2,500 to 4,000 words (including citations).
- Use in-text documentation by following the 9th edition of the MLA Handbook. Where applicable, a list of works cited and any other bibliographic information should also follow MLA style.
- Provide a statement guaranteeing that the manuscript has not been published or submitted elsewhere.
- Ensure that the manuscript conforms to the NCTE Statement on Gender and Language: www.ncte.org/positions/statements/genderfairuseoflang.
- Obtain permission for any student work featured in the manuscript.
- Submit images, photographs, charts, graphs, etc. in separate files per instructions in Editorial Manager. Contributors are responsible for securing rights to copywritten material.

Submit your manuscript to NCTE's Editorial Manager, Books Program at https://www.editorialmanager.com/nctebp and mark Special Issues-Racial Literacy as the article type.

If you have any questions, please contact the volume editor:

Ayanna F. Brown: abrown@elmhurst.edu.